BLACK ACTIVIST SCIENTIST ICON 🍁

BLACK
ACTIVIST
SCIENTIST
ICON 🍁

The autobiography of
DR. HOWARD D. MCCURDY
with GEORGE ELLIOTT CLARKE

NIMBUS
PUBLISHING
—— NIMBUS.CA ——

Nimbus Publishing Limited
3660 Strawberry Hill Street, Halifax, NS, B3K 5A9
(902) 455-4286 nimbus.ca

Printed and bound in Canada
NB1683

Design: Jenn Embree
Editors: Chris Benjamin, Marianne Ward
Editor for the press: Angela Mombourquette

All images courtesy Brenda McCurdy

Nimbus Publishing is based in Kjipuktuk, Mi'kma'ki, the traditional territory of the Mi'kmaq People.

Library and Archives Canada Cataloguing in Publication

Title: Black activist, black scientist, black icon : the autobiography of Dr. Howard D. McCurdy / with George Elliott Clarke.
Other titles: Autobiography of Dr. Howard D. McCurdy
Names: McCurdy, Howard, 1932-2018, author. | Clarke, George Elliott, author.
Identifiers: Canadiana (print) 20230221068 | Canadiana (ebook) 20230221114 | ISBN 9781774712313 (softcover) | ISBN 9781774712320 (EPUB)
Subjects: LCSH: McCurdy, Howard, 1932-2018. | LCSH: Civil rights workers—Canada—Biography. | LCSH: Politicians—Canada—Biography. | LCSH: College teachers—Canada—Biography. | CSH: Black Canadians—Biography. | LCGFT: Autobiographies.
Classification: LCC FC106.B6 M42 2023 | DDC 323.092—dc23

Nimbus Publishing acknowledges the financial support for its publishing activities from the Government of Canada, the Canada Council for the Arts, and from the Province of Nova Scotia. We are pleased to work in partnership with the Province of Nova Scotia to develop and promote our creative industries for the benefit of all Nova Scotians.

For Brenda
Wise, Scintillating, Scientist Beloved
&
Leslie, Linda, Cheryl, Brian
Beloved, Indomitable, Extraordinary Quartet

This was art, this was truth, this
Was *Beauty*....
— James Schuyler, "The Morning of the Poem"

Beauty is intelligence; it is the intensity of
an alluring and enigmatic expression.
— Fabrizio Ferri,
quoted in "Fabrizio Ferri," *Photo: Box*

CONTENTS

PREFACE
IDENTIFYING THE RIGHT SINGULAR
DR. HOWARD DOUGLAS MCCURDY, CM, O.ONT,
BA, BSC, MSC, PHD

BORN IN LONDON, ON, ON SATURDAY, DECEMBER 10, 1932, Howard Douglas McCurdy Jr. too soon passed away in LaSalle, ON, on Tuesday, February 20, 2018, at the patrician age of eighty-five. So, who was he? Why does this record of his life exist?

That anyone would ask such questions is one reason for this book. Canadians do a lousy job of remembering Black Canadians. Don't our lives matter? Doesn't our involvement in Canadian politics matter? To read this book is to become enlightened.

Still, those initial questions are pertinent, and they are not to be answered by listing achievements, though Howard McCurdy was amazing: first Black Canadian to become a tenured professor; first Black Canadian university department chair; second African-Canadian member of Windsor (Ontario) City Council; the foremost authority on gliding bacteria; the man who named the New Democratic Party; the founder of the anti-segregation Guardian Club (in Windsor, ON); a founder of the Canadian Civil Liberties Association and of the Canadian Association of University Teachers; the founder of the National Black Coalition of Canada (the nation's first national Black representational body). He was the second Black Canadian Member of Parliament (1984–93) and the second African-Canadian to seek to head a national party. He was appointed to both the Order of Canada and the Order of Ontario. He talked with King and he walked with Mandela.

But Howard McCurdy's triumphs are not the only reason to celebrate the man, to study his life, to understand how he got to do the things he did, becoming a respected scientist, a prominent human rights and civil rights orator and activist, and a formidable municipal and federal politician, while being always a proud Black Canuck. Yes, Howard combined his scientist's hunger for knowledge with the thirst for justice as an Afro-Ontarian descended from the Underground Railroad ex-slaves and never-slaves who built pioneer communities in southwestern Ontario, Hamilton, Toronto, the Bruce Peninsula, and even in Kingston and Ottawa between the 1830s and the 1860s. Howard kept that heritage close to his heart. Thus, he plunged into desegregation activism in Ontario in the 1950s and 1960s, forming the Guardian Club to review and document incidents of racial harassment. Thanks to these activities, the Windsor Human Rights Institute was formed in 1964 and then a Committee on Employment Opportunities in 1968. Also in 1964, Howard had the foresight to inaugurate an exhibit on Black history, "From Slavery to Freedom." Successful, the event spawned the North American Black Historical Museum in Amherstburg, ON.

Beyond these many accomplishments, there's still more to know, to recall, to honour. There's the man himself, a track-and-field star in his teens, who seemed permanently youthful and almost indestructible. Indeed, he raced against racism in southwestern Ontario; he raced into the academy, becoming a University of Windsor biologist (authoring fifty scientific papers and directing eleven theses and dissertations); he raced into track-and-field coaching; raced into becoming a Windsor city councillor; he raced into the House of Commons as a two-term Member of Parliament; he used to race back and forth, Ottawa to Windsor to Ottawa, covering each eight hundred kilometre segment in five hours and never getting a speeding ticket.

And the man was both racy and dashing in his suits—those dozens and dozens of single-breasted or double-breasted, pinstriped or solid-colour getups—that Freeds of Windsor gifted him with such bedazzling largesse. No wonder he was always being voted Best-Dressed Member of Parliament, and he wore all such honours well. Because he had that class, that panache, that snazzy, jazzy, hail-fellow-well-met spirit, so posh was his demeanour. (At a Windsor party big-upping my receipt of an honorary doctorate from the University of Windsor in autumn 2010, Howard materialized. Lanky, he ankled through the doorway and, suddenly, his neon-bright sweater centred all the available luminosity upon his mien.)

Nazrey African Methodist Episcopal Church is now part of the North American Black Historical Museum complex in Amherstburg, Ontario.

Another redoubtable and inimitable fact about Howard was his vocabulary, so rich with zingers and zap, slang and Latinate, scientific lingo and words that always sounded sweet as molasses but moved as swift as lightning. The man could talk—and out-talk—and was dangerous to debate, because he always had a lungful of Oxford Dictionary and a heart full of spirituals and a tongue that could issue some jive-talk rappin' too.

In his second term as a Member of Parliament, Howard contested the leadership of the national New Democratic Party. He didn't win, but he prepared the way for another personage of colour to later succeed, namely Jagmeet Singh.

Ironically, lifelong smoking shortened his elder status as definite éminence grise and just-beginning-to-be-acknowledged statesman. Yet even in his last months he seemed almost a teenager, vaping freely on his medicinal marijuana and eager to buy a new car. He loved to drive fast, to make that engine vroom and those wheels squeal, to turn everybody's heads as he zoomed-zoomed through LaSalle, Windsor, and his 'hood.

When I heard of Howard's passing, I was in Havana, Cuba. Instantly, my Cuba Libre became a Dark 'n' Stormy as my tears embittered an already sweet-n-sour cocktail. Why? I'd worked for Howard, on Parliament Hill, from 1987 to 1991, and he'd been my pre-eminent role model. His example preordained my PhD—and affirmed my own sense that intellectuals must be social justice advocates.

Nor was I the only one to recognize that a giant had fallen, that a library had been torched. A trio of prime ministers sang Howard's praises for the official *Globe and Mail* obit: The Right Honourable Brian Mulroney, The Right Honourable Joe Clark, and The Right Honourable Paul Martin. I doubt such empowered (white) men are much given to sentiment. But study Howard Douglas McCurdy's life story and you'll know why even these potentates had to stand in awe of that singular, Black, and radical dignitary—as if they were honourary pallbearers.

George Elliott Clarke (X. States)
Toronto, Ontario
1 Nisan (April) MMXXIII

INTRODUCTION
EDITOR RE: AUTHOR

O my body, make of me always a man who questions!
— FRANTZ FANON, BLACK SKIN, WHITE MASKS
(TRANSLATION BY CHARLES LAM MARKMANN)

DR. HOWARD MCCURDY (1932-2018) IS THE TITULAR AUTHOR OF
this autobiography. But in July 2017, seven months before his decease,
he requested that I edit this work, which was already progressing toward
a conclusion. Howard was like a father to me, and so, just as with my
actual father, William Lloyd Clarke (1935–2005), I resisted accepting the
fact that he could die. I wanted there to be time for us to draft his manuscript together, just as I had often writ letters and press releases alongside
him, thirty years before, when I was his constituency liaison in his Centre
Block, House of Commons office, from 1987 to 1991. Alas, that was not
to be, for Howard passed away in February 2018, and the news weighted
me down with sobbing while I strolled amid Havana's palms. His widow,
Dr. Brenda McCurdy, PhD, posted me the manuscript on several USB
sticks, either later in 2018 or by early 2019. However, they languished in
my home office, awaiting my completion of my own manuscripts of
poetry (mainly) and my own memoir, and, of course, my fulfillment of
the mandatory duties of a professor (teaching, marking, researching,
writing, publishing). Luckily, the bad luck of COVID-19-20-21-22-23
(and counting), which coincided with a sabbatical year, 2020–21, forced
me to hunker down on my premises, thus liberating me to get to Dr.
Howard McCurdy's memoir at last. (I thank Brenda McCurdy for her

sumptuous patience and only iron-fingers-in-a-velvet-glove nudges to me to get the editing done.)

But, lookit! Upon reading the opening paragraph of chapter I, I got fired up! That AI paragraph, somehow conjoining Einstein to Genesis, reminded me that, as I'd known when I was Howard's employee, *the man can write*, good people! Indeed, this autobiography, which he planned to title *The Book of a Coloured Man, Negro, Black Man, African-Canadian Scientist*, is likely the longest work he ever scribed, for the bulk of his prose backed topical ephemera: letters (to editors or to politicos), reports, articles, op-eds, and speeches. Descended as he was from Essex County preachers, church-builders, and *les hommes politiques*, Howard practised oratory in the mode of many African-American leaders, from Frederick Douglass (whose surname was given to him as his middle name, minus the second *s*) to Rev. Dr. Martin Luther King Jr., from Malcolm X to President Barack Obama. As with these esteemed speakers, whose most urgent speeches often arose spontaneously from an amalgam of emotion and intellect so that prose gets spiritualized into poetry, Howard delighted in the extemporaneous peroration, which, issuing in electrifying combustion out of heart and head, had audiences—especially Black people—presenting standing ovations so often that their chair seats never had a chance to warm. Yet, rotund and ornate speech can seem clotted and cloying, or so purple in polysyllabic, virtuoso euphemism that the sense of it is lost as one moves from a Latinate-laden opening clause to a syntactically slippery—if sonorous—conclusion. Indeed, Howard's two major careers—as scientist and elected politician (or tribune)—presented him with authorial challenges: to never allow either scientific precision or political circumlocution to render his style either bland or dully verbose.

So, in editing Dr. McCurdy's prose, I've striven for clarity and succinct expression, variation in diction and punctuation (Howard shuns question marks, exclamations, and colons), and I've added contractions (every single one is my doing) plus slang, French, barbarisms, italics, puns, nicknames, etc. Howard is a formal stylist: he writes *President*, which I render as *prez*; he prefers *mother* and *father* to my informal choices of *mom* and *dad*; he steers clear of profanity, but I coin the expletive "*mater-fouteur*" because the occasion that he narrates calls for a term somewhat stronger than *bastard*. He has a yen for *extraordinary* and a ken for *ironic*: I endeavour to reduce their occurrence accordingly. When he turns to cliché or overuses the same terms, I seek vivid synonyms and/ or images as antidotes. He adored polysyllables, but I have replaced them, frequently, with monosyllables, for the sake of extra bluntness, punch, bite, or lacerating comment.

One reason Howard can slide toward the prolix or utter conventional sentiment or draft the severely laconic phrase or sentence or paragraph? To avoid or evacuate emotions that render the author vulnerable. Like his father before him, Howard had difficulty expressing (as his widow has confirmed) his yearnings or laments. Outrage was easier for him to air—though, no matter how honest his anger, it was always a touch theatrical. He wanted you to know he was angry, but he was never as truly angry as he could sound. (Whenever a parliamentary staffer quit, Howard would suffer a type of grief; it was as if he felt that he had been shunned or betrayed, though he would never verbalize his sorrow or regret.) The most poignant moments in his life story—his first definitive *amour*, their too-soon breakup, his parents' divorce, his marriages, the births of his children, his jousting with administrators and bureaucrats, the death of his father, his political triumphs and defeats, and his personal experience of police brutality—are canvassed almost dispassionately. While I respect his impulse to keep personal matters private, I have essayed to voice hitherto unspoken emotions with empathetic accuracy. (BTW, his voice sounded a tenor brogue—molasses and smoke, peat moss and honey, Scotch and tobacco.)

When I worked for Howard, he trusted me to compose letters (mainly to Crown ministers or to constituents) for his signature and rarely saw need to edit. However, he penned his own Commons speeches; in that case, my role was just to pencil light touch-ups, act as a sounding board, and research tidbits of information or quotations. The time I worked for him, 1987–1991, is practically two generations ago, so I should not assert my recollection as evidence of a truly symbiotic, creative process. Yet, I recall that whatever we jointly edited was jointly authored, and we did publish an op-ed together in *Policy Options* (April 1992), a paper that remains, unfortunately, very relevant: "Section 33: The Demolition Clause in the Constitution."

The terms *Coloured* and *Negro* would have dominated North American references to people of Black African descent in the first thirty-five years of Howard's life (1932 to 1967), with Canadians preferring *Coloured* to *Negro*. By the later 1960s, *Black* or *black* began to enter into *vox populi* parlance as both adjective and noun, but the question of capitalization—or not—was both a matter of political accent and an aesthetic puzzle. Although Howard used both *black* and *Black*, we have chosen to make all instances of *Black* upper case in keeping with the publisher's house style. Up to chapter 10 of this book, Howard tends to use *Coloured*, *Negro*, and *Black* fairly interchangeably, in respect to both the era of his youth and young manhood. By chapters 10 and 11, however, Howard begins to use *Black* predominantly, and the earlier usages become less frequent. As of the 1990s, *African-Canadian* and *Afro-Canadian* become more common, and Howard's consciousness begins to register this shift in nomenclature. As for the "n-word," it is irredeemably hateful and merits our opprobrium. Yet, the pejorative was wantonly operative historically in North America, including through much of the last century, and so Howard uses it—spells it out—*on occasion* to accent its vile, terrorist affect.

Now that I have edited his autobiography, I ask you to savour his life of "firsts." Dr. Howard McCurdy was exemplary in self-sacrifice; he was stellar in avant-garde thought and vision; he was the most absurdly astute perfectionist in statement and study, and the most unforgettably august Black man I ever had the pleasure to know. His birth? Mirrored the dawning of a star.

George Elliott Clarke (X. States)
1 Nisan (April) MMXXI

CHAPTER ONE:
THRESHOLD

I WAS FALLING, PLUNGING DOWNWARD THROUGH AN INFINITE array of rapidly receding points of light in the agitated blackness, an inky cascade. Then, brilliant, blinding white light—an explosive burst, incandescent as fireworks—arrested my descent.

Is my oldest recollection imaginary? Or does it draft my genesis? If so, it occurred nigh 1:30 A.M. on December 10, 1932, at St. Joseph's Hospital in London, ON. Weighing just four-and-one-half pounds, I was a tad premature, testified my mother, Marion Bernice Logan McCurdy. Thanks to my birth, my father was—suddenly—Howard Douglas McCurdy the First. And I had conferred upon me the burden of being called "Junior," "Juney," or "June Bug" by almost everyone—until my "Dr." prefix annulled the "Jr." suffix.

Born in 1914, Bernice was but eighteen when she thrust me free of her womb. She was the daughter of Mary Phoenix and Thomas Logan. Tom, as he got nicked, was half-Jamaican; thus, he dubbed Great Britain the "mother country." I thought that odd: How could a land of lords and ladies foster a nation—Canada—of lumberjacks and railway porters? I also thought it strange that his brother Gilbert, whom I ever saw but once, had a different surname, Williams. All made sense once I knew my grandfather's ancestry.

My great-grandfather Henry Logan and his wife, Mary, were fugitive slaves from Kentucky. They came to Canada via Rochester, New York, where their son, Alex, was born in 1845. Because Henry was only a labourer, it was extraordinary that by 1852 he had acquired the frame house at 709 William Street in London, ON, where I'd spend my boy-hood. Sometime during the 1860s, Mary passed away, and in 1868, the widowed Henry married a Jamaican woman named Norah (or Lenore), age twenty-one. No one knows how a Jamaican woman so young became a Londoner. No matter—she bore Thomas Logan in 1869. (Henry died as 1881 was born.)

My maternal grandfather, Tom Logan—"Poppy" to my sister and me—worked long years as a dining car chef on the Grand Trunk Railway. Also a barber, he cut my hair when I was a child as well as that of others who came to our house—or for which, with clippers in hand, he strolled to theirs.

Once a strapping bloke, he'd been kicked by a horse in his farmhand youth, thus dipping his posture below his otherwise six-foot height. Though stooped in spine, he was natty in dress, sporting spats over his shoes and parading impeccable suits, plus flashy vests festooned with a watch and chain, all regulation gear for churchgoers and swanky dos (and pleasurable don'ts). Poppy defined *charmant*; dude was a choice ladies' man. To my sister and me, he could seem gruff and irritable. But this facade belied his elemental kindness, courtesy, affection. To those manners born was he. (I confess that my own comportment is a mix of honey and vinegar, or sunshine and blizzard. Perhaps I inherited these contrary traits from Poppy!)

Howard McCurdy's parents: Marion Bernice Logan McCurdy and Howard Douglas McCurdy the First, ca. 1950s.

My mother, Bernice, deemed her mother, Mary Logan, "so sickly as to be tragic"—like a Victorian poetess stricken with phthisis. The daughter of an Irish woman, Jeanette Martha McNaughton, and a part-Negro father, David Phoenix, Mary was so pale in pallor and her hair so straight, she looked pure Caucasian. She was generous and the very definition of a doting mama to both Bernice and the adopted girl whom I knew as my mother's sister, namely Helen Ball. Mary was charitable but fragile, and tending to her mother-in-law—notoriously cranky Norah—

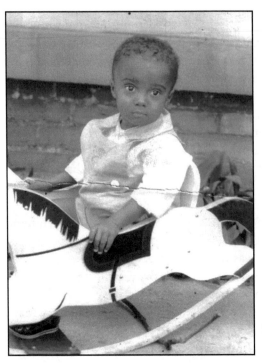

Howard as a toddler on his rocking horse. "Like the Beach Boys, 'I get around.'"

entailed utmost stress. Striving to help elderly Norah down some steps, Mary tripped and broke her hip—with fatal outcome. Her hospital bed bred pneumonia, and she died—aged only forty-two.

Upon Mary's death, Bernice's primary "mom" became the older girl, Helen, who at age sixteen eloped with Arnold Pryor, the "quadrupeds" on his bicycle, to wed in Windsor. Bernice lived with Helen and Arnold until she married Howard McCurdy in 1931.

My parents moved to London where they took up residence at 709 William Street in the house that Henry, my mother's grandfather, had bought eighty years earlier. In the similar house next door, at 711 William Street, dwelt several relatives, and others were nearby, including Aunt Maud who lived near the African-American–planted British Methodist Episcopal (BME) church. We'd lunch with Aunt Maud after Sunday services.

In my boyhood "hood," we McCurdys, Phoenixes, and Browns were the few families of colour about. My Aunt Helen and Uncle Arnold's two teenaged children, Yvonne and Woody, visited London a few weeks each summer. Their stays excited my sister and me because, until our move to Amherstburg, we saw few other Coloured kids outside of Sunday school and services. Most Negro Londoners "shacked" on the hardscrabble side of the CNR tracks.

Come summer of 1934, my sister Marilyn—or as I'd say, Sissy—was born. My first memory of her? Displacing me from my high chair! True: I was seated upon a wooden stool which, placed atop a regular chair, let me dine alongside adults. But I hated having to let Sissy have my seat! Mollification? I was no longer the runt, I was suddenly the big brother. I held dear the responsibility: to keep her out of trouble and protect her

MY BROTHER 4 MYSELF
"TIME WROUGHTS MANY CHANGES"

Howard and his sister Marilyn (Sissy): Home on the range!

from harm. However, when she'd misbehave, I often got blamed—or even injured. In fact, a scar that marked my forehead for several years attested to her having pushed me from my crib!

Another bothersome fact? Due to Marilyn's July debut, she always snagged a birthday gift. But because I was born so nigh Christmas, my birthday present(s) vanished—indistinguishably—into Santa's once-a-year bequests. Hell! Christmas nullified my birthday!

Once Sissy was born, Poppy, who'd often ridden the rails, left the trains to tend us grandkids. That was a boon! His cookery stressed frugality, aye, but with a Jamaican flourish. Thus, we devoured chicken dumplings, eggplant, smoked and salted cod, salmon steak, pork tongue, heart, or kidneys, dandelion and beet greens. Beneath steam or smoke always stewed or simmered a feast!

For one thing, Poppy planted a backyard vegetable garden that flaunted, fascinatingly, peanuts—if a modest yield. Also a backyard vintner, he let me taste his wine—a flavour like grape juice infused with lemonade. Well, I liked it so much that one night, I snuck out, uncorked a bottle of probable wine, and swigged a mouthful. *Surprise! Vinegar!* Not only did I get sick, but I had to fess up to my precocious oenophilia. Instantly, my bottom assumed a burgundy tint and a scorching feel!

William Street boyhood decided my racial attitudes. That Coloured oasis had existed for seventy years as a respected portion of an elsewise paleface neighbourhood. I wandered freely, dropped in on white folks—who always beckoned Sissy and me to sit and stay awhile.

So, I was not self-conscious about my colour, although I did wonder why God had gifted me with supplementary melanin. My hair was a bother, not because it had been demonized as "bad" but because melanin-deprived folk felt compelled to touch it curiously and ask, "How did you get such curly hair?" No, the irksome thing was, when I tried to pretend to be Superman, my hair wouldn't form the blue-rinse curl so prominently angled cross his "flesh-tone," comic-book forehead!

Yet, while acting as my radio hero The Shadow—invisible to the eyes of men—I knew that, thanks to my dark skin, I could don invisibility at night, unlike my too-brightly-complected chums. (How's that for "Black magic"?)

Still, Superman exercised stupendous, absurd influence on my six-year-old self. That he was pasty did not deter me from attempting to emulate his individual superiority—*to excel*. If I could not outrace a bullet or leap tall buildings in a single bound, I could still seek to outrun and out-jump my buddies. My most persistent dream (one repeated even now) of being able to soar—like Superman—above others (a metaphor for achievement) dates from earliest youth.

Then again, as a boy, to me "white" was just a colour. After all, to be officially "Coloured" could encompass various shades—from "indigo" to "ivory." Aunt Pearl, my sister, and I were a molasses tint, whereas Uncle Fred resembled snow. Everyone else, including my mother and father, were amber, copper, tan, and beige gradations. Given this rainbow of melanin among us, "colour" meant nothing to me. We were all the shades of Neapolitan ice cream—as if plunked as a "float" in root beer or ginger beer.

My peers would tease other kids for being fat or for having red hair rather than razz them for their pigment. Shamefully, I admit that I was as guilty of non-racial yet irksome teasing as they.

Still, Sissy and I met with intolerance. One kid—a stranger—would screech, "Eeny meeny miny moe, catch a nigger by the toe," then scram. Once, buddy Donny Ruddy and I chased down brats from the slummy side of the CPR tracks who'd hurled ugly names at Sissy.

Wise Aunt Pearl advised, "Sticks and stones may break your bones, but names will never hurt you." Sure. But Dad disagreed—adamantly. If anyone ever called me "nigger" or mocked my colour, I was ordered to kick the malefactor's mangy butt. No shucking and jiving! Little to no turning of the cheek! I was commanded to definite fisticuffs. Or be sly and sneaky, but exact revenge.

My father gave one other daunting warning: if I were ever to get the strap at school, let me beware my homecoming. These two dicta would later pose a dilemma.

For her part, my mother embraced a Jamaican Africanist movement, I mean Marcus Garvey's Universal Negro Improvement Association (UNIA).

I remember a hefty and thus intimidating Black man, Carl Woodbeck, who'd circulate UNIA literature and speechify roaringly. He exalted Haile Selassie, the Ras Tafari of Rastafarianism, who won global plaudits for his brave resistance to Mussolini's Fascist aggression that pit Italian machine guns against Ethiopian spears.

Such influences informed my ma's tales of our Africa homeland and how our ancestors were warrior kings—like Emperor Selassie. (A bust of a turbaned Black man resting atop Aunt Pearl's dining room cabinet depicted one such potentate.)

Said my mother, my skin was dark because Africa had a torrid sun, and my colour protected me from the sunburn that afflicted my albescent friends, causing their skin to burn and peel. Thus, to be Black is divine. Moreover, many Caucasians expressed exotic fascination with me as a child, thus enhancing my pride in my lustre.

One searing summer day, Mom had dressed me in blue overalls with the legs rolled up. On my head I wore a Mexican-style straw hat with a broad brim trimmed with pendant cotton balls. I was sitting on the curb counting marbles in front of our house when I was interrupted by a woman cyclist. So pale she was, so tall, her dark hair tied in a bun, a dark dress sliding bout her limbs. Sunlight? Her smile. She asked how I came to possess such great big brown eyes and pretty brown skin. "Because I come from Africa," I told her with inflated chest, repeating my mom's version of Genesis, ignorant of its anthropology but avowing it as accurate. When the stranger asked if she could paint me (*like my dad painted houses?*), I thought *that* a weird desire and ran home to tell my mother. She laughed—but met the artist; and then, once a week, I walked the block to the artist's house on Oxford Street for several sittings, each rewarded with a lollipop. The painting of that smiling little four-year-old brown boy wearing the blue overalls, a Mexican hat, and holding a red lollipop now hangs prominently in my den—a reminder of the days before I understood what being "from Africa" and living in Canada really meant.

Although Poppy's father had freed himself and landed in Canada via the Underground Railroad, we never discussed his trek. My entree to slavery? "Negro spirituals." Soulful songs uplifting all. When Mahalia Jackson, Marian Anderson, Paul Robeson, or the Deep River Boys throated these songs from our radio, our whole household wafted cross the River Jordan to Canaan. Freedom songs were our anti-slavery heritage, naming our liberation from hateful Yankee Caucasoids "down South," who abused Africans by forcing them to sweat for zilch. Yet, we also repeated the brain-clouding propaganda that we Coloured

Londoners were fortunate because, being part of the British Empire, which had abolished slavery, Canada had offered our ancestors true liberty.

Assuredly, in my childhood, Blacks were zero in most media. So, when they did materialize, they mesmerized. Alongside spirituals, we audited jazz and blues from the likes of the King Cole Trio, Duke Ellington, and The Ink Spots. Though radio aired pabulum-bland, nasal voices, the exception was Rochester who played the dignified, comedic foil for Jack Benny. Oddly, Poppy's fave program was *Amos 'n' Andy*, two Black characters voiced by Jewish actors.

Although Paul Robeson and Lena Horne headlined a few flicks, most silver-screen Blacks played demeaning roles. *The* movie that excited William Street? *Gone with the Wind*! Every adult saw it; none said why. Naturally, the reason was its two-toned cast, featuring Hattie McDaniel. She became the first Black star to carry off a golden Oscar statuette. Better yet, her character projected gravitas. Still, that was balanced by the "black-face"-inherited "comedy" of Butterfly McQueen (who was, in reality, a cerebral Black-rights activist and a true-blue atheist). Contradictorily, *Gone with the Wind* imbued Blacks with atypical humanity—*and* exploited stubborn stereotypes. As late as the 1960s, Hollywood portrayed Dixie as a noble society, tragically victimized by the North, while slavery got white-washed as a jolly-good praxis, in which saintly "zwiebacks" or "crackers" (whites) cared for happy-go-lucky, obedient, and loyal Negroes. Problematically, any Negro who contested these depictions, proving "uppity" or defiant, could be strung up—left hanging from a tree branch.

One lesson I regrettably gleaned early? Some Black people haste to turn a profit from ridiculing our "race." Yep! Attending a London carnival one year, Donny Ruddy and I reconnoitred a sideshow that featured a "half man, half ape" billed as "outta Africa." This Neanderthal travesty occupied an on-stage cage. Ultra-black with wild, frizzy hair, this missing-link, stooping fool jumped up and down while grunting, growling, jabbering, all to appear abhorrent—an atavistic, throwback fright. Unable to afford a ticket, Donny and I snuck in via the tent's back flap. Backstage, our star ape-man stood perfectly, *Homo sapiens* erect, sipping a Coke and intoning the King's English.

My father held down a job at General Steel Wares or McClary's. We had to live in London because such job sites did not hire Negro Windsorites. Dad also worked part-time (or when laid off, alongside my Uncle Fred) as a painter and decorator and at other times as a plumber or carpenter. My father was a "jack of all trades" to better be the master of debt.

My mother was equally resourceful, working as a seamstress at home and at the tony Artistic Fashion Salon on Richmond Street where she was the first and only Black saleslady in London. She tailored the "dress-up" clothes my sister and I sported. She ensured especially that we always had spanking new threads so we could stroll alongside the Easter Parade. (That cognomen was weird! I never spied the Easter Bunny leading believers to the tomb of the resurrected Jesus!)

Despite paternal "workaholicism" and maternal home-ec, the Depression still dirtied our thirties! Financial stress dogged us. Once, my mother hid my sister and me under the dining room table so we could dodge a bill collector by pretending no one was home.

When my parents lacked the twelve-cent fare for the Patricia Theatre, Sissy and I'd beg Uncle Fred for a "kick in the pants," which was his playful term for the crucial coins. Then, he'd jangle the pennies into our palms. On Saturdays, then, we had the moolah to watch Hopalong Cassidy, Gene Autry, Roy Rogers, and other cowboys gallop or lope cross the screen, or to learn if a weekly serial hero had defied death yet again, his six-gun blazing at a diabolical, top-hat villain.

In September 1937, at age four and a half, I started in kindergarten at St. George's Public School. Vivid is my first day. I see my mother standing in front of our house, tears waterfalling her face, while two older neighbour girls, flanking me, each took me by a hand to escort me the half-mile to school. One gal was Rose Lombardo, sister of the famed bandleader Guy (of the Royal Canadians), and the other a Harding girl, whose brother was Gord Harding, then just a snot-nosed squirt, but who I would know later as Windsor's astute and capable Public Works Commissioner.

I liked school and my teachers, especially Miss Roundtree, who taught kindergarten and grade 1, and Miss Coughlin in the later grades. Vice-Principal George B. Aberhart was always kind to Sissy and me. Never was I ever frowned upon. I even had a little blonde girlfriend, Brenda (the precursor of my beloved helpmate, Brenda?), whose Shirley Temple curls both her mother and mine judged as cute as woven sunshine!

My parents expected me to excel in school. I preferred daydreaming to study though, and that caused concern. Early report cards labelled me lackadaisical. Heck, I enjoyed pondering things—plus blueprinting "inventions" like airplanes powered by giant rubber bands. I also drafted imaginary, futuristic cities. I was more Dr. Seuss than da Vinci but still drew attention.

Worrisomely though, I blinked and stuttered. What motivated these tics? Imitation of my pal, Donny. Polio had hiccoughed his speech. It all drove Pops bonkers! Soon, I got threatened with a thrashing if the over-active eyelids and the fitful tongue did not cease. Well, they did—immediately!

In 1937, a polio epidemic swept through Canada, paralyzing thousands of children. Donny was among the fortunate survivors, his uncontrollable stutter being the only sequela. Luckily, I'd been quarantined within our fenced yard, while Donny had roved the streets, leaving him prey to infection. In contrast, "to ward off the demon," Mom tied a foul-smelling little bag on a string around my neck. (The amulet was indebted to Grandma Norah's Jamaican superstitions.)

Sundays started with Bible stories for kids followed by Rev. Johnson's adult-aimed sermon at Beth-Emmanuel BME Church on Grey Street. Pastor Johnson's wife, Aunt Hattie, made every Sunday seem like Easter. My dad and mom, plus Aunt Pearl, Uncle Fred, and just about everyone we knew, staffed the choir. My dad had a bass as persuasive as Paul Robeson's and a baritone as elegant as Nat King Cole's. His solos islanded you in gravitas or landed you amid paradise.

For Black Canuck London, the church was our Leicester Square and our Piccadilly Circus. Our annual picnics at Springbank Park entailed rides on a mini-railroad. Our Port Stanley picnics boasted an electric train ride. It was also nifty to watch parents shimmy, boogie, and waltz to the bands serenading the pavilion.

The BME church is where I wed for the first time—at the age of four! 'Twas a "Tom Thumb wedding," a fundraiser do. My bride was Pearl Clinton, a pretty li'l gal. Our kiddy nuptials were lauded, and I adored the star turn. Yet, the reception brought a sour note. Awaiting Pearl and me was cake iced superbly with chocolate. I lusted for it, but disaffection lurked! Hidden beneath that sumptuous icing were masses of bug-like tidbits that would forever offend my palate: raisins!

The BME church was not my sole exposure to religion—or to the pious. Some Sundays, a plump, pale "missionary lady" escorted Sissy and me to the big white (in paint *and* congregation) Baptist chapel on Adelaide Street. Thanks to the combined BME and Baptist lessons, I figured out how to distinguish Delilah from David and Samson from Saul. A cinch: dungeons versus *altruism*.

So, Donny and I—as if we couldn't get enough of church—also partook of Thursday eve meetings at the Gospel Hall on Pall Mall. These events always staged a Bible quiz, which I'd ace and thus scoop a chocolate bar reward. (Pass the tryptophan and Praise the Lord!) I later uncovered another fundamentalist church matchingly lucrative in doling out gold-star chocolate confectionery.

However venal I may sound, I believed thoroughly in a God residing *above* the sky (although *where* puzzled me) and in the Garden of Eden, in Jesus and Mary, the Christmas story, and also that the cosmos had been created in six days. Yet, I also believed in Santa Claus, fairies, the bogey-man (lurking in Aunt Pearl's cellar), and, most of all, Superman!

Nightly, before going to bed, Sissy and I recited "Now I lay me down to sleep…" and at every meal thanked God for the food that needy Indians and Chinese did not have and that, therefore, we dare not waste. Yet my mania for reading was already germinating doubt. (For example, why did God not feed the famished Indians and starving Chinese? If not rice, wasn't manna available?)

With parents at work and Poppy sometimes away, nannies watched Sissy and me. The first was Aunt Essie—a light-skinned, thin woman, giraffe-tall (but I'm short on further recollection). Also a vice-mom was Mrs. Hepburn, or "Tanty Hep," an English woman next door. Whenever I packed up my toys in my wagon to flee domestic tyranny—as if a fugitive fleeing slavery—I'd make a beeline to her door!

I'll never forget sitting with Tanty Hep and hearing Adolf Hitler growl from the radio. His aerosolized spittle was riling Europe but also roiling North America. At the Patricia Theatre, between films, the March of Time newsreel soundtracks clopped with jackboots tramping. Though only aged six, I could sense a horrendous war in the offing.

As a boy, Armistice Day ranked fourth in special days after Christmas, Easter, and Halloween. Every November 11, Poppy would don a suit, pin poppies on Sissy and me, and swish us to Victoria Park. How rousing to eye soldiers high-stepping, their rifles aimed at the sun, while drums beat, bugles blared, and bagpipes siren'd! Next, volleys of rifle fire tendered boys a chance to recover a spent shell or two. Booty as precious as Halloween or Christmas candy and Easter eggs!

But what was a lark for me was a solemnity for Poppy. He mourned the Canuck heroes slain in the Great War. For Poppy, the "mother country" was not Ethiopia, nor any other African realm. It was Great Britain where our King and Queen resided and ruled over the British Empire. The Empire had painted red one quarter of the globe. Every race and colour knelt to the Windsors—as if the Brit sovereigns superseded the King of Kings. Each school-day began with pupils begging God to "save the King." Songs like "Rule, Brittania" and "There Will Always Be an England" riveted St. George's Public School. Even as primary scholars, we'd have gaily perished to defend the chain-smoking George VI's right to pig out on cigs!

Schoolboys love gangs, eh? Joining Donny *et moi* was Bill Harding, Jerry from 'cross the street, and Archie Metcalf. A redhead and our elder, Archie seemed to know all that lads crave to know. He led our escapades: hikes to the Big Pond, raids on pear trees, and nervy dodging of the railway cops along the box factory sidings. Like Cockney rascals (bellies sacking pints and throats floating cusses), we scourged north London! Hooray!

Most treasured was our secret underground hideout that Donny and I tunnelled—according to my blueprints. Sissy—Marilyn—chatelained a miniature doll house (constructed by our dad) in our backyard (take that, Virginia Woolf!), but we pint-size "gangsters" needed a place of *our* own. So, in a vacant lot, we dug a seven-by-four-by-four-foot hole with a roof of boards covered by dirt and grass and an entrance tree-branch-camouflaged. Tossing about smokescreen-thick shade was a large maple inhabited by my pet squirrel, one that would jump on my shoulders to nosh passionately on peanuts.

In our subterranean "bunker," Archie revealed sex secrets via "Tijuana bibles." Agog were we as the outsized appendages of Popeye and L'il Abner plumbed the squirting depths of Olive Oyl and Daisy Mae Yokum. Much joy took we in musing on such joys—until our hideout met a dastardly end! In April 1939, damnable bulldozers filled in our trench! "Royals" were set to tour our deputy London, and our tot lot now had to accommodate hustings, bleachers, and portable "johns." Hell!

During their whistle-stop, cross-Canada tour, King George VI and Queen Liz surveyed the troops parading at Wolseley Barracks, and Princesses Elizabeth and Margaret passed right by our house in their elaborately festooned horse-drawn carriage! Years later, at the Commonwealth Heads of Government Conference in Vancouver (in October 1987) during an impromptu one-on-one with the Queen, I told Liz Windsor of the sacrifice of my "bunker" that her long-ago visit had necessitated. She was bemused—if not amused. Perhaps she saw the bleak irony that, not long after I lost my trench, her wartime PM, Winston Churchill, had had to duck into his own, to shelter from the Blitz.

The royal family's 1939 Canada travel was undertaken to ensure the Dominion's loyalty because the war clouds over Europe were thundering, klaxoning a cataclysm. Though but a child, I knew that Hitler and Mussolini were brutish wackos who deserved to be whacked. So, as August vacation ended at my Aunt Helen's Windsor abode, I exulted to hear a Border Cities' *Star* paperboy hollering, "Extra, Extra—WAR declared!" Wouldn't the goose-stepping monsters be fast dispatched—ideally by electric chair? As it turned out, well, not so fast. Soon, the war would dominate all, but its impact developed gradually. Life in "London II" changed glacially. Still, I began to perceive that racial, religious, and ethnic differences were grounds of division that bred bedevilling loyalties and debilitating strife.

This lesson was borne out when the Hepburns moved. A rumour swept the neighbourhood: Catholics gonna smack down Protestants! So scurrilously were the "Papists" dissed, I expected to see their heads sprout horns. But when the Noonan family settled in, they were superbly normal and were soon our best buds and gal-pals.

Nevertheless, in wartime, repugnant ridicule of "Eyeties," "Jerries," and "Japs" was rife. And though Hitler's abuse of Jews was condemned, many Londoners were sickeningly anti-Semitic. But not us McCurdys! We accorded Jews special respect because they were good and welcoming to "us"—the Coloureds. Our MD, Dr. Tillman, was a Jew; a Jew delivered me at birth; and Jews hired my mother—at the Artistic Fashion Salon— thus publicly flouting "genteel" segregation.

When Joe Louis fought Max Schmeling for the second time, every radio about huzza'd the Negro boxer's lightning victory over the reluctant Nazi hero from whom he had suffered his only defeat. But our two Coloured clans at 709 and 711 William Street were deliriously ecstatic! We'd witnessed, twice in two years, another one of "us"—Louis following Olympic gold medalist Jesse Owens—disprove Hitler's claim to Nazi superiority and concomitant white supremacy.

We also recalled that when, during their first match in 1941, Billy Conn—the "Great White Hope"—outpointed Louis, Canuck Caucasians cheered lustily. Though Louis prevailed by knockout in a later round, I knew our shared melanin had bound me to hail his win. (Crystal clear for Coloured London was the stark hypocrisy of zwieback-bossed democracies attacking black-shirt and brown-shirt states, while condoning white-hood, ethno-racial prejudice in their own domains.) When the Daughters of the American Revolution, in April 1939, refused to allow Marian Anderson, perhaps the greatest contralto of the century, to sing in Constitution Hall, just steps from the White House, outrageously evident was the hideous salience of the colour bar.

In 1941, Uncle George, my dad's youngest brother, a brand-new army inductee, arrived for training at nearby Wolseley Barracks. George was my favourite uncle, my hero, and, for most of my life, my best friend. In those days, he'd march with his platoon past our house, and I observed his gallantry with unadulterated exhilaration. A gifted athlete, George bested all in the army's heavyweight bouts and sprint races. (Later, Uncle George coached me brilliantly in track and field. But he could not render me a pugilist; I had no desire to smash others but to soar to excellence. My ideal was the cartoon Superman—a do-gooder—not Nietzsche's sadistic Übermensch.)

The war preoccupied me no end. I studied every battle canvassed in the dailies, on the radio, and in the newsreels. Fighter planes fascinated me so much, every spare school-day minute I drew Hurricanes, Spitfires, Stukas, Messerschmidts, and later Japanese Zeros, rat-a-tat-tatting black rounds through blue sky. Constantly playing with toy airplanes, the sounds I made to imitate their engine noises elicited my father's sole nickname for me: Buzz!

By late 1941, the Allies had just managed to stave off defeat. On December 7, three days before I turned nine, we were munching lunch when broadcast music was silenced by the news that "Japs" had bombed Pearl Harbor. I knew immediately what this meant and leapt from the table to race to Donny's house to announce, "Yanks are gonna join the Allies!"

Almost simultaneously, Marilyn—Sissy—became a star by singing the Negro spiritual "Swing Low, Sweet Chariot" over the school loudspeaker system. Her spectacular rendition of "our" music blessed every Coloured pupil with electrifying and appropriate ego-enhancement. At recess, though, I got schooled in negativity. A lad tarred me as "Sambo." Curiously, I did not judge as racist the story of *Little Black Sambo*. After all, an Indian boy triumphs, heroically conquering tigers by turning them into butter! But I heard the epithet as an insult, and so the offender qualified for the response my father had recommended. I stalked my prey until he bent to a drinking fountain. Soon as he took a sip, I bopped him on the head, banging his mouth on the metal spout. He spat out watery blood as he hollered from the dental hurt. To the vice-principal's office I was promptly sent for this vengeful infraction.

Mr. Aberhart was sympathetic; he understood my reasoning. But punishment could not be abridged. I gulped with fear when he withdrew from his desk a strap as wide, black, slick, and hellish as smoking pitch laid on a roof. Expecting flame-hot pain, I held out my palm. The strap alighted feather-light, feather-cool. Grinning, Mr. Aberhart intoned, "Stay out of trouble." Although I had struck a bully just as my father had commanded, it was with a consequence that my father had equally warned against. To me, I'd been strapped. It was a dilemma and a guilty secret that I would never reveal to him—and feared for many years that he'd uncover.

Escaping the strap but vanquishing a bully marked successes—if also traumas. But unmitigated woe did occur. I owned a black Labrador Retriever I'd dubbed "Spot" due to the white fur on his chest. Though a new pet, he heeded my dicta. The last? I summoned him to cross the street. Car brakes screeched; metal thudded hide. Blood streamed from his snout. Days, yes, I wept, yes, disconsolate.

To become a Boy Scout was every lad's ambition, and I was no exception. So, donning my Cub Scout uniform for the first time, I felt as supercharged as Clark Kent must when he changes into Superman. (However, I'd never earn even one badge; we moved to Amherstburg before I got the chance.)

While war work was ending Depression joblessness, our family yet faced dire straits. Faith, Hope, and Charity—three bantam chickens given me as pets by Grandfather McCurdy—vanished. Shortly, we dined on meat so tough, you'd need an axe to chop the flesh. Guttling my fowl we were! When I complained, my dad retorted, "We have to eat something!" The one London pet that survived our meal plans and road traffic was the grey squirrel that lived in the maple beside our house. He would jump on my shoulder when I called and allow me to carry him around as I pleased.

Just after Faith, Hope, and Charity ended up on the chopping block, my dad landed railway employ. For Black men in 1941 (as in 1891), train work furnished a mortgage-paying wage plus lucrative tips. The Black bourgeoisie was all railroaders. Indeed, Poppy was a retired dining car chef. (Until the 1960s, Blacks could not aspire to be train conductors or engineers.) For us, railway men were aristocrats, but their tasks were as body-and-soul-destructive as slave work. (Pick up Stanley Grizzle's 1997 memoir, *My Name's Not George*.) But my father could not abide insults. Despite his nice haul in tips from a transcontinental run, once home, he quit the tracks. Soon, we moved to Amherstburg: Dad had snagged a gig at the Ford Motor Company in Windsor.

Amherstburg was the McCurdy ancestral home. Sissy and I relished our summer stays with our there-domiciled grandparents, for we had many Black playmates. One was Charles Hurst with whom I played shoot-'em-up games in the old ruins of the nineteenth-century "Coloured school." In Amherstburg too, there was a capacious town library, well-stocked with tales to prime a yen for derring-do. The five-and-dime store vended cap pistols as loud and as fire-spitting as cannon. So, relocating to Amherstburg—Ontario's oldest town—in the summer of '42 meant finding more fun.

Our departure was delayed due to my last London lark with Donny. We'd been purloining pears (just like the young, "wascally" Saint Augustine) from a neighbour's tree when a branch broke, so I slammed to earth, snapping a wrist bone so painfully, I wailed, "I'm gonna lose my arm!" Thus, I arrived in Amherstburg sporting a cast—thus cast as deserving sympathy.

CHAPTER TWO:
HOME TRUTHS

OUR ANTIQUATED HOUSE AT 106 GEORGE STREET, AMHERSTBURG, was Victorian only in archaeology, not architecture. Reputedly, a century earlier it had been the prestigious abode of an abolitionist, John Sloane. Now, it was a mouldering barn. My father needed two years, all his trade skills, and hard labour—with aid from my Uncle Alvin—to displace dilapidation with a dwelling. Saws had to screech, hammers bam, glass tinkle, and plaster blam down before we could inhabit a two-storey, white-clapboard home in simple nineteenth-century style, situated on a half-acre. Beside it, lush, beautiful lilac bushes separated a large lawn from a cultivated backyard in which potatoes and other vegetables took root and currant and blackberry bushes and pear, cherry, and apple trees flourished. We even had a chicken coop. (But I gave up keeping poultry as pets; too quickly could they fatten a pot!)

Until the reno was history, I had no bedroom. So, for the first year or so, I slept at my great-grandmother Mary Davis's demesne on Sandwich Street. Gran was my Grandfather McCurdy's mother. She'd divorced George D. McCurdy Sr., then outlived second hubby Fred Davis, a lawyer (and son of Delos Davis, the pioneer attorney and Canada's first Black King's Counsel). Gran was a petite lady whose physiognomy reflected her purported Indian ancestry. She had a double relationship to my grandmother Laura, whose sister had married Gran Davis's brother Robert. She was both mother-in-law and sister-in-law to Gran McCurdy. Gran Davis and I were pals. Once I ceased boarding with her, I still stopped by after school to say hi and do chores. I'd mow her lawn or ride my bike to collect rent from the Negro and Caucasian tenants of her Sandwich Street properties. She was a feminist before her time and a capitalist for the ages.

Gran loved to take me to movies; at times, my aunt Mabel Simpson, my grandfather's sister, joined us. The two grandes dames gossiped and bantered matter-of-factly of ghosts, spell-binding, and witchy goings-on. Was Gran's house haunted? True: I heard bizarre noises—but only due to rats slithering and scratching behind the walls. Really "haunting"? The stench of poison-slain rodents, rotting behind wallpaper, slats, and plaster.

Gran Davis also loved yakking on the phone, which, back then, still had a crank to ring up an operator. Party lines abounded, so Gran ranted about others wiretapping her gab fests; yet, she herself gloried in eaves-dropping! She also liked to tipple from a "medicine" bottle secreted in a dining room cabinet. Most fascinating to me—most coveted by me—was the nickel-plated, pearl-handled, snub-nosed revolver Gran kept in her night-table drawer. (Her persona mirrored a Bette Davis siren of unfathomable morals in a psychologically puzzling film noir.) An old law library was mysteriously closeted behind a door leading from the upstairs bathroom. Could this site shelter ghosts? (Well, every book is but a detached house haunted thoroughly by its spectral author.)

A year after arriving in Amherstburg, I was shaken awake post-midnight, bundled up, and taken from Gran Davis's to 106 George Street: Poppy had gone to Heaven. A devastating loss! Because our parents worked day jobs, Poppy had been nanny and tutor for me and Sissy. Even so, the sorrow that was his death delivered unto me the blessing of having a bedroom at home.

Now, I resumed my friendship with Charles Hurst, whom I had met during previous Amherstburg stays. However, other Black kids—classmates—spurned my sister and me. The Amherstburg Public School was smaller than St. George's, so grades 5 and 6 shared one room. Having skipped a grade in my last year at St. George's, I was in grade 6, but pupils my age and older were stuck in grade 5. Worse, I vaunted my smarts: I answered queries snappily, while my classmates stayed mum. My smarty-pants ways peeved some. And being short, and sporting short pants, I seemed puckish—adorable to teachers but unbearable in the schoolyard. Too, Sissy and I were dissed as privileged. Unlike many pupils, because we were our family's sole offspring, we didn't have to vie with multiple siblings for attention or for new clothes or for extra helpings of meat or sweets.

Bullies loathed my elocution, my vocabulary, my high marks, my preppy duds, my slight build, my lack of penury. I was accused of "acting white" or "trying to be white." How I feared the school-day's final bell! Lugs would lurk in the schoolyard—to browbeat me for scoring all the A's.

A zaftig, cheerful woman, Miss French—my first homeroom teacher—and Principal Alan Buchanan urged on my scholastic attainments. With few exceptions, from primary to university, teachers were supportive. I felt I could choose any profession, any career, and succeed.

The exception to this school-house indulgence? A teach—his name long since lost—who replaced Mr. Buchanan and whom my peers denounced instantly as "prejudiced." Once, when I was in eighth grade, he refused my request to go to the washroom. When I again raised my hand to say that I absolutely needed relief, he grabbed me by the back of my shirt and hurtled my entire seventy-five pounds past rows of desks, to smack the wall, then bounce to the floor. I reported this assault to my mother. Upset, she called my three uncles. The triumvirate—Alvin, George (who was on furlough), and Ralph—marched to the principal's office and, as the coward cowered behind his desk, advised that he upgrade his pedagogy. This avuncular intervention bought me street cred; thus, the after-school harassment ebbed to ribbing.

Another teacher, Sarafine Lanue, stands out in my mind because I once teased her mischievously by telling the class that her name could be loosely translated as *naked angel* ("Seraphin the nude"). Plush, scarlet blushing accompanied—agreeably—her congrats of my lingual sleuthing!

Trying to resume my involvement in the Boy Scouts (whom I'd joined in "London II"), I ran bluntly into Amherstburg's "black codes." Knowing that conclaves assembled at the United Church, off I went, to my first. But pallid adults objected to my Coloured self being mustered in their Caucasoid assembly. Wouldn't I feel more "comfy" leaguing with other Negroes? In letters between the Amherstburg Coloured Community Club (of which Uncle Ralph was secretary) and the local Scout bosses, the latter volunteered to form a Coloured-only troop. We rejected this apartheid idea; still, the Amherstburg Boy Scouts disbanded rather than integrate, so I never was again a Scout.

Considering that Blacks sat in the same classrooms as Caucasians and that our prowess distinguished the top sports teams, the positing of a segregated Scout troop was farcical. Yet, Negrophobia was as common in

Amherstburg as it was throughout the Dominion (railway porters told of Halifax fights, Montreal plights, and Vancouver slights). Everywhere, though, it was a hit-and-miss practice.

Like ours, most Black families dwelled nigh King and George Streets or in a blighted, eastern section dubbed "Back o' Town." Exceptions were Gran Davis on Sandwich Street and respected, old-stock, Black, blue-blood dynasties such as the Deans and Fosters.

Negroes also peopled the Texas Road, north of town. The Browns—descendants of a fugitive slave my great-great grandfather helped along the Underground Railroad—resided there.

The distribution of Amherstburg Blacks reflected unquestionably historical settlement patterns. Yet housing was not apartheid-level segregated; most Blacks had Caucasian neighbours. Even so, real-estate covenants excluded both Negroes and Jews from purchasing certain properties.

Excepting Clarence Simpson who hauled coal—and the Canadian Canners factory during canning season (when hands of all tints helped to top the tins)—no Blacks worked in Amherstburg. The coal-ash-discoloured red hair of many local Coloureds (the result of ingesting a noxious brew of lead, arsenic, and mercury) signified their stigmatized jobs at Brunner Mond (later Allied Chemical), just north of town. The Ford Motor Company, eighteen miles away in Windsor, only began to hire Negroes—including my dad, grandfather, and Uncle Ralph—thanks to that faraway, anti-Fascist war opening up home-front opportunities in industries helmed by domestic fascists.

The Boblo Island Amusement Park engaged summertime Coloured help. Yet, although it operated on Bois Blanc Island, on Canadian soil, its American owners refused Negroes admission. Luckily, segregated Black Detroit permitted Canuck Coloureds to obtain jobs commensurate with our training or skills. So, unable to staff offices in the Dominion—despite stellar academic credentials—my aunts Laura Jean and Dorothy went north, to Detroit (Windsor, ON, being south of Detroit, MI), to be secretaries.

Across southwestern Ontario, eateries refused Negroes service. Or, they'd seat us at a counter, not at tables. In the midst of the Second World War, the Canadian Armed Forces were integrated, but the local Legion Hall excluded Coloured veterans. The Brunner Mond Club was for ofays only. Most local beaches barred Blacks, save Colchester near Harrow. But in Harrow itself, the cinema only admitted Negroes to the balcony. Although few "Whites Only" signs were seen, rife was anti-Negro racism. Some Essex County towns even had "sunset" (curfew) bylaws aimed at Coloureds.

As in the 1930s, 1940s pop culture still played to noxious stereotypes. The pattern had been fixed in silver salts by D. W. Griffith's classic flick *Birth of a Nation*, which pictured blackfaced whites presenting Negroes as subhuman fools and/or ghouls. In ads and photos, we were "jigaboos," bug-eyed and saucer-lipped. In movies, Stepin Fetchit was slow-moving and slow-witted. Although his eyes and teeth lit up the dark, Mantan Moreland was scared of his own shadow. Depicted as thugs, pimps drooling after pink-toed jailbait, and as drug-mad junkies, we were cast as meriting, justly, violent suppression. Thus, pitiful death row Negroes sobbed bluesy spirituals while awaiting coffins. But paleface gangsters—perpetrators of massacres, instigators of assassinations—appeared on screen as manly, square-jawed, tommy-gun–toting outlaws.

Blackface crooners like Al Jolson (whom I delighted to imitate) were a staple of minstrel shows that raised funds for service clubs that no veritable Blacks could join. General Amherst High staged plays featuring blacked-up characters. (When Patty Foster agreed to play a shoe-polish-darkened Negress, we Coloured kids told her that she had disgraced her family's abolitionist past.)

Michigan radio and Detroit newspapers conveyed Negrophobia far and wide; so, Amherstburg whites parroted what they heard and read. Too, many Yanks had summer or even permanent homes among us; indeed, 75 percent of car licence plates about town had US origins. Surely, many ex-pat Yanks vroomed and broadcast Dixie attitudes to our burg.

While privately owned, segregated public facilities verified the bigotry of Uncle Sam clientele, many Canucks smiled smugly along. They would assert their abhorrence of racism while upholding it, claiming they had no choice but to cater to Negrophobes who did not want to associate with—or even be served by—our people: "Not our fault. Sorry!" (Are not Canucks such inveterate hypocrites?)

Racism also inspired the patronizing address of some *blancs* for Blacks, calling us "Sam," "boss," "boy." Others adopted a faux Dixie accent peppered obnoxiously with "y'all." Superficially, tolerant co-existence honoured Amherstburg's noble history as a haven for Blacks seeking freedom. Subliminally, however, racism smoldered, catching fire, here and there, in a tossed Molotov cocktail or in a blazing Ku Klux Klan cross.

London had not accustomed me to such racism, for Negroes there were less than 1 percent of the populace (approximately 300 souls out of 200,000). In Amherstburg, we were 10 percent (approximately 300 souls out of 3,000) and so viewed as threatening Euro "purity" and redneck job security. Even so, Amherstburg Negroes impugned the African heritage that my mother extolled. They adhered to a colour hierarchy, wherein Sissy and I, being dark-complected, were supposedly sinful and devilish. Straight hair was "good"; kinky, "bad." A passed-down, racist orthodoxy.

Lookit! Some "Coloured people" saw blackness as a contaminant. One group fought to obtain "Indian Papers." For some, *white* was right, *black* backward, *brown* a downer.

A lexicon of self-deprecating racial epithets—spooks, shines, darkies, coons, nappy heads, and, of course, the N-word—abused our egos. (Yet, any Caucasian who directed such terms our way was liable for a bruising.) How could expressions of self-hatred be reconciled with some Negroes being taunted for "acting white"? Well, our quandaries were four-square social, cultural, economic, and religious.

Most Negroes arrived via the Underground Railroad, so Amherstburg, ideally situated on the Detroit River, soon became a busy terminus. Even before the US Fugitive Slave Act of 1793, persons of African descent—including some who were free United Empire Loyalists or some who were slaves of cracker Loyalists (such as the Babys)—were already residents. With the British Emancipation Act of 1834 and the American Fugitive Slave Act of 1850, a trickle of fugitives became a tsunami. By the time of the American Civil War, about half of the 2,500 people living in Amherstburg were of African descent.

Contrary to what many credit, not all Negroes who landed in Canada during that period were fugitives. Many were free persons fleeing "black codes" and slave-catcher harassment, even in North Star states. They were generally better educated and trades-trained than were their ex-slave compatriots. They were also, often, mixed-race persons.

In pre–US Civil War Amherstburg, they owned and operated the only hotel, a tavern, grocery and hardware stores, barber shops, the blacksmith shop, and the stagecoach to Windsor. At Puce, Gilgal, and New Canaan, all-Black farm collectives flourished.

Free-born Blacks hobnobbed easily with Caucasians. Their voice was *The Provincial Freeman*, a broadsheet issued by Mary Ann Shadd (Cary), North America's first Black woman publisher and Canada's first woman publisher. Solidly integrationist, Shadd opened an interracial school.

Henry Bibb's newspaper was *The Voice of the Fugitive*. Unlike Shadd, he was an escaped slave and advocated separate Negro settlements and even emigration "back to Africa."

Separatists damned integrationists for "trying to be white," a charge sometimes justified. (This criticism—directed at me all my life—enacts racist self-hatred, eh? To think that literacy, enunciated speech, prosperity, and good manners are only "white" attributes enacts a most wanton self-sabotage. To prize dignity, though, is a natural, non-racial, human prerogative.) Their opposing orientations saw separatists and integrationists establish polar-opposite organizations.

My Uncle Alvin strove to preserve Amherstburg's Underground Railroad history. An amateur but scrupulous historian, his knowledge of family chronicles and local events aided the research of scholars such as Fred Landon of the University of Western Ontario and Yale's own Robin W. Winks, author of that formidable tome of scathing criticism of Black Canada, *The Blacks in Canada: A History* (1971). Al's papers now occupy a prominent position in the Archives of Ontario (see archives.gov.on.ca/en/explore/online/alvin_mccurdy/mccurdy-collection.aspx).

Certainly, Uncle Alvin's studies turned up Nasa McCurdy, the manumitted son of an enslaved woman and her master. While still enslaved, Nasa was permitted independent carpentry labour. Did he fight alongside George Washington in the American Revolutionary War? Maybe. Signed by Rachel Kennedy in 1793, Nasa's manumission document cited his valuable support during the "insanity" (likely Loyalist sentiments) of her husband, his master. Next, Nasa acquired hundreds of acres of farmland in Greene County, Pennsylvania, and wed (perhaps his second wife) Hannah McGill, a slave master's daughter. He even served on a jury, which was a rare deed for a Negro, for service required that the person be literate.

Hannah and Nasa had eleven children, the descendants of whom were Caucasian *and* Negro. Five of their sons wound their way to Amherstburg, and one, Nasa Jr., was not only an ardent abolitionist and an Underground Railroad "agent," but fellow-travelled with radical abolitionists Martin Delaney and Frederick Douglass. In his honour, Nasa Jr. named one son George Douglas(s). Since that time, one male in every generation of Nasa's descendants has carried the name Douglas(s), including me.

Nasa Jr.'s name materializes in Amherstburg in 1846 as the chair of the Building Committee of the First Baptist Church. A realtor for and builder of Black churches, either African Methodist Episcopal (AME) or Baptist, in Amherstburg, Sandwich, and the county, his name is legibly carved in the Amherstburg AME church on two wooden pulpits he crafted. Nasa Jr. became one of Amherstburg's model citizens—a constable, a bailiff, and an elected school board trustee. He and his wife, Permilia Bailey McCurdy, were blessed with seven children, among them my great-grandfather, George Douglas McCurdy Sr.

Other notable McCurdy antecedents include William Henry McCurdy, dubbed "The Squire," an agricultural aristocrat in Colchester, and Joseph McCurdy, who established the McCurdy Coal and Lumber Company in Michigan. (His offspring—who became white McCurdys—included William Harvey McCurdy, an illustrious industrialist of the first half of the twentieth century, associated with both the Coldspot and Whirlpool corporations.)

Another part of our family's history and prized possessions are the manumission papers of my great-great-grandmother Susan Holten and her children. Their mistress, Mary Kirk, brought them from Kentucky to Ohio to be set free by a "Buckeye" court. Said Uncle Alvin, Susan's hubby, Randolph Holten was born a Burr and was the son and ex-slave of President Aaron Burr. (Gentle reader, of the forty-five US Presidents to date, 25 percent owned slaves.)

The Civil War done, Negro Canucks dove stateside in droves. Amherstburg's Black bourgeoisie? Gone! However, the McCurdys and other Black clans stayed. They would not abandon the churches and the farms in which their forebears had invested so much, nor the social and familial ties established with neighbours of all hues.

A grandson of George Douglas McCurdy Sr., Melvin "Mack" Simpson, initiated the Amherstburg Black Historical Museum. Another descendant, Merlin (Merle) McCurdy, was a star African-American public servant in the 1960s. To pay for his law studies, Merle deckhanded on Great Lakes ore boats. After Merle garnered his LL.B., Prez Jack Kennedy appointed him a US District Attorney in Northern Ohio. Next, Prez Johnson named him the first Consumer General, to advocate for the interests of consumers regarding prices and product safety. Set to become the first Black US Attorney General, Merle dropped dead of a brain hemorrhage in May 1968. George Steinbrenner christened a Great Lakes bulk-ore carrier in his name: the *Merle M. McCurdy*.

My grandfather, George D. McCurdy Jr., at sixteen, also caught the merchant marine bug; he was the youngest chief steward on the Great Lakes. He and Laura had six children: my father, Howard, was the first-born, followed by Ralph, Alvin, George Frederick, Dorothy, and Laura Jean.

The males all earned nicknames. My dad was "The Big Six" or "Peanuts" (because "goobers" crammed his pockets); Ralph was "Skinny"; Al was "Gravy"; George was "Cowboy." With my grandfather, they formed a supreme quintet, harmonizing on such chestnuts as "I've Been Working on the Railroad" and "O Mary Don't You Weep." Their concerts? Part church choir, part shindig.

Most weekends, the McCurdy homestead saw milk, eggs, sugar, flour, all grandmothered into fried cakes, chocolate cake, or apple pie. Monday visits ensured that leftover pastries and baked beans had no shelf-life beyond twenty-four hours.

Indeed, the family ran a general store and associated bakery. But neither outran the Depression. With the businesses shuttered, then winter freezing out freighter work, my grandfather turned to the law he'd acquired in his stepfather's office. Becoming a paralegal and notary public, presiding over routine legal needs, he pursued this employ until retirement.

Grandfather George was esteemed. Offering for Amherstburg town council in the 1950s, he led all polls—and did so in all of his electoral summits. Admired for his astute analyses and eloquence, he soon became deputy reeve. Fifteen were his years of elected service—and of his expansive influence over municipal policy.

Despite his success, my grandfather never sought the mayoralty; he knew that ambition would rile envious Caucasians. Still, one marker of his lasting celebrity is Amherstburg's McCurdy Drive—a half-kilometre-plus of residential street that begins straight and narrow, ends similarly, but vaunts a north-pitched, middle "bulge" resembling an expectant womb. (The street design allegorizes George McCurdy's rhetoric: to the point, yes, but also curvaceous with flourishes, unto the clinching rectitude.)

George's children were also stellar. Not only a historian, Alvin headed the local carpenters' union. Ruling over Ford Canada's chemistry lab, Ralph developed a revolutionary new method for water purification, which saved the company millions by avoiding potential pollution fines and/or law suits. He jetted to Ford plants globally to oversee the adoption of the new process.

To achieve racial equality, Ralph primed sit-ins in Dresden, ON, and was an officer of the South Essex Citizens' Advancement Association (SECAA). Like his father before, Ralph sat on Amherstburg's town council as well as the school board. Due to his fanhood for local sports, the town's athletic park bears his name.

George and I allied in jousting against bigotry. He led the SECAA to close the last segregated school in Ontario in Colchester, and we eliminated job discrimination in Amherstburg. Once prez of the carpenters' union local and executive secretary of the Carpenters and Joiners of Ontario, he joined the Canadian Human Rights Commission, then directed the Nova Scotia Human Rights Commission, and was a Canuck appointee to the United Nations Human Rights Commission. (George viewed civil rights, human rights, and labour rights as constructing three sides of an impregnable social-justice pyramid.)

Now Amherstburg-settled, my mother was an independent seamstress. However, the income was spotty, the task boring. Practical nursing became her trade, which she plied over two summers at Boblo Isle Amusement Park. Dissatisfied with that employ, she qualified herself to manage the Quality Control Lab at Canadian Canners, thus taking a position unprecedented for a Black woman.

My father, the oldest, the strongest, the handsomest, and likely the brightest of the George McCurdy boys, was an introvert. But also a paragon of industry. To him, lassitude was devilry. To hold down always two jobs at once was his champagne and caviar. The show-horse workhorse, he instilled in me the ethic to do my best—to be the best. To do is to be; to be is to do.

But Howard the First was not alone in emulating the craft of our ancestor, Nasa McCurdy. His brothers carpentered, yes, but my dad was a Michelangelo with wood. He crafted incisive, beautiful ideas. Thus, he led his bros to compose a woodworking studio in an old converted barn in Gran Davis's backyard. They crafted doors whose swing was whispers, windows that were themselves the view.

CHAPTER THREE:
BAPTISMS PLURAL

AFTER A YEAR, AMHERSTBURG WAS MY CRIB. STILL, VESTIGES OF
yearning for London and homeys—like bosom pal Donny Ruddy—pained
my heart. To salve my sense of Essex County exile *ex* Middlesex County,
I sheltered in the Amherstburg library where I, often the sole patron,
hoovered up the ABCs of astronomy, biology, and chemistry. How fascinating to learn that I was an abracadabra, alchemical amalgam of stardust
and bacteria, sulphur and sugar!

I also enlarged my already humongous comic-book holdings, which
numbered first editions of Superman, Captain Marvel, the Flash, and others. (Geez, I'd be a multi-millionaire had Dad not trashed my stash!)
Amherstburg Black kids distrusted literacy, so there was no comic-book
sharing among us. True: I did trade storybook graphics with paleface chums.
But, unlike white London friends, they never asked me to their homes.

No matter—I relished Classics Illustrated editions of *Kidnapped*, *Treasure
Island*, *Robinson Crusoe*, *Gulliver's Travels*, *Huckleberry Finn*, and *Tom Sawyer*. The
latter two works did seem racist, unlike the treatment of Friday in *Robinson
Crusoe*. Sho nuff, *ni**er* abounded, but also pronounced was author Mark
Twain's anti-slavery view. *Uncle Tom's Cabin* furnishes like pluses and
minuses. (To ask Black pupils to read such works aloud is mischievous;
but to discourage reading them is misguided.)

Gradually, Sissy and I forged new alliances, including with next-door siblings Junior and Doreen Harris, plus their cousins, and friends like Charles Hurst and his sister, Barbara. Never sat in the same grade, Charles and I were extramural buds. We hunted frogs, fished, hiked to the old quarry or Big Creek, and war-gamed among the battlements of Old Fort Malden. Other leisure? Park pool swims and gloveless softball matches. But no hockey! Because Amherstburg is nestled in Canada's tropic zone, winter whelped little snow and froze little water. My skates just rusted away.

Inseparable were Charles and I, but indispensable to our escapades was my prized dog, Butch. Whatever the game or frolic, my mostly collie canine leapt and loped, fetched and barked, non-stop. Let anyone bully me, even jokingly, and snarls were growled and fangs were bared! Butch was—as a dog can uniquely be to a child—my most copacetic and simpatico chum.

Yet, boyhood ain't all puppy dogs and snails. Charles and I had chores that mandated discipline. Because his family was sizeable, his duties were more numerous, more onerous than mine. If left undone or done grudgingly, Charles would feel the bite of the cat-o'-nine-tails. A tad extreme, yes. But the *threat* of a whupping can call up inspiration!

A weekly task for Charles was hauling home cartloads of free corncobs from a grain elevator. They burned as well as wood or coal. (Many folks still used coal oil—kerosene—lamps.) My duties? Cut grass, trim bushes, plant and weed the vegetable garden, and whitewash stones edging the lawn.

The last job calls to mind an anecdote proving book smarts useful! Once, while I was whitewashing stones, Junior Harris happened by. Emulating Tom Sawyer, I convinced him that the daubing was so much fun, he just had to finish the job for me! (*The Art of the Deal*, à la Trump!)

A profitable chore? To feed and water our chickens, clean the coop, and harvest eggs. Those exceeding our culinary needs were sold for pocket change.

My most hateful labour? Carting home fifty-pound bags out the coal yard. So sweaty and sooty was it, to heave and heft my own body weight! Smearing my ebony self with Vantablack streaks!

The Amherstburg First Baptist Church so preoccupied my family that we basically occupied it! My parents harmonized in the choir; Sissy and I warbled from the pews. Our church involvement also meant joining the (Af-Am) Prince Hall Masons and its sorority, the Order of the Eastern Star. (Granddad was the Lodge's Ontario Grand Master.)

A descendent of Delos Davis, Cleo May Dean, a superb Sunday school teacher, was so super-fine that I had to shut my eyes—in prayer—to try to temper the tempestuous feelings that she aroused. Yep! When she wed and left Amherstburg, the town turned to thorns and dust. (Cleo bore Tony Dungy, later the top coach of the National Football League's Indianapolis Colts.)

Amherstburg First Baptist church members descended from white-gloved, black–top-hatted, abolitionist McCurdys, et al. Another Nasa Jr.–erected edifice, the Nazrey African Methodist Episcopal (AME) Church, had afforded fugitive slaves refuge.

The Black Baptists and Afro-Methodists were, to use a Yoruban term, *bolekaja* (that is, *brawl–and–battle*) Christians: militant anti-racists. But the fundamentalist, Negro Pentecostals were do-nothings, their piety just pure, let's-eat-pie-in-the-sky-once-we-die folderol.

Other Amherstburg Coloureds adhered to the Church of God in Christ led by Bishop Elder C. L. Morton, whose sermons, broadcast on CKLW Windsor in the 1940s and 1950s, spurred many to pack up bottles and pick up Bibles. His program's cheery hymn, "I'm on My Way to Heaven and I'm So Glad," is an earworm yet that quivers my brain, shivers my spine.

Each year, while flashbulbs popped, hundreds of Morton's Detroit-based "saints" convened on the banks of the Detroit River to waltz into the waters, get dunked, and shimmy out, all a-shimmer. Black conservatives sneered at "ringmaster" Morton. Yet, Morton was such a radio miracle-worker, such a Motown-melodic, old-time-gospel showman, he spawned an army of clones led by ambitious but cloddish—even thuggish—pastors, dudes who'd keep straight razors tucked in their Bibles.

Note: my chum Charles perched in Morton's church. So, I'd often companion him to Sunday school. Teach was Rev. Morley Stewart, a scholarly esquire, whose fundamentalism wasn't just bottled-up alcoholism. As in London, my Biblical expertise again gleaned reward but now with silver quarters rather than dark-n-dreamy chocolate bars.

We McCurdys disparaged the jump-up-and-down hollering of "Holy Rollers," who were so fanatically Bible literalists, why didn't they stab out their always lustful eyes? Yahoos all, they were sure that scientists—as sordidly backward as sodomites—were bound to fry in Hell. These would-be snake-handlers would eschew the double-winged, double-serpent symbol of medicine and resort to the "laying on of hands" to treat perilous ills. Being a compassionate nurse, my mom would attend to "pennycostals" suffering sickness due to their fidelity to ignorance.

His ample flock gifted Elder Morton ample luxuries—all sweet as peaches, doused with brandy. A "Kubla Khan pleasure-dome" was his Mt. Zion Tabernacle! For down-at-the-heel parsons, propped up by the pennies of indigent believers, it was all too much. They damned Morton just as Father Divine damned—famously—the judge who jailed him for a year for his late-night singing. (When the judge perished three days after sentencing, the savvy preacher quipped, "I hated to do it.") Yet, Morton catered to his congregants, unlike holier-than-thou pastors who were standoffish—probably so they could plead to call down hellfire and dodge its flames.

Damn joyous were the Church of God in Christ services at Mount Beulah Church, an architectural phoenix resurrected from the ruins of ye olde Amherstburg Coloured School. (Charles and I had cavorted in its wrack.) No wheezing hymns! No snoring organs! Aroused by salvation, AME, BME, and Baptist choirs were wildly arousing in song. Ecstatic were the tambourines, the pianist's fingers dive-bombing the keyboard, the organist hallelujah-ing the air. *Drum-matic* (my coinage) beat the tom-tom feet. The congregation, one instrument incarnate, swayed and clapped to loping rhythms and Morton's leaping cadence. White-clad "nurses" assisted those overcome by the intoxicating "Spirit" or those exhausted from speaking in tongues. Services sustained serial collections of offerings until God's inexhaustible demands emptied the purses of many whom I knew could ill afford the tithe. (The Black Church enshrines ritual, assembles community, and enacts worship as fanfare. But *faith* accepts irrational contradictions and urges intolerance of others' beliefs. Thus, for me, Darwin and Mme. Curie and Einstein began to eclipse—in credibility—Adam, Eve, and The Messiah.)

Windsorites were Mom's adopted family. Until my dad became her husband, she lived, with my Aunt Helen and Uncle Arnold, in the frontier Gotham. While still Londoners, Sissy and I spent some summer weeks with the Pryors. Now, ex-Amherstburg, we'd jaunt weekends to Windsor to savour their company and their chow.

Aunt Helen cooked up yummy calories, while Uncle Arnold and Cousin Woody acted yuk-yuk comics. A Detroit luggage porter, Uncle Arnold dispensed jokes like candy, plus paraded funny faces as elastic as gum. Teenage Woody was a shoe-shine "ragtimer": his rag slapped leather to sassy, syncopated timing.

Despite lacking a golden touch, Aunt Helen and Uncle Arnold bet avidly on thoroughbred races. So, they hipped me to "playing the numbers"—a gamble that Windsor and Detroit Negroes trusted. Daily, a "numbers man" would collect penny bets on whatever three-digit number a bettor chose. The winner? Decided by that day's "hoss"-race results. Flamboyant Negro racketeers milked this unique and lucrative ghetto-profit niche.

Socio-economically, Windsor Blacks lorded it over their Amherstburg cousins: their populace was linked to Detroit's Black bourgeoisie. But Windsor also boasted Black businesses and professionals, including two MDs, two tooth-docs, and an LL.B. who was the city's ace solicitor.

My mother volunteered for the Hour-a-Day Study Club and the Armistead Club. The former assembled mature ladies who, lauding scholastic achievement, passed precious dollars to Coloured students (me among them). Composed of young, middle-class men and women, the Armistead Club valued galas and salons. These pretentious Negroes lunched with intimates of a mirror, hoity-toity Detroit entity, the Cotillion Club. The Black Windsor elite (no, the *e-light*) numbered railway porters, secretaries, clerks, and some tradesmen, as well as doctors and lawyers.

At times, Armisteaders would homestead, yep, in our Amherstburg digs. Marilyn—Sissy—and I would spruce up the house and confect elaborate, tempting hors d'oeuvres, which we'd dare not sample. True: not every Armisteader was a prig. But way too many were.

Mother's acquaintances in the Windsor churches and in the Detroit Institute of Arts, the Detroit Historical Museum, and the Detroit Zoo opened doors for me to meet other Black youth from other provinces or from distant states. Thus, I got to eye feminine dazzle!

The best chance to ogle Black beauties was the annual Emancipation (or "First o' August") Celebration held at Windsor's Jackson Park, where thousands gathered for the "Greatest Freedom Show on Earth." Organized by Walter Perry and his semi-mythical British North American Brotherhood, the extravaganza was likely the vastest assembly of Negroes in North America. Vaunting a coronation-long parade, a pageant of absolute lovelies, talent shows to shame Motown— and Broadway and Hollywood—plus the sweet-n-sassy BBQ pits, it was a spectacle irresistible to presidents, prime ministers, and preachers (cigar-chomping, silk-suited panders in plush-seated Cadillacs, so nattily interchangeable with pimps). The event also bestowed its Freedom Award on such transcendent luminaries as Mary McLeod Bethune. My fondest memory? The exhibition race between my Uncle George, Canada's nominal go-to sprint idol, and Af-Am Olympian Jesse Owens. Uncle George lost, yes, but his fleet feet got defeated by less than a foot.

As I matured from boy to teen, the Second World War permeated daily life. Yes, we had to defeat Hitler's master-race thesis, which was imping on Axis atrocities, particularly the mass slaughter of Jews. But white supremacy also needed to be overthrown right at home.

So, Essex County Negroes debated whether it was sensible for us to fight for European freedom overseas when domestic Europeans were frustrating ours. Indeed, Blacks desiring to liberate Europe were themselves barred from prestige roles in the Canuck military. In the Navy, we slung hash. In the Army, we scoured latrines. In the Air Force, we stood around in grounded crews.

My family feared that our fathers would be drafted. Nicely, my father and Uncle Ralph weren't. But Uncle Alvin was. He was spared induction but not the teasing about the "flat feet" that earned his rejection (or, I'll say, escape).

Black Amherstburg soldiers? Uncle George, Jack Foster, the Conway Bros (Lester, James, and George), Clayton Harris, and Jesse Henderson. Jesse returned a hero, bedecked with medals for combat in Belgium, France, Sicily, and Germany. His nephew, Edward Guyon Henderson, returned in a coffin, felled by a training mishap in the sky above Saskatchewan. Harold Wilson was also killed in action but overseas—ironically, in Africa—on July 17, 1943.

As of 1942, sugar, coffee, tea, meat, butter, gasoline, wine, spirits, and beer were rationed. The alcohol limits? Loathsome! Heavy drinkers traded food stamps for spirits. Shortages caused runs on (not "in") nylons, plus hoarding of tinned foods.

Unable to buy metal toys, boys carved wooden guns that "shot" elastic bands and used rubber inner tubes for slingshots. Chemistry-set elements, gunpowder, and a blacksmith's metal filings sired fireworks. Roller-skate wheels affixed to wooden boards became scooters. Pork-rib-bone, homemade xylophones let us "play the bones."

War-effort child labour meant collecting newspapers, tin cans, and other metals (which junk dealers bought for a few cents). We aided Red Cross food drives. Memorable, too, were school field trips to search out milkweed pods whose contents, as fill, made life jackets float.

Army Cadets commenced in grade 8 but was compulsory in high school. Every lad had to show for drills, learn to fire .22-calibre rifles, and stand in formation for inspections. Cadet officers had prestige. But I was thrilled to emerge as a sharpshooter: with my one-shot BB gun, I slew several pheasants and a squirrel (the last consumed with consummate guilt due to my once having made a pet of one of its brethren).

War cranks out jobs. The Depression jobless were now grunts. Blacks—and gals—now composed a real-time proletariat; Negroes could even join the United Automobile Workers (UAW). (Thus, in concert with churches, synagogues, and social justice groups, the UAW began to promote civil and human rights—right alongside labour rights.)

On D-Day, the Allies thrust a beachhead into Nazi-governed Europe. Only eleven months later, VE-Day (Victory in Europe Day) got deliriously celebrated.

Hitler was dead by gun-sucking suicide, Mussolini by a partisan machine gun; in contrast, Roosevelt was slain by brain cancer. Soon, the new US prez, Harry S. Truman, dashed Japan by detonating a just-invented weapon of mass destruction, the atomic bomb, which vaporized—in a heartbeat—the city of Hiroshima.

Even as a twelve-year-old, it struck me as horrific that a single bomb could level a city, incinerating thousands of innocent people. I thought exploding a second bomb upon Nagasaki cruel and excessive, thus evacuating the high moral ground "our" side arrogated to itself. Though smokestack capitalism promised "Atoms for Peace" to power cities and appliances, the 1950s saw missile-rattling via the Cold War and Korean War, plus an escalation in annihilation capacity—from A-bomb to H-bomb—and concomitant fear of carcinogenic toxins from atmospheric tests. Backyard and basement bunkers became a craze, public fallout shelters posted, and pupils drilled in measures too silly to slough off a nuclear blast. The doctrine of Mutual Assured Destruction (MAD) was, for my generation, no insane acronym but a true doomsday scenario.

Anyway, 1945 saw not only feats of arms. The historic, ninety-nine-day Ford Strike that fall inflicted G-force stress on us all: no work equalled no pay, save the miniscule sum allotted for picket duty. The strike—and an unprecedented, two-day auto blockade of Windsor's Riverside Drive—won the epochal backing of stellar Bolshevik Paul Robeson, Negro titan of stage and screen. Dad and I couldn't get into Robeson's strike-support concert at the Capitol Theatre. Instead, we merged with the boisterous masses outside, belting out "Solidarity Forever"! Radically, workers defeated Wall Street and Bay Street! Plus, the strike-settling Rand formula set the pattern for collective bargaining in Canada, even introducing company-contributed medical coverage.

Soon came my first self-made trip to Windsor—to obtain a haircut at Harry Olbey's Barber Shop. (Euro barbers wouldn't clip Negro hair.) After scissors had topiary'd my head, I shot downtown. On Riverside Drive, I chanced upon shop display windows whose merchandise consisted of busty, leggy, dolled-up, real-live "mannequins." Back home, I told Howard Sr. that the ladies resembled fortune tellers—like the "Gypsies" who'd traverse my boyhood London. Pops snapped, "Those ladies weren't soothsayers, nor were they ladies." Innocence retired, I now knew that, bordering on Detroit, Windsor was a hub for mobsters, drug pushers, gamblers, and molls. Our ancestors had escaped the iniquity and criminality of US slavery, but Canada was no Canaan impervious to the Republic's vices of racial segregation and mass criminalization of the Coloured, the immigrant, the Indigenous, and the poor.

CHAPTER FOUR:
RACE ACE

IN 1944, I STARTED GRADE 9 AT GENERAL AMHERST HIGH School at age eleven-and-a-half. I was the youngest in my class and the lone Negro. (I maintained this demographic distinction all through high school and university.) Weighing but eighty-five pounds, and small, I acquired the nickname "Pipsqueak" (in addition to "Buzz" and "Junior"). My Aunt Laura Jean, a top athlete, was the only other Black pupil at Amherst but would soon graduate. All teachers adored Aunt Laura, due to her acumen at study and sports. Hers was a daunting success *pour moi* to strive to match. Yet, I no longer lusted after the highest grades. Instead, I just wanted to outscore other lads—a shameless justification for minimal effort.

I relished history and Latin. Miss Veronica Coyle, Gran Davis's next-door neighbour, made Latin thrilling. With her, dead words lived again—in our eyes, ears, and mouths. History teacher Georgina Falls, too young to be stuck in the aged past, became the butt of my endless pranks. One bright spring afternoon, while serving detention in a second-floor classroom, I saw Miss Falls, who was presiding, exit the room, whereupon I opened a window then snuck behind her desk. When Miss Falls returned, she was told that, "suicidal," I'd jumped. She paled, quailed, shrieked. Quickly, I revealed my "survival," and her panic became rage, then frame-shaking jollity.

Miss Falls fell victim to another shenanigan: torpedoes made by tightly wrapping caps with crepe paper over BB-size lead shot, so that when hurled at a hard surface, impact would cause a booming report. When the teacher had her back to the class, the blackboard was an ideal surface.

The shock effect of the bang, while startling the "teach," amused all pupils. In spite of these "playful" exceptions, I was generally assessed as good-behaved. I never played hooky and only ever missed class due to honest sickness.

Miss Aylsworth, whom my aunts said was "prejudiced," was, yes, a tad malicious. Due to illness, I missed a trigonometry exam, and Miss Not-Worth-the-Ails forbid a make-up test. Thus, I failed a course—for the single time in my life. Heck! No probs—I aced the next school year.

Interest in science continued to take an explosive turn. Potassium nitrate, sulfur, and powdered charcoal were all I needed to fashion gunpowder—and any pharmacy could dispense all. At first, I mixed gunpowder with metal filings and spices to generate rainbows of fireworks. Next, I decided to engineer blasts.

See, Charles and I had gotten caught up in a rinky-dink gang war. We teen combatants were to square off in the field behind a derelict slave hut (dubbed "Uncle Tom's Cabin") on the riverside. For the battle, I constructed a primitive bazooka from a carpet tube; via gunpowder, it could rocket-propel a tin can. Charles and I were hunkered by the cabin ruins when our foe took the rear of the field, half a block away. Outnumbered? Us! Charles went to negotiate battle terms while I "had his back"; the bazooka nestled showily on my shoulder. Agitated parley ensued; enemy fingers pinpointed *moi*. Our foes vamoosed. How pleased I was that my invention cowed the hooligans without being fired—it could have blown up in our faces!

To enable another blast, I contrived my own nitroglycerine by mixing glycerine with nitric acid—a two-ounce, medicine-bottle sum, pilfered from the school lab. I expected my experiment to explode the Parish Hall on King Street (nowadays, the Lighthouse Baptist Church) and thus razzle-dazzle my peers. At the scheduled moment, like a cartoon anarchist throwing a dagger, violently I hurled my small-bottle "grenade" against the target. But my "bomb" bombed! The bottle didn't even break! So, the Parish Hall stood, while my "Einstein" rep was downgraded. Fair enough! Had my grenade included a vital catalyst, sulphuric acid, I'd've crumbled a chunk of the edifice—and disintegrated myself into chunks and crumbs!

A new kid in town, Bob Van Ettinger, engineered crystal radios. These sets could receive only strong signals from local stations, and one needed earphones. No matter—the Detroit Tigers seemed to play better baseball when I eavesdropped on their games via my home-built radio.

I also acquired a microscope and was soon manufacturing infusions and studying microbes. Next, I began to make wine—secretly. (Surely, this "double major" in microbes and chemistry pushed me to become a microbiologist and biochemist?)

Despite my pipsqueak height, I found, in grade 8, that no one could beat me at the high jump. Then, all through high school, I was the Negro "Superman" in track and field. I could sprint; I could outdistance; I could leap. Long jump, high jump—superb. One of only two coaches I ever had, my Uncle George, sparked me at sprints. The London Central Collegiate coach pushed me to race the 440-yard dash.

How sad that I couldn't have made tracks, however, from cadet camp at Ipperwash! An ex-army barracks, the site was Arctic cold and no-man's-land bleak. Extra misery? I was the sole Black among a battery of N-word-articulate, kiddy KKK. Despite my father's admonition to meet all slurs with fists in faces, I couldn't punch out the whole corps. I felt isolated and alone.

I was still quite small—so small, yes, that when I fired a Bren gun, it kept dragging me forward! And noxious it remained—even with gas mask donned—to face chlorine gas in a shut-door room.

In my last week at Ipperwash, a track-and-field competition got me some glory—and gave others grief. I kicked ass! I out-ran, out-jumped, out-leapt all comers, thus humiliating the most hostile cadets who, judging by the congrats I received, were disliked by many.

Once sprung from Ipperwash camp, I went to London to rusticate with Aunt Pearl and Uncle Fred. Though Donny and Archie had moved, I was able to resume boyhood friendships with other guys.

But I met with cold shoulders, not open arms. Disquieting was Donny Ruddy's reaction to my fly-by. His father now dead, he and his mama inhabited a duplex on Dundas. Eager to see my number one London pal, I asked a new chum, Jerry, to ride the bus with me out to that midst of the horizontally elongated city. When I saw Donny, his teen growth-spurt had made him nigh a man—in height. He had company: an aloof, sourpuss guy. Once, the twain left the room and Jerry and I could hear Donny being cussed out for letting a "nigger" into his home. We hightailed it. I was starting to realize that Euro folks can smile upon Black children, but once we become teens, we males begin to be classed as sexual rivals and economic threats (and vice versa).

Still, these estranging encounters did not spoil wholly that dreamy summer. Uncle Fred and I were regulars at the London Majors baseball games. Semi-professional they were, but skilled. We staked out seats behind home plate—to study every swing, foul, hit, and run.

Too, London Rec held track meets at Labatt Park for teens up to age sixteen. Representing McMahon Park, I entered the high jump. My chief opponent was Paul Johnson, reputed to be the supreme jumper in town—and also "Black like me." Paul's fans, a harem, cheered him cooingly and booed me sneeringly. Despite his beauteous groupies' vocal inspiration, Paul only drew a draw in our hour-long, monumental contest wherein neither of us missed a height. Our soaring feud ended once dusk dawned, thus erasing any chance at precise calibration of the jump and measurement of the height gained. Nevertheless, his ego would continue to be stroked by his bevy of admirers, while I would have to fade away, lonesome as usual, into the night.

That McMahon Park matchup is where I met the Central Collegiate coach who so admired my long-legged stride that he spent hours schooling me in the *echt* technique for the 440-yard (400-metre) race. In the final track meet that summer, I snookered trophies, medals, laurels, and praise—including in my high-jump rematch with Paul. And I snagged his friendship.

The London coaching groomed me so well, the 440 became a favoured event. Except for grade 11 (when I injured a groin ligament and couldn't jump), *I* was the hero! Sprightly in the sprints, I had wings in the high—and triple—jumps. I didn't run; I didn't leap; I flew!

Smoking was my Achilles heel! At a provincial meet, I placed second in the high jump. Then, in a 440 race, I led the field until my lungs pooped out. Hating to lose, I quit the tobacco. Soon, I topped all at the high jump again. In the 440, I didn't conk out, and I got to do a victory lap.

That track meet remains vivid, not just for my "firsts," but for an incident at a Chatham hotel, where we wished to dine. Our driver went in to check out its restaurant and returned, agitated cursingly. Why? The manager had seen me and thus refused me entree: I'd have to munch a sandwich segregated in the car. My teammates were upset, but I shrugged: "Amherstburg's just as bad for segregation." Our drive home was as mute as a dude with a noose slipped round his neck.

Besides track and field, I loved basketball and placed on the junior team in grades 10, 11, and 12 and on the senior team in my final year. My comic-book trading partner, Bill Hall, was a centre and I the right forward. Although he overshadowed me, I was quicker at attaining the optimal altitude—in the jumpoff—to tip the ball in my team's favour. Jealous of my basketball prowess, Bill strove to outdo me in the high jump. He dominated the event only when my groin injury sidelined me. A year later, healed, I out-jumped him easily.

In my final year as a junior, in a razor-close game against Kingsville ending with a breathtaking climax, we won the county pennant. In that Leamington matchup, we were ahead by two points, a minute left on the clock, when do-or-die Kingsville rebounded the ball. To beat their fast break and intercept their Hail-Mary pass, I mimicked Speedy Gonzalez.

Hey, I was the real McCoy because, by flouting the Kingsville play, I secured Amherstburg's bragging rights. But my ecstasy died fast. In an ill attempt at humour, coach Phil Gibb described my sleek, slick stride as "a black streak going down the court." My once-smile pinched fast into a frown.

My senior-year basketball team dribbled, passed, and dunked. Just not enough to net glory.

Baseball I also loved. Grandpa McCurdy intro'd me to Briggs Stadium in 1946. The World Series Champion Detroit Tigers were hosting the Yankees. Ah! The beauty of Joe DiMaggio's swing even as Hal Newhouser struck him out! To see Hank Greenberg hitting the first major-league home run I'd ever witness—wow! One thing was wrong: Blacks dotted the stands, but zero were on the field. Nor would the Tigers' racist owner, Walter Briggs, hire anyone for the front office or the coaching staff. He thought the game should be as ivory as the ball the bat strikes.

After his postwar "demobbing," my Uncle George played for the Amherstburg Cardinals and for the Dayus Roofers. A Coloured team, the Roofers turned Sundays into "home-run fun" before cheering fans at Windsor's Wigle Park. But baseball boys were my heroes. Guess I was following in the cleated steps of Amherstburg's first athlete to play pro baseball, the none-other-but-ignorantly-nicknamed Jay Justin "Nig" Clark (1882–1949), who hit an amazing eight homers in a single game (Texas League, summer 1902). (BTW, Clark was Indigenous—a member of the Wyandotte Nation—and thus not at all a Negro.) I sought out Amherstburg Cardinals practices—to snag fly balls and to learn how to pitch.

(End of practice, June 17, 1946: unforgettable! As we shed bats and gloves, a stiff breeze built; the mercury shrivelled by umpteen degrees, and the northern sky pitched midnight dark. Soon, a lurid, mucus-streaked, lightning-spitting, black funnel cloud, swirling trees—from canopy to trunk—plus other hunks of debris, twisted through LaSalle, a town halfway between Windsor and Amherstburg, crafting surreal wreckage. Like nails, straw got spiked into telephone poles; a car's exploded metal resembled a butchered horse; railway boxcars flipped sideways; a house was split open, half of it torn away, exposing upstairs bathroom and downstairs kitchen. The dark aerial monster picked up buildings and shook people out as if they were salt and pepper, pelting seventeen souls lethally against the earth or solid objects. Raining stones crushed faces.)

In spring, this young man's thoughts fixed on baseball. Although I was nearly an atheist, I prayed, "Dear God, please don't let rain pester practices!" My classroom doodles of nude, chesty darlings now graduated to depictions of athletes in catching, pitching, or batting "ballet." Conflict grew between my piano lessons and baseball practices—and, therefore, between my mother and me.

True: I completed the ninth grade of the Toronto Conservatory of Music and even gave two public recitals in Windsor, during one of which I plunked my own composition. But I excelled in theory, while seeming execrable at practice. I scored supremely in exams but marginally at performance.

Problem was, I hated the piano! It's a nit-picking instrument! Maybe God sensed my loathing? In the fall of 1948, my mother asked me to add fuel—paper and wood chips—to the kitchen stove. I did so. Soon the chimney pipe glowed red. Then, we saw smoke seep through the kitchen ceiling. Firemen put out the erupting blaze quickly, but their pressured water flooded us, smashing our home. Voila! I'd have to board with Gran Davis, far beyond earshot of the summons to seat my keister afore the ebony-and-ivory horse-coffin, which itself, to me, merited inundation if not incineration. (During the fire, a school lesson got put to the test. To retrieve an item for my mom, I ran upstairs to my parents' bedroom but was soon smoke-blinded, smoke-dizzied, and nearly smoke-choked. Fortunately, I remembered the classroom instruction to get down as close to the floor as possible. I did, and I was then able to breathe, see, and escape.)

My dad was devastated at seeing his hard work destroyed. I feared that I was to blame. Still, our home was improved—electricity and fuel oil replaced the wood stove and coal furnace.

So, passé was the piano, but back was baseball! Jackie Robinson was in the majors, other Negroes en route; yet I inexplicably remained a Tigers fan, despite that Big Racist In Grey Gabardine Suits (BRIGGS), that SOB. Going to Briggs Stadium was an adventure. On Michigan Avenue—all drunks, panhandlers, and rascals—I dallied amid pawn shops and bars. Burlesque joints on Woodward Avenue teased my eyes with their graphic posters of stripped-down starlets.

A night game against the Cleveland Indians—who'd signed both Larry Doby and legendary pitcher Satchel Paige—is anchored in my brain. At game end, Paige came in as a reliever. Due to his "hesitation pitch" and his throws behind his back, he displaced Newhouser as my idol. (I had to feel divided loyalties when my hero Paige struck out Windsor's very own Reno Bertoia in his major-league debut with the Detroit Tigers on September 22, 1953.)

Ol' Jesse Henderson, a neighbour, came out one day to watch me catch. Though a war hero, Jesse was a loner, only appearing when he needed to shoo us from his peerless pear trees. But he was still an AI pitcher, not just due to his acme as an anti-aircraft gunner, capable of aiming his weapon at perfect pitch! Geometry also informed his curve and knuckle balls.

Despite having no uniforms or a league, a bunch of us composed a junior baseball team. Our first year, we staged exhibitions. Then, "Skirts" Robinson agreed to manage us, and uniforms showed up. My old high-jump opponent and basketball teammate Bill Hall was our other pitcher. Again, I was our squad's lone Negro player. (One other local Coloured sportsman was Marvin Grayer, a rival at sprints. Now, I admit to a legendary defeat. Another sprinter, Charlie Hurst, couldn't catch my backwash, let alone me! But one July night, as I left baseball practice, he boasted that his new sneakers made him quicksilver fast, slippery as wind. He challenged me to a 50-yard race. I guffawed, "Do your damnedest!" Hell, he strutted cross the finish line, thus granting him exultation he still proclaims—seventy years later!)

Our baseball games drew crowds. Stalwarts came out to see "Satch" McCurdy pitch. But not my mom and dad. Neither attended any more than a single high school game. But my dad did catch for me now and then when I practised pitching in the backyard. He praised unstintingly my ability to hurl a ball forcefully enough that its impact stung his hand!

We played teams from Harrow, Kingsville, Tecumseh, and Leamington. Leamington always fielded skilled hands, even forwarding major-league prospects. One such pick, a pitcher, had a ninety-five-miles-per-hour fastball, which, to everyone's shock (including mine), I hit for the longest hit of my baseball career! If that ball had appeared on radar, or had been mistaken for a UFO, or had gone into orbit, the report would have been justified!

Not so nice was being called ni**er and other slurs during a game in Tecumseh. Yet, two other contemporary incidents influenced significantly my thinking about race bias. The intersection of Sandwich and Richmond Streets, before the Liberty cinema, was a magnet for malingerers. One night, the yobs mobbed a grocery store, denouncing it as a "Red" business. They lobbed insults and epithets at the owners, shouting, "Get out of town—or else!" What rot! The owners, the Yakima family, always as courteous as could be, were not "Reds" at all. They were "White Russians," actually "DPs" (displaced persons), who'd fled Ukraine to escape the Communism they were now accused of backing. Police soon dispersed the menace. Yet, the disgraceful episode exposed the potential harm that ignorant bigots can inflict.

Next, the "mobsters" thronged at the library to harass a "commie" meeting. The louts exited sheepishly when they realized that Christian Scientists were kibbutzing, not "Reds."

The lessons? Prejudice is stupidity. Yet, those biased against one group are oft biased against many. Racism itself is fuelled by Wall Street impulses: fear and greed.

I loved baseball, but I did not continue beyond the junior level due to the demands of university study. My one memento of those days was a business card from a St. Louis Browns scout. (How came it into my hands? I was no major league prospect!)

Baseball games? Only one reason to go to Detroit. My mother shopped for clothes for herself and for Sissy and me at sprawling department stores such as Hudson's (hosting, at Christmas, the "authentic" Santa). For socks and underwear, there was Sam's cut-rate clothing store on Broadway. But I craved the Sanders Spanish peanuts and Vernors ginger ale (available free at the bottling plant).

Racial tensions there were high, with the Belle Isle riot of 1943 still fresh in mind. True: thirty-four people had died, mostly Blacks shot by cracker cops. One Black man was literally cut in half by a Gestapo-manned machine gun. Prez Roosevelt had to summon the army to quell the unrest. The acrid smell of smoke drifted across the Detroit River from the fires of the burning, looted stores. Not to mention gunfire. Mom warned Sissy and me not to look directly into pasty-faced Detroiters' eyes because, she said, "they would just as soon shoot you as look at you." (But violence was casual every-where: a double hanging in Windsor in August 1943 took out two Detroit murderers who slew a Windsor restaurateur in a botched robbery.)

Even so, Detroit skyscrapers awed us; the presence of Negroes—in numbers—instilled a sense of solidarity. To wheel to Motor City was also exciting because our purchases had to be smuggled back home. How? Wear old clothes to Detroit, ditch 'em in the US, and wear the new threads back to Canada. A smart technique! (I adhered to it myself, when requiring flashy garb as a dapper teen.)

Lookit! A suave dude modelled black, draped pants, black, square-toed shoes with built-up soles, and jackets with school colours. The go-to place for must-have duds? Todd's on Broadway. One day, wear-ing a jacket, pants, and shirt I'd bought at Todd's—and with too many packs of smokes hidden in sundry pockets—Canada Customs stopped me as I crossed the border at the Detroit–Windsor Tunnel. My shoes were Canuck-bought, but only they secured scrutiny. I'd purchased them at a Windsor shop, but an officer made me sweat a half-hour while he "checked" my story. He cleared me. I think he knew I was smuggling the rest of what I wore.

(Fast-forward sixty years: though I was smuggling zero upon returning to Windsor from Detroit in the twenty-first century, I was de facto racially profiled, roughed up, arrested, and jailed. So, what *truly* changed between 1948 and 2008?)

As a teen, on my own or with Charles, I'd head to Detroit for Sunday matinees at the Paradise Theatre on Woodward Ave. Bland Hollywood fare was chased away by premium Black singers and musicians. The Ink Spots, Lionel Hampton, Duke Ellington, Count Basie, Billy Eckstine, and Erskine Hawkins pleased our ears with sass and teased our eyes with swank! Billie Holiday's Paradise concert still haunts me. En route to the stage, she passed my aisle seat. A spectre in spangles and a siren in sequins. Pale, scrawny, disoriented in her eyes and unsteady in her gait, her junkie deterioration was clear. Still, her voice levitated the theatre.

But the Paradise was paradisiacal for another reason: I'd chat up sepia angels! Yes, my pursuits proved vain! Charles claimed better luck. Yet, his amours induced such guilt that he would repent, renew church attendance, and abstain from dancing (if not—*ahem*—"fornication").

Ballet also spelled Detroit. Sissy enrolled in a Black ballet school, and I was her escort. Mahogany butterflies and sable swans abounded! Back then, the school, mounting the annual Delta Sigma Theta sorority's talent show "Jabberwock" (a tradition dating back to 1935), rued the absence of testosterone in tights. Mom bribed me to fill the void: I'd learn enough ballet to "dance" in "Jabberwock" in exchange for a Harlem Globetrotters ticket. As it turned out, I merely had to lift a female dancer, which was, given her celestial pulchritude, an uplifting experience!

I frequented Detroit much but forged no friendships—until the Hour-a-Day Study Club bade me meet three Detroit lads: Leon Rivers and David and Bill Smith. All were Cass Tech students, all from outstanding and upstanding families: *Ebony* mag photo-ops. Rivers and the Smiths were nice enough but exuded an off-putting Yankee arrogance. How irksome that, due to his ignorance of Canada's contribution of two million troops from a population of but fifteen million, papa Smith trivialized our Second World War role. Once, he opened ostentatiously a cabinet to display a trove of canned goods—enough to outfit a grocery store. He was acting as if his kitchen was Fort Knox. Yet, he was a mere Ford prole—just like my dad.

Bragging offends. Why? Because accomplishment speaks for itself. But Yanks seem to need a megaphone to assure the world that they know how to whisper. Also mystifying was the sense of patriotic superiority among so many US Blacks, though they were treated so much worse in comparison than we African-Canadians. They kiss off Uncle Tom so indignantly, kiss up to Uncle Sam so avidly.

Seldom did I lack coin-of-the-realm in high school. For one thing, Charles Hurst and I would score a buck each by unloading flour bags from trucks at Marra's bakery. A superb bonus? Loaves of hot, fresh, butter-ready bread that we snagged for free.

Charles and I also got a buck each by weeding tomato plants. Earning the same pay was an Italian ex-POW who had to do farm work for umpteen months to be permitted to remain in Canada. To me, it was grotesquely unfair and akin to slavery.

For two years, Uncle George and I sold Christmas trees from our backyard. Another year, in the McCurdy Bros' woodworking shop, I made toy swing sets that I sold door-to-door. Another enterprise saw me peddle imitation fluorescent light bulbs.

In 1948, Sid Hinch sold me his *Windsor Star* route for fifty dollars, and I became its first Coloured newspaper carrier. With over one hundred customers, it was lucrative, yielding about seven bucks a week and nearly one hundred dollars in Christmas tips. I gave up the route to go to college.

At age sixteen, I got hired at Canadian Canners to stack ketchup cases trundled along by warehouse conveyers. It was toil, but Charles and I had fun. Crazily, we used to glug the still warm condiment straight from the bottles—until, that is, I broke out in massive hives!

In summer 1950, Charles and I punched clocks at Boblo Isle, picking up trash for a Negrophobic boss. He cautioned us, for instance, against ever bantering with the Euro patrons. One Sunday morn, he sent us home due to a squall. By afternoon, the sun was back, so Charles and I took to the ballpark. How shocked we were to find out that we'd been fired for not responding to a call to return to work! Charles had no phone, and no one had called my house.

Fearful of being snubbed, I skipped high school socials. One day, a young lady asked me if I'd attend a dance. I told Mom about it, and she pushed me to go. Suitless, sporting a plaid shirt over a white shirt and tie, I felt I was unsuitable. At the shindig, several gals tried to tempt me to jitterbug. But not only was I too shy, I felt patronized, dorky, and pitiably, self-consciously Black, that is, an intruder, unwanted and out of place.

Fifty years later came a reunion at Assumption College. As I entered the reception room, I heard a gaggle of lithesome likely grannies giggle. "There's Howard McCurdy!" All former General Amherst students, they told me how much they had admired me as the school's star athlete who, they said, was so stuck up, he would never come to dances, and when he did show up—just once—he'd refused to waltz their ultra-willing waists.

CHAPTER FIVE:
ACCIDENTS

HIGH SCHOOL GRADUATION: NO PLANS, NO PROSPECTS.
I grieved the incipient termination of my athletic cachet. I chose to repeat grade 13 to repeat triumphs in shooting baskets or sprinting and leaping skyward to cheers. Due to the consequent diminution of focus, my marks slid. My laxity was so taxing, Principal Sidey displayed his frustration by interrupting chemistry class to forecast—before all my classmates—that I'd not take home a diploma.

Openly upbraided, I felt shamed into upping my grades. I crammed for the matriculation exams with insomniac single-mindedness, even overdosing on caffeine. Did cognition suffer from lack of sleep? Well, during the English Lit exam, I could recall every author and every line of poetry that I'd studied, but not a single title. Luckily, a short nap refreshed my recall, and I aced the exam.

Yet I dreaded the Province of Ontario's fateful envelope. After weeks of daily post-office jaunts, my hands shook to hold the missive; my fingers trembled to open the flap.... Elation! I'd gloried in all nine subjects. Moreover, I'd bested my peers. Only four of us—in my cohort—had qualified for university study across a nonet of interrogative categories.

That summer, Marilyn (she'd outgrown "Sissy") and I visited Oberlin and Cleveland, Ohio. In Oberlin, we stayed with our Thomas relatives. A boutique town, Oberlin had been a hotbed of abolitionism (fired up by Oberlin College); for years, the McCurdy and Thomas clans alternated reunions between there and Amherstburg. We then spent a week in Cleveland.

My mother had always dreamt I'd become an MD or an LL.B. But no one in my family had ever gotten a degree (excepting the "third degree" from two-legged, K-9 flatfoots). General Amherst High had no guidance counsellor, nor had any teacher proffered college as a goal. I had some savings: enough for tuck and textbooks, yep, and nada for tuition.

Later, I ascertained that Principal Sidey had sought college cash for me, and that secretive initiative explained his blunt rebuke of my academic slacking. Luckily, bursaries from the Hour-a-Day Study Club, the Armistead Club, and others helped fund my freshman year.

Windsor's Assumption College (handing out University of Western Ontario degrees) was my first post-secondary choice: it was affordable, feasible. My panic over price tags caused me to overlook Michigan State University. Not only was its tuition within my reach, it offered both athletic and academic scholarships (unavailable in Canada) for which I was righteously qualified.

So, in the spring of 1950 my father and I (still just seventeen) appeared in the registrar's office to enroll me for classes at Assumption. When Miss Barbara Birch, Assistant Registrar, asked what major I had chosen between arts or science, pre-medicine or pre-law, I couldn't say. Time for a coin toss! My father gave me a quarter. I flipped it; it came up "heads." Thus, I majored in science.

Despite that decision, I had no direction—and less cash. Dad refinanced our house to realize the four hundred dollars required to cover my first-year tuition. Paper-route and canning-factory savings secured me books and wardrobe. Had not my Aunt Dot given me rides to Windsor every morn, and had I not hitchhiked home most eves, I could not have sustained attendance. Eventually, summer jobs and part-time work let me earn enough to repay my father's loan and fund my education.

High school had been facile; I'd "shazam'd" through exams just by cramming. Yet, desperate memorization cannot suffice in college, where profs muse like mystics and students must decipher the logic. Pedagogues eschew rote imparting of knowledge; they wish to spark wonder.

A monkish student, I lacked study buddies. So, I eked out a B average, though flunking in chemistry and failing at library science (as if an illiterate). Calculus was witchcraft, so my pass was magical. (I discovered that calculus is just math as a verb.) Chemistry and history were both so dottily taught that otherwise fascinating subjects became unsurpassed drudgery.

Joe Trooper and Frank Demerit (I've changed their names) were rotten eggheads. My Intro Chem prof, Trooper, too arrogant for teaching, just hated his students. The next chem prof, Demerit, charged me with that odious, academic sin of cheating. (His proof? His prejudice.) Also taking Demerit's organic chemistry class was an older guy, a Jamaican, "Smitty," who gabbed more than he read. After one test, Demerit summoned Smitty and me to his office to accuse us darkly of, well, telepathy! Smitty and I had not sat near enough to permit rubbernecking, nor were our scores unusual. Yet, Demerit thought that his only two Black students could only have passed his exam via voodoo. Outraged, I stalked out, clattered the door behind. Smitty followed as if my shadow.

One first-year course was outstanding: English 19, on public speaking. The prof? Conrad Swan, bro to college registrar, Father P. J. Swan. Although a Canuck-born Pole (the family name had been anglicized), Conrad had a stiff-upper-lip, Brit accent, which suited his status as an ex-officer in the colonial Indian Army. (Ah, the genius of the Brits: to make their accent the tongue of the King-James-Version God!) My classmates and I thought Swan amusing. I liked the course, and Swan liked me. Therein, through his tutelage, I developed debating skills that helped me excel in politics.

Basketball was Assumption's only varsity sport. My commuting schedule and part-time jobs ruled out a tryout for the team. I did play intramural basketball as a part of the phys ed requirement, and I dunked enough baskets to hook an A.

Favouring the high jump still, I trained alone, in my backyard, using homemade standards and crossbars. Thus, I acquired the Western roll. Instantly, my vertical jump now surpassed six feet. Yet, I did not engage the "aeronautics" again until I relocated to the Maritimes for work.

I sold off my paper route; mandatory now was a part-time job. Charles Hurst was setting pins at the Brunner Mond bowling alleys, so I joined him there. We earned seven precious pennies per line. Hard work, but we could bowl—free—during downtimes and after hours. However, if we wanted to pay to bowl during regular hours, we could not: Negroes were forbid play.

The Brunner Mond Club was not a rare no-Negroes joint. Neither Ouellette's nor Beneteau's—two pool halls—would let us play. Charles and I had to protest these detestable restrictions. We complained to my grandfather, parents, and uncles; they decided that a delegation headed by my grandfather should ask the town council to enact an anti-discrimination bylaw.

My grandfather's submission to council—and Charles's and my testimony—elicited lip-service sympathy. A committee was tasked to examine enacting a general licensing bylaw with an anti-prejudice provision. (I advocated for a standalone bylaw.) Following unexpectedly protracted deliberations, the committee, chaired by Ferman Sinasac, voted *nyet*. Councillors concluded that patron choice was the prerogative of a private business. No hard feelings!

My grandfather was as nigh to outrage as his civil demeanour could allow. Charles was ballistic; I was apoplectic. Sinasac hinted that we were hallucinating our own suppression. (That outcome was predictable given the character and associations of committee members. In a separate article on the same page of the *Amherstburg Echo* detailing council's action, two committee members were hailed for their performances as blackface minstrels!)

Also that year, 1951, I got a summer job at SKD, an Amherstburg auto parts manufacturer. I had to transfer metal parts from one electroplating bath to another. Tedious and tricky—I risked acid burns—the work paid sweetly. Unfortunately, my contract ended before my finances had been repaired. So, I gigged at Canada Canners: a rinky-dink job, no real silver, just tin-tin-tin.

Then, Charles and I dug up a gold mine! Learning that the town hall auditorium was available free of charge, we made it a venue for Sat'day nite dances. We just had to keep it swept and mopped—and spic-n-span morally (no Elvis-pelvis groin-grinds). Grape vines and party lines criss-crossing Windsor and Essex County talked up our sock hop. Asking a buck a ticket, we lads cleaned up, clearing about fifty dollars apiece.

Then, Windsor toughs hassled us at the next dance. They refused to pay admission; they threatened a thrashing. (One thug assured us his jacket hid his gat.) I kept my cool, demanded payment: now, grumbles scored the riffling of pockets and wallets. But the hooligans didn't want rock 'n' roll; they wanted rumbles. Next, the town set a steep rent for the hall. Further dances became unfeasible.

Year two at college? Abject! Confused about goals, I drifted. Cramming remained my dumb-ass study strategy. Too, cracks in my parents' marriage now widened into a separation. Howards I & II? Suddenly de facto dad-and-lad bachelors!

I was closer to my mom, for she'd always encouraged me to succeed. So, I blamed my dad for their split. When I feared he'd do my mama harm, Howard Jr. raised his fist at the face of Howard Sr. His aspect? Hangdog defeat and pitiful remorse. (Yet, it was he rather than she who would back me most as I tried to find my way forward.)

Windsor was about weekends—with or without Charles. I ran with guys like Eddy Whitehead and Donny Milburn, who knew which bootleggers were willing to sell the seventy-five cents Catawba wine and beer to "minors." (I didn't get "carded" until I was twenty-eight!)

Often, we congregated at a street corner or at someone's crib. Sometimes there were parties at Eddy's or a buddy's. I was still too shy to rap to—much less fox-trot with—gals who thought me handsome. Sure, I could dance. But I didn't deem my "good looks" good enough for hookups.

Black music was as scarce on radio as Negroes were on silver screens. Soul music (rhythm and blues) and rock got strummed or drummed or hummed by the likes of Illinois Jacquet, Lionel Hampton, Bo Diddley, and Sister Rosetta Tharpe. Dinah Washington's subterranean dirty blues lit up our ears. Only Detroit had these records—just like only the US had an atomic stockpile. To hear Black music on radio you tuned way up the dial to find some weak Memphis station, whose only strength was Coleman Hawkins or Hank Ballard.

Then again, Black vibes got ripped off—first by Bill Haley & His Comets (whose "Shake, Rattle, and Roll" was first a Big Joe Turner song). Next, Elvis Presley just Xeroxed Black singers in sound and movements (and got condemned at first as acting "too Black"). Resentment arose due to paleface artists raking the green off Black rhythm and blues while the Black originators couldn't.

Donny jaunted us to Chatham (ON) or Ypsilanti (MI) in search of gals and kicks. But his driving could unnerve the bravest. One hundred miles an hour was a casual speed to him, even when he was sober!

Because my father worked afternoons, I began to hold parties at our house sometimes with—or sans—his permission. When I partied disobediently, all hell would break out if the clue to filial "disrespect" was the disappearance of some of Dear Old Dad's stashed away drams!

My pals had jobs, cash, and steady women. I was too shy to date; I lacked a date fund, anyway. Still, I pondered, *should I quit college; snag a j-o-b; try out fast cars, fast hooch, fast gals?*

Reality check: my running mates weren't no intelligentsia. They wanted booze and babes, not college and careers. Who among them would ever urge me to become a scientist? Luckily, the only other Black guy (besides Smitty) in the Science faculty, Dick Miller, invited me to join Kappa Alpha Psi—the Negro fraternity that had a chapter, Alpha Beta, at Detroit's Wayne State University (WSU). To become a Kappa, one had to be initiated. This involved a silly hazing ritual that I took seriously because I craved membership in a Black academic community. With Dick as my witness, I went for one week without speaking to any of my classmates!

Assumption hosted no fraternities, but they were vital entities at US colleges and universities. For Black students at ostentatiously Caucasian, post-secondary schools, such bodies countered social isolation. They also fielded Negro professionals as mentors. Besides Kappa Alpha Psi, two others had numerous members at WSU: Omega Psi Phi and Alpha Phi Alpha (the latter was purportedly open only to "tan" or "beige" Blacks). Each fraternity was linked to a sorority. Nicely, Kappa Alpha Psi brothers "matched" Alpha Kappa Alpha sisters.

Being a frat member, I met suave, successful Af-Am men. Many of my Kappa bros became lawyers, doctors, and one, a deputy mayor of Detroit. Many bros were well-heeled, but others were down-at-the-heel, from "the projects," and had been wafted into WSU on the wings of athletic or academic scholarships. ("Ghetto" dysfunctions now blighting Detroit had not yet burgeoned.)

The irresistible Assumption sport? Pure amateur pugilism! Lads went into "huts" in a little gym, emerged in trunks, and put up dukes, to swat at skulls or bat at bellies. The "sweet science" was a healthy set of skills supplementing my judo training. Both were assets.

Lornie "Leonard" Hurst, Charles's cousin, was a resentful lug whom I'd avoided as much as possible in Amherstburg. My junior by a month (born January 7, 1933), he probably outweighed me by thirty pounds: and all muscle, no *molesse* (French for flabby softness)! We were working in a warehouse when he began shoving me about. I pushed back and he swung at me, but his fist hit at air. Instantly, I counter-punched—stabbed a left jab into his face. His look of shock? Beautiful! Our combat became a grudge match because I was out-boxing him as we wrangled through the warehouse and burst through the exit doors. Finally, overwhelming me due to his burly heft, he wrestled me to the ground and could have cracked my noggin on asphalt had co-workers not hauled us apart. To that extent, I yielded the fight, but the sense of elation I felt for having nevertheless thrashed a pest has never been forgotten. Never would he try me again! (And good on him that he became a soldier!)

Psychology was one second-year Assumption subject that held me spellbound. A charming young priest, Father Fehr, was our prof, but he preferred moral philosophy to scientific psychology. So, I researched—on my own bottom—Freud, Jung, and others.

Thus, I chanced upon a hypnotizing book, a how-to manual for inducing hypnosis. Reading directly from its pages, on my first try, I entranced Junior Wilson before pals in our living room. All were wowed, though I don't think I had Junior do anything peculiar or stupidly juvenile. Later, at a party at the McCurdy domicile, *père et fils*, I mesmerized two girls alternately so that I could two-time each without either one knowing. When the third arrived, whom I wished to romance, I spellbound the first two ladies until number three departed. None was ever aware of the virtual (but non-sexual) "*ménage à quatre*" I'd thus effected!

On two occasions I was able to demonstrate unusual hypnotic phenomena. At Donald Harris's house, I hypnotized his sister, Betty-Lou (future grandma to Dallas Cowboys football player Tyrone Crawford). I had her stand ten feet from me as I opened a Bible to a random page, with my back to a large mirror. Despite the distance, she was able to accurately read the suddenly backward letters. Everyone was astonished. Next, another rare Black Assumption student, Ray Crawford, and I were visiting my Gran McCurdy when the subject of mesmerism arose. My grandmother was skeptical. Thus, to prove my skill, I so transfixed Ray that I was able to stick a four-inch hatpin clean through the web of skin between his thumb and index finger; then, upon snapping Ray out of his spell, he not only reported no pain, there was no sign of his epidermis having been pierced. Ray did not even remember the event. Gran's reaction? "Sons, quit my house now! Out with yer devilry!"

My hypnotist career ended when I observed that, contrary to folk belief, a subject can be brought to self-harm. This fearful anecdote unfolded in London, ON, in my mom's second-floor apartment. After mesmerizing my sister, Marilyn, I warned her a tiger was bounding toward her! At once, she bolted for the balcony. She would have leapt from it had not I grabbed her to hold her back!

After being expelled from the nursing program at Windsor's Hôtel-Dieu Hospital (because she couldn't abide the codes and curfews imposed by its Hun-like nuns), Marilyn was in London living with our mother and working as a secretary. With family now in London, I stopped in often, even bagging a mail-delivery gig during two Christmas seasons.

In the spring of 1952, I went job hunting in Windsor. Starting at the far east end of Tecumseh Road, I walked to its western end, and then traversed Sandwich Street, stopping at every site of possible opportunity. Most had no openings—or none for which I qualified. In other cases, the black-and-white fact was that my being Black was a non-starter.

By sundown, feeling dismal, I reached my last chance: the personnel office of the Canadian Salt Company. Here I scored a cordial, bantering interview wherein my chem courses got me hired. Ecstatic that I'd landed a lab job, I raced home to tell my father the good news. To my chagrin, I soon saw that I'd be only a prole, hauling ash from the scorching-hot furnaces in the power house and also acting as an "oiler." I was disappointed; but, in reality, for a college student, the job was letter-perfect.

Pulling the ash or slag from the furnaces necessitated muscular effort in tremendous heat—and I weighed but 135 pounds. Yet, I could accomplish the task in thirty minutes—if I attacked all with purpose. This fact irritated the older, unionized workers who didn't want management to realize that we could all work harder and faster.

Pulling slag was required only twice during a shift. Oiler shifts were a cakewalk. That involved checking several generators for their oil levels twice each shift. A fifteen-minute walk sufficed.

I thus could talk labour politics with my co-workers, or doze, or, most significantly, read in my "library"—a platform among the walkways above the furnaces where I kept a pillow and books. (In one section of the plant, I could even fish for perch.)

Another bonus: I received union wages that far exceeded what I'd've earned elsewhere. I even bought—for seventy-five dollars—my first car, a 1928 Ford Model A. Since I purchased it in Windsor, I had Charles Hurst join me to drive it home; I'd only ever had one driving lesson! I learned to "motorvate" (a Chuck Berry verb) by covering the fifteen miles to and from work.

In the spring of '52, Mom and I were bussing from Windsor to Amherstburg when she noticed an ash-blonde eyeing me ardently. I looked over; the beauty flashed a lightning-bright smile that elicited mine. Then, she sashayed off the bus at Anderdon. Flirtation done.

Simultaneously, Charles Hurst and his brother LeRoy and other fellows were gabbing about an unusually amicable white family, the Browns, who had welcomed them into their home. Soon, Charles bade me join him in rapping on the door of the genteel, Caucasian collective.

The Browns were exotic nonconformists. Headed by John, a sable-haired, charismatic thirty-year-old with shockingly electric-blue eyes, the clan included his sixty-year-old wife, Liz, and his two younger sisters, Alice and Marlene. I recognized instantly Marlene as that stunning girl from the bus. All were from Saint Paul, Minnesota, and it was poetic symmetry that John bore the cognomens of the American antebellum, anti-slavery insurrectionist, who'd visited southwestern Ontario (when it was Canada West) in the 1850s, seeking men, money, and munitions to spur on the violent, immediate liberation of enslaved African-Americans.

But this John L. Brown was a social worker, on staff at Palmer House, connected to WSU, Detroit. Though an atheistic communist, capable of sobbing over Joey Stalin when the USSR's butcher-dictator turned a stiff, John was memorably cerebral, engaging, and intellectually provocative.

At Assumption College, I immersed myself in philosophy and economics. Catholic social philosophy—such as that espoused by Monsignor Moses Coady (the rad Cape Bretoner)—now catalyzed the commitment to social change that was in my DNA. Hadn't I joined the UAW local 195, which represented the salt plant workers? I also became a card-carrying

Marlene Brown: My bella, *my* donna, *and my* belladonna?

member of the social-gospel, "socialist" Canadian Commonwealth Federation (CCF).

My recruiters? Co-workers: old Jimmy Wakeman and Alex Mackenzie. Jimmy was a loner and a Scot, all peat Scotch and bardic brogue. Along with championing unionization, he gave me a tattered volume of the poesy of Bobby Burns. In contrast, "Mack" was a never-mute politico who took me out to canvas for the CCF in the 1953 federal general election campaign and got me all hunchbacked, crouched and painting lawn signs in a basement.

During that twenty-second federal election, my aroused political consciousness led me to rebuke a candidate who had brought a case of beer to an Amherstburg flesh-presser. I berated him for trying to buy Negro votes instead of debating our concerns over jobs, affordable college tuition, racial equality, and financial security for workers. His face? Scarlet as a broadcast napalm strike!

Catholic social philosophy bordered on liberation theology, but exposure to the Thomistic proofs of God, plus notions of a First Cause and original sin, had me rethinking religion. Too fantastic was a telescopically distant God who pays microscopic attention to every atom of Creation.

Take original sin. The concept? Occult. I asked my Catholic classmates if they could credit that because Adam and Eve had eaten from the Tree of Knowledge, we are all born sinners. To me, more sensible is the Aristotelian idea that we are born with a tabula rasa. Given that *Homo sapiens* (Latin for *wise man*) defines a rational animal, it is obvious to me that it is via intelligence that one sounds Truth and divines the Good. In the absence of that enlightenment, to be described as sinful—and thus mortally damned—is fundamentally *irrational*.

Issues of this sort were hashed out in the third-year introductory philosophy course taught by Father W. J. Dwyer, CSB (Congregatio Sancti Basilii), PhD. An intrepid teacher, he fostered a galvanizing, electrifying climate, and he lauded my ability to articulate abstract concepts in concrete terms.

St. Thomas Aquinas harmonized Catholicism with rationalism, an extension of Aristotle. All scientific thought required validation in light of this classical ideal. So far, so good. Yet, the concept of substantial change and how it related to evolution exposed me to the sophistry of Thomist thought. Say Aquinas devouts, while physical evolution is demonstrably true, it involves mere, accidental change; however, the change from primate to man is so substantial a change, it would be impossible without an external cause, a prime mover. To quote Father Dwyer, "A pig is a pig! An ape an ape! Man is a rational being. It required God to provide the definitive intellect." Well, that just puts God on a par with the humming monolith in Kubrick's *2001: A Space Odyssey*!

I perused Aquinas, Plato, Socrates, Aristotle, and other church-nodded-at thinkers, but I read—on my own (often in spare time at work)—Kant, Spinoza, Schopenhauer, Hegel, Marx, Nietzsche, Rousseau, Descartes, and Voltaire. I read the Bible from Genesis to Revelation. That deed scared my daddy-o into thinking that Assumption was pushing me toward the priesthood!

He needn't have worried. I was now a solid skeptic: no so-called proof of God's existence was valid. Worse: the anthropomorphic, ethnocentric, and genocidal God of the Old Testament did not accord with abstract notions of God's perfection. Even less so did a God who fathered a mortal son in the manner of the gods of Olympus or those of Egypt or other ancient myths.

I came to posit that God is the pattern of the order in the universe that we have evolved the intelligence to understand. I gravitated toward Jesuit paleontologist Pierre Teilhard de Chardin's humanist notion of "The Phenomenon of Man." Inherent in all matter are the properties that make evolution inevitable—and *thus* the evolution of a humanizing intelligence. That intelligence, that order, that process inherent to the universe and our conscious awareness of it, IS God. Period. As we come to understand ourselves and our place in the universe, ethics develop in tandem with reason and morality with purpose (or choice). Religions preach (but don't practise) such conscience. Their divisive dogmas just back Stone Age tribalism, Iron Age barbarism, and Atomic Age nihilism.

How energizing to Ping-Pong ideas back and forth! I headed a coterie of undergrad *philosophes* who loved stimulating, intoxicating debate. But the problem of Determinism versus Free Will got me into a quagmire of a quarrel that almost muddied my studies fatally. In my last year, I took Father Norbert J. Ruth's Philosophy of Science course. (The Dean of Science, Ruth also taught physics.) Father Ruth had landed at

Assumption *ex* Texas. I suspect that he had had little contact with anyone of colour—either Negro or Latino—for he speculated about my background and the extent of the "persecution" I had experienced.

Generally, Ruth was a man who liked jests and was a give-and-take conversationalist. Being a priest, however, his authority had to be palpably papal, and being a small man, he nursed—I sensed—a Napoleonic complex. This attitudinal combo was both abrasive and combustible. So, one day, while sipping tepid cafeteria coffee, we got into a hot dispute vis-à-vis cause and effect. I'd forwarded a series of sensible propositions that established that every human choice has a cause, in other words, is determined. Unable to extricate himself from this logical trap, Ruth jammed his fedora on his head and—*ruthless*—banned me from his class!

Told of the fatwa, my classmates poised a boycott to oppose my expulsion. Reinstated I was. Yet, despite scoring the highest exam marks, I hooked a punitive B. A clear case of cause and effect: Caucasian Napoleon sabotaged by Black Louverture!

My now-solo visits to the Browns were also now daily. Infatuated with Marlene, a feeling which both John and Liz blessed, I got to ogle delicious her—and to argue nourishingly with John. Marx versus Keynes, Darwin versus Genesis, Galileo versus God, Mesmer versus Freud!

Once I got the gumption, I asked Marlene out. The most beautiful (in today's slang, the hottest) of the two sisters, Marlene was feather slim, candle-flame lithe, and her blue eyes showed me heavens to wing toward. Her dirty blonde hair—gold ore sandy-dark—was cut medium-short. She was *shy*: Chinese for "poetry par excellence."

Soon, but not without trepidation (interracial couples were rare and taboo), I escorted my lady to a Windsor restaurant. Marlene was unfazed by our public date, but I was wary. Seated, we ordered; the meal appeared; we took up our knives and forks. Then, I spied a diner eyeing us. When he abruptly stood and approached, my legs were coils, set to spring—to high jump and land a blow to lay the sucker low. Instead, beaming, he said, "You'll need these." He set down before us white salt and black pepper shakers: symbolic, divine approval for my first great love affair!

Love? We were Hank Crowder and Nancy Cunard, or Jean Toomer and Georgia O'Keeffe. Or Paul Robeson and la Pasionaria! (They weren't a couple, but should have been!)

I fell in with John and our colleagues, including his brother (who objected—archly subjectively—to Marlene and me). Was social work a viable calling? I joined the Windsor Group Therapy Project (WGPT). We sought to uplift fourteen delinquents, mostly Negro, who had minor scrapes with the law but were at risk of devolving from being criminalized to becoming actual criminals. I was able to intervene successfully only with a magnificent septet.

One lad—I'll call him Dunky Grouse—had seen his family shattered by the fatal shooting of his father. Having relatives in Amherstburg, he spent much time with me—as if my second shadow. His role model, I sparked him to excel. Lacking grade 10, he still earned a college degree—and became a high school teacher and principal.

Through my duties with the WGPT, I soon learned that psychiatrists, psychologists, and social workers have so many emotional problems and mental hang-ups of their own, their praxis is just dressed-up drivel and polysyllabic bunk. Even more vital for me now, however, were my readings in psychology and sociology, those pertaining to race—and sex!

After a year of blissful, sweet, sweet coupledom (yes, recurrent bliss), I'd bought a ring and proposed—on bended knee, just as cinema idealizes—to Marlene.

My ardour ended us. Asking her to marry me was asking too much. And not just of her.

Later, I sussed out that my proposition had precipitated a family crisis. All I knew then was what Dad chose to convey: John forbade me seeing Marlene again. That moment occasioned the only conversation I ever had with my pops about sex. His single sentence? "I understand that you have been intimate with Marlene." (Yes, sir: sable and milk, malt and salt, amalgamating.)

Sadly, it was really the McCurdys who were scandalized by the prospect of an ebony-and-ivory marriage. Would not Marlene and I produce brown offspring? Bad enough that we'd been "intimate," but we shouldn't marry, nor be parents. For his part, radical, Stalinist John thought his sis Marlene too young to be my bride, my wife, my helpmate.

"They" broke us up, and I agonized immeasurably. Pain seared my brain, torched my heart. Not to hold her waist; not to follow those visionary eyes to her open heart; not to smell her hair; not to kiss again those cherry-red, strawberry-with-cream lips…depression! Long, intolerable, suicidal. Why couldn't we have been Othello *and* Juliet, defying one Shakespearean tragedy of race and another of youth? Wasn't I good enough for her to risk all to elope with me? (Hypocritically, my father and my Uncle Ralph, who'd objected to Marlene and me, "wed white" second wives! I guess my own predilection was too avant-garde: still too much McCarthy about, not yet enough Hefner.)

Months later, I sought Marlene. She was with John, in Newmarket, at a treatment centre in a capacious mansion, one that he'd converted into a home for disaffected girls. Once an Anglican charity for "wayward girls" (referred there by courts), St. Faith's Lodge was rechristened as Warrendale in 1953, when John was hired to replace discredited, moral-based disciplinary treatment with a humane and psychological approach. My heart bursting, my eyes sodden, I trekked half of the southern third of Ontario to seek my soulmate. But, oh, she spurned me as if I were some poltergeist! Love was gone, and I, the "ex," was as good as dead.

(John went on to create, beginning in 1966, an international network of Browndale Homes in Canada, the US, and Holland for juveniles, including Black and Indigenous, requiring group therapy. Then, revising his once-outspoken contempt for social democratic parties, he entered the Ontario legislature in 1967 as a Torontonian social democrat! However, parliamentary procedure, decorum, and partisan discipline were intolerable for him. He quit politics in 1971.)

Thirty years after finding John and Marlene in Newmarket, I saw John again, in the mid-1980s. I was a rookie MP, still new in office, when security for the Centre Block (where sits the House of Commons) called to alert me that I had a visitor: John L. Brown! My once-mentor was a grizzled shadow of his once-stellar self. No fire lit now his eyes. He needed funds for a project on a Nova Scotian Mi'kmaw reserve. He informed me that Alice had died prematurely and that Marlene had married and returned to Saint Paul, MN. Never again heard I word from him. He had passed through my youth like a comet, radiating intense light and heat, with Marlene along, inflaming my heart with her imparted bolts; then both were gone, leaving only smoke and ash in their wake.

In my third and last year at Assumption College, I took to microbiology, with Bob Doyle as my prof. My passion was now microbes and chemistry. I preferred predictable bacteria to chaotic human beings.

Financially, I was solvent to the point of pseudo-affluence. My salt-plant job would last until November, then I'd qualify for Unemployment Insurance cheques of eighteen dollars a week, tiding me over Christmas. Also, I was a paid Teaching Assistant (TA) for the general biology course. The WGTP—where I remained a counsellor—also brought "ka-ching."

My final year at Assumption was not only books and blackboards. Monthly, I'd hitchhike to Toronto alone or with Paul Johnson. Thus, I met Nelson Seabury (whom Marilyn would marry in 1954). My Toronto entourage soon numbered Archie Alleyne, jazz pianist (Conrad) Connie Maynard, (John Richard) Sonny Branton, and Lorraine Shepherd. One eccentricity about Toronto, whose Black population was less than that of Essex County? Black women held down nice office gigs, while Negro men worked hand to mouth. (Sonny Branton, who would become the first

African-Canadian train conductor, was an exception.) Guys had to be part-time musicians: witness Nelson, a saxophonist. Even I slapped bongos and sat in on some shows. Archie Alleyne became an acclaimed drummer, then an owner of Toronto's famous Underground Railroad Soul Food restaurant (1969–1990). (Lorraine Shepherd was an AI student and then a first-class educator. In 1990, as Hon. Zanana Akande—the new first name and marital name both honouring her new Afrocentric identity—she joined Ontario's first social-democratic New Democratic Party government as Minister of Community and Social Services.)

Closer to home, Paul and I were partying much-much-much, not only in Windsor, but in the county—in Puce and Harrow—where we hung out with the Grayers, Scotts, and Walls.

A Walls-sponsored party in Puce kicked off a night when I should have ended up in the grave, or in jail, or assuredly in a dust-up—with my pops. Our quintet voted to quit Puce to boogie in Detroit. Wheeling to Windsor, I had to navigate a long curve from Highway 2 onto bumper-to-bumper Dougall Avenue. Rounding the curve, an opposing car sideswiped us. All pulled over; my dad's car sustained scratches, the other car had dents plus scratches. No IDs got exchanged, for the other driver was too drunk to think, let alone speak. So, I restarted my—Dad's—car and ran my homeys to the Detroit do of whisky and reefers.

I sniffed and sipped the drink. I puffed relaxing whiffs of spliffs. Then, we left.

After riding about Detroit, we glided to Windsor via the tunnel. Now, I sideswiped *all* of the pillars on the entrance curve, scraping the car all along the driver's side. The awful, grating noise was a truncated version of what the *Titanic* captain must have heard as he brushed his vessel up alongside a hulk of ice whose substance was as hard and sharp as a diamond.

When I parked at home, the sun was high. My father met me at the door to tell me that Amherstburg Police Chief George Hanna had called to say that his men had tracked my movements all over the county. I dodged jail. Why? Likely only due to Chief Hanna's respect for our family.

Inspecting the harm done his prized 1950 Ford, my dad was speechless. Tears slid from his eyes. But he didn't punish me: I'd totalled his car, yep, but he'd wrecked me and Marlene.

As 1952 touched on December 31, I'd just turned twenty, and my future was vague. Ideas abounded. Med school was on my radar—but an old (WASP) boys' network would block my admission. (True: one *blanc* got into the University of Western Ontario with grades so low, they could only have qualified a doctor's

The Birth of the Cool. (Alton Parker, Shirley Coleman [later Wilson], Paul Johnson, Sonny Branton, and Howard —during his Assumption College days.

son [which he was]. Quotas capped Jews, but Negroes got zapped: zero would be accepted.)

Admittedly, medicine bored me anyway. I contemplated dentistry, but admission criteria stressed—crazily—he-man muscles, as if I had to be Charles Atlas to pull teeth, or perhaps to keep a drilled and needled, squirming, howling patient pressed down in the chair!

I scoped out the Royal Canadian Air Force. A fellow student, Otto Salo, and I darkened the recruiting office where we were told that our science background made us fine prospects. But every army feeds off of xenophobia, racism, homophobia, and sexism. Ain't no place for a leftist!

Another Assumption TA, Norman Goldin, had globe-trotted, sailing on freighters. His tales so intrigued me, I dreamt I'd seesaw the "Seven Seas." Besides, hadn't several McCurdys steamered about the Great Lakes? Could those waters be my "main" domain too?

Luckily, landlubber prospects materialized. I researched graduate programs in microbiology. The Canadian schools emphasized medical microbiology as a subset of MD studies. But Canada gave zilch aid. Michigan State University (MSU) offered the best program at the least cost—and chances for "scholar-dollar-ships." I dispatched envelopes to MSU and two Canuck schools.

Come spring of 1953, I drove to London II where I became 1) a member of the last class from Assumption College to receive a BA from UWO; and 2) the first McCurdy to become a college grad. All were jubilant—and me too. Even Barbara Ann Scott, Canada's 1948 Olympic-gold skating sweetheart, kissed my cheek!

Assumption having split from Western, I could only further study microbiology by pursuing a Master of Science degree. Study skills once casual now knew my exacting mastery.

I found a job posted by the federal Department of Health for a student bacteriologist to undertake clam and oyster surveys in the Maritimes. And in May, I was accepted at MSU.

I was also invited to appear before the selection committee for a National Research Council (NRC) grad fellowship. (Bob Doyle forced me to apply.) Soon, I bussed to Ottawa for the interview. Heck, when I came before the NRC panel, that trio reacted as if I were a cat checking out a party of mice! They did not expect a Negro. The interview became a trial. The questions posed to me would have stumped Darwin, let alone Einstein. The fellowship was clearly a "white-guy-ship."

But my reception at the Department of Health? *Healthy*! Following interviews and paperwork, they had me test clams for a toxin absorbed from algal blooms in the Gulf of Saint Lawrence. The tests involved emulsifying shucked clams in saline and injecting the brew into the peritonea of white mice. If present, the toxin's effect was ghastly! Seconds after injection, the mouse would quake, shake wildly, leap into the air, stiffen, then drop dead. Ah, Cold War science at its finest!

After two days of sacrificing mice in the national labs, I caught a train to St. Andrews by-the-Sea, NB, to meet Ilmar Ernst Erdman, the lead microbiologist, and Mervin Kelly, technician. The latter—an Irish extrovert from an Ottawa undertaker clan—was a wit. Ilmar was his opposite: an introverted diabetic. A nifty team! Even before finding my digs, we were off to sample clams. Now I viewed the waters of the Atlantic Ocean from what was, as I stood upon it, a cliff some twenty-five feet high. Later that day, the world's highest tides would tsunami the Bay of Fundy—as it did every day—and the cliff would be a beach. My life was half Steinbeck's *Cannery Row* and half Hemingway's *The Old Man and the Sea*: a landlubber out of my depth, I was a scientist in my element.

Our lab was a converted bus, and gratifyingly stocked. Easy-peasy was it to shuck shellfish and emulsify them to test for fecal bacteria. Most were shore samples, but to harvest oysters entailed—yep—floating a boat!

St. Andrews? Bee-you-tea-ful! Situated at the base of a hill on Passamaquoddy Bay, the resort town had a year-round pop of a thousand. Off Main Street, I boarded with the Browns (a chance reminder of Marlene), an abode needing only half of my allowance. (Added to my salary, the allowance saw me salt away about one thousand dollars, equalling my past salt-factory income.)

As my first day became dusk, townsfolk swarmed the docks. A once-in-a-century gargantuan tuna had been hooked. Onlookers got handed chunks or slivers, including Mrs. Brown. I ate fresh tuna for lunch the next day. Its taste? Champagne with truffles.

Being the sole Coloured downtown, and exuding "soul" style, I strutted cachet. Attracted to me was a lovely Japanese-Passamaquoddy gal-pal, Alice Akagi, who dwelled at Indian Point. (Could her glossy black hair salve pangs related to a gilded dirty blonde?) Romantically, wind teemed waves at a dither where we beached—in a sinecure of beer and fish-fry. Later, light-footed in the star-milky, draping dark cakewalked the Bobby Browning, whose Liz Barrett was redolent of pine and brine, whose kisses…Ah! Didn't each haggle for—finagle—further kisses?

Shortly, I ganged together a ball team for whom I was coach—and lone pitcher. League-less, we played exhibition games. In one amazing match against a Mi'kmaw squad from Calais, ME, I struck out eleven, allowed no hits. I starred. Still, we lost eight to zip.

Besides baseball, I pursued track and field anew. Qualifying for the Maritime championships, I won the 440-yard run and the triple and high jumps. I got scouted for the 1956 Canadian Olympic training camp in fancy-footwork events. But attending the camp—in Vancouver, BC—was outside my private-citizen means. The fact felt tragic.

But the Maritime Championship was actually almost tragic. Our quartet steered to Moncton by car. Halfway there, we skidded as if we'd hit ice and tumbled down a hundred-foot incline. Uninjured, we checked the damage: Substantial. A death-defying escape. Aye, I shook—like a toxin-injected mouse. For years after, I refused to plunk in any car's front passenger seat: Hadn't my teammates dubbed it the "dead man's seat" as we'd persevered—limped—to Moncton?

We did make the contest, but only I had time to compete—in the high jump, for which I set, as I leapt, a local record. I scored celebrity treatment, even a radio interview.

Back in St. Andrews, at the CP Railway–owned Algonquin Hotel with its Tudor-style exterior, with Merv and Ilmar instructing, I swung at golf balls—hit-n-miss—for the first time.

That St. Andrews summer was seminal. At age twenty, I now lived purely on my own—and on my terms—with a haul of dollars sprawling my wallet. Now a scientist, an athlete again, and my lovelorn blues (maybe only temporarily) receding (thanks to A.A.), I locomotived *ex* St. Andrews by-the-Sea, at summer's end, with emotive regret—and yet never did I return.

CHAPTER SIX:
BECOMING "DR. MCCURDY"

FALL 1953. FALLEN WAS NIGHT WHEN I TAXIED TO THE HORIZON-less expanse of Michigan State University (MSU). Thoroughly intimidating was an institution whose student body of 21,000 was five times the population of Amherstburg. Even MSU's police force was fifteen times larger than that of my ex-home!

My dormitory was Brody Hall. I got to my assigned room, where I'd bunk with two roommates. Shut suitcases staffed one of three bunks. Once he showed, their owner—a blond dude—seemed un-American: he was amiable! After we exchanged names and speculated about roommate #3, a chunky Negro in rainbow motley materialized. Dramatically, he exclaimed, "I'm Harvi!"

Harvi was a flamboyant harpist—and buoyantly Queer. Uninhibited, he quoted unabashedly *ex* his boy-toy's "sux-n-fux" letters. The blond and I struck a live-and-let-live attitude. We had to! Yet, homophobes (and Negrophobes) hurled hateful epithets relentlessly our way. To our ashamed relief, Harvi soon reconnoitred more simpatico quarters. I still see his departing eyes. (Harvi Alonzo Griffin [1936–2005], of Detroit, became a world-renowned harpist, playing the White House some twenty-five times! Audit youtube.com/watch?v=RGzbh5P5EaA. Thou shalt be enchanted!)

Shortly, I met Prof. Henrik Joakim Stafseth, head of the department of Microbiology and Public Health. A veterinary microbiologist, the elegantly goateed Stafseth was a classic Norwegian scholar: suit, tie, spectacles. Incorrigibly cordial, Stafseth viewed me not as a Negro but as an "exotic" Canuck. Believing me grounded in chemistry, he advised, "Minor in physical chemistry."

My debut MSU courses? Microbiology, immunology, statistics, physical chemistry. Not distracted by love or vice, my study was rigorous. (The "McCurdy Postulates for Effective Study" are thus engrained in my kids!) What I lost hold of in class, I grasped by clasping books. Stats and phys chem having exposed my deficiencies in math, I absorbed an extraordinary text, explicating all from primary arithmetic to Nobel-level calculus. Once a klutz, I became a computer.

Phys chem brought my first midterm. I feared I'd flunk. Nope! Scored 97 percent! Unbelievably, my grades in all subjects ranged tightly: 95 to 100. Stats awarded me 100 percent! I now stood out as a singular achiever, and I was inducted into Phi Kappa Phi, the oldest honour society in the US and one devoted to lauding academic distinction in any field.

A pioneer in sanitary microbiology, Walter L. Mallmann was *the* expert on exterminating germs. (Did his middle initial stand for "Lysol"?) Short, thin, and fifty-sumpin', flaunting a luxuriant shock of Einstein-silver hair, jutting Mount-Rushmore brows and nose, and eagle eyes, Mallmann had joined MSU in 1918. He smiled, but his speech was grunts. A no-nonsense prof, his first assignment saw me devise a simpler medium for the detection and enumeration of coliform bacteria—E. coli mostly. (Fecund in fecal matter, coliform bacteria are used to detect—yep—shit particles in drinking water.)

Mallmann's roster? All Korean War vets, including Fred Post, Robert "Coop" Cooper, and Thomas Randolph Neblett. Fred and Coop were opposites. Both Californians, Coop was an extrovert Democrat, Fred an introvert, liberal Republican. (The Grand Old Partisan—not the jackass-backer—was my constant correspondent.) An Egyptian, Tawfik Younis Sabet, was quiet and either aloof or alienated. (Dissatisfied, or Cairo-homesick, he paused his doctoral research to rake up manna at Detroit's venerable Difco Laboratories.) Tom Neblett later directed microbiology at Detroit's Henry Ford Hospital. (Via Tom, my beloved wife, Brenda, secured her first job.)

Meanwhile, through chats with the few Af-Am students at the Brody Hall residences, I assisted in initiating Delta Pi, the MSU chapter of Kappa Alpha Psi Fraternity. Partying with these guys off-campus in Lansing, I met several ex-Spartan (MSU) football players. Their trophies gleamed amid rooming-house rat droppings and used-needles biohazard. (This doom has befallen too many Af-Ams: recruited for their athletic ingenuity, then discarded due to academic collapse.)

As I commenced research work, onerous now stretched the mile-and-a-half distance between Giltner Hall and the dorm. To Shaw Hall (just across the Red Cedar River from Giltner, the domicile of bacteriology), I moved. Awaiting me? Fresh roommate upset. The new guy was an authoritatively pleasant, pallid Mississippian. But the ex–Korea vet bore 350 pounds, and for that reason snored so raucously, either homicide or suicide became my dilemma. Relocation was the judicious option.

My next roommate was a memorable eccentric. Indeed, virginal to Michigan winters, he lacked wool threads. Worse? He eschewed soap and water; olive oil did for both. Rancid, his odour overpowered any hint of oxygen. I'd gone from a guy whose lungs reamed my ears to a guy whose aroma had me gasping. Again, I sought out the dorm manager (a Canuck) to "clear the air." I was giddy to hear that grad students merit a single-occupancy room. Hello, solo! More good news: I qualified for a foreign tuition and maintenance scholarship. That—coupled with my lab assistantship—eliminated any financial frets.

Come February 1954, a sinkhole gaping at the salt mine—what was now the Canadian Rock Salt Company—sunk summer job hopes. (Fifty thousand yards of fill were needed to level off the abyss.) An alternative to a Windsor gig? Oh, to vamoose to New Brunswick, to get back to Alice A.!

By spring of '54, I'd triumphed in all classes (including a thesis), incurring just one B. Dr. Jack Jenks Stockton in instrumentation (an applied science cum engineering course) had conferred that demerit, though I'd scored straight As in all tests. And he refused to justify his grade. (My involvement in Canada's greatest racial protest of the 1960s–'70s was due to allegedly racist grading by a biology prof at what is now Concordia University. My experience with Stockton afforded me insight into the complaints levelled by Blacks about racial bias downgrading—degrading—their marks.)

The most notable event of that spring was the May day I returned to Shaw Hall to find an uproar. Everyone everywhere dissected the headlines that declared the US Supreme Court had struck down segregation in its decision on Brown v. Board of Education of Topeka (Kansas). Caucasian and Coloured students yahooed! The civil rights era had begun!

Though I'd hoped an MSU degree would lob me an industry job, I now planned to be a prof and researcher. After I passed my oral exam, I was ecstatic to meet with Dr. Mallmann to plot my future. He observed

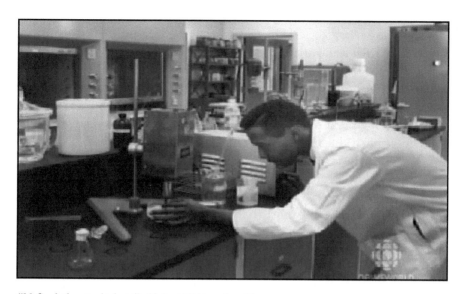

"McCurdy the microbiologist"—likely at Michigan State University, ca. 1957.

that I was an "ideal candidate for a doctorate." Why? "You are not a Negro!" Translation? My IQ transcended my melanin. A Republican of Abe Lincoln creed, Mallmann perceived me as distinctly unlike the "customary" Yankee "darky." I contested his assertion. Yet, I disregarded truly the subtleties in the existential politesse between US Caucasians and "dem" Blacks—an air of thuggish smugness from hog-it-all palefaces (lynch mobs at the ready) and a kind of hostile deference from Negroes, camouflaged by happy-go-lucky grins—with pocketed guns cocked. (Behind every smiling Sambo stands Malcolm X, lighting a Molotov cocktail....)

An incident re: my then pal Calvin Davenport illustrates my point. A Korean War vet, once domiciled in Mexico City (which he called "raceless"), he came one eve to the lab with a bag of books to employ as pillows. Why? To "transfer their contents by osmosis"! Then he complained, "How else can I pass? Our profs are so prejudiced!" Forgetting my situ with Stockton, I said I hadn't observed any untoward attitudes. His answer? "You're not Negro, you're Canuck!" (I answer both Mallmann and Davenport with James Baldwin's retort: "I am not *your* Negro.") Later, Calvin became Head of Microbiology at historically Black Virginia State University and invited me there to conduct a curriculum review and direct a seminar. A remarkable moment! Black science students heard an Afro-Canuck prof expound on his own published research!

In summer 1954, I rejoined Ilmar and Merv on the clam survey, beginning with a month in the Gaspé, Quebec, where French was *de rigueur*. I struggled with the tongue, for idiomatic traps abounded. For instance, after lunch one day, my landlady's daughter asked if I was hungry still. "*Non, j'suis plein*," I answered. She eyed me peculiarly and disappeared into the kitchen. Gales of laughter erupted. Why? Via gestures and fragmented English, I learned I'd said, "No, I'm pregnant!"

The Gaspé was seaside pastoral with its hilly terrain and with Percé Rock and its thousands of seagulls. Yet, it lacked the seductions of St. Andrews (cue: Alice A.). Nor was our Prince Edward Island idyllic, as I learned while competing there in track and field that summer. Noted for its North Shore beaches, bucolic seascapes, and for being "The Cradle of Confederation," a noxious miasma—the reek of xenophobia—encumbered the lobster mecca. Thus, at the Maritime lists I contested—again winning the high jump and 440 race—my mother, who had come to watch me stride to the podium, had to cover her ears (with gloved hands) to muffle the torrent of racial epithets roared at me from the stands. (*Anne of Green Gables* should have been entitled "Anne of Whites-Only Beaches"!)

An honestly sickening episode unfurled near Summerside, PEI, where, while taking samples of shitty water, I met two paleface clam diggers. I warned them not to eat the raw clams; they yelled indignantly, "You're just a rotten, Black egghead come-from-away!" Soon, the local rag's headline screeched: "TWO INFECTED WITH TYPHOID: Ate Toxic Harbour Clams"!

Back at MSU, I confronted a no-nonsense academic: Charlie D. Ball. Iron-tough. Denied a doctorate, yet a full professor. Legendarily, rather than alter his dissertation's rad conclusion, he'd refused the degree. Ball was, well, ballsy. Thus, vicious was Ball's disdain for those he thought boastingly huzza'd the designation "Doctor." Feeling such scorn was Dr. C., my virology prof, a pro at vet medicine. Doc C. was doing PhD work but repeating Ball's course having failed it at first try. Ball hazed Doc C. relentlessly. He'd assert a lecture point, then hector his prey, "Isn't that right, DOCTOR C.?" Doc C. was a pretentious, friendless fop. And Ball, feared and fearless, was a P. T. Barnum type: he'd leap up on the front table to demonstrate an idea. Like Lear's fool, he could seem comic; yet, like Lear's fool, his logic was dead serious.

On my first biochemistry exam, Ball notched me an 82. The mark disappointed, but it was an A and the top mark that Ball gave. Still, I shook with fear of failure. Thus, I did lab work even while my mother attended the convocation at which I received my MSc!

Until that day, Ball had never addressed me directly. But as I laboured solo in the lab, he threw open a door, barked, "Mc-CURDY!" I nearly dropped my flask. With my pulse still skipping, he hollered, "I know you're CANADIAN! Do you play soccer?" "No." My answer dismayed him, MSU's soccer coach. Despite this letdown, he was complimentary about my academic work. Thereafter, he'd wink at me while chiding Dr. C. (Ball had friends in high places. Two-time Nobel Prize laureate Linus Pauling was one. He came to Ball's class to lecture on protein structure and DNA composition, just when the link was spurring viral debate. Like most world-class scientists, Pauling was able to depict tricky concepts in a kindergarten-savvy, connect-the-dots manner.)

Simultaneously, I was conducting contract research to identify a bacterium that causes cutting oil (a metalworking-useful lubricant) to deteriorate. Thus, I *discovered* an enteric bacterium (that is, E. coli–related). To character it, though, I had to test it serologically. Rabbits did fine for raising antiserum. But MSU had more poultry than lagomorphs. Still, chickens are dimwits, always dying during bloodletting because they won't be as passive as rabbits. So, at the end, I had fifty clucking hens, and so I deputized Coop and a chap named—*ahem*—Christian to assist in head chopping. Each of us took home a share; I stored the rest in Dr. Sadoff's humongous freezer.

Dr. Harold L. Sadoff was a grad student fave. An iconoclastic yet eat-drink-and-be-merry Jew who treated us as comrades, he taught microbial physiology. (Later, along with microbial genetics, the field would get rebranded as molecular biology.) Where the action was! Sadoff's focus was on clostridia (anaerobic bacteria), which revoltingly, nauseatingly *stink*!

Yet, not even Sadoff's smelly cultures could out-stink what happened when someone unplugged the freezer where my headless hens were rusticating. Shut up for months, so that the de facto poultry mausoleum baked in summer's searing heat, once the freezer door gaped wide, the disintegrated fowl belched an epic stench, befouling all of Giltner Hall. That soggy mess of feathered flesh and sloppy bones was left to me to clean. I gagged nigh to vomiting. Anaerobic bacteria were doing jumping-jack aerobics in my nostrils, gorge, and belly!

Classes and lab research frustrated socializing. Not that I lacked distractions! Free campus concerts featured A-list performers, such as jazz diva Ella Fitzgerald. Football games were spectaculars: opposing plays resolved into short bursts of colourful, earthbound pyrotechnics, while contending fans were as rowdy as Fourth-of-July patriots.

A few hundred yards off-campus was the State cinema where I'd catch a flick. East Lansing was dry, so if I wanted suds, I had to transgress the town limits. I aggressed, egressed, and transgressed!

Supreme recreation? Golf. Courses were plentiful, although I mostly traversed Groesbeck. Nor did my black skin ever inhibit me from clubbing a white ball across any Michigan green.

Outside MSU, my buddy was Chester Holley, a hulk of a good-natured, brown-skinned US Army vet. Half-deaf due to bombs and bazookas, Chet had to second-guess half of my words. (To his ears, my speech was one-quarter jive and one-quarter scat.) A table tennis pro, he improved my play. My best man for my wedding would be, natch, who else?

Dating I was, sporadically. Now, as I envisioned employ in academia, I worried I could end up a nerdy, tweedy, leather-elbow-patched bachelor. Needy for a steady lady? *Moi.*

Shaw Hall was peopled partly by Spartan—but epicurean—footballers. One was Howard Neely Jr., from Ypsilanti, a town with familial ties to Windsor. In fact, his mom was Canadian; we had the Dominion in common. Hanging out with my namesake Howard Jr., I learned that his sister, Patricia—Pat—was also at MSU. Shortly, she and I were canoodling at length.

Meanwhile, US politics had gone ass-over-teakettle (again). McCarthyism was at its fascistic peak (or nadir): loyalty oaths got imposed on grad students receiving taxpayer bucks. (A Marxist microbiologist was more seditious than a Mormon one?) As a Canuck, spared the "patriotic" assaults and insults, I still hewed—skewed—leftward, anyway.

African-American and (some) Caucasian students became movers and shakers for the burgeoning Civil Rights Movement. Pat and I enlisted. I started a campus branch of the National Association for the Advancement of Coloured People (NAACP). Thus, I honed a talent for public speaking and a style that could excite and direct an audience.

I got elected prez; then, once other campuses spawned offshoots, I became prez of the Michigan Association of University Chapters of the NAACP. Next, as Prez and First Lady (so to speak), Pat and I were delegates to a national NAACP congress in Washington, DC. Disgracefully, the NAACP had long disavowed the radicalism of its prime mover, W. E. B. Du Bois (the NAACP was largely the brainchild of Du Bois, who called its originating Niagara Movement together at Niagara Falls, ON, in 1905); and, as a CCF member (the socialist Co-operative Commonwealth Federation), I resented the rank, anti-socialist yakking of Black Yanks backing Red scares. Rightly, our Michigan branches were free thinkers about freedom! *How else to think it?*

I led the Michigan NAACP until I left MSU in 1959. My replacement? Ernest Gideon Green of the Little Rock Nine, the nine African-American students who integrated the Little Rock Central High School in Little Rock, Arkansas, in 1957. He was the first of them to graduate from the school, in 1958; he enrolled at MSU thanks to the patronage of MSU's governor. Though astonishingly young, and despite his cinematic experience—requiring an escort of paratroopers to enter into and thus desegregate an Arkansas high school—Green seemed quite unassuming about his "profile in courage." His heart was heroic, and his backbone seemed to bear feather-lightly the lead weight of leadership.

Our NAACP activism necessitated campus recruitment, non-violence workshops, placard marches, bullhorn protests, and contesting race bigotry on campus and in East Lansing. Pat and I tested off-campus housing discrimination ourselves but could prove little. Given the few Negroes at MSU, the few complaints about academic bias got resolved; prez John A. Hannah acted with dispatch.

One indelible event was a panel debate on South African apartheid that transpired before a Black-majority audience. Two chalky South Africans faced off against two "Native" fellow citizens, the latter disputing the image of racial harmony presented by the Caucasoids. The conciliatory tone of the discussion belied the violence that the conflict over Boer-minority rule would engender. Three years later, in 1960, the Sharpeville Massacre would ignite the fuse of apartheid's destruction via mass mobilization of peaceful, domestic protest, Cuban-backed guerilla war, and international economic sanctions.

Now, I had to scheme a doctoral research project. I contemplated studying the microbiology of compost or the peculiar myxobacteria (soil-dwelling, slimy, microscopic-minuscule organisms that chew up insoluble matter). In the end, a spectacular move to another department would satisfy my desire to dodge traditional, ho-hum bacteriology. In 1957, Coop took a course in general mycology in the Botany department, taught by Edward C. Cantino, the inaugural editor of *Experimental Mycology*, that he deemed phenomenal. Coop badgered me to try the course, confident that not even I could scoop an A. Every bit as admirable as Coop advised, Ed Cantino was a stellar lecturer, whose course featured studies on morphogenesis and differentiation using fungi as model systems. This research could illuminate how various organs in the body are formed by presumably genetically identical cells. Therein, I scored my A. (In fact, I received the highest mark Ed ever awarded.)

I had to transfer to the department of Botany and Plant Pathology. When I told Dr. Mallmann about the necessity, he agreed graciously to joint supervision of my degree. (Then again, he was preoccupied with a domestic matter. The only female grad student in microbiology was thirty-year-old Virginia, a picture-show beauty. Imagine: not only were she and Mallmann dating, they would soon elope. Over some fifteen years of marriage, they disseminated several joint-authored research papers that underscored their—I'll say—harmonized interests.)

Fraught with speed bumps, nevertheless, was my move to Botany and Plant Pathology. Indeed, Robert Stanley Bandurski, a plant physiologist, queried my knowledge and objected to my refusal to satisfy extra course requirements. Still, my schooled stubbornness carried the day. Next, a New Brunswick Canuck, who taught the genetics of molds, handed me a B on an exam in a course I had taught to fellow students—all of whom scored As! I was apoplectic! I told the doc that prejudice had doctored—docked—my grade. Blushing, he righted the B to an A!

Just past thirty-five, Ed was a youthful full prof. He'd made a name for himself via an artful theory of how carbon dioxide triggered the aquatic fungus *Blastocladiella emersonii* to form a resistant, structurally different plant. My lab colleagues were James S. Lovett, a grad student, and Evelyn Horenstein, Ed's research assistant (and later a PhD at the National Institutes of Health).

Our lab environment was smartly casual. Thanks to Ed, we knew about yet-to-be-published work in microbial genetics and metabolism, including DNA study, all of which positioned US research at the global forefront. Shocked were all of us then, when the Soviets launched the Sputnik satellite—and thereby triggered spasms of Yankee self-doubt.

Often we'd gab about socio-politics. Though sympathetic to the Civil Rights Movement, my colleagues knew only one Negro: *moi*. Herself a Jew who had experienced bigotry, Evelyn was most insightful. Jim's ancestors had backed abolitionism, but he was conservative—like Ed—and both dreaded McCarthyite attack. So, my open avowal of socialism made me a pinko bête noire.

Research on the developmental biochemistry of *Blastocladiella* had been based on comparisons of mature static cultures in plants of various ages. I chose to use bacteriological techniques to enable the harvesting of pure spore suspensions. Once initiated, their growth would then be synchronized to magnify the behaviour of a single plant, thus yielding far more significant data.

In the meantime, there sprang up love (or maybe supercharged affection), and so marriage was on the agenda. Pat Neely and I had forged a bond apparently good enough for "tying the knot."

Wedding day to Patricia Neely. Hope was springing—not eternally, but desperately.

So, in the spring of 1958, Pat and I wed in Ypsilanti, MI. The bride was late but copper-cinnamon beautiful in her luxurious gown, so lavishly albescent. I savoured her neat, lithesome form; I took for my bride a loving Black activist in a lovely, white-wedding ceremony amid candled aromas of apple blossoms and pear nectar. I had reason to hope for (our) happiness. I said "I do" with no pursuant, dubious inhalation. The champagne was crisp, the nuptials silky.

Yet, swiftly, misgivings became regrets. (Compare Hardial Bains, *Thinking About the Sixties*: "[W]ithin this aura of loveliness, an ugliness intruded.") Pat blamed her lead-balloon grades on racism. Yet, assisting with her study, I detected carelessness—and noticed tardiness. (She'd been so late for our wedding—an excruciating ninety minutes—that I'd almost backed out.) When she was grumpy, I was jumpy, for she'd turn pots and plates into missiles!

We managed—and/or struggled. We lived in the "Huts," a village of ex-army housing, rentable for $48 a month, all-inclusive. Pat worked for the Home Ec department, and with my $3,600 per annum in scholarships and fellowships, plus free tuition, our household was debt-free.

After flat-out toil (often in forty-eight-hour stretches) all week, I'd take a break and avoid the lab from Friday night until Sunday afternoon. During football season, we'd shop for groceries Saturday morn and then party before going to the game. Deeming a car essential, I purchased a used 1950 Oldsmobile.

My last academic requirement? To qualify in German having passed French. (To be able to distinguish *Sekt* from *sex*!) During my lingo course, my appetite tanked: my 165-pound frame shed 40 pounds. Diagnosed with infectious mononucleosis, I had to complete German while hospital confined. (No *Sekt*, no sex.)

In fall 1958, the Huts got gutted. Pat and I selected a newlywed-oriented high-rise; our rent leapt to $85 per month. Coins got clawed back from our pockets.

My research was concluding. Shortly after New Year's 1959, just as Castro was running Batista out of Cuba, I began scribing my dissertation. It engrossed me—well into the summer of what was Pat's *grossesse* (pregnancy). From dawn to midnight, I typed scientific sentences to the music of Richard Wagner (*Die Walküre* and *Tannhäuser*), Max Bruch, Ludwig van Beethoven (my dark-complected bro), and Felix Mendelssohn. I battened onto German Romantic discord and distress and even wanted it "darker" (à la Lenny Cohen)—the *Sturm und Drang* of *Faust*, the Wagner-scored (this time—sorry, Hans Erdmann!) *Symphonie des Grauens* that yields the theme of *Nosferatu*. Music sheets perfect for fire! Why? I'd entered a pitched grief: I yet longed for Marlene, but Pat was my wife, and I her husband.

My sorrow was not relieved until Ed approved my manuscript (sustaining merely cosmetic changes), and I was done by August. My MSU degrees: Master of Microbiology & Public Health with a minor in chemistry (conferred December 13, 1955), and Doctorate of Microbiology & Public Health (conferred September 4, 1959). My dissertation became my first publication. And so commenced my academic career. To establish unabated brilliance, aye, plus drop-kick back to Dixie every bigot's ass!

CHAPTER SEVEN:
NAMING
THE NDP

AS SUMMER RUSTED UNTO SEPTEMBER 1959, PAT AND I domiciled in Amherstburg. Expecting our first child, we took over my boyhood home (Dad vacated it to afford us space). Simultaneously, I was now a prof at the new Assumption University of Windsor.

I'd nixed joining the faculty of (historically Black) Virginia State University. To the chagrin of Ed Cantino, I'd declined a Yale post-doc post. I wanted to be back in Canada—albeit my "home *on Native* land." The Dominion? The "white devil"—to quote Malcolm X—I knew best.

During my MSU studies, I'd stayed in close contact with Bob Doyle of Assumption. Now, he wanted me back—as faculty; and Father Grant agreed. Hired at the rank of lecturer, I thus became the first African-Canadian to secure a tenure-track post in a Canadian university. My colleagues? Winfred G. Benedict, Father Jack R. Dougherty, Bob Doyle, Father A. J. Grant, Calvin C. Kuehner, and Mike L. Petras. Like me, Benedict and Kuehner held PhDs. (We star in a Biology Department photo in the 1965 Assumption University of Windsor yearbook. On page 21, I'm seated, far right, looking as dapper as Miles Davis but impish as the Cheshire cat! See core.ac.uk/download/pdf/72791829.pdf.)

For my debut, I taught nurses bacteriology and chemistry plus a half-course in general mycology. Sleeplessly nervous, I over-prepared, practising and practising my first lecture—in mycology—so I'd seem spontaneous and authoritative! Yet, I wound up speaking to but five students, only slightly my junior. Indeed, in spite of affecting a Hugh Hefner pipe, I was often mistaken for a student. Once, thus insulting my professorial ego, a bus driver insisted that I need only pay the student fare!

Fifteen women—mature students—sat the nurses' courses. (In dreams, my eyes still slide their way.) They enjoyed my lectures and I enjoyed teaching; and the more I taught, the more I improved.

My initial contract saw me paid $4,800 for nine months: I earned less than a public-school teacher and but half of an autoworker's pay. (My salary was as raw as celery, for it wasn't real "bread.") Fortunately, Calvin "Cal" Kuehner, Bob Doyle, and I scored a research contract with Stroh's Brewery that padded our summers with "extra green."

A University of Detroit grad, Cal was a pal of John Stroh, who hired us to fix the fermentation characteristics of yeast then spoiling the taste of his brewery's beer. A flavourful challenge! Though we couldn't remedy his fickle yeast, the brewery found a culture of "good" yeast, yielding the sweet-spot suds. Still, Stroh's cash let us acquire dreamt-of equipment and start our own research program.

Cal was a towering, talkative American with whom I shared an office. Thus, he was there when I took a phone call from a search team for Douglas Aircraft Company, seeking a microbiologist trained in disinfection. Dr. Mallmann had pitched me as the ideal candidate, so the caller sought a personal interview. But why would an aircraft company need a sterilization bacteriologist? Easy: the space age search for extraterrestrial life would be compromised if the rockets utilized were not preserved against earthly microbial contamination. The idea wasn't, really, "rocket science"!

Shortly, my telephone interlocutor was at my office for our interview. He knew my CV—chapter and verse—and had schmoozed my ex-professors to suss out fraud or failures. Our face-to-face tête-à-tête would top things off. My comportment proved agreeable and my perspectives spot-on. Next, I beheld a document for my signature, which would commit me to becoming an American citizen. A Canuck patriot, I objected. So, no Apollo moon-shot project *pour moi*!

Before joining Cantino, I'd become obsessed by myxobacteria, whose life cycle is either deviant or exceptional. Few of the bacterium had ever been isolated and grown in pure culture (a priori for any experimentation). In fact, classical botanists had described much of the material via utilizing dried specimens at the Harvard Herbaria. Although I published on *Blastocladiella* as well as the cyanobacteria (blue-green algae), my study of the taxonomy of the myxobacteria is what brought me research moolah, grad students, and modest recognition.

In the fall of 1959, Pat bore our first child, Frederick Douglas. A heart defect ended—so abruptly—his infancy. My own heart dashed and smashed, I mused:

Destiny
Must deny
Scrutiny.

Pat? O! Plunged deep into postpartum sorrow *and* funereal woe! She sought solace in striving for a diagnosis of the speaking, hearing, and apparent mental impairments suffered by my sister's son, Nelson. (These defects were likely attributable to my sister having contracted German measles during her pregnancy.) Our research took us to hospitals in London, ON, and Michigan. (Sadly, Nelson was an adult before he was diagnosed as deaf.)

Pat and I began our activism just after we interred our first-born. (An unholy sentence, that!) We deceived ourselves that we could thus relieve our grief. Having lost *our* Frederick Douglas, we acted to recuperate history's Frederick Douglass. (Compare W. E. B. Du Bois, "Of the Passing of the First-Born.") So, Pat brought together teens whom we mentored, while dishing out much home cooking. I coached the guys in sports. (Their ranks included Windsor boxer Charlie Stewart, who became the 1970 Eastern Canadian heavyweight hefty, the 1972 Canadian light-heavyweight boss, and then a 2000 Olympics Team Canada boxing coach.)

Though many African states were seizing independence and Dixie Coloureds were beginning to vote again, our "raps re: race" were revelations domestically. Few Ontarians knew our African roots. Told of our African heritage, their first reaction was horror, evincing an atrocious degree of self-hatred among Negroes in Essex County—the crucial terminal of the Underground Railroad.

Once tutored in history, instilled with knowledge? Pride took root and flowered into strength.

Now, as "Red" as I was, my uncles pressured me into what seemed a retrograde decision: to join the Prince Hall Masons, also known as the Black Masons. This body had been integral to the survival of the ex-pat Af-Ams of US-border-hugging southern Ontario. And it was familial tradition: my father and my uncles were all members, and my mother belonged to the sister organization, the Order of the Eastern Star. (As the Worshipful Grand Master, my grandfather presided over the Ontario Lodge, 1952 to 1956.)

Black Masons were *bourgeois*, not radical. Even so, I was initiated to the level of the Third Degree in a ceremony reminiscent of my initiation into Kappa Alpha Psi. Soon, my activism saw me damn as moribund a body whose significance was historical and irrelevant.

Race relations in East Lansing (that is, "on campus") were affable. Yet back home, in the Dominion, I was reminded rudely that the Great White North was no North Star Canaan for we "Negroes." For the 1960 Labour Day holiday, the McCurdy and Thomas clans held our annual reunions in Amherstburg. After church, four of us sought to putter about a green. At MSU, I'd ranged freely all the local courses, swivelling my hips as I sent balls bounding cross grass or sky. So, I loathed the Canuck nixing of our leisure. My quartet tried first the Kingsville course, where we were told only members could play. Clearly though, white golfers had only to pay green fees. At the Roseland (in Windsor), Essex (in Walkerville), and Dominion (in Oldcastle) courses, the same gambit got bruited. In contrast, white golfers looked to be the pink of perfection for the green.

I sent a letter to the *Windsor Star* recounting our experiences. That elicited a supportive comment in Richard Moorsom "Dick" Harrison's double-column, page-length "Now" op-ed. Harrison's stress on my being "Dr." McCurdy encouraged the attention I got. For some readers, race discrimination was merely an irritant, but class discrimination ("lower" versus "upper") was catastrophic!

However, nothing happened until I entered a complaint against Kingsville under Ontario's Fair Accommodations Practices Act. I also retained the counsel of A. Alan Borovoy of Jewish Labour Committee– sponsored anti-bigotry protest. (A fellow CCF-er, Al soon earned a national rep due to his backing Africville residents to battle the City of Halifax, NS, to frustrate its effort to wholesale expel Black families from their city-government–segregated community. Al also championed the Ontario Human Rights Act.)

The prompt reply from Kingsville? Their attorney solicited the intervention of Father Eugene Carlisle LeBel—the first Catholic priest to be prez of a non-denominational university, namely mine, and, thus, my boss. So, Reverend LeBel (CBS, CD, LL.D.) urged me to treat with Kingsville and accept a now-proffered membership. Couldn't I "play an Uncle Thomas"? Um, well, never! (This would not be the last attempt from outside it to use my university position to suppress my anti-racism activism. Although I separated social struggle from my professorship, academic freedom was yet the fraught question. Thus, I was spurred to help establish the university's faculty association and then the Canadian Association of University Teachers.)

In the summer of '61, with allies from the Black community, the Unitarian Fellowship, Labour, and the CCF, including Borovoy, I dispatched teams to "test" golf courses for Negrophobic praxis. We also investigated two public beaches in Emeryville near Belle River. My procedure: pairs of Blacks followed by pairs of Caucasians sought admission to each of these facilities. Always the result was a depressingly unambiguous revelation of racism. Moreover, proprietors or managers would excuse themselves by slagging their clientele for objecting to the presence of any save "prominent Negroes." Often I heard that I'd've met that criterion—to be an "honorary white." That I would not accept to be a "token" stirred no slight consternation among the supposedly "charitable" palefaces. (So, you scorn golf-club integration as just an upper-class fancy? Need I remind you that racism aims to immobilize us—by residence, work, and class? Slavery paralyzed us by whip and chain and barracoon; segregation impeded us via illiteracy, ghettoization, overpolicing, and underemployment. Our *Freedom always* entails the ability to *move*—our limbs unshackled, our vehicles unhindered, our neighbourhoods green and flowering schools.)

Our anti-racism "tests" received thumbs-up press cross-country—except for the *Windsor Star*. Instead, columnist Jim Cornett, a patio-lantern-enlightened, folksy paternalist, critiqued us and vented customary malarkey: Windsor had the Emancipation Celebration, a long-weekend-long, Windsor-based festival uniting Windsor and Detroit in the celebration of the British termination of slavery in colonial Canada on August 1, 1834 (Windsorite Walter Perry, a Garveyite showman in Las Vegas packaging, helmed the crowd-pleasing extravaganza from 1937 to 1967); Negroes occupied key city positions. Naturally, Cornett huffed that two golf courses welcomed Black patrons! "So there!" (Two years later, "Jimbo" Cornett, in his column, sallied to defend blackface minstrelsy. He won scathing rebuke from George F. McCurdy, striving to banish "defaced Negroes"—my term—from stage plays at General Amherst High School as well as in service club fests. To me, Cornett's opinions—all that bigoted nattering—showed him to be a stuffed-shirt black shirt.)

Our struggles to eliminate all-white golf courses and white-only beaches attracted the backup of the labour council, churches, etc., all willing to boycott Negrophobic recreation sites. Notably, not one segregationist facility accepted integration willingly.

While these actions were being undertaken, the CCF was seeking to redefine itself as a social democratic party in partnership with the Canadian Labour Congress. "New Party" clubs were being formed cross-country to expand—we prayed—our partisan ranks. Like many young(er) activists, I wanted the New Party to add white-collar, pink-collar, and no-collar to the CCF's blue-collar base. The New Party's convention—in August 1961—also had to launch its name. Contenders? The "New Party" or the "Social Democratic Party of Canada." (The latter choice honoured Canuck praxis wherein parties' names echo their bedrock ideology. Even "Progressive Conservatives"—when they still existed—could be progressive on social programs, if retarded on social policy.)

CCF Windsorites favoured the "Democratic Party of Canada," for we admired US Prez JFK's "New Frontier": more space shots, fewer have-nots. Too, we adored former Michigan governor Gerhard Mennen "Soapy" Williams's staunchly leftist Democrats. Our local compromise was to conjoin "New" to "Democratic." We'd advocate a "new democracy."

In that "Bay of Pigs" April of 1961, Pat and I welcomed our first daughter—in time for the "New Party" convention in August. I announced teasingly that my child's name was "Vanilla." Well, the jest spread like wildfire! To squelch it, had I to circulate her true-true name: Leslie Lorraine.

Anyway, the convention was showdowns and shindigs, steelworker brio and garment worker charm, fists pounding tables and shoes tapping floors, plus cigar fumes, cigarette smoke, the acrid smog all sweetened by perfume and cologne and whiffs of ale. I audited ideologues at loggerheads with dreamers.

Assigned to give the inaugural speech to claim the name "New Democratic Party," for the "New Party," I faced a struggle. The national exec had already selected "New Party" and was printing info to make that cognomen a *fait accompli*. To beat back this propagandistic and psychological head start, I had to combine King's cadences, Kennedy's wit, and Nat King Cole's timing. I hit on the allegorical theme of Pat and me as prospective parents debating what to call our newborn. That predicament saw me ridicule the notion of any parent dubbing a new baby, "The New Baby." The point resonated, and the "New Party" became the New Democratic Party. Kudos flooded my way.

Following this historic vote, CBC Radio's Norman DePoe labelled Windsor delegates "radical left extremists." Justly pissed, a Windsorite trio tromped up the stairs to the CBC booth to lambaste DePoe for his blacklisting Red-baiting (a wooden-noggin Charlie McCarthy as ventriloquized by flint-hearted Joe McCarthy).

A new NDP exec member, Roy A. Battagello (later revered as Windsor's "Riverfront Warrior"), told me that he'd nominated me to join this leadership body. However, foreshadowing disappointments to come, my name was rejected, Battagello said, because the national exec thought it "premature" to have a Negro in their midst! These "New Democrats" were as retrograde as old-hat Dixiecrats?

By mid-June of 1962, the federal New Democratic Party faced its first test. Two candidates vied for the Essex West riding nomination: Bill Tepperman, a young man in a hurry, and Battagello, a teacher. Strategic, Tepperman seized the nomination by signing up new members.

For their part, at a bedlam-raucous roundup at the Tivoli Theatre, the Grits needed three ballots to pick Herb Gray over Valerie Kasurak. As a partisan of the Windsor Interracial Alliance, Valerie was well-known and well-liked. Herb was a lawyer, the scion of well-liked and well-connected parents. The well-known versus the well-connected? No contest!

A buddy and I shadowed Gray's events and loved lobbing questions as spiky as razor-wire. Our queries needled Herb, but our jabs were, he said, as healthy as acupuncture or a vaccination!

Prior to the pursuant election, Ron Trider and I realized that Bill had goodwill but few committed voters. We advised him to show his electors his face, but Bill was inordinately confident in his invisible and inaudible charisma. Although as laid-back as Northern Lights weed (an Afghan and Thai combo), "Gray Herb" did outpoint Bill. (Latterly, the greying H.G. became fabled for his love of head-banging hard rock, all electroshock and acid schlock.) A loser, Tepperman decided to skip politics for business.

Soon, non-union types deserted the party. The NDP ignored all who carried a briefcase instead of a lunch pail. Pontificated some, the NDP wasn't meant for entrepreneurs or eggheads.

Donald Cameron MacDonald headed the provincial CCF and then the Ontario NDP (1953–70). Drab, he could've packaged his snooze-button self as a guaranteed sleep aid. His successor, Stephen Lewis, brought the ONDP unprecedented success in the 1970s. Yet, even he seemed—to me—to regard academics as one-part irrelevant and one-part irritant. (More than sixty years after joining the CCF—then helping to establish the NDP—I will say, in my experience, the "pinkos" do not welcome People of Colour. My later involvement with the party, from the 1980s to the early 2000s, saw me quit in disgust over its subterranean—yet seismic—racism.)

Soon again, Parliament was dissolved and writs dispatched. I refused to run but urged Trevor Price, a Welsh high school teacher (and later University of Windsor political scientist) to carry the party banner. His campaign? Exasperating. To him, being on the hustings was akin to by-the-book lecturing. No! It's intellectual combat wherein mud gets thrown. Lacking guts and spine and heart, his defeat was only delayed by election day itself.

Easily re-elected as he would be *forever*? Herb Gray. (Not until my upset victory in 1984 would a New Democrat win a federal seat in the Windsor area.) Disaffected with the party, my focus shifted. Time for the parental McCurdys to furnish a homestead for Leslie!

Commuting twixt Amherstburg and Windsor became a game of chicken as I outfoxed both sluggish "turtles" and tailgating "hares." What to do? Build a house in South Windsor! Our realtor—Chaucerian-surnamed Bob Pedlar—warned us that when a previous Black clan had desired to move into our dream locale (the Cabana Road–Mt. Carmel district), a redneck petition had gone round: "Keep Our Neighbourhood White!"

Heck, our bungalow at 3910 Mt. Carmel Drive not only went up sans incident, our pleasant neighbours included, in time, other Negroes, namely, the Black Whites and the Black Greens. Just down the street? St. Gabriel's Roman Catholic Church. No sooner had we unpacked than Father Martin Johnston was standing on our doorstep! Spouting apostolic zeal for ecumenical, coffee-fuelled communion, he was a liberation theologian, if more in the mould of Dale Carnegie than Karl Marx. Pat and I did darken (I pun) the church—a one-storey, yellow-brick, sprawling ranch-house structure. (The worship portion boasted a vaulted ceiling and warm tones of maple and oak and cedar.) Johnston was truly magnetic. Yet, I was already receiving papal bulls from my father and sister, didn't need extra. Soon enough, though, Father Johnston was defending me publicly when I was being blackballed by yellow journalists.

Surveying that period, 1959 to 1961, I'll admit that my marital unhappiness (a side-effect of lingering feelings for Marlene) saw me invest psychologically in science. Then, the death of my first-born led me to hurl myself—with Pat—into social causes. (Ah, the sublimity that is sublimation!) Yet, Leslie came laughing (and instantly the drama princess) into our lives, and by naming her I was inspired to "brand" the NDP. Because I scrutinized bacteria, I also knew that we had to war against the pathogen of prejudice. So what if I didn't go to NASA? I had the NAACP experience, which fed into the NDP, and I was now a husband, a father, a professor-scientist, and a Freedom strategist. And yet still a Coloured man en route to becoming Black. And the countdown was on.

CHAPTER EIGHT:
ENTER THE GUARDIAN CLUB

THE YEAR 1962 SAW ANTI-DISCRIMINATION LAWS GEL INTO THE Ontario Human Rights Code and Dr. Daniel Hill kick-start the Ontario Human Rights Commission (OHRC). His debut marked the culmination of a two-decade struggle in which Dan, his wife, Donna, and civil rights allies (numbering multitudinous Windsorites) in labour or ethnic or faith organizations, steamrollered warrens of anti-Black rules throughout "Southern Gothic"—that is, Alice Munro's—Ontario. A gung-ho director, Dan urged the "downpressed" to call the OHRC into combat wherever prejudice unsheathed its dagger. When Pat and I and comrades were struggling to integrate golf greens and white-sand beaches, the OHRC didn't exist. We were alone. No matter—Black Southwestern Ontario emerged in anti-slavery. It originated in the Underground Railroad to defy both Dixie and white supremacy. The Great Depression spawned spirited defence of civic, social, and economic interests. Thanks to over-lapping memberships, Black Christians became the base and backbones of the Central Citizens' Association (CCA), the Armistead Club, the Hour-a-Day Study Club, and more.

CCA dynamos numbered Walter Perry ("Mr. Emancipation"), Dr. Henry D. Taylor, Hilda Watkins, Pat Watkins, Rev. Mack Brown, J. Lyle Browning, and Lyle Talbot. The CCA broke many colour barriers but struggled mainly to hike Negro employment. The reckoning? Having the right to eat and sleep and live where one wished could not count for much if one could not afford to dine in a restaurant or lodge away from home or even to buy or rent a roof!

The first bastion the CCA breached? The City of Windsor. Alton Parker became the first Black police officer. (Later, Parker instituted the juvenile bacchanalia and charitable notion of "Uncle Al's Kids Party," from 1966 up to his octogenarian death in 1989. A Windsor park is named in his memory.) Jim Watson became the first Black city solicitor. In a city where Black workers were barred from the auto industry and the retail sector—and where we were relegated to servile employ such as railway and hotel porters, maids, and cooks—municipal posts bore high prestige.

But private corporations rebuffed the CCA. Dominion Stores (a national supermarket chain) and other retailers scoffed at hiring Negroes. Black women could not be sales clerks or cashiers; Black men could not stock shelves or stack boxes.

Typical was my Aunt Dot's experience: a qualified secretary, she could only—in Windsor—cook and clean. Other Black women chose to cross the border, daily, to sweep and mop the dirty premises of a foreign country. Ultimately, Aunt Dot did only clerk in Detroit's Black-owned enterprises.

True: the Second World War opened the auto assembly line to Blacks. But it took until the 1950s for Chrysler, forced by law, to hire its first Black worker. Some CCA members, such as Mahlon Dennis and Lyle Talbot, were union—*and* anti-racism—militants.

After the anti-Fascist war, the CCA, renamed the Central Citizens' Association for the Advancement of Coloured People (CCAACP), under Talbot's leadership became more vigorous, more vociferous. 'Twas a sharp departure from the moral-suasion approach and the brokerage skills of "go-slow" Negroes in negotiating concessions! Talbot and company's "radicalism" scared the old guard, who feared the erosion of their status.

First billed as a struggle against Fascism, the Second World War soon emerged as a battle against racism and colonialism. These causes now had many proponents; simultaneously, long-suffering victims of pernicious prejudices now abandoned patience. Often aided by "righteous whites," many Afro-Southwestern Ontario communities—chiefly Amherstburg, Dresden, Chatham, and Windsor—forged groups to forge change.

In solidarity with labour radicals, the CCAACP established the Windsor Council on Group Relations (WCGR). With Lyle Talbot serving as chair, its members listed Rev. Lloyd Jenkins, Nancy Watkins, Mahlon Dennis, Charles Brooks, and Valerie Kasurak, among others.

The WCGR launched a community "audit," surveying employers, hospitals, public institutions, hoteliers, and landlords and interviewing Coloured citizens. Its purpose? To choose strategic targets for integrationist campaigns. Yessum, the WCGR did not shy from "direct action" tactics. The WCGR mounted sit-ins, flying pickets, and stand-ins that conservative Negroes disdained and the *Windsor Star* condemned. Hugh R. Burnett's National Unity Association was also aggressively progressive! Burnett was a liturgical blame-thrower and a surgical flame-thrower.

In Windsor, the WCGR succeeded, controversially, in proving the pervasiveness of Negrophobia. Its research, published as *How Does Our Town Add Up?*, documented that 98 percent of all Black men were precariously employed labourers, while de facto segregation seemed a matter of civic pride.

But whenever Canucks are condemned, rightly, for racism, they accuse their critics of either being insane or ungrateful. Thus, restaurateurs and publicans denied prejudice but justified anti-Black policies by blaming Caucasoid clientele for objecting to Negro patrons. Realtors and landlords refused to sell or rent to Coloureds because we were "unhygienic" and "recidivist." In cahoots, these chalk-faced hypocrites informed us, hysterically, "Blacklisting is legit business praxis."

Thus, in the autumn of 1961, during a dinner party whose guests included Dan Hill and Alan Borovoy, the lack of a civil rights insurgency in Windsor dominated our discourse. I agreed to start a new body to manifest equality of opportunity so as to improve the quality of Black lives.

I consulted comrades and we met at the home of Mahlon Dennis. Present? Harold R. Johnson, Spurgeon Garland Montague, Henry White, Lyle Talbot, *et moi*. Unanimously, we voted to start an "uppity" organization, as sly as Castro's guerilas, and just as purposed to harry the foe. We selected an evocative, non-racial, and mysterious name—The Guardians (my coinage), in keeping with its purpose: to guard the interests of the Black community. Thus was the Guardian Club, with a shield as its symbol, originated, and I got voted prez. (I confess: given my NACCP chapter presidencies, I'd begun to like feeling "presidential.") Other debut officers? My veep Howard Watkins and our secretary Eugene W. Steele.

Howard was a star detective with the Windsor police. We went back years; indeed, his brother, Lloyd, was my Aunt Dot's helpmate. Eugene was Windsor's first Black firefighter and was heroically battling—all alone—horrendous racist abuse by those who were officially colleagues but who acted like racist firemen. His wife, Frieda (Alton Parker's daughter), overcame racism herself to become a supervising nurse at Windsor's historic Hôtel-Dieu Hospital. (That Frieda Steele had to overcome prejudice at all says much, because Hôtel-Dieu of St. Joseph Hospital was established in 1888 specifically to serve Af-Ams who'd migrated from Dixie to Windsor in search of industrial jobs but whose children were excluded from Caaucasian-oriented schools.)

Other premier Guardians counted my wife, Pat; Mrs. Howard Watkins (Leverda); Af-Am sociologist Dr. Wilson A. Head; plus Cliff Walls, Mahlon Dennis, Henry and Doris White, Lyle Talbot, Lyle Browning, Philip and Pat (Eleanore) Alexander, Spurgeon Montague, and Rev. Lloyd Jenkins. Harold R. Johnson, whose advice informed our strategies, soon "went North," where he became the first Black dean (of Social Work) at the University of Michigan. (Barack Obama assembled for his Prez Cabinet a Lincolnian "team of rivals." Well, the Guardian Club was a team of firsts: first Black tenured prof, first Black cop, first Black firefighter, first Black supervisory nurse, first Black dean. And not one of us "firsts" believed we need take a back seat to any zwieback ever again.)

The Guardian Club asserted vehemently the provisions of the Ontario Human Rights Code. We backed complainants and publicized complaints. We tested colour-blind entree to bars and restaurants. We also sent volunteers to do survey work to support sociologist Rudolf A. Helling's study, *The Position of Negroes, Chinese, and Italians in the Social Structure of Windsor, Ontario* (1965).

Natch, our efforts brought blowback! I recall having my hair cut at Harry Olbey's Barber Shop, while listening anonymously to an "E-lite" lady berate myself, "that Negro prof," for engendering "a stink."

Dr. Roy Perry voiced like sentiment. Slamming Helling, he alleged that the sociologist had used unscrupulous survey methods, dispatching student interviewers to glean predetermined results. After all, hadn't they failed to interview "successful Negroes" such as himself? Perry poohpoohed racism. To him, only sourpuss or backtalk Blacks suffered discrimination—which they deserved. Perry was a city councillor, so the *Windsor Star* banner-headlined his self-hating slurs. (Perry pursued a Grit nomination but lost to Bernard Newman, who aced the provincial election vote. Seeking my endorsement, Perry's wife, Charlotte, dubbed her hubby a "race man." I demurred, opining—gently—that her man could only be a "race man" if he ran track!)

In February 1963, just four months after the US trained nukes at the USSR to thwart nukes being operationalized in Cuba, the Government of Canada was defeated in Parliament for refusing to accept Yank nukes being stationed on Canadian soil! (Prez JFK's valentine to PM Dief-the-Chief!) That same month, I treated with the Canadian Council of Christians and Jews (CCCJ), who sought my insight regarding asking Martin Luther King to speak in Windsor and garner its Brotherhood Award. Yes, I had misgivings: the CCCJ had a sad record of handing out "merit badges" to those who were mum about human rights. I suspected that the CCCJ aimed to profit their lucrative Brotherhood Week banquet. I swore that if King were asked to praise Windsor while ignoring the racism that the Guardian Club had documented, we'd protest that travesty—with bullhorns.

To secure Guardian Club buy-in, the CCCJ arranged my one-on-one with King. Our half-hour meeting? Cordial. I outlined the issues confronting Ontario's "Black Belt." I warned King that comparisons with Dixie and the local history of the Underground Railroad could be used to imply—falsely—that Windsor was "Canaan reborn."

Well, in introducing King, the "sucker MC" acted exactly as I'd worried, whitewashing Windsor's history. To my vast satisfaction, however, King specified that Windsor also allowed execrable anti-Negro praxis. Never ask, he said, for whom the bell tolls; it tolls for thee. Did the *Windsor Star* ignore King's John-Donne-derived critique? Do birds fly?

Three weeks after quitting Canada, King launched the Southern Christian Leadership Conference (SCLC) campaign in Birmingham, Alabama, and the news of it inspired the creation of a fund to aid the SCLC. Fifty leading Windsorites were sponsors and elected me as chair. Walt Perry—the barker—tried crassly to exploit our effort. He even reprinted a *Star* op-ed extolling the fund. In response, I released a statement disavowing any connection between the MLK moneys and Perry's cabaret of pinstriped preachers and star-spangled showgirls!

King was back "in da hood" in June, when he led "The Detroit Walk to Freedom" to its terminus on the riverfront. I was among the 125,000 "dreamers" who heard King rehearse the baritone quaver of his "I Have a Dream" speech for the upcoming August March on Washington. To my ears, as King repeated the visionary refrain, the emotions of the throng surged to a combustible and explosive pitch. (How fortunate for the Yanks that King was not a demagogue!)

Also that year, Dr. Wilson Head joined the Guardian Club and took avidly to "testing." In one case, he and Cliff Walls attempted to golf at the Roseland course. As usual, they were told that one must be a member—or be recommended by a member—to play. Next, Wilson's request for the membership list was denied. Then, inexplicably, the pair were allowed to golf for free, which, to Cliff's embarrassment, exposed Wilson to be no golfer but a duffer!

One legendary testing expedition occurred on a Sunday afternoon. Our two families motored to the Kingsville area and spotted this sign at the entree to a public beach: "Whites Only Please." ("Whites Only" is Yankee; "Please" is Canuck.) A snap of Wilson and me posing with that sign got snapped up by wire services—and viral it went. Next, an Ontario Human Rights Code complaint deep-sixed the sign, and "Segregation Forever" transformed into "Segregation Nevermore." (Wilson's Windsor days would soon end, but "Doc Head" and "Doc McCurdy" crossed paths evermore. A York University prof and chair of the Toronto Urban Alliance on Race Relations and then prez of the National Black Coalition of Canada, Wilson was a staunch proponent of human dignity and citizen equality. We were "brothers from different mothers.")

By 1964, the Guardian Club had proven the existence of gonzo local racism in hiring, housing, and slinging hash. We adopted this mantra: "Make shame more shameful by making it public." Conjoining the Windsor Labour Council, the Windsor Council of Churches, and my university's department of Sociology, we set up a weekend Human Rights Institute.

Giving the keynote, I summarized the Guardian Club's findings (which jibed with those of Doc Heller). Catalyzing 10 percent of all racism complaints, Essex County had proportionately the worst record in Ontario. (Across Canada, only Nova Scotia vaunted more documented anti-Black incidents.) Still, I held that most Windsorites would back anti-racism measures. After all, Negroes held prestigious city positions. However, I also noted that while local broadcasters had often sympathetically reported cases of alleged race-prejudice, the *Windsor Star* usually turned a blind eye and a deaf ear.

Local radio, TV, and Toronto's *Globe and Mail* thought my remarks newsworthy. The *Windsor Star* did not, despite reprinting the *Globe* article. Then, in an editorial and two op-eds, my speech was condemned. I was hissed at for collaborating with the *Globe and Mail* to blacken (yes, I pun) both Windsor and my own university. (*Star* journalists even hinted that I could be—should be—fired!) Heading up the parade of denial? Mistah Emancipation hisself—Walt "Disney" Perry!

Well, Windsorites who'd audited my speech inundated the *Star* with protests. Even Dick Graybiel, the *Star*'s owner-and-publisher heir-apparent (his parents still ran it in 1964), expressed umbrage and told editors to print my rebuttal. Maddeningly, the editorial board told Uncle George and me that my op-ed would be published only with "the usual editorial changes." Rejecting that reply, we walked out. Adamant we were that Graybiel's proviso be respected. And so it was.

In July of 1964, the Institute (now a permanent OHRC advisory committee) was the subject of a full-page spread in which an executive triumvirate—chairman Rev. Canon J. G. Lethbridge, Frieda Steele, and I—sat for an interview with the *Star*'s editors. Permitted carte blanche to expose Negrophobia in Windsor and table resolute solutions, we prepared the way for the first OHRC office outside of Toronto to open, in Windsor, in 1965.

That same year, I took a surprise telephone call: civil rights activist Dick Gregory wanted a Canuck home for his family. He feared a race war in Chicago, whose tense atmosphere felt to him "like TNT awaiting a spark." King had advised him to contact *moi*. So, Dick asked that I recommend a realtor. (The Af-Am comic was acquainted with Windsor, having played dates in the city in 1962 when his appearances on the Jack Paar TV show first brought him cross-border fame.)

Soon, Dick was a regular presence, and I chauffeured him about to assess properties. (Since Dick was forever fasting, I had to keep on hand for him a carboy of triply distilled water.) His non-stop, hilarious, autobiographical gags kept me laughing so hard my breaths were gasps and my eyes sheer tears. But he was also canny. Sagely, he advised, "Howard, buy soy beans." I should've. They were then valued at about two dollars a bushel. Shortly, they were eight dollars a bushel.

Finally, we located a Riverside Drive mansion whose price was a steal. The estate extended from Riverside all the way back to Wyandotte Street. Before closing, however, Dick brought his wife and his guru to examine the property. His wife adored it but Dick deferred his decision until he and his seer (a bearded, beanpole psychic in a monarchical, ivory-snow robe) could inspect the acreage. Their ramble done, Dick announced that, according to astrology and/or feng shui, the residence was a no-go. "No deal," exclaimed the Universe.

In February 1965, the Guardian Club, alongside ten Negro groups, launched a Black history exhibition at the university, *From Slavery to Freedom*, the first such celebration of our history anywhere in Canada! Assuredly, our volunteers were unprecedentedly cultured. Frieda Parker Steele, Howard Watkins, Pat McCurdy, and Alice "Verna" Chatters outdid themselves.

Throughout Essex County, museums and families loaned priceless artifacts. Hundreds showed: Detroit sent the curious, Toronto sent the ignorant, but all were inquisitive. Alongside Dan Hill, a progenitor of the Ontario Black History Society, Wilson O. Brooks, Toronto's first Black teacher, electrified the kick-off banquet. Also present? Lenny Braithwaite, the first Afro-Ontario MPP (elected in 1963) plus Dr. Charles Wright, who set up the International Museum of Afro-America in Detroit in 1966, now the Charles H. Wright Museum of African-American History.

Also in February 1965, Malcolm X—the firebrand "Black nationalist"— was shot dead by his once "Black Muslim" confreres. He'd extolled Black pride, our crucial pivot. But we dismissed, heartily, his gospel of violent, "revolutionary" retribution. Still, that man afflicted us—shook us—with his diatribes, his elegant elocution, his elegies for lynchees, his Garveyite anthems, his acidic retorts, his bluesy sermons, his geopolitical editorials, his recitations of Europe-beatified genocides and Europe-beloved tyranny, his machismo compounded of brio and *menefreghismo*.

My cousin Melvin "Mac" Simpson was so converted by the exhibit that he devised—with his wife, Betty—the North American Black Historical Museum (now titled the Amherstburg Freedom Museum), whose Amherstburg doors opened in 1975. Mac and Betty's accomplishment was immense, and George McCurdy's oration soared at the dedication. Yet, Mac overlooked his first cousin and pioneering Black historian, Alvin McCurdy. Thus, the Alvin McCurdy Collection now resides in the Ontario Archives.

While we Windsorites were beginning to prize our history, African-American history was being made afresh in Alabama. An attempt by John Lewis of the Student Nonviolent Coordinating Committee (SNCC) and Hosea Williams of the SCLC to lead a voting rights march from Selma, Alabama, to the state capitol in Montgomery was smashed by "Stasi" goons and their deputized and brutal hooligans. Thus, March 7, 1965, got branded "Bloody Sunday."

Being the veep of the Unitarian Fellowship, I asked Anglican, Eastern Orthodox, and Catholic churches to parade on St. Mary's (Annunciation) Day to agitate, ecumenically, for Equality. (Catholics used the *fête* normally to counter commie-inspired May Day events.) So, on Sunday, March 28, 1965, seven hundred marchers thronged Ouellette Avenue. Christians wore sneakers; Unitarians donned sneakers; B'nai Brith laced up sneakers; most UAW locals put on sneakers; and university profs and students and Negro activists proved their "rubber soles." Who was MIA? Negro pastors plus their sheepish lambs! (They'd feared that wild-eyed radicals could hijack the march.)

Meanwhile, the year-old South Essex Citizens' Advancement Association (SECAA) was confronting brazen school segregation in Colchester. Backed by the Guardian Club (led by Uncle George), SECAA swore that School Section (S.S.) #11 was not only Black-only, but deplorably unhealthy and extremely unsafe. Shutter it *NOW*!

Opposition arose from principal Beulah Cuzzens and teacher Hilda Dungy, the county's sole Negro (and inconsolable) schoolmarms. They blasted upset parents as "distrustful," that is, not accepting that the pedagogues were "doing their best" despite a live rat being caught on the rundown premises and then taking a star turn on the front page of the *Globe and Mail*.

Finally, then Education Minister (and later Premier) Hon. William Grenville Davis revoked all Negrophobic permits. Thus, #11 closed. Hurrah for integration!

In summer o' '65, on Boblo Island, five Black teens mixed it up with Detroit ofays. Negro fists had the upper hand until twenty redneck Chrysler workers, their annual picnic transpiring nearby, waded into the melee. *Call the cops!* Sure! But who got charged, cuffed? Only the Black kids. (In 2017, I'm depressed to note that this incident of 1965 got replicated in 2005 or so [see chapter 21], in Windsor, with the like result: Black kids charged, white offenders set scot-free.)

Another altercation erupted at a slot car raceway in Amherstburg; two more Black youths got arrested. After a cross was burned on Main Street, the words "Home of the KKK" were scribbled cross the town's welcome sign, and hateful epithets blasphemed the walls of the (Coloured) First Baptist Church. Several Black citizens, including my Uncle Ralph, a town councillor, uncradled ringing phones only to hear foul-mouthed, Ku Klux Klan death sentences.

Because Blacks were feeling anxious and distressed, SECAA reached out to the OHRC (Dan Hill) and Borovoy. I doubted that any true Klan was pestering Black Amherstburg. Like the chief of police, I figured cracker jokers for cowards. Yet, these worrisome episodes spurred Mayor H. Murray Smith to form a joint Race Relations Committee, whose membership featured SECAA militants Ralph and George McCurdy, plus three town councillors.

SECAA submitted recherché briefs to the committee, tracing race preferences in housing and jobs. Meetings ensued with thirteen of the town's industrial and commercial employers, and a few Blacks gained local jobs. George and I also called on Bell Telephone to open up opportunities. Thus, we inaugurated affirmative action programs in Canada. (In 2014, Amherstburg hailed its first African-Canadian mayor, Wayne Hurst, his tenure a reflection of the success of our struggle of half a century ago. *Half a century!*)

Then, on a bright Sunday morn in July 1967, a buddy and I, returning from a round of golf at Little River and bound for South Windsor, drove by the airport. Our clear view of the Detroit skyline saw it smoke-smothered. Fiery insurrection was ablaze. Chop-chop of helicopters, rat-a-tat-tat of machine guns, wooh-wooh of sirens.... Rancid, squalid, fetid stink of burning.... Rats supposedly abandoning a Detroit of firestorm-blistered supermarkets and splashing across the Detroit River to Windsor.... Accused rioters kept marinated in urine and garbage.... Bitter embers, sour char.... An epidemic of bullet wounds.... Snipers intent on assassinating firemen.... Haphazard massacres at the Algiers Motel.... Et cetera.

Although the 1967 conflagration was apocalyptic, it wasn't Detroit's first. I was at my Aunt Helen's house in June 1943 when an armed, peckerwood mob attacked Blacks on Belle Isle. Next, a gun-and-badge "fifth column" invaded Black neighbourhoods, even Black Bottom and Paradise Valley, to burn and loot, beat and shoot, thus slaying nearly thirty-six victims. "Policing"? No: a pogrom.

King's movement was demolishing explicit Dixie racism, but implicit apartheid, long cemented in Detroit, had become an "edifice" attractive to Molotov cocktails. "Urban renewal"—that progressive-sounding claptrap—bid white-helmeted city planners replace white-helmeted cops but with mirror outcomes. By instituting freeways to convenience Negrophobic suburbanites, thus aiding "white flight" from Detroit (so depriving the city of a significant tax base), stable Black neighbourhoods were bulldozed into rubble, their residents transferred into slum ghettoes (served by poor schools that were just pipelines to prison or the morgue), and the city hollowed out. The Motown sound? Sniper fire, gunfire, drive-by "hits," cacophonous no-go zones. How bad did it get? In 1982, I spied a burnt-out, charred-black fire hydrant, right downtown!

The catalyst for the 1967 insurrection (no mere riot)? A KKK-Keystone Kops corp roaming Detroit, arresting, assaulting, and/or murdering Blacks at will with zero justification. (I myself had witnessed uniformed-and-badged sadists beat and/or club to the gutter defenceless Negroes—in broad daylight on Woodward Avenue, Detroit's main street.)

During the wee hours of July 23, Blacks had gathered at a speakeasy to salute the return of two Af-Am Vietnam vets when constables storm-trooped into the joint, to cuff all eighty-two patrons. For the crowd observing the takedowns, the brutal manhandling catalyzed *Resentment* into retaliatory *Rebellion*. To denounce law enforcement's crimes, some Blacks turned to looting and arson. *Les flics* then blockaded the entire neighbourhood (as if it were Cuba menaced by JFK). But outraged Black folk smashed the encirclement! Stymied, Detroit had to call in martial reinforcements.

By the time the flames wilted—on July 28, due to US Army and National Guard boots tramping streets—43 persons were dead; 467 injured; 7,200 jailed; and 2,000 buildings torched. Once the manufacturing colossus of the US Midwest and a reputed model of Prez Johnson's Great Society (*Welfare* at home, *Warfare* abroad), Detroit was so wracked by these Northern Ireland–like "troubles" that it remains to this day a living corpse, one "devoured by the maggots of political cynicism and the pestilence of corruption" (to lift a forensic phrase from Pierre Elliott Trudeau; see his "New Treason of the Intellectuals," an essay excoriating nationalist Québécois politicos, in *Federalism and the French Canadians*).

The riot closed the border, locking commuters into their passport identities. Only firefighters, reporters, and emergency services personnel escaped the stay-at-home orders. Panic swept Windsor. Euros feared Detroit's implosion would imp Windsor Blacks to like violence—led by "firebrands" such as myself (!); Windsor Blacks dreaded a local backlash.

Assuredly, the Detroit blaze cremated the annual binational Windsor-based Emancipation Celebration. Despite pleas from mover-and-shaker Walt Perry (who'd sought to "advance the race" via sermons, sequins, and spare ribs), zwieback and backward Windsor politicos nixed the fest. One dissenter was Eugene Steele, who asked rhetorically, in an interview, "If the Detroit riots had happened before Thanksgiving, you wouldn't cancel Thanksgiving, would you?"

Because he'd prepped for the extravaganza at huge personal expense, Perry panned the cancellation as exemplifying the municipal racism that he'd always had to combat. Thus, he presented a bill to Windsor Council to cover his outlay, plus—to general consternation—wages for his family. Sure, councillors scoffed at the dunning. Then, Perry died. I speculate: His premature decease was attributable to the demise of the most important thing in his life?

Almost instantly, Edmund "Ted" Powell, a union local prez and an ebullient hustler, assumed control of the Emancipation Celebration. But Perry had nixed his "Greatest Freedom Show on Earth" on the smart condition that it be revived in 1968. Such would require a fresh round of licences for the parade, the carnival, and a dance. During the winter months of 1967–68, Windsor Council voted to ask the police commission to recommend licence renewals. Naturally, the badged killjoys chorused, *Nyet, nyet, nyet*: death to (the) Negro Freedom (Fest)!

Now, Powell had early broached the question of the licences to Windsor's top cop, Gordon Preston, but had been patently ignored. To the OHRC, thus, he complained of police racism. So, alongside trade unionists and churchgoers, the Guardian Club and SECAA backed Powell's charge that he was suffering a bureaucratic form of police harassment.

On March 29, Black Windsorites—including SECAA prez Ralph McCurdy and me as Guardian Club prez—met with Mayor Wilfred John "Jack" Wheelton to air our concerns. All bonhomie, if not lawyerly blarney, Wheelton advised that we get to the next police commission hearing, on April 5, when Powell's licence applications would be reconsidered.

On April 4, I was partaking—with my Uncle George, *et al.*—in a fed Human Rights Commission workshop in London. That evening, while we were hanging out in George's hotel room, the TV news whacked us: MLK had been shot dead. Incited was a blood-and-fire apocalypse. King's death weighed leadenly on my mind as I wheeled back to Windsor the next morn for the police commission meet. I was in no mood for the tenor that gathering would take.

As Ted Powell, Uncle Ralph, and I entered, we were neither welcomed, nor introduced, by the gendarmes' bosses. Once Powell was, at last, recognized, Judge Bruce J. S. Macdonald (OBE) barked, "If you think that this commission is going to permit ten thousand Negroes to come across the border for the purpose of creating civil disorder, then you have another thought coming!" (See Herb Colling's 2003 book of investigative journalism, *Turning Points: The Detroit Riot of 1967, A Canadian Perspective.*)

King's martyrdom lit the fuse; now I exploded! Across the room, I pointed a scornful finger at the blanching, repellent Macdonald: "Your statement reflects exactly the mentality that makes it possible for someone of King's stature and leadership, with his capacity for reconciliation, to have been shot!" As his face shaded from pallid to pink to apoplectic purple, I added, "Most American Blacks consider Canada a respite and are most unlikely to cause trouble here. Yet, not a single Caucasian-sponsored event has been cancelled due to the threat of possible importation of Yankee racists! But you likely don't mind importing such because you're used to their ilk in Canada—and maybe right here in this chamber!" Spontaneous was my fury and as serious as a heart attack.

Now, Macdonald conjured the spectres of Black Panther radicals, "H. Rap Brown and Stokely Carmichael," set to invade Windsor and lob Molotov cocktails. I jeered: "The jurist's *Jurisprudence* has sloughed off all *Prudence.*" Macdonald accused me of "predicting the future"! "No," I said, "the definition of prejudice is to pre-judge, and it is you who are doing so." Now, Macdonald and Judge Gordon R. Stewart chimed they could expect Caucasians to be civil but not Negroes. (Note: Judge Stewart was removed from office in 1986 due to a seeming unbecoming misuse or abuse of authority respecting the Windsor police department. See *Report of a judicial inquiry regarding His Honour Senior Judge Gordon R. Stewart, a judge of the Provincial Court (Criminal Division) Ontario*, 1987.) Once a war crimes prosecutor, Macdonald yelled, "Our commission tells people what to do! No one tells us what to do!" I thought, *Someone's spent too much time with the Nazis he was prosecuting*. It's unlikely that attorney-war-hero Macdonald had ever been court-martialled—figuratively—by a Black man who is/ was as Joe Biden said arrogantly of Obama in 2007, "articulate and bright and clean and a nice-looking guy." Still, my *chutzpah* scandalized even *moi*, save that it was 1968, the year of the Tet Offensive, the Prague Spring, France's *mai* upsets, RFK's insurgent candidacy, and the kiss-and-hug, Anglo-Canadian version of grassroots revolt, that is, "Trudeaumania."

Ralph explained that Mayor Wheelton had asked us to treat with the commissioners. Macdonald huffed but Ralph set out the compromise: Macdonald should bid key, bilateral officials consult Black Windsorites before deciding whether *our* Emancipation would be celebrated.

Shortly, the commission okayed the parade but not the carnival. Powell withdrew his permit applications because the event, minus the carnival, would bleed red ink. Council then rescinded writ to use the park. Meanwhile, Dan Hill of the OHRC, at last hearing Powell's racism complaint, dismissed it, paradoxically, due to erroneous police-officer warnings of potential subversive acts by "Negro radicals"—such as myself—who were under surveillance. Thus, Hill got suckered by prejudice rooted in the genesis of cops as ragged peckerwoods paid to nab fugitives fleeing their "massas."

Powell then sought the aid of the CCLA's Borovoy, who launched an appeal before the Ontario Supreme Court, which upheld Hill's decision. Whatever the technical basis of these rulings, Black people could not ignore the blatant racism therein expressly articulated.

Thus, on the night of August 1, 1968, at UAW Local 444, a well-attended "funeral" was held for the Emancipation Celebration. Sponsored by SECAA, the Guardian Club, the Windsor-area labour councils, etc., the featured speakers listed Canuck UAW boss Dennis McDermott, Borovoy, and Michigan State Senator Coleman Young (later mayor of Detroit), who lamented the scar on Canada's reputation. "Does Canada seek to repeal Emancipation itself?"

That 1968 "wake" was, sadly, prescient. Though the *fête* resumed in 1969, it was—just like post-riot Detroit—a hollowed-out entity. Once seeming granite permanent, it was now papier-mâché fragile. Fire dusted the Jackson Park grandstands; the Ouellette Avenue extension divided the park itself. Moved to Mic Mac Park, the once-august gala lost pizzazz, lost glitz, and lost money. The bash was now a bust. With so many more attractions opening up to Blacks as racial barriers fell, perhaps Walt "Disney" Perry's one-man-impresario "Freedom Show" was a throwback. Yet, here's the truth: nothing has emerged to take its place, to link Canada and the US, Windsor and Detroit, in celebrating the liberation of Black peoples from the tyranny of slavery and to boast fiesta—Bibles for Blacks, bathing beauties for "the boys," and BBQ for border-crossing bellies! Thus, many Windsor Blacks yearn still for its return, recall it with nostalgia and wonder, hold Walt Perry in their hearts, and speak about him and his celebration in heroic terms to their children and grandchildren.

Instantly, I was a non-stop public intellectual and/or "talking head," called upon to describe the extent and effects of racism and to demand justice. Some masochistic Caucasians luxuriated in being damned for their sins. In contrast, Blacks wanted to hear not only the inventory of injustice, but also how to engineer empowerment: to end our exclusion from opportunities.

Now, I rejected the term "Coloured": we were not wannabe whites tainted by African tints. No! It was as citizens *ex* Africa, slipped from chains and shackles, and with defiant flaunting of our blackness, that we would enact equality. We would now be *Black*!

Not everyone accepted the new self-identification. My grandfather became Black happily, but my grandmother thought "Coloured" best mirrored our mixed-race heritage. Nevertheless, "Negro" upscaled to the militant "Black." Folks who had once minimized their African heritage started wearing African garb and sporting Afro dos, even if straight hair had to be kinked into the style.

In late 1968, I addressed a Windsor Rotary Club luncheon. In due course, I recounted the April brouhaha with the police commission and quoted Macdonald's injudicious words. Present, he thought my castigation intolerable, but his words were undeniable. Furious, he tossed aside serviette, clattered down cutlery, scraped back his chair, stood up, and stormed out. (Macdonald and I crossed paths again sixteen years later during the federal election of 1984. Knocking on Walkerville doors to identify my voters, I came face to face with the old judge. "Well, I guess you won't be voting for me." His smiling answer? "You may be surprised.")

Shocked by the judge's behaviour, one Rotarian asked Pat and me to be his *Guess Who's Coming to Dinner*–style guests. (Note: though I criticized the Rotary wheeler-dealers for their lack of a Black member, I wasn't invited to join.)

Ironically, 1968 was UNESCO's International Year of Human Rights. To observe it, Hon. Dalton Arthur Bales, the Ontario Minister of Labour, convened the Windsor Advisory Committee on Employment. Honorary chair? His Worship Jack Wheelton. Chair? City councillor Mrs. Cameron Montrose (a.k.a. Ms. Edith Georgina "Georgie" Leggett Montrose). Other notables? Valerie Kasurak, George Burt (ex-head of the Canuck-branch UAW), Armando F. Deluca (lawyer and everyone's fave board member for *all* causes, from sickbed to symphony), and myself.

Guardian Club research registered job gains for Black Windsorites, exceeding easily the paltry figures of the WCGR and the Helling Report. Even so, many employers remained racist. Moreover, "integration" was a one-way street, not an interchange. Once Black consumers began to patronize Euro businesses, Black professionals and shopkeepers—already too few—disappeared. Black youth could now enter predominantly Caucasoid schools but were classed as troublemaking interlopers, "impossible to teach," and assigned ass-backward counselling, steered into low-brow courses, and treated to passé ideas and derogatory texts. (Racism is always anachronism and archaism and, finally, fascism.) Those not expelled on the flimsiest pretexts were only slightly exceeded by those yearning to drop out as soon as possible.

While these findings were being reviewed, the Guardian Club suffered the sudden, grievous loss of our beloved Howard Watkins. After a do at my house, Howard complained teasingly about the "indigestion" he'd suffered because he'd downed a double serving of my double-hot chili. This jest was a longstanding *canard* between us double Howards! O, if only it had been the chili—and only indigestion! A heart attack slew him; all Windsor mourned. He'd been the epitome of activists, gifted with Black consciousness *and* a humanitarian conscience.

In 1969, the Club offered membership to any and all, and that income replenished us. Cliff Walls became the veep; Florence White, our indefatigable secretary. Through his efforts, Cliff obtained $1,500 from Chrysler, Hiram Walker, and the UAW, funds designated to retrain or "skills upgrade" the difficult to employ. He then strove to match job seekers to positions with recruited employers. As a result, nine individuals gained placement.

One scandal that we laid bare was employers conspiring with Canada Manpower (now Employment and Social Development Canada) to back whites-only job sites. How atrocious that public servants could cancel—in a star chamber—the job prospects of Black taxpayers! Thus, we demanded investigations to ensure that Manpower staffers were not colluding with payroll-controlling bigots.

We also treated with school board officials regarding the system's failures. We identified problem students and secured them help. Our plea? "Jettison racist teachers and stereotyped caricatures in textbooks!" Lookit! Our critiques helped spur John Tomlinson at Windsor's Hon. J. C. Patterson Collegiate to create the first Black Studies course in Canada.

Every silver lining has a cloud. Thus, the expansion of the Guardian Club membership was good for our numbers and cash-on-hand but deleterious for our morale and direction. The plethora of new members infected us with the same ideological splits that were havocking "liberation" movements everywhere. We'd pursued integration; now it divided us. We sported Afros, but that was a fashion statement, not a manifesto. To be free, proud, and prosperous: Was that not the goal—"by any means necessary"? Or was it to "stay Black and die"? Even if such meant remaining poor and powerless?

CHAPTER NINE:
HACKING THE "BLACKBOARD JUNGLE"

AS A BLACK CITIZEN OF WHITE WINDSOR, I HAD TO STRIVE FOR real equality, real opportunity. Little did I know then that the struggle is ceaseless, for white supremacism shift-shapes continuously: ex-slaveholders become men of state; Klansmen become cops. Yet, the 1960s—that tumultuous decade—was not only about anti-racism lobbying. Other "liberation" causes were my concern.

As a tenured, *Ebony*-mag-class academic in the ivory tower, I exemplified the merits of integration. But the quest for liberty—begun by Blacks and beatniks, then demanded by francophones, women, Indigenous persons, gays, and students—also loosed at its iconoclastic extremes a philistine libertinism that backed ecstatic, wild, anarchic individualism. So, the cry, "We want Freedom and Equality" degenerated into "If it feels good, do it," a slogan that can license mass murders as well as orgies: Manson misinterpreting The Beatles, The Weathermen misinterpreting Dylan's "Subterranean Homesick Blues."

Despite my extracurricular deeds as a "freedom fighter" and as a father (on May 11, 1963, Pat and I welcomed the birth of our second alliteratively named daughter, Linda Louise), I was still a research biologist. I released landmark papers on the myxobacteria; I taught UW's General Microbiology course. In that standing-room-only class, I exposed students to the latest findings regarding the biology of microscopic organisms—their evolution, genetics, biochemistry, and interactions with other living things. Father Alexander J. Grant exiled himself to Arizona to seek medical relief from a skin allergy that Windsor's humidity rendered intolerable; thus, Bob Doyle now chaired Biology.

When I'd begun to study myxobacteria, the top researchers were Soviet. The single US scientist with whom I corresponded was John Peterson at the University of Missouri. His travel "bug" prodded him to collect a prize cache of microscopic bugs. So, in jetting to his Columbia, MO, lab, I took my first flight! (I hummed Wagner's "Flight of the Valkyries" in joy at my God's-eye view of the backs of clouds!) At my hotel, the staff were extra-solicitous. Thanks to John, I was the first Black to stay at the once-segregated abode.

At the University of Windsor, due south of Motown Detroit, it was faculty parking that sparked a political crisis. Our pay was so poor, profs resented a parking fee the mandarins had slapped on us. Dramatized now was the need for a faculty union! It gelled in 1962. In 1964, I became its veep; in 1965, its prez. During my tenure, the Duff-Berdahl Report (1966) appeared. Among its recommendations, the Senate, to be faculty-dominated, was to approve curriculum integrity and academic appointments, plus conditions for tenure and even the appointment of the U of Windsor prez.

Given the Duff-Berdahl recs, as faculty association prez, I proposed a new university governance model to gird up academic freedom. Opponents? Those dreading the incipient irrelevancy of the Basilian Fathers at a secularized university. Thus, my reforms were sabotaged by colleagues who'd approved my liberal proposal in committee, then orphaned it after it sustained surgical, "clergical" attacks. Yet, after I quit as prez, the approved doc echoed my reform ideas. U. Windsor's prez, J. Francis Leddy, sympathetic to admin renewal, assigned, in 1967, the reform dossier to Dean of Law Walter Tarnopolsky. Later, Mark MacGuigan, the new dean (and a future Pierre Elliott Trudeau cabinet minister) completed the work.

Decisive also was student action. Once the faculty association's proposals were approved, radicalized students—sick of Cold War prohibitions and hypocritical, puritanical inhibitions—took seats on the Senate, the BOG (Board-o-Guv'nors), and at all levels of university governance. They espoused "participatory democracy," a spinoff concept of the Civil Rights Movement.

Amid the passion and effervescence of *bourgeois* whites seeking to emulate Red Guards and Black Panthers, or burn-the-bra *sans-culottes* and ban-the-bomb peaceniks, the university's student newspaper, the *Lance*, reprinted an excerpt from Jerry Farber's 1968 book, *The Student As Nigger*. The article damned—rightly—ham-fisted censorship of the student press. Yet, I thought Farber's title and profuse use of the N-word a gross insult to Blacks, so I was astounded that not once in the debate about Farber's squib was the hateful epithet denounced. (Offensive also was Québécois nationalist Pierre Vallières's view that French Canadians were oppressed "White Niggers," yet nobly anti-racist themselves. This *canard* obscured Negro and Indigenous slavery in Nouvelle-France, as well as the prevalence of Negrophobia and anti-Semitism during the era of Québécois Adrien Arcand's Nazified "Blue shirts.")

The irony? At the exact instant that North American Blacks had cast off "whitey"-assigned terms "Coloured" and "Negro" and were inching toward adopting "Afro-" and "African-" as self-descriptors, our purportedly progressive allies were adopting "nigger" as a revolutionary label for all the "outcast"—including the descendants of slaveholders! Then again, the unreflective avant-garde, in using arrogant scatology to allegorically assassinate the powers-that-be, only spout potty-mouthed drivel. Thus, when John Lennon sings, "Woman Is the Nigger of the World," whatever his affinity for feminism, his anthem also forwards the regressive idea that "nigger" is a fine word—if employed for positive reasons. I disagree—no matter all the "gangsta" rappers and even Harvard's "house nigger" Randall Kennedy speechifying the opposite! (I refer teasingly to the Af-Am doc's scholarly defence of *nigger* as voiced in his eponymous book published in 2002.) To many of us combating oppression, student militancy was just the privileged fighting, via tantrums, for yet more privilege. Even when Canuck palefaces marched for the Civil Rights Movement, as some admirably did, they headed to the US to stand against Dixie as opposed to confronting the domestic "Confederacy" of ye olde Confederation.

Once the *Lance* brouhaha subsided, a student sit-in started up to protest the termination of the probationary contract of an academic theologian. Thanks to the students asserting their "right" to insert themselves into faculty appointment and tenure decisions, the *clerc* was permitted to remain a taxpayer-funded scholar of Eden and Hades, Jesus and Judas—whatever, *if any*, his obsolete methods, insufficient thought, and evident grandstanding. I repeat: *if any*. My point? How can students vet doctoral-level scholarship? By what means can they assess post-dissertation—or thesis publication—achievement?

Despite my seat on the Academic Freedom and Tenure Committee (AFTC) of the Canadian Association of University Teachers (CAUT), I played no role in these two campus tempests, beyond that of bemused, lab-coat critic. Instead, my CAUT involvement brought me into the orbit of a certain Pierre Elliott Trudeau (PET), soon to be Canada's celebrity-politico answer to JFK.

How? Sensing that I possessed royal jelly and could purvey honeyed tones, CAUT exec secretary J. Percy Smith appointed me to the AFTC. In September 1966 I got to my first meeting but could not greet the fran-cophone nominee from the Université de Montréal as that bloke "had other plans" and skipped the opportunity. *Now, just who did that chap think he was?* Pierre Elliott Trudeau. (Another stand-out personality? Judge Bora Laskin, an ex-CAUT prez. In 1958–59, he had co-investigated, for the CAUT, Prof. Harry S. Crowe's *cause célèbre* political firing from United College [now the University of Winnipeg] for "disloyalty" [perhaps to Queen, country, Christianity, and capitalism]. A decade later, Prime Minister PET sat him—the first Jew to serve—on the Supreme Court and later lauded his appointment as Chief Justice in December 1973.)

In 1967, I was elected CAUT prez (one more presidential honour!). Thus, in May 1968 (that month of glorious near-revolution in France), I presided over the historic CAUT meeting that imposed the first censure on a Canadian university—Simon Fraser University (SFU). I was not unaffected by the censure decision. Shortly after, at a University of Windsor meeting of the Canadian Society of Microbiologists (CSM), John James Ramsay "Jack" Campbell, a University of British Columbia microbiologist (and later a CSM prez), vented his fury about the SFU *situ* by spitting scornful invective (some aerosolized) in my direction. But I stood my socially distanced ground and reminded him that it wasn't me, myself, and I who had censured SFU. No: I'd merely chaired a meeting where, in a vote nigh unanimous, the critical motion carried. Now, "Jean-Jacques" apologized. Naive had been his intransigence but intrepid my rationale and unhindered my truth.

CHAPTER TEN:
FOUNDING THE NATIONAL BLACK COALITION OF CANADA

ALTHOUGH MY 1960S ANTI-RACIST MILITANCY HAD CENTRED ON Windsor and Essex County, national notice had graced our successes—staging a Black history teach-in; proving the efficacy of affirmative action; shutting down whites-only schools, beaches, and golf courses; confronting police prejudice (an endless task); and constructing healthy alliances among faith groups and labour. Moreover, our prime protest agencies—the Guardian Club and SECAA—had generated priceless notoriety for such newsworthy acts as conducting marches and surveys. Too, having been a Michigan NAACP prez (plus prez of this and prez of that) and also a tenured scientist with ties to democratic socialists ("Reds" representing the pink of perfection), Unitarians, labour mavens, civil-liberties and human-rights "agitators," as well as prominent African-Americans, my name accrued some fame.

So, I was pleased to be summoned to address a national summit of Black orgs, sponsored by the Caribbean Conference Committee (CCC) at Montreal's Sir George Williams University (SGWU). This October 4–6, 1968, weekend meeting was historic: the CCC was hosting the first coast-to-coast gathering—in a century—of Black people in Canada.

It wasn't "Ten Days that Shook the World," but there was still "a whole lot of shakin' goin' on." True: in 1968, Montreal was a cosmopolitan, commercial, and cultural centre, a "kissin' cousin" to New York, Chicago, Paris, London. It didn't just trade furs, it vaunted furriers; there's a difference. It toasted singing poets like Leonard Cohen and Hollywood babes like Geneviève Bujold. It even had, in its radical FLQ, a terrorist underground modelled on the Front de Libération Nationale of revolutionary Algeria. In compare, Toronto had "the Ex"—the Canadian National Exhibition, a "national" fair that was embarrassingly municipal, except for imported Las Vegas has-beens crooning over cocktails. So, it was a revelation to be in that raucous, *joual*-gabbling, jazzy metropolis, where everyone said *je m'en fou* or *taber*—, or a gal could call herself *"une pepsi."* (Really, if it were not for Quebec, Canada would be one hellish, deathly boring suburbia of hockey arenas and donut shops.) Montreal's ambience? Smoking was prayer, drinking Zen, and to *"cherchez les femmes"* was to encounter beings—even in nuns' habits—as maximally titillating as miniskirted pseudo-nudists. The air was pure perfume: nicotine cut with alcohol. And everybody seemed to be on perennial strike—taxi drivers, teachers, even *les flics*. One couldn't help but think of Paris, the spring of the *soixante-huitard*. There's much to be said for a city boasting a rue Shelley and an avenue du Président-Kennedy, but also one where, in 1734, a Black woman, Marie-Josèphe Angélique, escaping slavery, may have sparked a fire that incinerated ye olde "Hochelaga."

My bespoke analysis to the colourfully pixilated faces before me (back then, *African* also denoted *Asian*) held that Blacks were doubly challenged. Externally, we confronted *ensemble* prejudice and powerlessness. Internally, we were so divided geographically, ethnically, ideologically, and socially, our anti-racism clout was minimal. Unlike every other ethnic or racial minority in Canada, we had no national body to represent our interests. That needed to change. "Thus," I said, "we must be as relentless in pointing out the deficiencies in our own community as we are in accusing whites of discrimination."

The conference split up into workshops to discuss employment, immigration, and education—the big *aiiiieeee*! (Does it sound like a screech? Well, our hardships do make a body holler!)

After our debates, clear was the solution to multifarious crises: the creation of a coast-to-coast organ. However, I cautioned that we'd require scrupulous care to formulate a structure appropriate to Canada. *Agreed!* Thus, this resolution passed unanimously: "Be it resolved that, in the interest of achieving the goals and objectives of the Black population of Canada in a coordinated way, a national organization be established to gather and periodically dispense for the effective use by regional groups, information, programs, and activities of particular interest to the Black people of Canada, and that the chairman of this organization be Dr. Howard McCurdy, with Dorothy Wills as secretary."

Dot Wills and I presided over an instantly materialized steering committee numbering delegates from three Associations for the Advancement of Coloured People (all provincial, nil affiliated with the Du Bois brand): Nova Scotia's Gus Wedderburn, bro to later BC MLA Rosemary Brown— first Black woman elected to a Canadian legislature; New Brunswick's Joe Drummond, an outspoken and impatient leader; and BC's Fred Collins, a laid-back dude, as mellow as BC Acapulco Gold.

To oversee our books, economist Clarence Bayne, a Trini-born, SGWU expert on oil pricing, sat as vice-chair. Other pillars? McGill grad student and leftist firebrand, Roosevelt "Rosie" Douglas, who had been, surreally, a Dief-the-Chief Tory (in the 1960s, Canada-landed West Indians were arrivistes from monarchical and High Tory duchies, applauding the gallows as much as they worshipped the crucifix; authoritarian were their schools, London-tailored their politicos); the Haligonian Burnley "Rocky" Jones (Canada's "Bluenose" Stokeley Carmichael); Peter Robinson of Toronto's Afro-American Progressive Association; OHRC director Dr. Dan Hill; and my uncle, George McCurdy of the SECAA. Yes, too much testosterone, not enough estrogen. But, hey, a start. (Incidentally, Secretary Wills was an excellent partner in carrying out our entrusted mandate. Our relationship became virtually synergistic, characterized by profound respect and, yes, affection via our daily communications by telephone and telegraph. It was primarily through our almost telepathic sympathies that the vision of the National Black Coalition took shape.)

So, we declared our existence to federal and provincial governments and called on each to appoint royal commissions to investigate racism. Only Ontario Premier John Robarts—always expertly retiring and pertinently charismatic (Frank Sinatra off stage; Sammy Davis Jr. on stage)— and his Attorney General Art Wishart replied, to say that such an investigation was underway. Thus did the two Cheshire cat politicos outfox us.

Nevertheless, the unprecedented decision to meld Canada's Blacks into a national strategic force generated much publicity, even a *Time* magazine article, wherein the existence of Canadian Negroes was suddenly revealed—as was our struggle for equality—likely surprising many Yanks.

Certainly, the prevalence of racial incidents and the emergence of oppositional radicals necessitated our movement. Indeed, just a week after the CCC gathering, a Congress of Black Writers occurred at McGill University, October 11–14, summoning not just Afro-diasporic intellectuals like C. L. R. James, but the Trinidad-born theorist of Black Power, namely, Stokely Carmichael, plus Af-Am psychiatrist Alvin Poussaint, plus Michael X (Michael de Freitas), later the catalyst of London's Notting Hill Carnival. Though writers tapped keys, "revolutionaries" rapped, clapped, and snapped up the headlines. But that made sense: the conference theme was "Towards the Second Emancipation: The Dynamics of Black Liberation." A Nat Turner theme, not an Ike and Tina Turner theme!

The congress sought to highlight Black history and its relevance to anti-segregation in the Americas and anti-apartheid in South Africa, plus opposition to Euro and Yank imperialism in the Caribbean, Africa, and Asia. Marcus, Malcolm, and Martin were dead, but Castro, Mao, Ho Chi Minh, and Nelson Mandela stood yet for the supremacy of BIPOC versus NATO, IMF, CIA, FBI, and all the other congeries of monocled *Monopoly*-figurine oppressors. Thrillingly, hundreds of eager, turned-on militants rendezvoused.

As the congress unfolded, with orator—not author—Rocky Jones inaugurating the sessions, the steering committee of the fledgling national Black org received our first summons to action. Gus Wedderburn demanded a "national" response to the refusal by a cemetery in St. Croix, NS, to permit the burial of a Black girl. A telegram was dispatched to "Red Tory" Premier G. I. Smith, who responded promptly and positively, yielding our first victory.

As the steering committee prez, I had to entice Af-Can groups in Montreal, Toronto, London, Ottawa, Halifax, Chatham, St. Catharines, and elsewhere to league with the newborn coast-to-coast advocacy agency. I spoke from church pulpits as well as school auditoria, but also from cushy living rooms. Back in sweet-home London town, I treated with Indigenous groups; the idea of a Black and "Red" front versus white supremacy took blueprint form.

On another occasion, I shuttled to Port Elgin, ON, to energize the Canadian United Auto Workers Union Leadership Summer School. Not only did I converse capaciously with Walter Reuther, the international union's prez, we even jogged together along the beach. Intrigued by the African-Canadian equal rights struggle, he pledged the UAW would both spearhead and backstop. But he was a master of the coalition only when all the "men" marshalled were Caucasian.

Soon, I touched down in Halifax, the Royal Navy's ex-North Atlantic capital: chilly, foggy, salty, and exuding memories of war—even of Sebastopol in Charge-of-the-Light-Brigade Crimea. But slavery was also honoured in *Nouvelle-Écosse*—not as an antebellum, Dixie phenomenon but as a set of inherited, racist praxis. So, "Scotians" dubbed their redoubt "Mississippi North." Many Blacks lived in segregated circumstances but preferred it, for ofays disparaged, exploited, and prosecuted them as if by divine right. The seaside Black community of Africville had just been dispersed to "fix" the desperate condition that Euro-Nova Scotian political and economic abuse and disregard had brought it: Atlantic Canada's largest garbage dump placed steps away from Africvillers' homes; water having to be boiled before consumed; no sewage service; no fire protection. Africville could have been Soweto: just fewer Black people and no Boer accent.

Hardly had I gotten my bearings in the Warden of the North (whoever controls Halifax controls the sea lanes between North America and Western Europe) when a panicky Gus Wedderburn thrust a letter into my hands. It warned of an impending crisis. Stokely Carmichael and his wife (the South African-born *chanteuse* Miriam Makeba) had just vacationed in Halifax with Rocky Jones, had "radicalized" local youth, and had posted two Black Panther cadres to Nova Scotia—allegedly to buy a farm "to train guerillas" in target-practice! Hearsay! Fear-mongering! Rubbish! Despite being a barrister, Gus was impressionable. Could Halifax explode like Detroit? (It did blow up, literally, in 1917, due to a munitions accident in the harbour.) There had been riots, infamously by soldiers and sailors in May 1945. Still, class seemed a more combustible element than "race." The Panther scare was productive, however: it forced Premier Smith to agree to enforce the province's Human Rights Act and set up a provincial human rights commission.

So, I said I'd keynote a human rights conference. When I landed in Halifax, Gus and Buddy Daye, an inspiring ex-boxer, ushered me to a closed-door session whose tension made the air feel humid, acrid, and sticky—like kerosene awaiting a coal-fire spark. Why such bother? Buddy and Gus recited names, mine included: a purported Black Panther "hit list"! Heck, why would the Panthers care about me or any other Black Canuck when their sworn foes were other Af-Ams—culture radicals—*plus* peckerwood cops gunning down wantonly every Panther that they couldn't jail? (J. Edgar Hoover's Federal Bureau of Investigation had identified the Panthers as the prime threat to US internal security and was colluding with racist police nationally via COINTELPRO, the Counterintelligence Program, to infiltrate and divide "radical" Black organizations, arrest and jail members on false charges, and, yes, simply gun-down any Black sporting a black leather jacket. This program accelerated once Richard Nixon infiltrated the White House in 1969. Consequently, many Panthers were skedaddling to France or Algeria. One Panther—Ronald Hill—did hide out in Nova Scotia. Using the *nom de guerre* Francis Beaufils, he rendered services to the local Black community and worked as a marine draftsman before his true identity was ascertained and he got frogmarched back to the US.) Neither unsubstantiated hooey nor alarmist hysteria were a-gonna bamboozle *moi*.

Yet, as a freshly minted "national leader" (a label that Gus slapped on me ASAP so I wouldn't be disparaged as an outsider—a "CFA" or "come from away"), I realized I had to achieve two ends: calm the impetuous, the fearful, the foolish; and buttress legitimate Afro-Nova Scotian grievances.

Later that night, I conferred with Rocky Jones, the lanky leader of Haligonian Black youth. Branded a radical and right proud of the label, Rocky was a gregarious, fun-loving, ultra-charming personality, the kind of chap who could dance, jive-talk, hook a salmon, down a buck, shoot snooker, sink baskets, and dominate charismatically either lecture hall or tavern, street corner or caucus meeting. His "up-against-the-wall-*mudderfokker*" rhetoric belied his sharp and constructive mind. (Rocky was under intense Mountie surveillance, and he suffered incidents of arson and burglary that were so mysterious as to be plausibly credited to flatfoot "dirty tricks.")

We congressed in a hotel room presided over by Roosevelt "Rosie" Douglas, the Malcolm X-ist *Montréalais*, more akin to Castro's percussive Cuba than to Gregorian-chant Dominica. (However, his surname echoed my middle name, so I regarded Rosie with wary bonhomie.) Memorably vivid to me still, Rosie laid on his bed in the unlit room while Rocky stood, a statuesque silhouette in the moonlit window. The scene? Pure neo-realism but as pacific as a household moment in Pontecorvo's *Battle of Algiers*.

Tobacco smoke strafed our nostrils. Scotch—in New Scotland—was an icebreaker. Or it was Keith's India Pale Ale? (That brew? Locals poetically pronounced it "Keats.") Outside, the streets smelled of dark chocolate due to an adjacent factory. (Halifax ladies unfurl Chanel, with top notes of chocolate....)

The "brothers" were upset. They'd staged a brouhaha before the "cop shop" to solicit arrest so as "to sharpen the contradictions" and catalyze community reaction. But their storm-the-Bastille strategy died a farce. Rosie pulled a twenty-five-dollar fine. He'd intended to become a jailhouse martyr, but the police chief told him to just pay the fine. Halifax's head *gendarme* imitated B-movie actor Chuck Connors more than he did the Birmingham, Alabama, "heavy," "Bull" Connors. (Soon, Rosie rose to international notoriety as the leader of the 1969 protests at SGWU, snagged an eighteen-month prison sentence for arson [a falsehood], inked a book from his prison cell, authored a Trotskyist [Pathfinders Press] pamphlet declaring the Canadian immigration system "racist" [which it is], then got deported from Canada as a national security "threat" in 1976. Yet, he became a short-lived Prime Minister of Dominica in 2000, succumbing to a heart attack after only eight months in office. In contrast, Rocky made a sustained contribution to the advancement of African-Canadians. He pioneered strategies to combat systemic discrimination and was the creative force behind the formation of the Black United Front of Nova Scotia. In fact, Rocky constructed institutions: the NS Human Rights Commission, the Transition Year Program at Dalhousie University, and then the Indigenous Black and Mi'kmaq Law Program also at Dal. Peruse his autobio, *Burnley "Rocky" Jones: Revolutionary*.)

Come dawn, my photogenic visage was sheer newsprint but also shellacked across screens; an earthy lilt, my voice slid from TVs and radios. As I was chauffeured about, plainclothes Mounties—their red-serge, equestrian outfits transformed into nondescript, button-bursting haberdashery—held me in their sights.

Even so, that night I orated before a throng, hundreds strong, whose expectations seemed impossible to satisfy. I called up Mahatma Gandhi; I recalled the Frederick Douglass of my middle name, quoting his perception that crisis breeds opportunity. I disavowed both paleface and "reverse" racism, for prejudice is always sheer ignorance. Aye, I called for Black Power! I defined it as economic and political power that could only be achieved by pride in ourselves and unity as a people.

My speech was foot-stompingly applauded, drawing laudatory headlines in the Halifax papers and national network news. In contrast, the *Windsor Star* featured a large photo of me, snapped not during my suit-and-tie speech but when I was dressed casually later, derisively entitling it, "McCurdy Leading Light for Blacks," somehow equating slacks and pullovers to hippy haberdashery. (Their choice was not accidental: they could have pictured me in my ultra-white lab coat!) No matter—attained was the conference goal. Premier Smith announced that a Nova Scotia Human Rights Commission—"with teeth"—would be constituted.

But never send a Red Tory to do a real Red's job! Disappointingly, Smith announced that Marvin Schiff, the *Globe and Mail* reporter who'd covered the Guardian Club in Windsor, would be its director.

Pinstripes can be battle fatigues!

Yet, the long-oppressed Black Nova Scotians wanted, demanded, a Black director! Schiff could not do. So, after much dissension, none of it Schiff's fault, he vacated the post, which, under Liberal Premier Gerry Regan, got assigned to my uncle, George McCurdy. I am pointedly not guilty of reverse nepotism when I assert that George's leadership made the NSHRC the most effective in Canada, given the daunting troubles that he faced in apart-heid-structured Nouvelle Scotland.

Meanwhile, a simmer-ing controversy at SGWU was about to boil over. Six Afro-Caribbean students accused biology prof Perry Anderson of racist grading. They alleged that he system-atically gave poorer marks to Blacks compared to *les blancs* and referred to Black students by their surnames—a curious complaint, for it was a common practice in Canuck universities; yet, there was testi-mony that Anderson referred to white students by their Christian names, a fact that revealed, for some, a policy of favouritism. In spring 1968, the sextet of complaints prompted the Biology department chair to investi-gate. But his report—six months later—exonerated Anderson. Br'er profs were told of Anderson's "innocence" but not the veracity of student com-plaints. Worse: the report disappeared somewhere between a Gestetner and a dumpster. Students felt patronized, insulted, and played for suck-ers. Amid the on-campus tensions, outsiders chameleoned into slick insiders. Enter Rosie Douglas. Thanks to his bullhorn's racket, sit-ins resonated. But Vice-Principal J. W. O'Brien was also an instigator. Allegedly, he insinuated that Black students were "threatening violence." When a picketer buttonholed him about this reckless assertion, O'Brien said he felt "kidnapped." Thus, three students got charged with that criminal offense, although never was O'Brien prevented from accessing his liquor cabinet.

A new committee convened to review the original complaints. Upset by what they viewed as a stalling tactic, Black students tasked the Black nominees, namely Profs. Clarence Bayne and Chet Davis, to resign. SGWU then replaced ebony faces with ivory mugs and scheduled a hearing for January 26, 1969.

At that inquest, Black students once again ID'd racism and then walked out—to protest the snowman composition of a committee (from which they themselves had urged Black profs to quit). Still, that the SGWU guv'nors thought it okay to replace African-derived visages with European ones signified their blithe paternalism. The student newspaper the *Georgian*, in its January 28, 1969, edition, denounced the admin. Militancy escalated to mutiny.

Blacks held rallies while their leftist, Caucasian student allies noisily disrupted the next admin meeting on January 29. Deploring SGWU's smug, retrograde leadership, they all thronged to occupy the university's computer centre, the ninth floor of the Henry Hall edifice. Four hundred students. Two leaders: Rosie Douglas and Anne Cools, transplanted Dominica and Jamaica. (Or Rosie Grier backed with Annie Oakley?)

From Ottawa ("Bytown") I called O'Brien and obtained copies of the disputed biology exams. In my review, I judged Anderson's marking unskewed. (I was reminded of the former Pat Neely's difficulties at MSU. She'd charged racism; I saw, instead, failure-to-buckle-down-and-study-ism. I tended to trust liberal-education institutions to be paragons of professionalism and proponents of meritocracy. But maybe she *was* right?) Inexplicable, though, was the discrepancy in marks, for the same labs, twixt Negro and Caucasian students. Perhaps the CAUT could mediate the dispute?

I phoned Rosie at the ninth floor of Hank Hall's hall. He assured me a resolution was imminent. True: a deal was struck, but SGWU profs "stoopidly" canned it. In response, the occupation annexed additional floors. Then, somehow, the computer centre sustained an inferno that caused over $2 million in damage and led to the arrest of ninety-seven occupants. Fewer than half were Black, mostly Caribbean students.

Dorothy Wills observed the climax firsthand and wrote the following account:

> *The struggle is still a difficult one in Montreal, one that will not easily be resolved or forgotten. Particularly so for people like myself who stood outside Sir George Williams University in silent vigil—watching, waiting, hoping, praying—but finally saw the*

inevitable come to pass. The riot squad arrived in seeming droves. They all appeared six feet tall and over, with their sticks about half their own size. It's true that fear of the unknown is the worst fear, and as we stood outside, not knowing what was happening to the brothers and sisters inside the building, tears flowed. And along with them came the insults of white folks: "Let the niggers burn! You Blacks should be sent back to wherever you came from!"

The conference steering committee launched a defence fund for the accused, with the largest donors being Dot Wills, the Guardian Club, *et moi*. Otherwise, tepid was the response from an Afro-Canuck populace loathe to support persons they perceived to be spoiled migrants and the irrationally uppity.

In Montreal, the SGWU incident spawned absurd police abuses. Weddings and social events were disrupted; arrests occurred on light pretext. Random raids were executed on homes (including that of community pillar Roy States) in fruitless attempts to intercept such dangerous but long-dead "subversives" as Marcus Garvey and Nat Turner. (Some twenty months later, during the October [FLQ] Crisis, the same high-school-dropout cops would confuse books on Cubism with tomes on Communism.)

Months passed before the SGWU students were tried. Meanwhile, the steering committee was preparing for the incipient inaugural convention of our new national body.

Our first plight was financial. My preference? Black Canucks must fund our new organization. But until African-Canadians could agree to be called "Black," self-funding was not an option. To ensure broad representation of delegates from across the world's second-largest country (5.5 time zones), we required outside funding to subsidize travel. I therefore applied for and obtained $3,000 from the Citizenship Branch of the Secretary of State. Contrary to later, conspiratorial accusations, the government imposed no conditions—apart from income-outcome accounting.

The establishing convention for what I had already begun calling the "National Black Coalition" was finally scheduled for the weekend of October 17–19, 1969, only a year since our Montreal inception. At the Lord Simcoe Hotel in Toronto, opening night saw sixty delegates entertained at a hospitality bash floated by the Toronto Black Business and Professional Association (BBPA). Gathered therein was a true cross-section of African-Canadians—in business dress, dashikis, gowns, Afros, brogues, and pumps. All of us perfumed and poised, cologned and chic. Our varied accents—African, Af-Am, British, Haitian, Parisian,

Québécois, "Scotian," Carib—comprised a jazzy medley. Our skin tones? A breathtaking panoply of gold, beige, black, chestnut, chocolate, cinnamon, cocoa, copper, ebony, indigo, ivory, mahogany, molasses, sandalwood, tan, teak: a celestial symphony of melanin. We were all, once, the offspring of plantations—of banana, coffee, sugar cane, cotton, tea. Now, we were literate sophisticates, charged with a mission of unified uplift. We were swishy in garb, spirited in wit, and sassy in *any* tongue.

Saturday's agenda: a roll call of human rights militants dissecting the perils plaguing our regionalized communities. Speakers: George McCurdy, Dr. Dan Hill, Bromley Armstrong, ex-boxer Buddy Daye, ex-trucker Rocky Jones, Jules Oliver, ex–sleeping car porter Stanley Grizzle of the BBPA, and Jose Garcia, secretary of the Central Committee of the Black Liberation Front. Most were ex-lumpenproletarians cum intellectuals and activists. We were striving to fulfill Marcus Garvey's command, "Up, you mighty race, accomplish what you will!" We were the "Talented Tenth" that Du Bois prophesized and novelist Austin Chesterfield Clarke alternately satirized and sanctified.

Yet, I felt unease. Missing were our automatically respected orators: schoolmarms and church ladies, preachers and priests. To be progressive, we thought, was to be secular, but Blacks are Anglicans, Baptists, Catholics, Methodists, Muslims, Pentecostals, Rastafarians, and *their* leadership is salt-o-the-earth: the barbershop pulpiteers, the beauty salon bluestockings, and even "gangstas" and "playas." How much sway could we exercise had we not the ear of church hall and blind pig, gym and mosque? That this middle layer of leadership was absent meant that there was no grassroots mediation between "Young Turks" (or "wild radicals") and responsible elders (or "old fogeys"). We had "elect" managers at the helm and anarchistic "fools" as our base, but we were bereft of the stolid, bourgeois middle.

Thus, in the workshop on Black Youth in Canada, chaired by Olivia Grange-Walker, the nine-month-past SGWU fracas was bruited. But its hashing out could not placate or mollify the disproportionate number of Montreal youth reps and their allies, who acted as an obnoxious, braying rump.

The first impediment? What were the precise organizations that the forty youth delegates represented? How many legitimate votes could their bloc cast? Quarrels answered these queries.

Also nettlesome was the registration fee. Although their bus seats, train tickets, and hotel rooms had been paid for, the hotheads argued that their *Négritude* justified "*gratuit*" entree. That point applauded, they soon insisted that the government dole that had paid their way also impugned our legitimacy! (A subsidy was a bribe!) Had they thought their infantile argument meritorious, they should have checked out of their hotel rooms, returned their tickets, and hiked back to Montreal. Did they? Guess! (Ain't immorality and illogicality always Siamese twins?)

Next, the hooligans argued obstreperously that the SGWU imbroglio take precedence over all others, including the girding up of the new national organization. They were like builders squabbling over a flooded basement instead of getting on with placing a tarp atop the premises under construction!

Then, I stood accused of trying to sideline the SGWU crimes-and-punishments, when, having been scheduled for the Youth Issues workshop, it could've also been raised in the plenary. When I explained this fact, and called for eyes-on-clock-hands, the SGWU-plagued rads—led by Rosie D.—torpedoed the plenary to posit a resolution that would've scuttled the convention agenda.

Basic punks now commandeered the mic, stirring furious reaction from many who wished to speak, including my young cousin, Barry McCurdy. Anger shook him as he yelled that people where he came from had experienced far more discrimination than the troublemakers ever had and that they had no right to obstruct a meeting intended to create a national organization for all.

In a helter-skelter scrum, I called those who had precipitated the chaos "jet-set brats, alien to Canada." In contrast, those living here—who would always do so—sought a body that would speak to the concerns of all Black people and not fixate on one case of apprehended racism, however blatant and disgusting.

Yep, my statement was inflammatory: The rabid labelled me as anti–West Indian; yet, those who'd elected me chair and who opposed the harum-scarum destructiveness of the rabble were also West Indian! Worse, it was West Indian *Montréalais* who lost most due to the employ of anarchic tactics—all those placarded canards; all those monologues of doggerel; all those Garveyite gangsters, high on piss and vinegar.

Some dissidents swore that only they had legitimate insight into racism: Canuck Blacks had been passive victims until take-no-guff West Indians browbeat them into "growing some guts." Really?

With the conference unravelling, I went to Dot's hotel room to plot solutions. I saw her roiled in a dispute with delegate Richard Leslie Lord—so foul, so appalling—who lunged at *her*, that slender, graceful being. My gallantry? Galvanized! (Was not Superman my boyhood idol?) "Tricky Dicky" got decked: the Nietzsche-plagiarizing "Lawd" was no *Übermensch*. (Dickie Lord—or Lord Dick—in a 1968 speech submitted that politics is not about principle, it's about "fighting"! His Nietzsche-derived "vision" weds Darwin and Ayn Rand. Recall the Italian Fascist slogan: *Believe, Obey, Fight!* See bscportal.wordpress.com/2014/03/30/89/.) In the scuffle, I sustained a four-inch-long hand gash. I was rushed to hospital, and the cut got stitched in the wee hours. Gossip said I'd been "stabbed in the heart." When I returned to the conference, some attributed my survival to a voodoo spell. (If I'd possessed *vaudou*, I'd've used it to fix that insufferable cad, Dicky Lord: yellow belly, gangrene heart.)

From the hospital, I scheduled a caucus of supporting organizations for a time when the youth would be too busy shaking off "Sat-nite booze" to muscle the mic. Thus, delegates from twenty-seven orgs unanimously agreed to a resolution to found the National Black Coalition and to establish a constitution committee and name an executive. I was elected chair; Dot, secretary. Vice-chairs: Gus Wedderburn, Nova Scotia; Clarence Baynes, Quebec; Joe Drummond, New Brunswick; Edwin Clarke, Ontario; Roy Williams, British Columbia; and Lloyd Perry, QC, Ontario. Yep: still too many dudes and one dame. But, again, a start.

Half-inebriated but wholly indignant, the drowsy, belated students awoke to my *fait accompli*. Peeved, the dissidents vaunted a non-confidence motion; it fizzled, buckled like a flaming Zeppelin! (Their own dumb fault! Had they paid their membership fees the day before, they could have voted and outvoted *moi*. But having been irresponsible, they were now ineligible.)

Naturally, the *Black Liberation News* and *Uhuru*—Montreal student rags— warbled otherworldly, malicious versions of our proceedings. They harped on and on about our federal subsidy, alleging that the Coalition was a lapdog. They accused us of muzzling dissent. Yet, the steering committee had publicized nationally the SWGU cause. The tyro journalists thought to publish *Pravda* but just flogged cheapo versions of *Allô Police*, demagogic, pettifogging scatology.

Most unprincipled were their attacks on Dot Wills. Once their enabler, she'd dipped into her own purse to help ingrates swagger free of their cells. The steering committee had also set up a defence fund for the SGWU-alleged arsonists. The Guardian Club, on my say-so, had also contributed dollars. But never were these palliative disbursements acknowledged or graced with a *merci beaucoup*!

Symptomatic of their arrogance was the claim that the SGWU affair was "the most…pressing issue for blacks in Canada," though "ignored" by the "moderate puppets" of the newborn National Black Coalition of Canada (NBCC). Due to this restrictive analysis—a kind of self-inflicted castration—they showed no interest in the plights of other Black Canadians.

Notably, the mouthpiece monologues descended from the loins of Carib plutocrats. See: Cheddi "Joey" Jagan Jr., son of Guyana's prime minister (and later a preening capitalist); Anne Cools, daughter of a Bajan pharmacist; and Rosie D., whose daddy was a Tory honcho of Dominica.

The trials of the alleged "arsonists"? Interminable! Finally, ringleader Rosie pulled two years in prison; Anne Cools got four months. After running unsuccessfully for a federal seat in Rosedale (a constituency of mostly poor voters plus several of Canada's toniest manors), "Queen Anne" got kicked to the Senate by Pierre Elliott Trudeau. (This credible Tory at heart, sitting in the Senate as an Independent, voices ideas incompatible with her "rebel" youth but perhaps compatible with her Establishment salary?) Well-to-do, if a leftist ne'er-do-well, Rosie trotted the globe before returning to his native Dominica where, righteously, he markedly improved the lot of the workers on his father's farm. He bagged Dominica's premiership, then returned laurelled to Canada—after having been a Canuck convict—as a Commonwealth head of state. He passed away—way too young—in 2000.

A SGWU committee cleared Perry Anderson of all charges of racism. Truly, the only good outcome of "the affair" was the appointment of the first ombudsman at any Canadian university.

Much revisionist mythology has been spewed concerning the NBCC. First, the NBCC was *not* the bastard offspring of the SGWU arson or prosecutions. True: students who'd backed Cools, Douglas, and Lord had tried to strangle it at birth. Nor was it a Frankenstein creature crafted by mysterious conspirators seeking to orchestrate Black protests.

The first significant action of the new coalition was a presentation to the biennial meeting of the Canadian Council of Churches (CCC) in Montreal in December of 1969. I circulated a draft paper: *The Canadian Black Manifesto*. It was inspired by a similarly entitled document advanced by James Forman in the US in April 1969, which demanded $500 million USD from American churches and synagogues (as reparations for their alleged participation in slavery and racism), and which completely failed. Ours was a modest, moderate (and successful) call to the Canadian churches for moral and financial support for the NBCC program. Yes, Joe Drummond thought my wording too mild, but it was too militant for Lloyd Perry. Both strove to find synonyms—some more bitter, some sweeter—for my wording but produced either a tirade or a bromide. Thus, in the end the *Manifesto* echoed my diction. Excerpts follow. (Reader, please do forgive my "Parliament of man"-style, Tennysonian, sexist diction. It dates from an archaic moment in my—*I think*—progressive momentum.)

The quest of Black people and of other non-whites for full recognition of their human- ity and their right to full political, social, and economic participation is no longer a plea but a demand. It is a demand predicated on new terms of reference and a new definition of the relation of non-whites to the society in which whites dominate. It requires noth- ing short of a complete revolution and a redefinition of the goals of society to ensure that no group will occupy a pre-eminent position and that none will be oppressed or exploited.

If Black people are to be full participants in the new democratic ordering of soci- ety, the psychological and social wounds within the Black community must be healed, it must reaffirm its roots, reconstruct or build anew viable institutions, and give voice to its unique aspirations.

The National Black Coalition has as its objective the complete elimination of all forms of discrimination and oppression and the attainment by Black people of full participation in all aspects of Canadian life before the end of this generation. Its strategy will be based on building strength and establishing initiatives within the Black commu- nity as well as seeking action outside of it. . . .

Clearly it is not solely or even primarily the responsibility of Black people to ame- liorate the effects of racism. It is white society—whether as a result of unconscious or gentlemanly bigotry or institutionalized racism—which must assume the major burden. And it is the Church above all other institutions which must assume leadership. If white society has failed to see in every man the image of God and function according to that premise, then it is due in large measure to the failure of the Church to adequately fulfill its mandate.

To speak so, however, is to talk of the past. We are here to address the future. We are here to extend an invitation to the churches to participate in concrete action of the kind that will give substance to the noble phrases and pronouncements which all too often are the only response to racial injustice by the Church.

The next paragraph is a request for outright grants of $10,000 a year for three years and additional matching funds to those raised in the Black community up to an additional $10,000 a year for three years. The *Manifesto* then continues:

What the National Black Coalition has asked has not been presented as a non- negotiable demand buttressed by threats, for we are sure you share with us that what is demanded is adherence to the very religious principles that this body was established to foster and that it is those principles that are non-negotiable.

The only threat is the threat that should we fail, social instability will increase to cataclysmic proportions as frustrated hope forces increasing recourse to violent vehicles for change.

Thus we offer you the opportunity to join with us in helping to redress the wrongs of the past and in building a strong new society based on a new measure of Man. The time is NOW. Black people are on the march and will no longer be denied full share in all that Canada or the world has to offer. A social system which fails to meet these demands cannot justly continue to exist.

When our delegation arrived at the first CCC plenary session, we learned that the *Manifesto* had not been circulated. So I read it to the assembly—to an amen chorus. Thereafter, I repaired to Windsor and was not present on the morrow when the CCC delegates then became embroiled in the question of a proposed $200,000 action fund directed to various minority groups to support a wide spectrum of social action as also proposed in the *Manifesto* in addition to receiving draw-downs for the NBCC. (I must take responsibility for this brouhaha. As I hinted in chapter 8, when Black activist bodies cease to focus on immediate tasks for the Black community, or when they bifurcate over ideological approaches, directed action dissolves in distraction and/or confused aims.)

The pivotal interrogative? Who'd mint the funds? How'd they be administered? All bogged down in the quicksand of questions of solvency and prudence. Drummond declared his frustration with the stalled process and threatened to leave. Rev. Dr. Floyd Honey, the CCC's general secretary, broke the impasse as dramatically as God parted the Red Sea. He moved that the CCC accept the NBCC's dollar request.

The CCC voted for the annual allotments proposed in the *Manifesto* of $10,000 per annum for three years as well as the matching funds for money raised by the Coalition itself. It also endorsed the action plan. Our presentation and the CCC's unprecedented response received media fanfare, giving the NBCC a practical as well as a public relations success—and a robust national profile.

Regrettably, one of the NBCC's major failures would be its inability to ever raise sufficient funds to take advantage of the CCC's matching provision. Instead, too many organizations not only saw the money we had received as an excuse not to fundraise themselves, but sought Coalition money to fund their own activities, as if the NBCC were an endowed charity.

During the winter of 1969–70, the NBCC steering committee had to draft a constitution; raise funds (which saw us beg affiliates—fruitlessly, *naturellement*—to meet their financial obligations); and recruit new members. In both deeds and desires, we were stymied.

Our constitution became a tar baby. I'd imagined the NBCC as consisting of a coalition of independent organizations. My vision was cautious, so as to respect regional differences. For instance, Halifax was—to apply a Maoism—"conservative in form" (the church had all the power and prestige) but "radical in essence" (Rocky's Panther-instructed youth were forcing change). In contrast, Vancouver was disorganized and unorganized because racism was thought to be magically neutralized by totem poles and Emily Carr's paintings, the nurturing power of dim sum, and the pharmaceutical pleasures of saki, ale, and weed. Thus, friction sparked twixt Lloyd Perry and me. His draft constitution was a vague document. I penned a critique, and he took my comments as "fightin' words." He swore that "arrogant impertinence" constituted my style. He informed Dot Wills that he should chair the NBCC and suggested—she felt "inappropriately"—that he could be a more compatible "colleague." (A character perhaps malleable to fraud, he submitted reimbursement claims—*allegedly*—for meetings incidental to his travel.)

Then, at a do in my home, Lloyd questioned my capacity to lead while advancing himself as a worthy and mature alternative. No. Rather, he was a worthy and mature candidate for darkening my doorway on his way out. In a huff, the blowhard puffed into the night. (Later, Perry served as the official Guardian of Ontario, 1975-85.)

Meanwhile, few NBCC affiliates had either ratified their memberships or paid their dues, much less fundraised to earn matching funds from the CCC. They were as zombiefied as are the mindless stumblebums in George Romero's *Night of the Living Dead*.

In December 1969, NBCC execs participated in a human rights conference in Halifax. In the year since the autumn of 1968, Scotians had spawned the Black United Front (BUF), as originally proposed by Rocky Jones, and had won the sum of $400,000 in federal moneys. Our efforts then and during return visits, although always cordially received, never succeeded in bringing the BUF into the NBCC. Yes, the NSACCP joined, but Gus Wedderburn's club had no ground-game. 'Twas all acronym and no agency. (Unknown to us at the time, however, was the truth that BUF had been so luxuriously endowed—and rendered relatively conservative in leadership—as a result of ministerial directives, prosecuted via funding from P. E. Trudeau's Prime Minister's Office.)

Tasked to launch our fundraising was Toronto's Ed Clarke, our "man in Ontario." Yet, when I asked to meet "Big Smoke" (Toronto) reps, so few delegates materialized, I realized that Ed truly was too much a "Clarke" (Old English for "cleric") to accomplish anything worldly. Thus, I tapped Stan Grizzle, a can-do "Hogtown" (Toronto) activist, to replace the "clerk."

BC was also discouraging. Despite Dorothy's efforts to maintain communications, BC felt ignored. If we had not had prior consultation with the Left Coast, the "Columbians" took special umbrage at any national media coverage received by myself and Dot. 'Twas a politics of sulking—as tear-sodden as were the provincial rainforests wet. To try to placate kindergarten-level concerns, Dorothy jetted to Vancouver to defend the NBCC. Her speech was huzza'd, but no amount of applause or Black Power salutes could dislodge lard-asses from their easy chairs or pacify schizoid egoists!

Yet, Dot and I persevered. By spring 1970, the draft constitution was approved, and we scheduled the constitutional convention for September 17–19 at Montreal's Windsor Hotel (sumptuously modelled on the Waldorf-Astoria). By then, I'd decided to quit as chair. A California sabbatical was nigh: time to forget about wrangling illogical busybodies and get back to angling my peepers at microbiological bodies.

Moreover, I had home problems: my wife's, I thought, spendthrift, uncaring ways.

Then, as far as the NBCC went, I was weary of frank opportunism from the left and rank careerism from the right. The middle? A constant fault line, a wonky fissure, either drooling lava or pooling quicksand.

Yet, to my delighted shock, the convention was a success. I oversaw the constitutional discussion on Saturday the 18th. The next day saw a symposium on educational initiatives such as the DaCosta-Hall Program of the Quebec Board of Black Educators and the Transition Year Program at Halifax's Dalhousie University headed by the redoubtable, indomitable, and definitely capable Rocky Jones.

Consideration of the constitution was a long but constructive process. However, it was necessary to appoint a special drafting committee to produce a statement of purpose, which was ratified on Sunday when I had already left for home and then to take up my sabbatical at the University of California, Berkeley. I would no longer be significantly involved in the NBCC or its subsequent troubles until the attempt to revitalize the consistently moribund body in the late 1970s. One last hallucinatory flirtation with a body utterly skeletal and its flesh so pox-riddled it was see-through sheer!

CHAPTER ELEVEN:
HUSBAND, BACHELOR, HUSBAND

ALTHOUGH MY SOCIALIST AND CIVIL RIGHTS CAUSES WINGED ME throughout Essex County and then all about Canada to Halifax, Ottawa, Montreal, and elsewhere, making my 1960s (the decade of my thirties) a constant round of tarmac and asphalt, I was still a biology prof. Microphones trained on protests did not replace microscopes trained on bacteria. Thus, research carried me to California as 1969 yielded to 1970. Also a doting papa (having lost my first-born son, Frederick Douglas, ten years before) and a homeowner wanting to feel perfectly at home, I was also—alas—a husband so discordant as to become a divorcé.

Our marriage began well enough. Notably, Pat and I hosted frequent parties for the Guardian Club or Unitarians or collegial profs. The frenzied, happy-face socializing helped to tamp down any inklings of discontent. Thus, we McCurdys became famed for our sizzling and "besozzling" New Year's Eves. The first one, in 1964, was the result of my socialist comrade Ron Trider and I learning that our friends had planned zilch. We summoned them to a BYOB jag at my digs. The sizzle? His chowder and my chili. The "sozzle"? New England-style Fisherman's Punch (a potent concoction of white wine, brandy, and rum).

Our shindigs shook up everyone as much as a proper Bond cocktail gets shaken. Why? My Sensurround-style speakers bounced shock waves of soul and jazz round the rec room. No foot could loaf; all limbs boogied. The platter'd music sizzled, Motown spicing the airwaves, while swizzle sticks pepped up the sozzle. Dancing was unbalancing: once-vertical strangers soon converted to horizontal missionaries (later on, I'll muse, but definitely in their own digs).

Anyway, whatever else the 1960s was, it was when Motown shunted aside Las Vegas and Nashville. At last, melanin-deprived folks were bopping to the authentic Black musical styles that Euro-American entertainers had "borrowed" and bleached, turning grit and sweat into bluegrass and fog. Now, Black music's dominant influence on popular and even classical music would soon become obvious as one musical innovation after another originated among Black musicians to be shared with (rather than stolen by) others: ragtime, blues, gospel, doo-wop, soul, rock 'n' roll, funk, reggae, calypso, jazz, disco, rap, and so on. (According to musicologist Timothy Kimbrough, European musical notation cannot accommodate Black music's emphasis on rhythm and percussion. He's invented his own notation system to suit African-derived musical performance.) Even better, Black entertainers were regal: Duke this and Count that, Empress this and Queen that, the Supremes, the Temptations, Nat "King" Cole, and soon Prince and the King of Pop (Michael J.) and the Godfather of Soul (J.B.).

We also soirée'd at the Bert Weeks household and with couples such as the Daniluks (thinkers) and the Beneteaus (boaters). We'd muse on Vietnam, the Kennedys, Johnson, Pearson, and later P. E. Trudeau. We'd also play and discuss recordings of speeches of Martin Luther King, Malcolm X, and Stokely Carmichael. Talk of CIA, FBI, and other McCarthyite US government conspiracies abounded. I mean, true conspiracies: the assassination of Patrice Lumumba; the FBI attempts to undermine King; Muhammad Ali's persecution for refusing to go and kill Vietnamese who, as he famously quipped, never called him a "nigger."

And we walked the talk! We led marches contra the Vietnam War, initiated the local grape boycott to support Cesar Chavez and US Latino farm workers (still treated like slaves), and inaugurated the local branch of the Canadian Civil Liberties Association. We were in folks' faces; we planted bugs in their ears. We denounced quietude! We were enraged, outrageous *engagés*!

At first, ours was the sole "soul" household on the street. But others glommed onto the address, thus creating a "Dr. Huxtable"—not a *Mr. Rogers*—neighbourhood. The next Black newcomers? The Plumb family, all peaches and cream, our next-door compatriots. Soon, two other Black families settled nearby: Eleanor and Harold Green (who were also my parents' friends), and Henry White, a member of the Guardian Club, and his wife. I recalled my boyhood pleasure in being party to distinctive Coloured families living among nondescript Caucasians.

By the time we'd moved into our new abode, Leslie was walking and talking. In fact, her first steps came at eight months; by age two, she was learning to "enunciate"—a word she delighted to repeat. Already the attention-loving extrovert, Leslie would stand near the road shouting "hello" to passersby. Even as a baby, she loved all the music that sashayed through her ears. By the time she was four, she could solve algebraic equations of one unknown; and she read, read, read. At age thirteen, she bemused a get-together at our home. While reading Peter Benchley's novel *Jaws*, she tripped over a word that she proceeded to spell. "Daddy," she asked, "what does 'U-N-B-E-F-U-C-K-I-N-G-L-I-E-V-A-B-L-E,' mean?"

Leslie was a fearless tomboy. One eve, I pulled up just in time to see her falling from the top of one of the twenty-foot poplars that lined the ditch next to our house. As she thudded into the grass, my heart thudded in my throat. She lay so still. (I mourned afresh my lost son.) Then, her breath back, she leapt up, unscathed, hollering, "Hi, Daddy!" I prayed non-stop gratitude.

Linda Louise, two years Leslie's junior, was less rambunctious and cute as a ribbon, with Disney-huge, gorgeous brown eyes. From toddlerdom on, she was very loving (and so she remains—lawyering on behalf of the most despairing, most despondent Windsorites). As soon as she could speak, she would greet me as I wheeled onto our parking pad, yelling, "There's my daddy! I love my daddy!" (Priceless—*priceless*—is parenthood.)

As a girl, Linda saw herself in Leslie's shadow. But her dyslexia turned letters into puzzle pieces that seldom fit sensibly. Worse, teachers expected Linda to be a second Leslie, fluently talkative and born for the stage. Although Linda did eventually master letters in spectacular fashion and emerged as accomplished as her sister, she endured so long an unwarranted sense of inferiority.

Our third child, Cheryl Lauralyn, was born two years after Linda. She seemed very emotionally fragile. Imaginary entities were scary; siblings and classmates were nerve-wracking. Yet, she was the equal of her sisters, in some ways combining their characteristics.

Finally, we cradled Brian Douglas McCurdy. I had not cared that—until his birth—only our girls might carry on my genes, if not my name. In fact, Brian's arrival was a surprise—for Pat and I were already slouching toward the courtroom as opposed to lolling touchy-feely in the bedroom. My son was precociously active and somewhat more resistant to discipline than the girls, for whom I only needed to count "1-2-3" to terminate any misbehaviour.

Like Cheri, Brian dreamt up invisible beings, but his were, well, simpatico, such as the imaginary dog that trailed him everywhere. Once, at a store checkout, he screamed at a woman who he said was stepping on the tail of his phantasmal canine. As the youngest of our quartet—and the only boy—naturally, all the elder McCurdy women thought he needed spoiling! (My parenting philosophy? Much Dr. Montessori, little Dr. Spock.)

By the early 1960s, my parents—now reconciled after a decade-plus of dissension—and my sister's family resided in the same T-Dot district. We'd drone down the nerve-wracking Macdonald–Cartier Freeway (the 401) as rapidly as possible to attain reasonable safety in their precincts.

After two decades with Ford Canada, my father had quit. Why? After becoming the first Black foreman at Ford's Windsor foundry, way too much spit-in-yo-face racism came his way from co-workers. Parachuting into Toronto, he got to supervise a small factory. Yet, here, too, he had to confront afresh two-faced, backbiting racism. In 1956, Canada had welcomed refugees from "intolerant" Hungarian communists. Soon, some of these "Hungarian freedom fighters" landed jobs at my dad's workplace. Yet, because these "heroic crusaders for democracy" could not tolerate a Black boss, my father was again dismissed! Undaunted, he took a post with Galen Weston (the polo-playing grocery store magnate), receiving pay for two years for various duties before joining Royal Mail Canada (now Canada Post) where, due to his acumen, he was soon again a supervisor. He also pocketed handsome, private lucre as pay for his beautiful carpentry.

My mother worked for the federal Department of National Health and Welfare where she boosted the Public Service Alliance. Marilyn's husband, my brother-in-law Nelson Seabury, part-timed at the post office and worked non-stop the saxophone. (As I mentioned in chapter 5, in the 1940s to 1960s, the Big Smoke's "Coloured" dudes were often "between jobs," so many took up instruments and morphed into play-by-ear musicians, making Toronto a hotbed of jazz—at least in blind pigs. I'd beat up bongos, time to time, alongside guys who ruled the stage: Archie Alleyne and Connie Maynard, a white, blues/jazz dude.)

Mama adored our girls, who called her "Nanny." Each Christmas, she'd be Mrs. Santa, presenting bags stuffed with gifts as well as clothes that she had sewn or woven herself. She even decorated Leslie and Linda's shared bedroom in ultra-feminine fashion. Pink hues and pixie-dust curlicues; sparkles and spangles.

In 1969, my diabetic mother, Bernice Logan, succumbed to a heart attack. Thus, knife-thrusts skewered my heart. A grown-man McCurdy, I secreted my mournful howls in cultivated solitude. Like my father, I could let no one know me as subject to tears.

Before her passing, Mom and Dad had become close—inseparable— with another couple, namely, Jack and Fran Stansfield. Not even death divided this quartet; Jack went to his grave soon after Bernice. Thus, "Howard I" chose to marry Fran. Ironically, Fran was both white and Catholic. I could not forget my dad's strident opposition—two decades gone—to my marital hopes for Marlene. Now, here he was, "sleeping with the enemy." Malcolm X gone Sammy Davis Jr.

To Pat's Ypsilanti clan monthly we went and biweekly to my Amherstburg grandparents. Thus, my kid quartet savoured the opportunity, rare these days, to form prized, lifelong connections with aunts, uncles, cousins. Now, they have identified and have come to know more relatives than I ever thought we had. (The more you branch out, the closer you get to your roots.)

Sundays perched the rug rats in Sabbatarian school, while their parents pewed with Unitarians. Later, if not bound for Amherstburg or Ypsilanti, we'd drop in on another Unitarian, so our "chillun" could play with theirs. The younger McCurdys developed a healthy (to my mind)— and scientific–skeptical view of religion. The downside? They missed out on learning about how the Black Church nurtured our communities. (However, they do know that the first Canuck McCurdys planted churches all about Essex County, enough, even, to compete with vineyards!)

Unlike my generation, for whom the Black Church was the centre of leadership training—and dating—the socialization of the new-generation McCurdys occurred through school, athletics, and secular bodies. Other Black kids were either absent or few and far between.

As "juvies," my "fab four" relished bedtime stories. Their fave? The Headless Horseman! Sometimes he galloped his legendary black stallion. Other times he lurked on foot in our own neighbourhood, threatening night-creeping, defiantly sleepless squirts. As terrifying as he was, he had a standing invitation to our home so that the lights stayed on till our kids saw slumber.

In winter, I seated them on toboggans or stood them on skates. Both Leslie and Linda figured-8 the ice. In summer, at fishing, Cheri cornered all the luck. Amazingly, despite her girlish likes, she could wrangle any finned, flapping critter onto wharf, dock, or deck.

The McCurdy bunch had desks at Southwood Public School, only steps from our house. Being the sole Black students, their colour did not go (prejudicially) unnoticed. But the principal ensured that they felt praised and affirmed. Nor did we elder McCurdys fumble at finessing corrective pedagogy for any teacher given to off-colour instruction or who evinced paleface incompetence.

Leslie's scholastic excellence and sports prowess made her a teacher's darling. Yet, despite Einstein grades, head-turning science-fair entries, unmatched athletic records, and star turns in school shows she herself scripted, stereotypes persisted; so, Leslie snapped up sports trophies, not nerdy laurels. (Too, it's hard to discount athletes: "first," "highest," "fastest" demarcate "marks" indisputable.)

Due to my psych training and social work praxis, I did not believe in "tanning bottoms." Only egregious wrongheadedness brought my dexterously sinister hand to a backside. Leslie and Cheri needed no correction. Once, Linda got "whupped" when I detected, upon leaving a supermarket, that she had swiped a chocolate bar. (Best beaten for a "peccadillo" now than jailed for a crime later!) Brian's recalcitrance—"defiance"—caught him twice a wallop. (To keep his son safe, a Black father must be strict. I acted out of love *because* a cop or a guard could *react* out of bigotry.)

Even so, Pat and I disagreed about discipline. Thus, friction arose. She tended to scream at eardrums or want to play taps on bums. To me, both measures were immoderate. We survived the seven year itch okay. But not so well the eleven year itch, that is, 1970.

An associate prof, I had job security, but any auto worker could out-brag my income. Still, Pat coaxed me to rival our neighbours at whatever cost. Thus, I purchased a mobile camper, though a backyard barbecue would have been more tasteful.

Thwarted in her academic ambitions, Pat channelled her desires into upgrading our accoutrements, so she could have (I wager) a sense of class status—as a Black woman holding her own amid the pallid helpmates flanking. Her expertise was interior design, which ain't about rearranging furniture.

O, but I was slow to register her frustrations! She'd been pregnant five times over the decade, about once every two years, so 45 months out of 120—almost 40 percent of the time—and then had conducted the lioness's share of child care, plus running the household. In contrast, I was shuttling constantly between microscopes and microphones. I garnered hate mail, yes, but also adulation, while Pat saw only paltry demand for her university-honed skills.

So, once I joined the BOG at St. Clair College (Windsor), Pat asked that I secure her a teaching job. Nope, I said. That fractured us, even though she was hired by St. Clair, due strictly to her qualifications. This success did not arrest the corrosion of affection. For one thing, Pat poohpoohed the subjects that animated our circle of friends. Or, to be fair, *my* friends—scientists and lawyers and their placid mates. Too, Pat was jealous of the leisure time that I gave myself selfishly. (I think that, for her, my reading a book was a stealthy form of adultery.) I wish I'd recognized sooner how Pat could rightly detest my aloofness to our domestic affairs.

Then, suspicious of my hours at the lab, Pat began to accuse me of pursuing different assignations, for I was "indifferent" to her needs. Yet, had I been a skirt-chaser, my rep as a fair-dealing, Black male activist would've vanished in a nanosecond. (Recall Hoover's essays to discredit King by circulating recordings of the latter's extramarital escapades.)

Pat had bitter grievances, eh? So did I. She was oft late for everything, as she had been for our wedding. Pat could also slap—or punch. Bickering was our liquor. To be drunk on woes.

When Betty Friedan published *The Feminine Mystique* in 1963, Pat read it as if it were holy writ. Lookit! Unitarians require liberal debate of religion, philosophy, science, and morality, so it was inevitable that Friedan would be canvassed. I hoped, though, that our reflections would enhance the lives of women, not pinpoint husbands as oppressors. Though I was practised at delineating racists, unprepared was I to be framed as a sexist prick!

Racial and gender equality were one pursuit. Friedan et al. replaced Fanon et al.; and Pat joined with Janice McCurdy Van Dyke, Pat (Eleanore Patricia) Alexander, and Eleanor Tate (now Payne) to form the Panel of Concerned Women. Integrated, they warred against both racism and sexism. By 1980, they'd mothered the Windsor Feminist Theatre.

Pat now saw (or so I thought) every spat as manifesting racial and/or sexual oppression. I deemed her fanatical! (Dudes, read *hysterical* at your peril!) Indeed, after our split, I stopped by our house and was greeted by Brian sporting a girl's pyjamas and housecoat. I queried Pat about it, and she said that Brian was learning that gender differences are merely superficial. (A surprise to Darwin and a shock to God!)

The breaking point? Winter 1971. In a dispute over my sabbatical plans for Germany, I had proposed that Pat, Leslie, and Linda join me there once school ended in June. Pat held that we all must go April through August, a proposition that would torpedo our daughters' school year and sink our finances. When I refused, she quit our home, abandoning the children to my care.

Quickly, I made arrangements with my Aunt Helen and other relatives for child care in my absence. Pat's malaise prompted her spiteful flight, but to me, she was now the selfish parent.

Before that rupture, however, I'd enjoyed a respite from marital woes by taking up my autumn 1970 sabbatical. I motored down to Black-Panther–Free-Speech-Movement-Flower-Power–Make-Love-Not-War Berkeley to work with Professor Roger Yate Stanier at the University of California. An ex-pat Canuck, Roger was a Nobel-level microbiologist and one who eyed my work admiringly.

I was warned I'd meet a prof gruff and offputtingly tough. But in our communion, he was open, reflective, and lauded passionately Berkeley's famous student insurrection. (In 1971, to protest the policies of Guv Ronald Reagan and Prez Richard Nixon, Roger removed to Paris, France, where he'd die, in 1982, due to lung and brain cancer.) One day, I ventured to ask him about his departmental reputation for being insensitive, that is, a standoffish *éminence grise*. Hurt, he flinched—blanched—at my query. (Later in my own life, I recognized that a gruff exterior can too securely hide a vulnerable heart. I know some saw me as aloof, insular, even stuck-up. But I longed for acceptance, respect, and love and was too fearful and proud to ask. My old-school masculinity? Staunchly stoic, pathetically paralyzing.)

In winter 1971, my sabbatical shifted to the University of Western Ontario, so I commuted to London twice a week from Windsor. (The driving was perilous, but my relationship with Pat was parlous.) I hunkered down in the lab of Robert G. E. Murray, a bacterial cytologist.

Thanks to the influence of Stanier and Murray, I gained international recognition as the authority on the classification of myxobacteria. (Right on! I became stone-soul, bro scientist number one!)

My third sabbatical? In Freiburg, Germany, "in the the spring" (to quote a brain puzzle). I flew off but had to leave my young with relatives, for—as mentioned above—Pat had gone AWOL to protest my inability to support two adults and four children for sixteen weeks in Europe with a Canuck-buck salary (itself reduced by 20 percent, due to sabbatical subtraction). No matter—my time with Hans Reichenbach (1936–2018), the German microbiologist, was a bust.

Second World War bombing had rubbled and stubbled Freiburg. Craters and pitfalls abounded. But medieval Münster (once said to vaunt "the most beautiful spire on earth") had survived as intact as Marilyn Munster's maidenhead. Hans's lab? Trifling! Too, he was introverted, favouring next-to-nil interaction. Associated with the University of Minnesota's Martin Dworkin, a molecular biologist who studied differentiation in the myxobacteria, they'd advanced a classification scheme that differed from mine, and so we subsisted as rivals, not persisted as comrades.

Yet, by 1971 (West) Germany felt so much like a Euro version of "Funky Nassau" that one could almost forget it had ever hosted the Third Reich. But Germans were congenial, not amiable. Thus, while tarrying in Frankfurt, looking super dandy in a black suit and carrying a closed, black umbrella, I heard two Krauts exclaim, "*Eine schwartze Englander!*" (Yes, I was jolly well a Black Brit! Wasn't I from London II?)

I soon tired of German beer (too bitter) and German wine (too sweet). However, I did develop the Freiburg taste for Scotch and Coke: a summertime, good-time cocktail.

Late in my stay, Leslie and Linda, aged ten and eight, landed in Frankfurt after jetting, accompanied only by stewardesses, across the Atlantic. Until I met up with them, they were in the care of Frankfurt nuns. Soon, we vamoosed to Kiel for a social visit with bro microbiologist Peter Hirsch, a *mensch* enthralled by exotic, budding bacteria. We'd met at the Kellogg Research Station (now the Kellogg Biological Station) at Gull Lake, Michigan, where our families had vacationed together and where I'd introduced his kids and mine to the hijinks of frog catching.

My girls relished seeing the Hirsch children again, though they were surprised that their playmates now spoke German, not English. (No matter—my girls were speaking German, and drinking a little German wine, by the time we returned to Windsor!) Our stay was idyllic. How near came the midnight sun! How tiny were the deer (more like a flock than a herd)! How rocket-like was the phallic Laboe Naval Memorial nearby, commemorating the German sailors sunk in two world wars!

Sadly, I cut short the tour. Bob Doyle began his sabbatical, and I was now acting chair of the Department of Biology. A new recognition, with new responsibilities.

Our return home also registered, for me, a rebarbative reality: Pat had reoccupied the house, to restore the *status quo ante*. Say, what? I packed up, went packing: a bachelor reborn.

Mutual friend and lawyer Saul Nosanchuk (appointed an Ontario Court Judge in 1976) entreated Pat and me to sign a voluntary separation deal.

Simultaneously, Pat opined that we seek psychiatric counselling to repair our bond. The result? Two incompatibles. (True: maybe Marlene—my long-lost first love—and I would have broken up even if our families hadn't broken us up. I mustn't romanticize "us." We'd been only teens. And yet, never had I felt the same sparking chemistry with Pat that I'd felt with Marlene.)

The failure of Saul's diplomatic and compassionate mediation established that the paired McCurdys were irreconcilable opposites. Divorce should have been the no-brainer that the erstwhile groom had displayed on his wedding day: no brains! Instead of an amicable division, Pat's lawyer spat subpoenas at me with every exhalation and scrutinized forensically my every dollar, my every dish, for fifteen bankrupting years! Yet, not once did I miss a support payment; I was not just a father, I was a dad and glad to make sure my children wanted for nothing.

Still, that protracted wrangling zoomed my legal costs skyward. Ultimately, I had to out-lawyer a lawyer. Double billings amounted to nearly a third of the total that my attorney claimed. Our dispute came before an assessment officer of the Superior Court who verified, within one hour, the sums did not compute. Upset by their loss, my lawyer's assistant dared to upbraid me for having revealed their managerial ineptitude. No matter—the lawyer lived to bill again another day. He even became a Family Court judge!

Although Pat was now a St. Clair College teach, with a salary comparable to mine, my support cash never seemed, in my mind, to get expended on our children. I was always buying such staples as shoes or covering incidental costs for school, dance lessons, and athletics. (In the early 1970s, support payments from men were seldom enforced, leading to the "deadbeat dad" phenomenon. Yet, no one kept tabs on what divorcée moms did with the cash they received. Judges ruled, aye, but the real world of broken relationships was ungovernable.)

Our separation dox stipulated I could take the kids every second weekend, but Pat scotched that access. Seldom were they set to leave when I showed. Due to Pat's choices, either they were often hours late or not available at all. Yet, our children knew that, to get to track or baseball practices, dance lessons or gymnastics, Dad was dependable.

Indeed, said hearsay, my kids were left alone to fend for themselves, even overnight. I became so concerned, I sought sole custody but to no avail. (One ironic outcome of second-wave feminism was, though women demanded rightful independence from the burdens of child care, in cases of separation or divorce, they were almost always awarded full custody of any offspring by harrumphing judges, even if these very justices were classified as "male chauvinist pigs"!)

In 1978–79, Pat took a sabbatical leave at Michigan State University. Although I attended some of their athletic events in Lansing, I felt alienated from my own brood. The upside? For the first time, they inhabited a substantially Black environment. Their schools were *crème de la crème*. Linda and Leslie attended Everett High School, still newly desegregated (and the alma mater of Magic Johnson). They thrived there, academically and athletically. Leslie and Linda became high school "all-Americans."

But "stateside" was not 100 percent positive. One day, because of a premonition, Linda refused to go to school, thus provoking Pat's ire. When she did go to school the next day, she was told that the student usually sitting next to her had been shot by another student sitting nearby. For her part, Leslie dated a boy who stole her heart, yes. Next, he stole valuables from the house!

Leslie launched into ballet lessons practically as a toddler, followed later by Linda and then Cheri. All my kids? Born athletes! I made a dirt high-jump pit and set up standards in the backyard. So, when Leslie was eight years old, I taught her the Western roll, and she soon ruled the high jump.

Well, the entire McCurdy quartet cornered the high jump, snookering all records. When they joined the Knights of Columbus track club, I was the club's official high jump coach, through the late '70s and early '80s. Under my guidance, many club athletes took home provincial and national laurels. An article vaunting my coaching prowess soon appeared in *Canadian Athletics*, a publication of Athletics Canada, the chief track-and-field body.

Linda was a more talented and zealous swimmer than her siblings, but, as was customary, she wanted to do what Leslie did. So she decided she'd be a high jumper too, which actually made her asthma less of a factor. Instead of the Western roll, she learned the Fosbury flop, a more suitable technique for girls that became the number one approach for all jumpers. Linda would more promptly become aggravated than Leslie and often quit practices in a huff. Striking it was, then, that in her first competitive meet, she aced the national Legion championship in Newfoundland!

In addition, Linda was twice an Ontario Federation of Secondary Schools Athletics (OFSSA) medalist, a Michigan high school number one, a university all-American, a five-time Canadian national high jump first-place trophy recipient, and a member of the Canadian Commonwealth team. Her chief grievance? Not being included on the 1984 Olympic team even though she'd qualified. (That setback was far worse than my decision to forego tryouts for the 1956 Canadian Olympic team.)

Brian, Cheryl, Linda, and Leslie: beloved quartet (1988).

Alongside the high jump, Leslie was an A1 hurdler and was named as an outstanding athlete at Massey High School, where gymnastics and basketball were her forte. All the McCurdys wriggled, leapt, and skipped through school gymnastics; yet, such athleticism was tortuously excruciating for parent spectators. We ranged miles for meets and then were terrorized by what seemed to be arbitrary judging, inevitable falls, and the fear of our children sustaining a debilitating injury.

Leslie was an elastic gymnast, but a horrible fall from the high beam, which dislocated her shoulder and broke her arm in two places, also shattered her self-confidence. Happily though, her strength, gracefully embodied, achieved stage expression. A natural-born dancer and choreographer, Leslie scored a scholarship and majored in modern dance at the University of Michigan. Though wooed by several premium US dance groups, an injury and premature maternity diverted my daughter into drama.

By taking title to the beam at an OFSSA meet, Linda made history, outscoring all in both track and gym. She, Cheri, and Brian all snagged university athletic scholarships.

Scholarships bore Linda and Cheri to the University of Texas at El Paso. However, an injury pushed Cheri out of striving to outrun and outjump rivals; instead, she took keenly to cheerleading. Cheri also figured in beauty pageants, striking a star turn as Miss Black El Paso, among boasting other titles. Linda augmented her student income via modelling and continued to be an incarnate mannequin even after becoming a lawyer. She vogued the courtroom as much as she interrogated the runway!

Brian quarterbacked in Windsor minor football and for the Lowe High junior team and as a senior at Massey High. He led each to city trophies, even spearheading the Lowe Juniors' first-ever first place. A football scholarship conveyed him to Riverside Junior College, in California.

Like his father, Brian was, until age eighteen, small for his age, just five-foot-six. So, although an outstanding athlete, at times his "pint size" hindered his confidence. I recall one incident in a high jump contest where his rivals were six inches taller. In the preliminary rounds, it was clear that he could outjump the others, but their height intimidated him so much psychologically, he quit the match.

But, lookit! Football was his to-die-for sport. Now six-foot-one, he could be intimidating! But he never again played quarterback, a position denied Black players in that era. So he became a defensive back at Riverside and later at Northern Arizona State. He snookered all-American honors at that position and stood as a first-round draft pick in the Canadian Football League, playing for Toronto, Ottawa, and Hamilton. While at Northern Arizona State, he also set the high jump record for the Big Sky Conference. (Ah, my kids! Always reaching for the stars!)

In 1977, with my split from Pat judge-stamped, I wed Brenda Lee Wright, whom I had first met in May 1969 at a Miami ASM session. So scarce were we Black microbiologists then that an Eli Lilly corporate microbiologist from Indianapolis ("Indian no place," he'd quip), Larry Eugene "Doc" Doolin, and I decided to marshal Black attendees to meet-and-greets. (Lawrence E. Doolin was also active in the African-American-oriented National Organization for the Professional Advancement of Black Chemists and Chemical Engineers.)

The Miami get-together is where I first beamed upon Brenda, then a first-year graduate student at the School of Medicine of Virginia Commonwealth University—one of the top research universities in the US—located in Richmond, her natal city. Brenda was in Miami to present a paper on bacterial endotoxin, a subject dear to my heart, just as she herself would become. Compounding her classy pulchritude, she was pursuing a master of science degree in experimental biology.

To cite "love at first sight" is a cliché. So, I won't. Besides, I was a domesticated, dedicated hubby. Yet, to see Brenda was, truly, to ogle, to divine. I surveyed—with my microscope-trained-to-scrutinize eyes, a sleek, chic, caramel-*bella* mitochondrial Eve, a marvel of design. Dark, glittering eyes! Strawberry-frosted lips! A face perfect as Thutmose's bust of Nefertiti! So beautiful, she *almost* rekindled in me a belief in God. I observed Opulence incarnated as Elegance, Excellence, Intelligence, that is, Uncommon Sense.

Thus, once I was a bachelor again and I could date, I came to know Brenda as absolutely phenomenal: brains plus beauty! A svelte scientist and burgeoning with singing talent. (Hear Brynda, *If I Follow My Heart*, her excellent jazz-soul CD from 2013. Don't take my word for it! *Listen!*) Extraordinary as any accomplished star featured in *Ebony* or even, yes, on *Oprah*!

My former grad colleague at MSU, Tom Neblett, headed the micro-biology department at Henry Ford Hospital in Detroit and needed some-one of Brenda's attributes. I recommended her; she got the post and I took her under my wing while she scoped out a place to live. (After all, she was exiting Dixie to place near North Star Canaan!) Brenda proved to be a powerhouse at Henry Ford. Next, she entered the PhD program at Wayne State, which she completed in 1980, becoming Dr. Brenda Lee Wright McCurdy, a specialist in immunology and microbiology.

Mr. Justice Saul Nosanchuk did the honours, wedding us on the Colchester (Essex Co.) property of my cousin Janice McCurdy-Bannigan and her husband, Richard. My children also swanked spankingly the bridal party. After some panic over lost in-laws and, gosh, even the bride (but not to the level of anxiety and upset that I'd felt at Pat's late arrival, almost a generation previously, for *her* and my wedding), all transpired suavely. Our Caboto Club reception? Scientists and soul sisters, profs

Howard and Brenda Lee Wright's wedding day: September 2, 1977.

and fancy dancers. Ron Trider was my best man; my buddy Winston Walls served up hot buttered funk, plus disco: Aretha Franklin's *Sparkle* shone a fresh light on Parliament's *Chocolate City*.

Brenda and I bought a house in Forest Glade then purchased a fine, two-storey home on Rankin in South Windsor. First, though, racist realtors tried to dissuade us from buying into "an Italian burgh." We fired the realtors, moved in. Guess what? *Tutti* were so simpatico! To later relocate from that haven to the constituency where I'd be elected to Parliament was one of the dumbest things we—I mean, I—ever did.

CHAPTER TWELVE:
BIOLOGICAL (POLITICAL) HAZARDS

AS PREVIOUSLY MENTIONED, I HAD CUT SHORT MY SABBATICAL when I was elected acting head of Biology after Bob Doyle took to Spain for a research leave. I returned to Windsor and a marriage on ice. Then, back from sabbatical in 1972, Bob served one last year before stepping down. In 1974, I was elected to a five-year term as his replacement. Thus, I became the first Black chair of any university department in Canadian history.

Before cushioning my tush in that seat, I negotiated vital concessions from UW Prez J. Francis Leddy and dollars from the dean. I turned a poet: "Biology is life, and living costs money, especially with price inflation spiralling upward." Bucks soon winged toward and nestled in our accounts. Shortly, Biology possessed cutting-edge tech for classrooms and labs, picked up go-getter profs, and savoured a hefty uptick in operating funds.

I liked Leddy and he esteemed *moi*. True: I'd only been Biology chair for a nanosecond when Leddy called to tell me that, on his recommendation, the vice-presidency of Guelph University was mine for the asking. I said no. I would honour the commitment I'd made to my colleagues when I became chief of Biology. I had zero yearning, anyway, to change a lab smock and microscope slides for cocktails and schmoozing.

Job one? To reno our premises. An addition enlarged our space by 25 percent. Five new hires strengthened our focus on cell biology but also allowed us to pivot to ecology. The latter move was prescient, for, out of it, the Great Lakes Institute was born.

Unfortunately, some faculty indulged immature behaviour, such as burning farts in the ecology lab, assisted by childish students! To end those shenanigans, I frowned and glared, played *Father Knows Best*, eager to take a switch to their lab-coat-tailed posteriors!

More egregious, however, was the flagrant reassertion of Negrophobic racism—aimed at me. Curiously, the person guiltiest for expressing brazen prejudice was the chosen Canuck among the new hires. Solid were his credentials and later fulfilled was his promise. Yet, Dr. No (I thank Ian Fleming for the pseudonym) could not abide a Black de facto boss. The first hint of his attitude? When opposing me in a departmental touch-football game, as soon as the ball was in play, he made a beeline for me, blocking me so roughly, I struck the ground hard. On the next play, I returned the favour with extra oomph, and his collapse put an end to his bumf. Even so, his "free speech" stood for vile bigotry, such as calling a Jewish colleague a "kike."

Also notable was Dr. No's hiring of Dr. Humbert Humbert (I thank Vladmir Nabokov for the pseudonym) as a post-doctoral fellow. They were birds of a feather. Although Dr. Humbert became an adjunct biologist, Dr. No never officially introduced us. Never was the honky hand of fellowship extended to clasp my Negro own. (I wonder: Did my black skin invalidate—for Humbert and No—my donning of the pristine lab coat?)

On one occasion, I stopped by the home of a new ecologist (one of the lads-of-the-fiery-farts) to drop off mail, and his wife met me at the door. Seeing a Black man on her stoop, she paled, she quailed, she palpitated, she aspirated. Pitiful! When I identified myself and asked her to pass a package to her husband, she was further shocked. Her hubby's boss was Black! (Did she poop her panties as I turned away? Hope so. Would've cleared her head.)

In addition to the Negrophobia afflicting some faculty biologists, there were others who resented our new systems—which I'd forwarded zealously—for promotion and remuneration based on peer and student evaluation. Why? The deadwood could hear the chainsaws revving!

But we'd lacked a systematic process for appointments or promotions, leading to anomalies in judging achievement and assessing merit or suitability. Translation? Cronyism. An aristocracy of inbred mediocrity.

Following consultation with an appointments and promotion committee, I met with each faculty member to review the results of both student and peer evaluations and laud attainments or suggest improvements. Also considered was the success rate in obtaining research support from the granting agencies, which could also involve a partial rewriting of applications where necessary.

Some colleagues acted like cornered rats; others quivered like scared sheep. Some improved, others could not. This tidy clique became self-protective ornery.

Curriculum reform necessitated departmental gabfests that resembled long flights. Routine dullness led to snoozing, which was then upended by sudden jolts of pandemonium and panic: the shocked reaction of faculty members who realized that their research interests—once such expansive, dollar-pampered domains—had become dusty dead ends.

But onward had we to go! Quickly, lecture-hall classes began to feel as intimate as labs. Due to our ascendant status, I became the vice-chair of the Ontario Association of University Biology Departments. (Our chair, Gordin Kaplan, hobnobbed—like me—with Roger Stanier.)

My accomplishments as UW's chief biologist were aided by the strength and bonhomie of my first-class secretary, Elizabeth Theaker. She had an eye for figures and a nose for discrepancies. When I learned that she was being paid much less than male janitors (a common situation for Windsor's female staff back then), I was so irate, I urged Elizabeth and another secretary to form a union. Being on the BOG, I lobbied for gender-blind equal pay for work of equal value. Nothing doing: only unionization would enforce change.

Sadly, Elizabeth passed away first. One day, she complained of back-breaking pain; the next she was hospitalized. Although Elizabeth never puffed a single cigarette, she had inhaled such second-hand smoke that, within two weeks of entering the hospital, lung cancer robbed her life's breath. I wondered guiltily whether my tobacco addiction contributed to the buildup of lethal pollutants in her lungs.

Two new office staff, Gayle Roberts and Pam Russell, could not replace much-missed Elizabeth. Still, Gayle's partner, Max Henshaw, became my pal; our trio socialized exuberantly. A silver-haired Australian—irresistibly beautiful, dauntingly intelligent, exceedingly ambitious—Pam, whom I dated, would soon quit "life science" to take up

Windsor Star journalism (to echo the paper's hostility contra *moi*, perhaps), only to return to another form of "life sciences" by becoming a social worker.

In the mid-1970s, that era of soaring inflation (as once dirt-cheap gas became a stratospheric luxury), the cash-strapped Ontario Tories, to control university expenditures, boosted class sizes and capped salaries. Many Windsor profs now demanded unionization. But Law and Engineering opposed this hardhat vs. mortarboard manoeuvre.

I, too, had qualms about applying a mass-industrial model to independent-minded scholars and university professionals. Because profs could now elect department heads (that is, the most immediate level of management), I held that we should be excused from any bargaining unit. I detailed my position before the arbitrator. I lost, but the judge, in delivering his decision, congratulated me on my submission, considering it superior to that of the university legal team.

In any event, Prez Leddy's 1978 retirement meant that faculty would help to select the new prez. Dr. Mervyn Franklin, a University of New Brunswick veep, emerged as the nominee. I had met Franklin as a br'er member of the Canadian Society of Microbiologists (CSM).

Prez Leddy called to sound me out regarding Franklin's appointment to the department of Biology. No probs! No financial or academic implications! However, Leddy's second request was toxic: Could Franklin's wife, Maxine Holder-Franklin, also be tenured in Biology? I declined: her CV did not correspond to our research or teaching needs, which were in ecology. (That she'd attended Radcliffe-by-Harvard was not a qualification.) Leddy accepted my integrity-informed decision that Dr. Holder-Franklin be assigned only adjunct status.

That night after I'd retired to bed, a telephone call hollered—from far-off New Brunswick. Guess who? Franklin had been told that I'd take Dr. Holder-Franklin only as an "extra," not as a fixture. To change my mind, he pitched me a salary hike, a better-furnished lab for us all, "anything," so long as I'd agree to appoint his wife to a tenured post. I was adamant: "She does not suit the department's needs." My conclusion outraged a man who nursed grudges the way that drunks nurse their liquor: avidly, protectively, lovingly.

So, Holder-Franklin joined us as an adjunct. Appropriately, she had the primary use of her husband's lab (from which he was normally absent) and access to all of Biology's shared equipment. However, she bristled at my refusal to outfit her a lab in her own name or buy an ultracentrifuge for her research alone. Being an adjunct prof, she could not expect these niceties. (Sometime after I left UW and her husband was no longer prez,

Dr. Holder-Franklin filed a complaint to the Ontario Human Rights Commission asserting sex discrimination for having been denied her own lab as a sessional! Absurdly, UW agreed to settle this frivolous grievance, which made no reference to me. Properly, I was not named in either suit or settlement. How did sex discrimination occur, then, if there was no "perp"? Too, how was she—as an *adjunct*—victimized? In any event, Dr. Holder-Franklin became a biology associate prof at the University of Windsor in 1992, then a full professor in 1994. All's well that ends well. But one more thing: neither Leddy nor Franklin understood that I, being Canada's first Black department head, faced intense scrutiny for my hiring decisions. To have been accused—*rightly*—of smiling upon cronyism would have ruined my reputation for scientific objectivity and administrative probity.)

During my term as the department's chief biologist, I kept a full teaching load. Still, no colleague matched my research publication record. Simultaneously, I supervised two doctoral students. As folks looked up my work, then looked up from microscopes, I was suddenly peering down at 'em from floodlit billboards (so to speak)! Research funds rained down like manna, and I joined the editorial boards of *Bacteriological Reviews* and the *Canadian Journal of Microbiology*. I was also appointed chair of both the international and American Society of Microbiologists taxonomic subcommittees on the gliding bacteria. If I was not the Jimi Hendrix of microbiologists, I was defiantly the Prince of that scientific *internationale*.

Thus, I was responsible for establishing the Canadian College of Microbiologists (CCM), the body certifying professional accreditation. Working with Holocaust survivor Dr. Raoul Korngold from the University of Ottawa, who served as unpaid registrar, I obtained—despite red tape—CSM bucks and so designed and oversaw the administration of the first qualifying microbiology exams. I presided over the CCM for four years, 1976 to 1980.

A survey told me that my research, teaching, and admin duties consumed as much as seventy-two hours a week. That was just my University of Windsor employ. A typical workaholic, I was also bogged down in BOG matters at the St. Clair College of Applied Arts and Technology.

The virgin members of the St. Clair BOG eyed me as suspicious for being a civil rights enthusiast; I had publicly lambasted the anti-Semitic and Negrophobic exclusions that their country clubs practised. They feared that a science-backed, pro-equality socialist, with a modicum of media savvy, could imperil their sinecure.

Despite the opposition of some BOG members, it was Dr. Richard C. Quittenton, its debut prez, who'd nourished St. Clair. Quittenton, who liked to be referred to as "Q" (like the inventive James Bond "quartermaster"), manifested an engineer's can-do attitude and a gadget-attuned mind. Q wanted St. Clair to be student-centred and community oriented. To buttress his open-door policy for students, he installed a "hotline" so they could reach him directly. He held bear-pit discussions at assemblies and was the most boisterous fan at college sports meets.

In developing the South Windsor campus (via a $13 million fund), Q ensured that it included an amphitheatre, an Olympic pool, and a gymnasium and sports fields, open to the public. He was a democrat, in vision and expenditure. Thus, St. Clair became a stellar college in the provincial system. By 1977, student enrolment had exploded from a few hundred to three thousand. A satellite campus was launched in Chatham.

During the college's formative years, I chaired the curriculum committee, timetabling courses that could attract lucrative private sector partners (who'd hire our graduates, for one thing). I also ensured that faculty were recognized as professionals; in addition, I helped to blueprint the physical plant in which they would work.

In 1973, I became the BOG chair; I did two terms. And I came to helm the Association of Colleges of Applied Arts and Technology, a body created to counterpoise our provincial overseer, the Council of Regents. Too, I presided over the committee that harmonized our instruction in diploma nursing with that offered by university BScN programs.

Once I quit the St. Clair BOG, the remaining board members began to chafe at Q's unorthodox ways and to resent his media profile. Q fancied himself a *philosophe* and so voiced eccentric views other BOGgers deemed *insupportable* (French pronunciation). Too, he was a Progressive Conservative, that is, a Red Tory, but other BOGgers were blue-blooded Tories, who liked to be closeted with their cocktails, not electioneering before cameras and mics.

All came to a head when Tom Toth, a Windsor City Council appointee to the BOG, psst'd to the press that Q had been asked to resign. Mary Easton, now the board chair, pooh-poohed his assertion, so Toth faced calls for *his* own ouster. Due to contract disputes or board conflicts—or both—Q quit the college, slipping away, shrouded by murk of controversy and the smoke-and-fog of his philosophical emissions.

At the University of Windsor, I was soon to go the way of Q, if with much less public rancour. Indeed, by 1979 my chief biologist gig was up. Heck, I deserved re-election. Dean of Science Conrad Gravenor headed the process to either renew my term...or bust! However, his committee abided several adversarial members. (Yep, my "race" mattered!) Months passed and despite my sundry queries to Gravenor, I received no rationale for the failure to advance—or to terminate—the search. Was Gravenor, at Prez Franklin's behest, enacting a policy of stasis? Was this payback for my refusal, the year before, to appoint Holder-Franklin to a tenured post in Biology?

Fed up with the stalling (so rudely dismissive of my sacrifices), I called a departmental salon and stunned all: "Limbo is for Sambo, and that ain't me. I'm out!" O! How I relished rebuking the search committee's brazen prejudice and heaping disgust on Gravenor's weakness!

Enemies lusted for a purge? Hell, I ex'd *them*—from my preoccupations and priorities. Brenda and I jetted to Cancún. First winter idyll in a decade. Time for just us—if way past time for justice!

There, in a beach chair, musing on my stint as Biology chair and mentally dissecting my colleagues, I determined some were suit-and-tie fecal matter. Once KKK hoods got doffed, I eyed ghoulish, pasty faces.

Returning to teach, I was X-acto–blade definite: no more slaving for ingrates! To slough off UW would be, for me, akin to my ancestors liberating themselves from Dixie bondage. (*Liberty* is a synonym for *Dignity* for African peoples.) Still, I admit that I was heartbroken: students petitioned the administration to keep me as the head of Biology.

One evening, while controversy roiled, I was in my office when Armando Deluca (later O.Ont., QC) knocked. An esteemed lawyer from Amherstburg and a boyhood chum and schoolmate of my cousin Michael McCurdy, Armando knew us well. Also, being Italian, he could sniff out WASP prejudice. That's why, having just left a meeting of the University of Windsor's BOG, he felt compelled to confide what he had heard. Armando projected a calm demeanour; even his complaints got voiced via euphemisms. However, this night he was fit for a stroke. His outburst? Pent-up lava: "Howard, I'm absolutely shocked! Until tonight, I hadn't realized the hostility against you among Windsor's administration. And it's raw, unadulterated racism. I can't *believe* some of the things I heard!"

I could—believe. I knew the ivory tower could be as pink-pigment supremacist as the Klan, if lisping polysyllables rather than grunts. (Exemplarily extreme, though, was one physics prof, a *clerc* ironically Jewish, who spat that "Negroes had no business being professors"! This disciple of Einstein hadn't gravitated toward light; no, he'd tumbled into the black hole of bias!)

Never before had the fact of racism compelled me to assume its presence in my colleagues. Now, Armando had confirmed what most Black people assume is said among anemic cohorts when we are absent.

Their smiles are silent snarls; their handshakes are merely pulled punches. (An intriguing factoid? During all my years in Biology at UW, I was the only African-Canadian-born to hold an academic appointment. That speaks volumes, I wager, about the Negrophobia of the Great White North's groves of academe.)

I speculated that Prez Franklin had led the denigrations. To blackball me for not "playing ball" by hiring his wife! But, as she was no Ursula Franklin, neither was he Ben Franklin.

Still a UW Senate member was I. After I'd dominated a loudly contentious debate one day, Walter Romanow (initiator of Windsor's Communications department and a cousin of Saskatchewan's future premier Roy Romanow) approached me to ask whether I'd ever wish to seek political office. I thought he was kidding, but he swore he was serious. Hmm....

At the same time, my speech at a testimonial dinner for Windsor mayor Bert Weeks sparked uproarious laughter and a standing ovation. Senator Paul Martin, flanking me at the head table, deemed it one unforgettable "peroration"! He too advised that I stand for public office—as a Liberal. I began to imagine that I could "stand" as a candidate.

CHAPTER THIRTEEN:

GOODBYE, BLACK COALITION! HELLO, CITY COUNCIL!

SINCE THE CONSTITUTIONAL CONVENTION IN 1971, I'D DIS-
regarded the National Black Coalition. Likewise, my Guardian Club years
had ebbed into nostalgia. I was disengaged from both bodies that I'd inaugurated. Why? My 1970–71 sabbatical, then being Biology head, plus the
turmoil of divorce, all had diverted my energies away from the civil rights
cause.

Anyway, the Guardian Club was inactive, and the National Black
Coalition of Canada (NBCC) was irrelevant. Abidingly suicidal, it had
rushed breakneck down the dead-end path of radicalism.

I hated racism, but I refused to view all Caucasians as racist or racism as uniquely European. As a small minority in a white-majority society, Blacks need allies who share our desire for equality and social justice. While knowing our history and identifying with our African roots empowers us, our Afrocentrism must not repeat the sins of Eurocentrism, thus alienating non-Blacks.

Though facing deportation as a security threat, Rosie Douglas—astoundingly—was honoured at the NBCC's first awards dinner. A booklet on NBCC history, which included the Black Manifesto, neither recognized my authorship nor cited me as the agency's originating chair! I recognized that I was either being blacklisted by envy or whitewashed by ignorance.

Still, I was on call. Indeed, a top official in the US Agency for International Development, Dr. Thomas Posey, had come to UW as a research prof in economics. He had heard that if anyone knew anything about Black Canada, it was me. He was researching the history of the Black Canadian Church and the Canuck Civil Rights Movement.

I shared my views. I held that the Black community had too many churches, led by too many unlettered preachers, all overly ambitious to achieve token honours. However, I did lead Tom to those who were writing up churches vital to the abolitionist movement. Tom was astonished to find that those same denominations were silent on contemporary anti-racism.

I also told him about the National Black Coalition and its flaws. He expressed his dismay at my accounting; yet, it was in his Christian character to try to resurrect the moribund. Thus, Tom summoned all Black Canuck leaders to U Windsor. The question? How to—or should we—revitalize the NBCC?

Due to much discord (over identity quibbles) and allegations of fraud in relation to the NBCC's failure to account for federal funds donated to dispatch a Black Canuck delegation to Nigeria for the second World Festival on Black and African Arts and Culture (FESTAC) in 1977, rank-and-file disaffection and dissension had brought the coalition to the point of dissolution. Correctly! One sign of the inefficiency of the NBCC is that, though I was the premier Black scientist in Canada, I was never contacted by Dr. Dennis V. C. Awang, a herbal remedy guru, to feature in an NBCC science-theme display for FESTAC. I heard zilch about the festival! Ironically, Doc Awang became Health Canada's head of the Natural Products Bureau of Drug Research. After I became an MP, he contacted me to seek my help when his position was threatened.

(Geez! Some Black folk only become Black when redneck crackers attack. Once "Oreos," their white "filling" disappears when their chocolate exterior is censured.)

Due to the NBCC exec committee's shirking of its duties, Roy States, exec sec outta Montreal, was sweating to hold together a Silly-Putty entity whose stretched-out substance was merely its exponentially increasing debt. Thus, in Toronto in spring 1976, twenty-five summide vigilant militants assembled to try to resuscitate the NBCC—or consign it to Trotsky's garbage dump (in the style of the post-mortem castigation of Pope Formosus).

Dr. Wilson Head struck a task force to tackle the options: reboot or power-down. On their own dime, the task force members shuttled across the world's second-largest country, canvassing the disparate communities. Their recs, à la The Beatles? "Let it Be," that is, let it die. However, Dot Wills, Gus Wedderburn, Clary Bayne, I, and other prime movers of the stat-up NBCC argued in favour of a reconstituted roundtable instead. And we were not stymied.

So, a steering committee was tasked to settle the NBCC debts and to call a national meeting to second a redrafted constitution and forward an executive. In synch with his surname, Head was again the "head." Bromley Armstrong pledged to beat the bushes of Bay Street, Queen's Park, and Parliament Hill to nail down funding. Doc Ralph James of Winnipeg and I would revise the constitution. Another Montréalais, Eric Mansfield, chose—bizarrely—to report on the working conditions of NBCC employees! (A pointless study, yes, but a good applause line.)

Soon, James bowed out; I'd rejig the constitution solo. I viewed the coalition as no more than a "paper tiger" (like NATO) because its reps were biz-card organizations with paltry memberships, if any, and a yen for dozing. Head and I upheld the model of the NAACP: a federation of chapters with individuals permitted direct membership in the national organization. I rewrote the NBCC constitution accordingly, grandfathering in affiliated bodies with compatible missions.

We met in Halifax in 1978 to reanimate the NBCC. No fistfights, few speeches. Doc Head got elected chair; I was veep. Black United Front of Nova Scotia honcho Hamid Rasheed slotted as second veep. Members-at-large were Delicia Crump (British Columbia), Jean Gammage (Ontario), Eric Mansfield (Quebec), and Wanda Thomas Bernard (Atlantic). (Appointed to the Senate of Canada in 2016, Dr. Bernard became the first Black woman to represent Nova Scotia in "the Red Chamber.") Al Mercury of Toronto took over as our new exec sec.

The parbuckled coalition was still a big ship—hard to steer—yet I prayed for smoother sailing. The Guardian Club, now the Windsor Chapter of the NBCC, not only paid its dues but lent the national organization five hundred dollars. In all, seven NBCC branches were formed in the first year of the "refloat," 1978–79. However, most affiliates remained glacially slow to forward tithes.

Luckily, the fundraising efforts of Mercury and Head bore good fruit. Dandy! But government dole-outs remained our life's blood.

So, April 27–29, 1979, revealed the gargantuan potential of the NBCC—as well as the real danger of fresh, fratricidal splintering. On that warm weekend in Toronto, at the posh King Eddy Hotel, a who's-who of Afro-Canuck politicos gathered to discuss "The Role of Blacks in Canadian Unity." Inspirational, it featured such delegates as Rocky Jones, Nova Scotia's grandiloquent radical who would soon contest (unsuccessfully) a provincial seat for the NDP; Rosemary Brown, who had all but creamed Ed Broadbent for the national NDP leadership in 1975 and who was a member of the British Columbia legislature; Lincoln Alexander, who was Canada's first (and, at that time, lone) Afro'd Member of Parliament, first elected in Hamilton Mountain, ON, in 1968 and soon to become the first Afro-Can federal minister (of Labour) in Joe Clark's short-lived, thirty-first Parliament; Jean Alfred, the Haitian member of Quebec's separatist Parti Québécois government (who shocked all by saying that he cared *nada* for Black equality struggle, only for Québec's "*libération*"); Emery Barnes, an-ex BC Lions football player, first elected to the BC legislature in 1972 (like Brown) and later to become, in 1994, the first African-Canadian Speaker of any Canadian legislature.

The speeches? Forceful; all "electable" ideologies present. Canada was in the midst of an election, and there was a sense that Prime Minister PET could lose to the "Red Tory" Clark. (Clark and I later became pals when he served in Prime Minister Brian Mulroney's cabinet as his Foreign Affairs minister.) We realized viscerally that weekend that blacks were vital to any consideration of Canadian unity, despite political differences, and that settler-decolonization and self-government for Indigenous Peoples were also *our* concerns.

Yep, that April weekend was exhilarating. Still, I had to treat a West Indian chap to an "*affaire d'honneur*" for alleging—divisively—that Black Canucks were all Uncle Toms and Oreos. (I prefer debate, but some loud mouths just seem to invite a fist.)

In 1980, two Windsor incidents illustrated the indisputable need for the NBCC. A Black single mom and her daughters had just moved into a rented house when it was spray-painted over with a hateful, black-letter, fungal spaghetti. They were forced to relocate. Later that summer, two Black youths were punched out by a Caucasian quartet in KKK T-shirts. Simultaneously, I spied the word "Nigger," disfiguring the windows of my own car.

In 1981, Mercury stepped down as exec sec, and Jesse Dillard, a "friendly giant" from BC (whose nickname could have been "Just Do It"—apologies to Nike), became the NBCC's manager. The NBCC was now, it seemed, the Voice of Black Canadians, among whom it had gained unprecedented support. However, too many folks still worried that NBCC meant Notorious Black Conspirators in Corruption.

As I recall, dissension centred around Mansfield of Montreal and Crump of the Coast; their egos seemed as supersized as Canada itself. Problematically, both pledged that they held vetoes over matters pertaining to their "regions."

Then, at a meeting in 1982, Mansfield's Anglo-Québécois bloc insisted on the unconstitutional "right" to block the NBCC membership bid of a Haitian immigrant affiliate. Worse: Wilson's placating of uncredentialed participants gave browbeating blowhards largesse to frustrate all.

Necessarily then, Doc Head and Doc McCurdy decamped, and Mansfield became prez, followed by Crump. Together, Tweedle Dee and Tweedle "Dumb" presided over the demise of the NBCC.

On a Monday morning in the fall of 1979, after returning from a disputatious meeting—no, a fracas—with the NBCC exec, I lamented the death rattles of "my baby." But lying before me was a *Windsor Star* article indicating that the deadline for filing nomination papers for Windsor City Council was at 5:00 P.M. that very day. Considering the opportunity that political office might present for advancing my beliefs, I decided whimsically to offer for public service—as had elder and earlier McCurdys. I expected to lose in 1979 but to succeed "next time."

I needed twelve signatures on the nomination form from residents of Ward 3, which houses Windsor's core Black community (where my electoral chances were best). After making a few calls, I collected the required signatures from ye olde Guardian Club stalwarts and other allies: Alton Parker, Bishop Arthur T. Harrison, Howard Olbey, Harry Morgan, and Rev. Mack Brown. Few liked my odds, but I got their "John Henrys" and got baptized a candidate.

True: I'd embarked upon seeking an employ for which I was a naive neophyte. So, I sought advice via a luncheon with city council dynamo Roy Battagello, flanked by Ron H. Wagenberg, a UW poli-sci wonk who had joined council in 1974. Neither thought I could win, so both ladled oodles of advice. I was a "dark horse" (I pun) that they wouldn't bet on but who they were leading to the race.

My first challenge? Find a campaign manager. After consulting many politicos, firefighter (and Windsor's first Afro-Can Fire Department Chief and later a school board trustee and city councillor in his own right) Ron Jones emerged as the outsized contender. He was eager to serve, although he admitted, sheepishly, "I have no idea what to do." "Fine," I shrugged. "Neither do I!"

"Reverend Ron" was also a most unconventional preacher at the Tanner AME church on McDougall (having succeeded the Rev. George Alger Coates). His vision of Jesus mimicked Pasolini's in *The Gospel According to St. Matthew*: a funky man of the cloth who ministered to the salt of the earth—the *sans-culottes* and the crooks-by-necessity—while castigating the swinish, hoggish, piggish fat cats and fat rats. Ron's church catered to once-broken people that Charity had healed and Courage was improving; he scoured skid row and red- light district to gather them into his Faith. Yet, his nat'chal charisma lacked any taint of megalomania. (He was Ron—not Jim—Jones.)

So, Rev. Ron was a perfect comptroller and cheerleader. Anchored in activism, he knew the Third Ward "Third World" inside-out—everyone's sins, talents, crimes, dreams, fears, and hopes. I glad-handed voters *partout*: bars, nightclubs, boxing matches, house parties, juke joints—you name it!

Still, the most meaningful alliances were with Alinsky-styled fire-brands such as Donna Gamble, the angel of the Downtown Community Citizens Organization. She'd spearheaded the establishment of the Glengarry Non-Profit Housing Development furnishing subsidized rental units. Although Donna would run against me in a subsequent election, we became friends and allies. Many of my campaign workers migrated my way from among her associates. (Although Gamble would resign in disgrace in 2001 after being charged with—*ahem*—"inadvertent gambling" with donated funds, she was an assertive spirit and herself served Ward 3 well as a city councillor, 1985–1997. Once she agreed to resign, the theft charge disappeared.)

Our committee room ("campaign headquarters" in Yankee) was located at a strategic site in a Wyandotte Street strip mall at the intersection with McDougall Avenue, next to the Windsor Arena. Our offices? An extension of The Rev's congregation: smokes, jokes, laughter, and cusses and prayers and bits of Top 40 pop, all interspersed with the blue-grey-purple haze of our atmosphere. In that space, lightning was a limerick and thunder was guffaws. Policing our joshing camaraderie and joyous proto-anarchy was Lana Talbot, supervising our supercharged office and working managerial miracles. Old chum Howard Olbey plus Eddie Hogan (a bleeding-heart Catholic who chaperoned a bullish, dictatorial dog named Zeus) and other NDPers—"Knee-Dippers"—wrangled our high-spirited, high-stepping voters to the polls come election day. Charlotte Perry, the widow of Roy (my erstwhile nemesis), stumped the western end of Wyandotte Street convincing virtually every shop to post my eye-battering, Day-Glo-orange signs in their windows. (Our campaign signs were such a garish orange that they heightened my visibility—at all hours. Rev. Ron chuckled: "They're awful looking, Howie. But you can see them bright as day at night, like jack-o'-lanterns!")

At the campaign's outset, W. D. Lowe High School hosted a jam-packed, all-candidates forum. All brouhaha and dogma. In my remarks, I deplored the boorish behaviour of some incumbents (they'd engaged in brawls, *par exemple*, in council chambers); I stressed the need for consultative and responsive representation. CBC-TV reporter Percy Hatfield (later, a good pal and, later, himself an elected MPP) posed a number of provocative questions (quite befitting an "army brat"), including this dilly: "What kind of car do you drive?" This was not a neutral question in a UAW hub like Windsor, where the make and model of a personal auto says as much about an owner as can their taste in beer. My answer? "My wife and I own both a Chrysler and a Mazda RX-7. But if Motown still built a sports car (like it used to), we wouldn't have had to buy the RX-7." Note, too, that 1979 was a time of stagflation, recession, OPEC boycott shocks, the looming Thatcherite, slash-and-burn Reaganomics, and thus images of laid-off Detroit autoworkers taking sledgehammers to better-built, cheaper-to-drive, Japanese-flagged, "foreign" cars. In visual terms, Hatfield's question appeared an innocent flame but one that could have blown apart my campaign.

My TV clips were ogled and smiled upon, thus furnishing that fine, campaign asset: name (and face) recognition. Often, the clip was playing in the background when a voter answered my knock. (Yep, the cosmos was orchestrating my election!) My chastisement of slovenly incumbents for acting like slug-fest combatants won mild rebuke in a letter from Alton Parker, who chided (I paraphrase), "Put your best foot forward; don't dwell on others' backward steps."

The most stunning reversal? After two decades of hostility, the *Windsor Star* fostered magnanimous coverage! A *Star* columnist, Alan Halberstadt, penned an ultra-praising and sympathetic piece.

As soon as our committee room opened, my old Amherstburg buddy Armando Deluca barged through the doors, Santa-like, and honoured us with a five-hundred-dollar cheque. The cash fattened our kitty nicely. The bonus? Armando was a major Progressive Conservative. His donation meant that I had appeal across party lines.

Even better, Armando introduced me to a charitable men's club associated with St. Angela Merici Church in Little Italy. The "alpha male" of the assembly—a *mensch* everyone seemed to know and to whom all accorded respect—was the *amorissimo*, Alfio Papa. A gilded Italo-Canuck, Alfio was rumoured, stereotypically, to be Mafia-affianced. Although I saw no evidence of any such association, Alfio was a cloak-and-wallet figure who never revealed where or when he was born. (So as to ward off anti-Italian and anti-immigrant hostility?) His vital stats didn't matter once one entered into his charismatic orbit, whose attractive force was one-part gregarious bonhomie and one-part awesome charity. Indeed, Alfio introduced me cheerfully all around and bade all to "check" my name on the ballot.

(Alfio's pull on the Italo vote propelled me onto Windsor City Council and then twice into the House of Commons: He was my personal "Rainmaker"! [I refer to the federal Liberal Party's moniker for their magic-producing campaign strategist fundraiser, Senator Keith Davey.] Alfio's mortal weakness? A bum ticker. Premature death got staved off only by a heart transplant from a lady donor. His female heart nixed Alfio's macho image, however, thus abetting much teasing, along such—aye, sexist—lines as, "Alfio used to pick Formula One races; now he picks brands of baby formula." Tragically, although his heart perils were resolved, Alfio perished in a car crash in Italy in 1992. He was an extraordinary friend, and I miss him deeply. My 1993 defeat in my third parliamentary campaign is due, in part, to Alfio's passing. Without his gift heart thumping loudly for my cause, the heart was gone from my own campaign. I can't say "*Ciao*" to him but only "*Arrivederci*, grand citizen, loyal brother.")

Although our campaign outperformed those of council incumbents, we suffered the pitfalls of inexperience. For instance, our campaign signs were first emblazoned, "Doctor Howard McCurdy for Alderman Ward 3." Thus, I had to explain that I knew a microscope better than a stethoscope—a "fault" that had some voters cantankerously dismissing me because I couldn't and wouldn't jot them a supply of pain-killing, mind-altering pharmaceuticals!

Soon, I was battering nearly every door, chatting up voters while handing out flashy Time-for-a-Change pamphlets. That message was a hit: two billboard signs got donated to my campaign.

Meanwhile, Donald "Don" Clarke, our targeted incumbent, the sitting— I said, "slumbering"—councillor, suddenly awoke to a fight. His local fame was due to his ability to extend the memory of one's name by chiselling it into granite. Yes, he was a solid-citizen tombstone fabricator but as politically mute as his erstwhile customers interred in Windsor Grove Cemetery. At campaign's end, we circulated the ward with an orange-placarded motorcade. Then, one car went for a joyride. When it was recovered, it was parked right in front of Don Clarke's "breathtaking" business. Yet, in this game of paper-scissors-stone, the paper (my signs) had wrapped up his "stones."

Election day! I expected merely to show. Reverend Ron joked that it would be nice for me to get the $18,000 stipend that councillors then received. It was a measure of my naivety that I was astonished to learn that I'd earn a paycheque for my council service!

On E-day a cadre of Knee-Dippers and union partisans materialized, headed by NDP organizer Tom Suffield, just twenty-four, a hustings egghead, bespectacled and jovial, spouting stats, yes, but also skilled in slapping backs and/or kicking butt. His team led our volunteers in "pulling the vote," that is, yanking passersby off the street and into polling booths or flushing our voters out of the Glengarry apartments, door by door and floor by floor, and frogmarching them to mark their ballots. On call? Battle stations of coffee, sandwiches, cigarettes, babysitters, and cabbies, whatever was necessary to ensure that "X" number of constituents marked the right "X" on an overwhelming "X" number of ballots.

Thus, the instant the polls closed, the media announced that I'd henceforth be Alderman (Doc) Howard McCurdy. I thought of grandfather George D. McCurdy, who'd got elected quadruply to Amherstburg's council; I thought of cousin Merle McCurdy, one-time appointee to Prez Kennedy and Prez Johnson. Now, here I was, maintaining this aspect of "our family business" but as a scientist become truly a *political* scientist." But I was also registering impassioned pride in all the people who'd laboured to wrest me this podium: Howard Olbey, Rev. Ron, my children, Charlotte Perry, Lana Talbot, Alfio Papa, Donna Gamble, Tom Suffield, and Armando Deluca—plus all those anonymous faces and hands—who'd collaborated to secure this coveted-by-many, unexpected-by-me electoral privilege. Our campaign was a bargain-basement version of Jimmy Carter's dark-horse prez bid in 1976: Hemingway populist, not Steinway elitist.

I basked in the winning news at Windsor City Hall where candidates, our partisans, and media pundits were gathered to tally the votes—and rally allies. (Cheers for victors; tears for the vanquished.) Soon, I heard Lloyd Brown-John—a U Windsor political scientist and talking head—prognosticate that my election would jeopardize re-elected alderman Ron Wagenberg's dominance as council's fiat intellectual. I thought the idea flattering but absurd. Yet, Wagenberg figured I was his rival and credited that his Steinway keyboard could outdo my Hemingway keyboard. Well, I'd not willingly let myself be bested.

Not only had my campaign upset—miraculously—an entrenched incumbent, we'd also helped defeat five others. Hell, one of those unseated was Roy Battagello, who floundered in the backwash of my criticisms of Don Clarke. But the sad fact was, his fists had sought to bruise the mortician pallor of Clarke's visage, who had answered with the muscles born of carving out gravestones. It was their unbecoming, council chamber altercation—their fisticuffs—that had knocked them down and out.

My flanking novice "aldermen" (as we were then called) quartet? Businessman Al Santing, lawyer Mike Ray, activist Peggy Simpson, and CBC broadcaster Elizabeth Kishkon. Surviving incumbents numbered teacher Tom Toth, ex-mayor Frank Wansbrough, accountant David Burr (son of former CCF MPP Fred Burr), teacher Peter MacKenzie, and Wagenberg.

As we huzza'd our David-versus-Goliath *victoire* in the besieged council chambers, Rev. Ron whispered, "There're two Eye-talian guys in the adjoining lobby who demand an immediate audience, Howie." Rev. Ron looked as worried as if the perceived "goodfellas" were freelancing exorcists out to pummel devils outta me. I surveilled 'em: two black suits, two black fedoras, two grim pairs of coal-black sunglasses! Could they be Mafiosi? Swiftly, I rebuked myself for even briefly conjuring the Italophobia. Still, I neared 'em with trepidation, until their dour demeanours brightened with patented *Blues Brothers* grins as they declared they were Italian Socialist Party members come to toast me with gift bottles of Prosecco!

Celebrations done, the work beckoned. I knew nothing—or not enough to be the effective councillor I was determined to be. Therefore, I interviewed systematically the senior managers of each city department to understand their duties. (I was guided by my knowledge that rookie prime minister PET had undertaken a similar review of the federal bureaucracy.) How startling to learn that I was the first newbie alderman ever to do so!

"Welcome to the 1980s," said PET on the February night of his takedown of Joe Clark's Tories in the election campaign that sprang up with the sudden demise, on December 13, 1979, of Clark's shaky parliament. I felt a renewal of my own fortunes as I revelled in the fresh council's inauguration in January 1980. An open reception chased the ceremony. (At that *fête*, a grey-beard drew nigh to ask if I remembered him. Well, my faulty memory plagued me throughout my legislative days, so no, I couldn't place his mug. But he was "sure" I'd recall an accident nigh thirty years back on old Highway 2, for he was the drunk who'd sideswiped my dad's car that night so long ago when I was also driving—yep, while intoxicated—from the Walls' farm en route to Detroit! Luckily, we'd both dodged the morgue, the hospital, and the courts!)

My first duty as a tyro councillor was to decide the municipal budget, an excruciating process. The city's capital needs were endless, but interest rates would surge past 20 percent by 1982, so borrowing was no answer. A double whammy: auto workers were facing a financial squeeze, making property tax hikes impossible. Yet, the city's sewage system stank—in every sense—and was a suite of miasmic ponds at peril of becoming public cesspools. Roads were potholes or sinkholes or disrupted by rail crossings that were excellent sites for car-smashing train collisions. ("Collateral damage"? Pedestrians.) Somehow, we lopped the capital works budget by almost 60 percent.

I saw clearly that Windsor had to diversify its economic base so as not to be totally tied to the roller-coaster fortunes of the auto industry. Yet no one had forwarded any systematic approach to developing or attracting any other industries or small businesses.

Al Santing was a small-biz guy, which was fine, but also small-minded, which was not. His free-enterprise outlook spewed contempt for those he'd label "ivory tower pinkos." He'd ridicule any proposal leveraging the people's money to improve public assets or services but almost never posit ideas to grow investments and jobs. His most significant initiative was to promote pay freezes for councillors. But how would rejecting a pay raise for councillors increase the local jobs available? To heed his logic, one would have to abolish government altogether, a plan that would only benefit despots and their plutocratic cheerleaders.

Nominal allies? Pete MacKenzie (who served one term with me, 1979–82), Dave Burr, Liz Kishkon, and Peggy Simpson: *quatre* Knee-Dippers. Grits? Wagenberg, Mike Ray, Tom Toth. Only Wansbrough, a travel agent and likeable ex-mayor, defied categorization beyond being a good ole boy who never said a bad word 'bout anyone. (Good at glad-handing, not stick-handling.) CBC pundit Liz was a part of my old social circle that had smiled upon Bert Weeks. Mike and I were council seatmates, not political soulmates. Still, he, I, Burr, and then Cassivi would lift our glasses bottoms-up (after council sessions) at the Windsor Press Club: a civics-course-level "Gang of Four."

One memorable experience with Mike? In the VIP area at the Renaissance Centre during the first Detroit Grand Prix (F1) in 1982, within hearing distance of Mike and me, two men were hogging a table of hors d'oeuvres, noshing on the savoury snacks, while one was gesticulating with piled-high cracker and chewing out Canada's political system between chomps of the brandished fare. His remarks were Reaganite hooey, and so I gave an unsolicited rebuttal, channelling Jonathan Swift: "If you think Canadian democracy is so bothersome, why don't you send in the Marines? They'd do a bang-up job, eh? Consider Vietnam!" The poster-boy crypto-fascist purpled and almost choked on his gobble. I smiled, loped off. But Mike was beside himself: "Are you nuts, McCurdy? Do you have any idea who that turkey is? That's Henry Ford II!" (I was nonplussed by that knowledge. I remember that his pops, "HF1," was so anti-Semitic that Hitler's Reich presented him its highest honour for non-Germans: the Grand Cross of the German Eagle. "HF2" was, perhaps then, tacitly anti-democratic himself.)

Mayor Albert H. Weeks was a veteran of the CCF, the New Party Club, and the NDP, but he was a jeweller by trade and so was suspicious of expenditure and preferred to create parks, not controversy. Thus, his heart was in the "right" place—on the "left," metaphysically as well as physically—and he'd backed both the humanitarian and egalitarian Unitarian Fellowship and the anti-racism of the Guardian Club. He'd cornered the mayor's chair in 1974 due to a decades-long anti-corruption drive (which even saw him dine with Detroit gangsters so he could ID Windsor's sleaziest Stasi). I knew his virtues; thus, I laced up my boots and slogged through a blizzard to rouse his voters, on E-day, and cart 'em to the polls. Bert extolled my virtues when he ensured my seat on the St. Clair College BOG and my receipt of the Centennial Medal.

As mayor and thus a member of the Police Services Commission, Weeks had also been a major assist in a run-in I had with two Windsor boys-in-blue in 1978. Just the details? Hell, as I exited the Art Gallery of Windsor parking lot one evening, I turned east from Church onto Riverside, proceeding through the intersection at the behest of a green light. As I executed that legal right turn, I observed an eastbound prowl car still stopped in compliance to its facing red signal. I observed the speed limit scrupulously as I continued eastbound on Riverside Drive West. Even so, once the cruiser had the green light, it was instantly on my tail. Thus, upon approaching the Goyeau Street intersection, I was careful not to entertain the yellow caution signal and braked. When I did so, the patrol car breathing down my bumper got forced to a screeching, lurching halt. Its roof lights strobed and a door disgorged a purple-faced officer into the blue-and-red-tinted dusk.

The zwieback first questioned my ownership of my, yes, snazzy auto, then wanted my name. I replied authoritatively: "*Doctor* Howard McCurdy" (placing emphasis just so).

The paleface spoke with vulgar informality: "Well, Howard, you went through a red light."

"I certainly did not!"

"Shut up, Howard! Pull over onto Goyeau!"

After I had done so and repeated my spurning of the spurious allegation, he launched into a tirade about "you people" and how "sick and tired" he was of "dealing" with us. I was accorded tickets for failing to stop at a red light, not having my insurance papers available, and for failing to wear a seatbelt. I phoned Mayor Weeks and told him of the incident. He saw two charges dropped at once. The copper had pegged me as failing to stop at Ferry Street, a location well short of Goyeau, so the citation was incorrect. The insurance charge was cancelled as soon as I produced proof of my coverage. That left the seatbelt infraction. By producing photos of my Mazda RX7, I proved in Traffic Court that no officer could possibly have seen whether I was wearing a seatbelt while driving or not. My cross-examination left the badged witness blue in the face and seeing red, but the judge shortly dismissed the supposed seatbelt violation as well.

Though Bert and I had a two-decade-long friendship, our relations soon became testy, for his go-slow instincts were irritated by my activism. Our clash arose due to a blue-clad cop versus Black citizen strife. The cause? A Black Windsorite, Charlotte Berry, reported that a constable suggested she move from her neighbourhood in response to her complaint about racist harassment, which included the spray-painted graffiti of the letters "KKK" upon her door. The then-prez of the Windsor NBCC chapter, Phil Alexander, upheld Berry's concern about the nonchalant and insulting gendarme dismissal of the implicit threat of the visual vandalism, but Chief Jack Shuttleworth, an ex-detective, seemed just as devil-may-care as had been his underling.

I pursued the case, and council agreed that Shuttleworth's inaction equalled a dereliction of duty. Summoned to council to explain himself, Shuttleworth blustered; I rebutted; he bullied; I blunted. Then, I stoked his ire by advising that Windsor create a civilian-led police complaints review board. I'd hoped that Bert would be "in my corner," but he'd not antagonize Windsor's top cop. Thus, I became a target of incessant jack-boot pestering during my tenure as a councillor. (Yep, cops were always underfoot. Truly irritating were the parking tickets that I was sure to attract if I stopped at the Nut House at 419 Ouellette, just a pit-stop to pick up my weekly ration of fresh-cooked peanuts, smoked cashews, and popcorn balls. Such badgering was, yes, a nuisance. But, when public servants conduct private vendettas, an abuse of power—in other words, corruption—is in progress. Recall Hoover versus King; Nixon versus his "enemies.")

Another worry plaguing Black Windsorites soon confronted council. Edmund "Ted" Powell petitioned to shift the annual Emancipation Celebration from Mic Mac Park to its historical venue at Jackson Park. Though Ted could too often allege discrimination if he failed to get his way, he deserved much credit for trying to maintain "The Greatest Freedom Show on Earth"—the Emancipation Celebration—fostered by Walter Perry, which had died with him (amid the smouldering ruins of the Detroit Riot) in 1967 but that Ted revived in 1969 (and kept up until 1983, though never at the monumental scale and supreme heights that Perry achieved).

By then, the city had cast Jackson as a passive park (for gardens) and Mic Mac as an active park (for sports). For that reason, some councillors opposed Ted. However, thanks to a powerful submission from Rev. Ron, plus my own sympathy and motion in Ted's favour, most of council sided with me but also stated that no admission be charged for entry to the grounds.

So, Ted got his wish: the show got transferred to Jackson Park. Hoorah! When I attended the event, however, I saw that Ted was blithely, unscrupulously charging admission. Not only had he betrayed the letter of my motion, he'd also impaired my reputation as a no-BS councillor. I confronted Ted: "You're now *persona non grata*. You've slit your own throat! You're finished!"

Another matter offensive to Windsor's Black community were reports that the relatives of (Caucasian) firemen and policemen were fast-tracked for municipal jobs. This ensured that Black taxpayers would seldom be able to contend fairly for city-paid jobs. I therefore proposed, successfully, a new anti-nepotism bylaw that imposed a reporting requirement and council approval for the hiring of relatives, in restricted circumstances.

Early on, I felt compelled to expand comforts for Windsor rest-home residents. Their status was dire because the province had deinstitution-alized many individuals, thus dumping patients onto the streets, where they became the new homeless. Some took shelter in private rest homes or in lodging houses, many of these deplorably slummy. To remedy the mess, Dave "Cookie" Cooke, a local MPP (NDP), asked that Ontario pass legislation to regulate rest homes, but the Davis Government showed off its spats and cravats by saying, *Hell, no!* Council drafted its own regulations in 1981, but our bylaw was nullified as ultra vires, outside our purview.

Due to the complaints I received, I assessed several rest homes and catalogued tenants enduring conditions not dissimilar to refugee camps. Rest-home operators had hotlines to morticians, representing profit, but not doctors, representing healing. Advocating for municipal regulation, I suggested several provisions that got incorporated into a new bylaw, which was then submitted to the province for constitutional review and passed, with modifications, to become law in fall 1983. We sought to rectify deficiencies while dividing lodging homes into a two-tier system, so that residents requiring medical care could get it. Provincial law was abysmal. But we did what we could.

Early in 1982, the *Windsor Star* printed an article suite entitled, "Windsor at the Crossroads." The writers analyzed the city's economic and image problems. Windsor was a one-industry town, but auto-making was a wobbly crutch. Negativity and self-deprecation were so engrained that our malaise got dubbed "the Windsor Syndrome." Windsor was based on a dinosaur industry only possible due to fossil fuels that were themselves the result of extinction events eons ago. Worse, the Development Commission had plenty of hindsight about the smokestack past but little insight about what should come next, and it was as destitute of funds as it was impoverished in vision.

Prodded by the provocative *Star* pieces, Santing, with typical ideological breast-beating, blamed Windsor's stagnation on council's "left wingers," in other words, anyone who drove a Volvo, dialed up jazz, or went barefoot in sandals. Somehow, "eggheads" had convinced enterprise capitalists to sock away cash in high-return investments rather than in risky manufacturing ventures. Yet the era of the gas-guzzler was as dead as were dodos. Motown would have had just as much luck in getting folks back into uneconomical cars as the horse-and-buggy-trade had had in keeping them out of cars in the first place. Yet, chasing Santing's rant, there was, well, tongue-wagging Wagenberg validating—inadvertently—Santing's pejoratives by inking a non sequitur squib against "rapid growth." If one essay was more an irritant than a pollutant, the other was more a pollutant than an irritant.

I knew how other cities had dealt with parasitic suburbanites bleeding downtowns and draining residential services while reserving their tax payments for their plush districts; how deindustrialization entailed loss of lunch-bucket jobs; and how decrepit infrastructure backed by a disappearing tax-base was a recipe only for graveyard expansion. So, I persuaded council to establish a "Committee of 100," composed of visionary entrepreneurs, avant-garde artists, and community-engaged educators, to remake Windsor's image *and* reimagine its economy. It got traction.

Indeed, the *Windsor Star* even published an article recounting the success of just such a group in Tampa Bay, Florida. (Citizen-action-oriented "Committees of 100" have been instruments of citizen-government engagement in many jurisdictions, including Hartford, CT, where such a group preserves and upkeeps a city park.)

However, Liz Kishkon pushed a Town Hall meet as the means to launch a Windsor renaissance. The media loved it; I favoured it; Mayor Weeks yawned. (He was so tired as to be retired!)

Two meetings—public-relations "biggies"—transpired. Fifteen hundred souls braved the cold, wintry blasts off the Detroit River to twice fill Cleary Auditorium to voice dozens of ideas, some practical, some fanciful, some déjà vu (that is, proven failures). Others? Yep, dumb.

Now, council assigned every idea "democratically" to pertinent agencies and bureaucrats, sans any prioritization. A supposed sect of blue-sky dreamers gave way to an anarchic, shambolic orchestra, vaunting equally every conceptual "white elephant" and every financial "black hole." I argued *again* that a Committee of 100 could sift the Town Hall–spawned ideas, discard the unfeasible, and advance those that would profit development.

Then, Wagenberg wagered on kiddy name-calling: my idea was "idiotic," I an "insufferable ass"—*and* procedurally "incorrect." Kishkon quit the session huffily. Only briefly our meeting's chair, Dave Burr, endured unfair *Windsor Star* critique for letting Wagenberg *and me* indulge hissy fits. Burr corrected the paper: only Wagenberg's behaviour was disorderly. (I'll say *disgraceful*.)

Next, Wagenberg floated a "Windsor 2000 Committee." (Yes, my "Committeee of 100" idea by a different name). Kishkon aired her variation: an "Attitude and Promotion Committee"! Then, *Windsor Star* columnist Al Halberstadt reasoned that Mayor Weeks should strike a "Group of Creativity." Apparently, my idea could not gain favour so long as it bore my imprint. (Due to unconscious racism or conscious envy?)

Next, I sought to sell the idea via closed-door meetings (including one in my own home) to community leaders. My aim was not secrecy but privacy (a prerequisite for some participants). Regrettably, I agreed to ask Halberstadt to an off-the-record tête-à-tête. But Halberstadt blabbed about all in the *Star*. Thus, convivial chats among prominent persons of polar political hues were now scuttled as folks defaulted to adversarial positions. Worse, I was now compromised: I was either too sly for my own good, or not sly enough to do any good.

Bottom line: the "Committee of 100" idea died. (Developer Chuck Mady did attempt to form a similar body, but, again, that effort was in vain.)

An association with Glenn Dennis (entrepreneur) and his son Gene C. (a financier) permitted me a platform to call anew for strategic planning. Leaders in the plastic mold industry, they wished to exploit computer-augmented design and manufacture (CADAM) for the enterprise, but it turned out that Windsor lacked skilled workers. Indeed, neither the University of Windsor nor St. Clair College listed CADAM training. Astoundingly, despite their location in Canada's Motor City, neither institution listed courses in automotive engineering!

Thus, I sought the unprecedented privilege to make a personal pitch to council on the theme. The *Windsor Star* reprinted my entire speech. Now, manufacturers and educators would mobilize. At long last, the Development Commission formed a strategic development subcommittee, for which I later obtained a $250,000 federal drawdown. Windsor's future was finally worthy of strategic forecast and thoughtful investment. Or so it seemed.

Come January 1982, speculation began to mount about Windsor's "next" mayor. Halberstadt kicked off the guessing in a column bristling with *ad hominem* barbs. Counting Mayor Weeks out, he considered the chances of Santing, Kishkon, Wagenberg, and me.

I had zero interest in the mayoralty, but that did not stop Halberstadt from suggesting that I use a 1982–83 sabbatical to reflect on how my "arrogance" alienated allies. Simultaneously, Halberstadt promoted my now rival, "Rev. Ron" Jones, as a council candidate. I suspected that Halberstadt was leveraging Ron to get back at me—and to hope that white Windsor voters would reject the potential presence of two Blacks on council as a case of "two too many." Next, the "ink-stained wretch" (to wax poetic) accused me of "stealing" the Committee of 100 notion from Mike Ray! (Wrong!) Yet, Halberstadt also injured Wagenberg, who, he opined, had been overshadowed by other councillors. Still, Kishkon was Al's pick, for she was a natchal-bo'n politico and "sincere," albeit with an ego, an attribute which Halberstadt fancied as *de rigueur*—in her case. (The "stoopidest" charge against politicos is that we are "vain" or "egotistical." Geez! One *must* possess a quantum of self-worth to put oneself forward for public attention, adulation, critique, chastisement—and all to benefit the public!)

In the end, Docs Kishkon and Wagenberg contested the mayoralty. Given that "K-W" were "very close" friends (as journalists, winking, stated), that is, perhaps just as close as Kitchener-Waterloo, the campaign was textbook-case bizarre. Fought with kid gloves (suiting hugs, not hits), Kishkon won. She was now the Queen and Wagenberg was Prince Philip (metaphorically). Too, Kishkon had attracted strong NDP backing; her triumph rendered Wagenberg a political castrato. Their pillow talk (if any) must've involved Ping-Ponged, heart-throbbing apologies.

I expected re-election to be an uphill battle. I faced formidable candidates in Ward 3—two ex-mayors, my friend Donna Gamble, and seven other contenders. Worse, a contentious bugaboo threatened my seat. I'd voted to close alleys in parts of Ward 3 because they were costly to maintain and hindered garbage pickup. Although homeowners would acquire the right-of-ways and could incorporate them into their properties, the measure sired street protests! (A case of Not-In-My-Backyard-ism—even if my backyard will be legally extended thus enhancing my property!)

Yes, I exchanged bruises and lumps! But I beamed and trumped, winning back my seat by six hundred votes. I felt as ecstatic as I had in my track-and-field *victoires*!

Five new councillors were seated: Martin "Marty" Goldberg, Edwin "Ted" Bounsall, John Millson (a future mayor), Tom Porter, and Dave Cassivi. Peter MacKenzie retired. Defeated incumbents? Frank Wansbrough and Peggy Simpson.

Marty Goldberg's affiliations were as unsettled as his positions would turn out to be. He relished glad-hand photo-ops but disdained hand-to-hand combat to back a policy. Ted and Dave were stalwart New Dems; Tom was a Bill Davis Red Tory (shy about social muddles, bullish on business). Having no open affiliation, Millson was likely a "Trojan Horse" Grit.

Although Windsor City Council was static in terms of party lines, partisans morphed into fanatics. Committee appointments? Grudge matches! The "Glib"/"Con" majority rejected nominees forwarded by the socialist bloc—me, Cassivi, Bounsall, Burr.

The first test of my second term was the deathless quandary of taxi licences. We'd limited taxi licences available to two hundred. Before that imposition, anyone could get a licence just by applying at the city clerk's office. Now, the cap triggered an explosive inflation in the price of a licence from $400 to $4,000, while the number of hacks shot up to the 200-cab limit from about 170.

What we'd asininely created was a de facto monopoly in the taxi industry, for only bigwigs could afford to buy up the now prohibitively expensive licences—and bargain for reasonable fleet insurance rates.

Yet, hack operators are notoriously independent-minded, opinionated, and as tough as truckers, while also being, yep, public servants, as gold-hearted as social workers. They are an odd posse to wrangle; yet, several drivers asked me to oppose the monopolistic consolidation. Clandestine were our confidences. Indeed, violent retaliation was not hypothetical: I picked up notes left under my windshield wipers, warning I'd be "wiped out." (Behold "Anonymous" the punster!)

Urgent pleas arose from Brandi's Taxis, whose owner said that the licence freeze had cut down her fleet. To obtain cheaper insurance, she'd had to sign over to Bill Oag of Veteran Taxicabs her car ownerships and safety certificates, required to acquire licences. Instantly, Oag held a gross advantage over any start-up taxi firm. He be the King of the Cabs, the Pharaoh of the Fare! His one rival was Capital, which was as close to his firm as Kishkon was (ahem) to Wagenberg.

Windsor's cab biz was a cartel, a classic duopoly: prices soar, service deteriorates. (See Canada's telecom giants today. They need to be either broken up or vehemently regulated.) Soon, the school board warned that its student transpo costs were escalating because it could not consider a host of bids. Citizens declared Windsor hacks dirty and dangerous, and drivers discourteous.

As chair of the Licensing Committee, I moved to lift the taxi-licence freeze at a council session that became a roller-derby melee due to a shoving, shouting clutch of boisterous drivers who had shown up to defend the duopoly. Now, Brandi blindsided me by rescinding her objections (to the cheers of the "hackers"); then I was betrayed by that dependably fickle councillor, Goldberg.

My next tactic? To get the Licensing Committee to adopt a bylaw that imposed new regulations for taxi safety, driver qualification and identification, cabin cleanliness, effective roadworthiness, and meter integrity (many were tampered with, so as to double the fare). The duopoly survived, but we forced "Oag & Co." to abide regulation rather than remain sketchy firms fielding dodgy drivers.

Once elected to council, I resigned from the Windsor Chapter of the NBCC. "Rev. Ron" took over as prez. During his tenure, the Windsor Interracial Alliance was conjured to represent a wider constituency of minority groups. Lawyer Micheline A. Rawlins (now the Hon. Micheline A. Rawlins, having been appointed to the Ontario Court of Justice in 1992, becoming the first Black woman to be assigned that post) assumed the presidency, but thereafter, the organization just seemed to vaporize into (I imagined) stacks of unused letterhead alongside columns of unstuffed envelopes. My wife, Brenda, was elected prez of the Windsor Black Coalition upon Ron's exit. She served one term, then Clayton Talbert Sr. took the helm.

With the revival of the NBCC, I again laced the heavens with contrails, jetting to Toronto, London (ON), Hamilton, Ottawa, Montreal, Winnipeg, and Halifax. These Coalition-spawned speeches called on the Black community to solve our problems ourselves. Education was the linchpin. I pushed activists to steer Black youth from careers as teachers, clergy, and social workers, to choose to be engineers, scientists, tech wizzes, and algebra gurus. (Note: this was the successful playbook of Québec's Révolution tranquille, 1960–76.)

In 1983, for the inaugural Harry Jerome Awards dinner (the awards recognize excellence in African Canadian achievement), sponsored by the Toronto Black Business and Professional Association, I joined a century of guests tippling cocktails. We were then ushered into the banquet hall where I was shocked to see two thousand seated. A gala audience! I was relieved that I'd not have to speak. I relaxed, nursed my Negroni, and chatted up the Nollywood-gorgeous sis of Harry Jerome, the African-Canadian Olympian after whom the awards are named. Soon, I sat at the head table with Af-Can track-and-field royalty: Desai Williams, Ben Johnson, Tony Sharpe, Mark McKoy, Angela Taylor (later Issajenko), and Milt Ottey. Glad I was to chat with such august athletes—and pleased to have no cause for, well, "performance anxiety."

Quickly, a fellow diner dispelled my laid-back state. My name would be called. I would have to orate—*now*—sans notes. Extemporaneously! As I made my way to the lectern, trying to conjure oratory *ex nihilo*, I was inspired by the sight of Ottey, the high-jumper, and I recalled the ecstasy of clearing the bar. I knew that I could tell the four thousand ears before me that we can all experience masterful ascension, transcendent triumph. We can all reach the stratospheric realm of excellence *if* we improve upon innate talent and intelligence by applying discipline and know-how.

When I surrendered the podium, a maelstrom of applause—thunderous, all-encompassing, and sustained—swallowed me whole. Afterward, a tri-level who's who of Hogtown politicos lined up to salute what many said was the best speech covering (race) phobias versus opportunity they'd ever heard. These seasoned politicians suggested that I move up from Windsor City Council. (A decade later, I took home a Harry Jerome Award.)

Appearing before the Ukrainian Youth Association of Canada (CYM Canada) in Winnipeg, I gave another tempestuously welcomed peroration. In preparation, I'd sought the advice of my Ukrainian friend Valerie Kasurak, who had informed me of the bond between the Ukrainian bard Taras Shevchenko and the classic, Victorian-era, African-American actor Ira Aldridge. Armed with a phonetic version of a Shevchenko verse, I praised their common interest in liberation. Exuberant jubilee was the CYM reaction! I was hoisted on the broad shoulders of two burly *gars* and jigged about the hall to the contradictorily jumpy and sultry cadences of polka music. My speech even captivated the stodgy elders who had looked at me so warily at first, wondering what I could say to charm their ears. Now, they too were lustily applauding. A new career beckoned!

CHAPTER FOURTEEN:
LANDING IN PARLIAMENT

FOLLOWING MY MUNICIPAL RE-ELECTION, NEW DEMOCRATIC partisans (who'd helped to pinpoint my voters and push 'em to the polls) bade me recommit to the party. Unto the Windsor-Walkerville Riding Association I affianced. Fast, I detected it was so rigid with rectitude, it was frigid with lassitude. Strikingly alive, in contrast, was the Windsor-Riverside Riding Association, which had raucously rocketed both Fred Burr then Dave Cooke to the provincial parliament in Toronto.

By 1983, all knew that the tired Trudeau Grits would soon face an electorate sick of constitutional wrangling, angry over sky-high interest rates hammering down households, and fed up with PET himself, who'd slid from being Canada's "Fifth Beatle"—all sandal'd philosophy—to being Duplessis redux, doling out patronage with shameless alacrity. Even if PET resigned, pundits enthused, the Ottawa Liberals faced defeat. Though I'd no plans to run, my local high profile stimulated the Riverside NDP, or Knee-Dippers, to seek my candidacy. Who couldn't smell Grit blood in the air?

The impressive prez of CAW Local 444, Ken Gerard, squired me to a luncheon. Over steak, ale, and cigarettes, Ken and other union chiefs pressed me to run federally.

The decision of Mark MacGuigan, Liberal MP for Windsor-Walkerville, to leave politics made the prospect of our ascendency irresistible. I called a news conference to declare I'd run. That prompted David Burr—my council colleague and son of the ex-MPP—to rush the mics to say that he wished to be Windsor-Walkerville's "man" in Ottawa, "The Big Zero."

Soon, Dave Cooke disciples such as Beverley Jeannette Wood furnished me with membership rolls and key contacts. I dialled everyone on her list and quickly enlisted ready enthusiasts. Meanwhile, as pledged, Labour mobilized too.

Three hundred militants packed the nomination meeting held in the Croatian Centre. My supporters? Innumerable, deafening, energized activists. James Brown's hit "I Feel Good" was an inaudible earworm moving groovy inside my skull!

Dave Cassivi and Donna Beneteau Crowell moved my election. "Pops" Burr's nomination of "Baby" Burr accented the notion that the son was his daddy's li'l lapdog. Unhelpful, too, was his mom's supermarket-tabloid-like description of him as a "little bull."

Although the actual ballot count was never released, my numbers were indomitable. "Baby" Burr was gracious in defeat, moving unanimity and pledging his backing—a promise he kept.

Having already assembled my campaign team, I was "cool, calm, collected" when the serving "Gritty" Prime Minister John Turner called an election for September 4, 1984. Ron Varley was my campaign manager; Bev Wood, office manager; and Joe Comartin, treasurer. Experienced, union-financed, CAW-trained campaign "sweat hogs" were seconded to my electoral effort. We fielded over two hundred volunteers, numbering unionists, Knee-Dippers, long-time comrades, and activist allies. The wind at my back? Fireworks! A thunderous rainbow coalition!

The *Windsor Star* chastised me as "pompous and arrogant" yet also held that I was "sharp-tongued and articulate." The broadsheet even stated that I flouted stereotypes (see Craig Baird, canadaehx.com/2022/05/17/howard-mccurdy). *Quel surpris!*

My opponents: Tom Porter (my capable council colleague) for the Tories and Terry Patterson for the Grits. (A self-defeating lawyer, Patterson cast himself as a "sacrificial lamb.")

Seasoned electioneers Steven W. Langdon and Paul Forder were the Knee-Dippers contesting Windsor Essex and Windsor West, respectively. A CAW honcho and ex-boxer, Forder had run against Herb Gray in 1972 and had made it a contest, not another Herb cakewalk. Unlike Langdon, he was a Windsorite, born to tool the line at Chrysler.

An ex-Waffle (that is, anti-US Knee-Dipper) outta the University of Toronto and Carleton University, Langdon had battled the ballot-topping Gene Whelan in 1979 and 1980 after having sought a seat twice before in "Otter-wah." Whelan had retired right alongside Papa Trudeau, so economist Langdon faced only one true adversary—Ray Robinet, a Tecumseh councillor.

As the Liberal vote evaporated due to leader Turner's boardroom-dyslexic garble and locker-room mania for patting ladies' tushies (and also due to Trudeau's *"Après moi, le deluge,"* devil-take-y'all shrug), the Windsor area looked ripe for a New Democrat sweep. Hence, respected *Globe and Mail* columnist Jeffrey Simpson cited my academic and activist credentials as advantages, and that urged other reporters to hound me for face time and sound bites.

Plant-gating and door-knocking was a daily sprint undertaken so I could canvass the entire riding in a campaign-long marathon. The routine was 9:00 A.M. door-knocking—or 5:00 A.M. factory-gating—straight to a lunch at about 1:00 P.M., and then persisting until nightfall. Some days, there was no break at all, for Ron was—*ahem*—a slave driver: to show constituents that you'll toil for their interests, ya gotta toil for their votes. When not canvassing, I'd meet voters at our committee room. (Once, Ron interrupted a precious nap, calling me back to our office to curry favour with two sisters who would not meet me elsewhere. Why? The RCMP had planted "bugs" in their yard to eavesdrop on their chit-chat— and that of chirping birds and buzzing bees!)

Canvassing started as a solo do; then, unaffiliated "Reds" or NDP pinkos traipsed alongside. Other company? Dr. Mrs. McCurdy, or my daughters, and friends such as the Walls (Brian, Al, or Winston). Despite my smoker's wheeze, I was an ex–track star, and none could match my pace! Once, Brenda and I trekked door-to-door for three hours in searing, 103°F heat and then joined a broiling partisan barbie. As "Hot Hot Hot" as Arrow's song! (Note: Not once was a door closed in my face; not once did my hand go unshaken. My "race" never came up, not even in Tecumseh where I'd not been welcome as a teen. But Windsor-Walkerville had been a Grit safe seat; thus, some voters eyed leftist *moi* skeptically.)

NDP leader Ed Broadbent jetted to Windsor early on, and Brenda and I hosted a wine-and-cheese "bread-raiser" in his honour. We collected humongous dough for the federal chief, and the subsequent rally at Local 444 was as booming and as beatific as any Pentecostal assembly.

Now, I met my co-campaigners. Forder was bullish, ebullient, and a bullhorn orator—a union dude through and through. Langdon's voice

The McCurdys proving irresistible as they campaign door-to-door during the run-up to the 1984 federal election.

affliction strained every word his lungs vented; still, he conveyed Yeatsian "passionate intensity."

We exhibited solidarity at plant gates, all-candidates gatherings, and press conferences. Yet, Langdon's team projected—to my ears—a leftover Waffle self-righteousness that urged overly aggressive postures.

One example of effective collaboration? A press conference to back female bar and restaurant servers. They complained about being exorbitantly taxed, based on an *estimate* of their tip income. Our candidate trio assailed the measure as egregiously unfair. Thanks to our public stance against this assault on students, single moms, and part-time or second household-income-earners, Revenue Canada had to end at once its greedy, piratic actions. Even stone-hearted Tories applauded our stance in favour of workers, not government coffers.

In the all-candidates debates, my expertise at oratory allowed me a healthy edge. While Ron Varley, et al., were optimistic regarding "our" chances, the E-day polls were close. So, I was banned from our premises to spend the day running voters to the urns.

Once polls closed at 8:00 P.M., I returned to HQ to find that everyone had gone to the Croatian Centre to await the results. News reports from Atlantic Canada (an hour ahead of us) indicated a probable landslide for Brian Mulroney's Tories. That forecast a higher-than-usual Tory vote in my riding, but who would gain Grit votes? Me or my PC rival, Porter?

Once more into the breach! House of Commons Campaign Number One commences, July 1984, with all hands on deck—and cigarettes close at hand!

Soon I was summoned to the Croatian edifice. En route, I took a call saying that Porter had pulled ahead. Uh oh! No! It was a glitch, a fluke. In a tight three-way race, I took the riding by six hundred votes over Porter. I was now Dr. Howard D. McCurdy, PhD, MP!

Thus, I became the first New Democrat to be federally elected in Windsor *and* the first descendant of the Underground Railroad, fugitive ex-slaves to sit in the Parliament of Canada. (Due to my four degrees— BA, BSc, MSc, PhD—I was also the best-educated MP! And I was only the second Black Member of Parliament, following Lincoln Alexander, who served from 1968 to 1984.)

Langdon captured the seat he had so long coveted, but Forder was not so fortunate against formidable Herb Gray. In Essex-Kent, Jim Caldwell (an ex–CBC commentator) got the nod for the Conservatives, contributing to their massive coup and the Grit rout. (Of 282 seats available in the 33rd Parliament, the Tories now occupied 211.)

Ecstasy resounded wall-to-wall-to-wall-to-wall through the packed Croatian (soccer-game-viewing-oriented) hall. We smoked up, drank up—both there and afterwards at my home—until dawn, then sleepless, with steady hangovers, staggered about, dizzied by salvaging our election signs.

Exhausted, Brenda and I ventured, for R and R, to Toronto where we watched the Detroit Tigers clinch the American League title versus the Blue Jays. We next flew to Calgary, transited to Banff, and then took the scenic train route through the mountains to Vancouver. Every vista was spectacular—for either naked eye or binoculars. Next stop: Vancouver Island, where we sightsaw, golfed, and hobnobbed with ex-NBCC exec sec Jesse Dillard.

My premiere visit to Parliament Hill occurred during the Queen's Canadian tour that year. Although it was only late September, "The Big (Sub-) Zero"—Ottawa—was already frigid, keeping its record as the world's second-coldest national capital (after Ulan Bator, Mongolia). So rather than freezing outside, I watched from a Centre Block window as "Her" carriage drew up to elaborate fanfare: Mounties, top hats, top brass, tails, fascinator hats, cannonade salutes, gilded this, and silver that.

The lone Knee-Dipper about was Neil Young, the MP for Toronto's Beaches. Neil was quite the informative docent as he escorted me about the Centre Block and helped me select the office that I would occupy during my entire first-term tenure.

We also sipped Scotch with a Tory MP, thus introducing me to the collegiality that softened and blurred party lines. With his Scottish burr and dry humour, Neil would prove one of the most easygoing of my caucus mates.

How awestruck I was to shake hands with Lincoln Alexander, the first, the only, and now the previous Black Member of Parliament, bigger than life—his stance enhanced by his huge smile! (In his youth, Linc was a friend of my uncle George McCurdy, another iconic African-Canadian.) Linc was fantastically gracious in congratulating me as the second of our race to be elected to the House. (Little did I know that, for the next nine years, I would follow Linc in being "the only.")

PET's posting of Anne Cools to the Senate—the first Black woman so honoured—was an insult, I thought, to worthier, native Black Canadians. Yet, oblivious to our only previous rendezvous, she hailed me with profuse enthusiasm. She'd been jailed for her role in the Sir George Williams affair and had disrupted the NBCC's founding meeting, and, in the process, had heaped calumny on Dot Wills and me. But I was exceedingly courteous, my diplomacy standing in for bonhomie.

I soon dined with Steve Langdon and his wife. She was so gracious a host. But I resented Langdon's assumption of parity between us just because he'd been a "development economist" in several African countries and had a "DPhil in African Studies" from the University of Sussex. Grating on me was his effort to be ingratiating. From whence arose this animus for my Windsor stablemate? Well, I hadn't felt, during the election campaign, that he'd been as helpful to me as I had been to him. Also, how did his four years in Kenya qualify him to speak about the lives of Black Canadians? Too, while Liberal Herb Gray and I were of Windsor, of Essex County, Langdon was a parachute candidate, and I chafed at his perceptible (to me) air of entitlement to what was, in *fact* (for him) alien electoral turf.

My first daunting task? Housing! Apartments were high-rent, vacancy rates low. My colleague Les Benjamin recommended that I try Hull, QC, just across the Ottawa River. I turned up a tiny, two-room abode: an annex to my landlord's home. The rent was passable, but my privacy faced easy trespass. I fled my first landlord's peeping orbs by snatching up a large Hullois basement apartment. I wintered there before springing—in the spring—for a high-rise apartment on Bytown's downtown, tony Elgin Street.

Yet, Ottawa's skin-lacerating and bone-chilling blizzards almost had me wishing that Porter had won Windsor-Walkerville! I shiver to recall returning to The Big (Sub-) Zero after the first Xmas break to find my car so entombed in snow that I had to hire a backhoe to extricate it!

Never could I love Bytown or its defining season. Summers could be entrancing when the Rideau Canal became a picturesque oasis of canoes, kayaks, boats, and yachts. Splendid were the Byward Market multiculti restaurants, the museums, and the nearby Gatineau Park with its Day-Glo spectrum of autumn leafage. But I was lonesome for Black people. Lookit! There were never more than three African-Canadians on NDP caucus staff, and two of them were hired by me!

I needed staff for both The Big Zero and Windsor. I picked Kim Hennin to run my constituency office located on Wyandotte Street in Riverside. He would be assisted initially by Betty Cooke (Dave "Cookie" Cooke's mom) and Clayton Talbert Jr.

A supervisor at a Dominion (grocery) Store, Kim had been laid off. As my sign chairman, he'd performed well. I knew he'd excel in serving my constituents and scheduling my local events but also in identifying and taking the initiative on home-front political concerns. He was a geyser of cigarette smoke, intrigue, phone numbers, and schemes, yes, but he knew my strengths as well as he knew my political rivals' vulnerabilities. He kept tabs on unionists, other constituency aides, all the tri-level politicos, and had his peripheral vision affixed on moneymen and ethnic "chiefs."

A Parliament Hill hire was Diane Flaherty. A University of Guelph grad, Diane had been a Canadian Federation of Students (CFS) militant, so she was invaluable in establishing my bona fides with that lobbyist body.

However, rumours began to circulate among members of Local 444 that she and I were as "close" as—*um*—Kishkon and Wagenberg. False! Diane was betrothed to Ian Deans, our NDP House leader, and of course, I was happily married. The salacious gossip resulted from silly Othello & Desdemona matchmaking scenarios.

Another Ottawa assistant was Susan Saville, whose light-hearted humour floated a relaxed atmosphere. *That* I needed—plus dollops of Scotch—given the hostility of some reliable opponents and the animosity of some unreliable comrades.

An ex-campaign worker, Beth Rutledge became my third parliamentary aide and fast flew self and goods from Windsor to Ottawa. But alas, Beth was too laid-back (I felt) to survive blood-sport politics. So, I ended her Big Zero employ. Although I respected protocols, the Caucus Assistants' Union tried, inappropriately, to intervene. I prevailed, Beth exited, but the bad blood so fostered later poured into a poison-pen letter meant to scuttle my 1989 NDP leadership campaign.

Nicely, neatly, Dan'l Loewen replaced Beth; he was not only superbly talented, efficient, and steadfast at toil, but instinctively loyal. Even on Bad News Days, his inimitable capacity to find something (black) comic to say would turn our office blues into godawful belly laughs.

My parliamentary stint began with a caucus conference held at a ski resort in Mont Ste-Marie, QC. There, NDP leader Ed Broadbent—lemme dub him "Leadbelly"—called each of us, one by one, to a small outbuilding to present our critic assignments. My shadow portfolio was Youth and Post-Secondary Education because Ed knew I could confer amiably with students.

From the get-go, caucus was an Obama-Cabinet–like team of super-ambitious rivals. Knee-Dipper MPs would rally to beat up the other parties; yet, we all knew that individual re-election meant gaining a high profile, both in the constituency and nationally. To succeed, each of us craved headlines, "scrums" (rugby-like crushes of journalists crowding about an interviewee), "hot" microphones, and our faces emblazoning TV screens, newspaper front pages, or mag covers.

So, there was no "Kumbayah" moment. Nope! It was everyone for "dem" damn selves! The "winning" wisdom? Stab backs, cut throats, cater to voters. At stake? The parliamentary pension! Only members who serve for at least six years are eligible (meaning, usually, that they've been re-elected at least once).

My only extended conversations at that time were with amicable Judy Giroux in the NDP research office and Johnny Rodriguez, the irrepressible MP of Guyanese origin, who was, ironically, a pal to my old nemesis, Rosie Douglas. Our bond? A Caribbean camaraderie.

Most of the caucus knew Steve Langdon, yet, in stark, black-and-white contrast, no one recognized my role in having given the party its name a quarter-century back. (That wasn't Langdon's fault, but I smouldered at what I saw as his easy-peasy-acquired Knee-Dipper "golden boy" status.)

Irritatingly, too, I had to parry put-downs of Windsor and stupidity about African-Canadians. Some MPs bantered with me as if to elicit responses parroting lines of jive or rap. (How batty those *batardi* were!) Two Knee-Dippers dubbed me "Dr. Detroit"; they were ignorant—naturally—that most Windsorites are die-hard, Maple-Leaf-Forever patriots.

Gradually, I got accustomed to the Hill. Yet, there were staffers and MPs who, though anti-racist in principle, disliked having an "uppity" Black man in their midst. Nor was I imagining their enmity or discomfort. Other African-Canadians on the Hill felt the same. We were in the Centre Block, aye, but we were *not* central.

One actual friend? Ian Deans, the House leader, who helped me find my footing, pace, and direction. A Scot, Ian was a suave, talented parliamentarian who elucidated the dynamics of the Hill and the ins and outs of caucus. Thus, I regretted his departure when he left electoral politics—seconded by the Mulroney Tories—to become a public-service mediator.

Ian's replacement was Nelson Riis, a bland but fair House leader. More pro-capital than most Knee-Dippers, he too would be courted by the Conservatives, but he'd stave off their seduction.

My most gregarious, most amiable colleague? Les Benjamin—no question! A month after my landing, he burst into my office, shouting, "Hello! I'm Les Benjamin!" Leslie Gordon Benjamin had been handily re-elected in his Regina riding despite a heart attack sidelining him in bed! But he was Welsh and—like his boozy compatriot, bard Dylan Thomas—irrepressible in spirit and unforgettable in style. Boundless in roaring grandiloquence, he loomed as large in our corridors and precincts as a pink-toned blizzard. Beckoning me to his office across the hall, he confided that he could no longer swig alcohol ("doctor's orders"), which was disappointing; only a water jug sat on his coffee table. Briskly, though, he whisked a whiskey forty-ouncer from a cabinet, and I tippled a healthy dram. An ex-railway hand, Les was also an ex-telegrapher and ex-stenographer, so his sentences were poetic phrases—Morse Code haiku or short-hand tanka. He loved baseball, hunting, and being an MP. Of all of my colleagues, he was the heartiest, the most "real" (to use Af-Am slang), as was his wife, Connie. (When US Prez "Ray-gun" hustled our House of Commons in 1987, Les was the sole socialist to heckle ye olde Red-baiter, thundering, "He's mad!" That diagnosis was correct. Only after Reagan left office in 1989 did the world learn that his final years as prez, when he was succumbing to dementia, saw his policies guided by astrology and he himself guided by his First Lady's whispers.)

Our *chef* was one of the pinko baker's dozen that Ontario voters sent to The Big O(ught). A white-collar tribune of our blue-collar base, Ed Broadbent was, like me, an academic turned politico but was actually more ruffled-shirt Edwardian than he was "Uncle Ed"—supposedly everybody's fave T-shirt socialist to have at a patio burger-flipper with suds. I couldn't imagine him dirtying his hands, certainly not on an assembly line (save one fashioning fountain pens) and not even by, say, withdrawing Canada "bloodlessly" from NATO. In my critic's role, interacting socially with foreign dignitaries, our convivial soirees or luncheons were often helmed by Ed and his wife, Lucille. (For me, Ed is Leadbelly but intimate with B. B. King's black Gibson *get-tar* helpmate, Lucille!) Although he could be aggressively assertive when challenged, Ed only vented purple rage when having to comment on the too-scarlet-tinted Waffle or its ex–intellectual honcho James "Jimbo" Laxer.

Ottawa Centre "Commoner" Michael Cassidy had been a Laxer ally. Before entering fed politics, he'd been critiqued as strident in lungs but a ditz in direction. My singular contact with Mike was to hear his insolent conviction that he, not I, should occupy a prime Centre Block office. Given my abrupt rebuff of his suggestion, I confirm the dude had no "game" for persuasion.

Another Ontario caucus mate was Iain Angus outta Fort William/Port Arthur (T'under Bay, a.k.a. "Li'l Finland"). Iain had a public Coke addiction. Seldom lacked he a Coca-Cola can. But he was also a convicted caucus jockey, acting interchangeably as whip, deputy House leader, and caucus chair. He was one of the jokers who dared dub me "Dr. Detroit." (I thus gift him the moniker of "Dr. BS," but only because his surname can refer to a Scottish bovine breed!)

Herself an ex–Ivory-Tower inmate, Lynn McDonald nabbed Hogtown's Broadview-Greenwood riding. An ex-prez of the National Action Committee on the Status of Women, she was as much anti-smoking as she was anti-sexist. Quickly, she canned the "smoky backroom" of legend and got landmark, anti-fuming legislation passed. While I tease her for restricting a hazardous commodity (one killing me as I write), I admired her tenacity in her cause. (Once, she hurled an ashtray at me in a caucus meet to make me, yep, butt out!)

Ernest "Ernie" Epp—a second T'under Bay–area MP—was, heck, a super-*earnest* critic for Multiculturalism. His academic roots were unmistakable, too much so to let him branch permanently into politics. The fur-trade historian would be the only caucus member to support my national leadership candidacy in 1989.

To canvass a few non-Ontario caucus mates, I named two stand-up and stand-out guys: Jim Fulton and Bill Blaikie. Jim was the grizzly-gargantuan, gigantically extroverted, outstandingly witty MP for Skeena (BC). He was a burly, charismatic chap, a cross between Clark Gable and Alley Oop but favouring the more handsome of the duo. Neither the Environment nor Indigenous shadow portfolios ever had an abler proponent. Dude was congenial, all way 'round the yingyang.

Manitoba's Bill Blaikie was a United Church minister. His tongue could distill "grapes of wrath" or stream milk and honey. A Scot, his Bobby Burns fiestas entailed haggis dinners, belts of Scotch, and bouts of Burns, his voice volleying verses as if cannonballs of wit. I thought him an ideal candidate to replace Broadbent. (To consider him and Leadbelly side by side would be to place a bearded and fiery Che Guevara next to a wax-pallor Mr. Rogers.) A spring of sensible advice, Bill was one of but four colleagues to summon me to his riding to speak. That says a lot.

Who could overlook Svend Robinson? An unabashed smarty-pants and an ardent crusader for waifs and Mama Nature, he was one of those thin men who Shakespeare's Caesar would have cast as projecting "a lean and hungry look," thus making him "dangerous"—or, in plebeian terms, difficult. His martyr-complex narcissism saw him expound holier-than-thou positions—*and* a patronizing liberalism—so that he'd play Mau Mau to my supposed Uncle Tom. Dubbed the "Svend Family Robinson," his office exuded such politic righteousness that Christ Himself would have blushed to be shown up as not quite right (or left). (He'd've had to cry out from the cross, "Better call Svend!")

Like Svend and Nelson, Margaret Mitchell and Pauline Jewett were BC Knee-Dippers. Maggie was the consummate ally. We forwarded the affirmative action (employment equity) proposals later adopted by the caucus and by the party as a whole. Pauline *et moi* were Parliament Hill strangers. Although she became prez of Simon Fraser U shortly after I'd presided over its censure in 1968, she never once raised the matter of the long-dissipated, illiberal academic stinkeroo. Perhaps it had been, for her, a tempest in a Rorschach inkblot.

Simon De Jong possessed a storied past. Once imprisoned in an Imperial Japanese concentration camp in Indonesia, he'd flourished postwar as an artist, an orator, a student activist, and a community organizer.

He was a "Strawberry Fields Forever" flower child whose passions were greening cities and banning war. Unconventional was his cogitating: a mix of Haight-Ashbury "cool," Berkeley "rad," and Freetown Christiania "Greenpeace" (and "weed," perhaps).

Although we were all leftists (and some of us were *gauche*, some "sinister"—I pun!—and some of us "leftovers" from long-discredited political movements), we were not necessarily a commune, a community, or communards. Rather, we were an association of "free radicals," voted into the House of Commons to ensure that the government never forgot that its most important citizens are those who work for a living, instead of living off the labour of others. We were allies in a common cause but not, except rarely, friends.

CHAPTER FIFTEEN:
BABYLON SCHMOOZING (LIFE IN MULRONEY'S HOUSE)

TAKING MY SEAT IN THE HOUSE OF COMMONS FOR THE FIRST time, chills shivered my spine. Snaps of the House had not conveyed its architectural magnificence nor the palpable sense of history that it evoked. Yet, here I was, a descendant of US ex-slaves, taking my place among the elected, empowered Maple Leaf elite.

No more a spectator was I! Rather, the spectators, my judges, would be my constituents, yes, *and* all Canucks. As the 33rd Parliament commenced, I was joyous but also respected its majesty. I felt awed to be among persons—names and faces—spied usually in newsprint or on TV screens: George Hees, Flora MacDonald, John Turner, Warren Allmand, Joe Clark, Dan Heap, Pauline Jewett, Ed Broadbent, Stanley Knowles...

the beat goes on. I was somewhat star-struck to be seated across from the "Right Honourable" and seated next to "the Member from...."

Admittedly, my first reaction to Brian Mulroney was merely to accord him due respect as the prime minister—and admiration for his magnanimity in embracing all MPs. (Mulroney and his wife, Mila, were heartily courteous to me, although the PM relished joshing me about being a "socialist" when introducing me to Mikhail Gorbachev of the USSR *and* US Prez George H. W. Bush. Another meet-n-greet was actually an audience with Pope John Paul II. When we shook hands, so flaccid was his grip, I imagined that he was merely an animated scarecrow: if the manual greeting lasted a millisecond too long, his whole arm would flop off his body!)

My schedule was dictated by House routines. I'd be at my office by 7:00 A.M. Sip chicory-enhanced, scalding coffee; speed-read the *Globe and Mail*, the *Ottawa Citizen*, and the *Windsor Star*; scan the morning news shows. Caucus Research forwarded notice of hot-button conundrums, and there were recs for talking points from my own Big Zero or Windsor staff. Though I chortled over weird tales, my laser focus was on subjects within my critic area or on issues riling Windsor.

By 9:00 A.M., I'd meet with research staff to discuss the House schedule and to decide which MPs would participate in question period (QP), which was the key moment to allow Opposition or backbench MPs a chance to be on camera, in the public eye, and to relay a question or quip that could play well nationally and locally, thus holding the government to account but also giving the questioner a high-profile boost for re-election. Those wishing to ask a question would submit arguments to buttress the query. After some debate, the House leader would choose the subject(s) to be covered in QP or in the "Rule 21," one-minute statements preceding QP. When assigned a question or statement, or when I was to participate in debate, my staff and I would hunker down, do the research, pore over the books, newspapers, or Hansard texts, and then I'd author the question, statement, or speech notes.

One-hour French lessons each noon were *de rigueur*. I scrupled to exercise facility in the tongue. I became skilled enough to pose questions and parry them in francophone scrums. I even became a preferred MP for interviews on CBEF (Ottawa's francophone radio station).

If I had a guest, we'd sup in the parliamentary restaurant; otherwise, lunch was gulped in the Centre Block cafeteria. QP began at 2:15 P.M. and ended at 3:00. Press scrums in the lobby outside the Chamber followed. If I'd bruited a question of import, I could expect a barrage of cameras in my face and mics up my nose.

Howard and His Holiness Pope John Paul II. His hand resembles a sail, but the canvas was listless.

The rest of the workday was devoted to committee meetings, House business, phone calls, correspondence, or sitdowns with lobbyists or constituents. Since House affairs were televised to all Hill offices, I always knew what was transpiring. Sometimes, I'd rush down to the Chamber to help jump-start a debate—or to clinch it. I admit that I experienced an addictive, heady, heart-thumping adrenaline rush—furthered by cigarettes, coffee, Scotch, and, often, all of the above.

We weren't supposed to read speeches in debate. Though most MPs ignored the rule, I strove to uphold it but referred to notes for accuracy of data. Hence, a signal duty at day's end was to edit any grammatical or typographical "awkwordy" errors in the transcripts in the "Hansard Blues" (so called because they were printed on blue paper) distributed each evening.

Fridays, I'd jet to Windsor. There, I'd get whisked to meeting upon luncheon upon dinner upon meeting. Saturday morns were devoted to constituency matters. Most weekends, I took in several functions, including banquets, which were stressful because few ran on schedule, and my sugar and salt consumption was excessive—to ameliorate tobacco bans. Yet, I savoured the inspiriting reception invariably accorded my speeches.

If free of other obligations, I would relax at home Sundays before heading back to Bytown. Often that was perilous, especially in winter, when a blizzard could nix or delay a flight.

In my first years, Simon, Ian, and select staffers would hustle me across Wellington to drinks at the National Press Club or to downtown receptions floated by foreign embassies. Of the latter affairs, there were two extremes worth noting: heaps of fresh lobster at one Arab reception; a cornucopia of Coke and hamburgers at the US embassy (on the Fourth of July).

But the most coveted event on the calendar was the Speaker's garden party. Swank! Razzmatazz! Vodka-sodden cocktails and curry-soaked hors d'oeuvres! Elvis revived! Bujold in-da-house! (At every soiree, my Brenda was *la belle* of the ball; her dresses, if elementary in cut, flaunted the exponential impact of gowns; her dancing was a butterfly's lithe, delicate, heartbeat-skipping, hypnotizing movement or its fluttering alighting, as if to grace a bloom.)

Parliamentary recesses were welcome holidays, yet never were they free of political obligations. For most of my tenure, summers necessitated committee work or international travel.

Travel is onerous bliss. But after I'd braved the inoculations, packing problems, annoying lineups, and customs protocols, I sortied to foreign climes I'd never have set foot in otherwise.

My first sortie—in spring '85—saw me accompany Les Benjamin and veterans to Europe to salute the fortieth anniversary of the Canadian Army's liberation of The Netherlands and Italy. In Apeldoorn, Holland, which Canucks had cleared of Nazi brutality when I was but twelve, the appreciation and love for Canada and Canadians that its citizens expressed, well, that summoned tears to daub my cheeks. In Italy, we visited Cassino where our soldiers attained valiantly a ruddy conquest. We navigated a vast circle: from Rome to Cassino, Naples, and then Sicily; then, north to Rimini, west to Florence, and south to Rome. At each stop, parochial plonk—*vino locale*—topped our glasses, non-stop.

My next foreign sortie? Back to Amsterdam, to add a Black presence to the Association of Western European Parliamentarians Against Apartheid. How peculiar to hear the Euro-Dutch express loathing for apartheid when it was the Dutch—*qua* Boers—who were oppressing Black South Africans! (And I guffawed at juxtaposed piety and debauchery: A few feet from our meeting-place monastery? A sign blared, "Yanks! Live F—king on Stage!")

The year 1985 also witnessed a week in Israel. Sponsored by the Canada–Israel Committee, our NDP delegation numbered Svend Robinson, Ian Deans, and Brenda and me. The Holy Land? Wholly mesmerizing! We ambled Ramallah (the Palestinian capital), the Sea of Galilee, the ruins of Masada, the Dead Sea, the River Jordan, Jerusalem, the Western Wall, Tel Aviv, and the West Bank. We spent a night in a kibbutz on the Golan Heights; we spent a day in Lebanon.

Israeli politicos were as intriguing to me as were their nation's fabled biblical sites: Yitzhak Rabin, Shimon Peres, Menachem Begin, and Benjamin Netanyahu were personages as storied as Solomon and Moses. Rabin and Peres corralled us with Labour Party captains. But the Likud party's Begin and Netanyahu met us individually. With all, we reviewed their relations with Arabs, the unabated Palestinian crisis, and the still unfolding Civil War carnage in Lebanon, a multifaceted, labyrinthine, internecine conflict involving communal militias, the more-or-less disintegrated Lebanese Army, and foreign actors such as the Palestine Liberation Organization, Syria, and Israel (1975–90). All had trigger fingers, *puis* red-wet hands; all manifested atrocities.

Our most abrasive—or bruising—pit stop was with Netanyahu. Aggressive, blunt, candid, defiant, he swore that Israel was not only always right, but was Righteousness embodied in the Middle East's only true democracy. Asked whether Israel possessed nuclear weapons, he demurred but noted that the Hebrew God was known to annihilate Israel's foes, zapping the flesh from their bones: a divine form of nuclear obliteration?

Truly, I've always ogled Israel with admiration unto adulation. Given the perfectly diabolical Nazi perpetration (with assists from too many other Europeans) of mass murder—genocide—against 6 million human beings and the struggle of the Jewish people to build a state where they would not be a persecuted minority, I exult in Israel's creation and survival. Later, I saw Israel's co-operatives as a global-level model of "actually existing" socialism. Our jaunt to the Golan Heights kibbutz enhanced that impression. Yet, my fanfare for Israel became more muted when I learned of its collaboration with racist South Africa, including their shared development of nuclear weapons. Israel's then-alliance with a repressive, racist regime had to taint its own propagandistic assertion on being an open, liberal, human-rights-backing, and civil-rights-supportive democracy.

B'nai Brith reps query candidates for Parliament before each election. When first we met, unequivocal was my endorsement of the Jewish state. The reps were delighted. When next we met, they were dismayed. But how could I be an unhesitant apostle of a country that treated with a regime that oppressed members of my own race?

Yes, as a tribune of human rights and civil liberties, I'm concerned about the misbehaviour of the Jewish state (and I'm likewise dissatisfied with Canada's often criminally behaving "settler" governments). Yes, I deeply respect Jewish leadership in anti-racism as well as treasuring our conjoint history in overcoming various pharaohs and fascists, dictators and dogmatists. Thus, I was part of a tri-party delegation (joining Tory Bill Attewell and Grit Lucie Pépin) that jetted to the USSR to investigate the plight of Jewish would-be émigrés to Israel.

Naturally, previous delegations had been harassed and spied upon. A member of one such body, Nelson Riis, had experienced a KGB attempt to compromise him, so we expected the worse.

But it was "Springtime for the Soviets"! Its leader, the global pop-star politico Mikhail Gorbachev, was extolling glasnost (openness, transparency) and perestroika (humane reform). Thus, at entry into the USSR, our bags went unmolested and customs cleared us as easily as if we were entering the US. Nor could we see that we were under any kind of surveillance as we met in Moscow and in Saint Petersburg with Russian Jews wishing to become Israelis.

We rendezvoused with perhaps two dozen such souls in small, spartan Soviet apartments. They complained of lost status, lost jobs, bureaucratic and police chastisement, and even being imprisoned for seeking exit visas. (To do so was considered "treasonous," unpatriotic.)

One Politburo official told us that, thanks to perestroika, Soviet Jews could now receive exit visas; however, the process was obstructed by bureaucratic inertia: a lack of glasnost was hindering perestroika. This assertion was plausible, for our parliamentary trio knew that every Canadian government initiative relies upon potentially fickle civil servants for effectuation. (Truth: senior Canuck civil servants view MPs as *their* servants, for they have job security, careers, and pensions, but any MP might lose all as soon as the next election occurs.)

Indescribably drab was Moscow—a bunch of bleached or sooty, Brutalist boxes; scarlet flowers seemed gaudy bloodstains reserved for busts and statues of Lenin. Our high-rise hotel was almost occidental ritzy. Architecturally, the Kremlin was nothing less than a czarist Taj Mahal. Yet, the nearby underground mall had more customers than goods, while its restaurants pushed menus interchanging borscht and vodka. (The top vodka? Bore the tang of bison-pissed-on grass!)

Saint Petersburg was, in contrast, a seductive gem, with its inexpensive but incredibly gourmet-dish menu at the Literary Café (which hosts a life-size statue of Pushkin), its bronze monuments, the august canal system (if choked with algae), magical museums, and storybook castles. (See the Hermitage, so magnificent in its postwar restoration, not to mention its classics of Russian and Western—even "decadent, bourgeois"—art.) I doubt there is another city anywhere where one can order coffee infused with red wine. (In *The Cantos*, Ezra Pound advises taking "tea and cake on Nevsky Prospect." Sure did.) However, disconcertingly, there were also many legless vets of Russia's ongoing Afghan occupation pushing wheelchairs, their wheels stumping along the uneven, poor-cement-concretetized, "crippled" and "jumpy" sidewalks.

Saint Petersburg also staged this indelible incident. We were looking for a taxi (with Marlboros in hand to ensure one would stop), when a snow-haired babushka, glimpsing me, erupted into a tirade. Translated by an embarrassed Canadian embassy staffer, I heard that my Red comrade had shouted, "Black bastard, Hitler should have finished the job!" (I thought suddenly of Marlene, my almost-four-decades-lost, soft-on-communism, so soft-soft-soft, teen-dream sweetheart. *Where was she now? What did she believe in now?*) I was not flustered by the woman's comment at all; I was glad that she spoke openly her prejudice, for too many Canucks do not (or think they don't), thus voicing sham sympathy for African-Canadian demands for justice.

(Not a year after my election, Brenda and I were navigating a Windsor street when I spied a tailing police car. The cruiser tracked us for several blocks, then I pulled over and parked. Well, didn't Windsor's finest scuttle behind us and just sit there? Two biped crabs. I got out of my car and strode back to theirs to demand that they explain why they were hounding us. Their cockamamie excuse? I'd given a signal and failed to turn. I told them to either give me a ticket, or I'd call a press conference. Upon realizing who I was, they squealed wheels in peeling off.)

As our 33rd Parliament work began, we four Windsor MPs agreed to co-operate across party lines on local dilemmas. That agreement had its first test when I received info that our local CBC-TV station would be closed or sold. Along with Knee-Dipper Langdon and Gray the Grit, I raised the issue in the House in one of my first interventions. But Tory Caldwell broke ranks to stand with Mulroney. The Windsor "common front" would be a troika, not a quartet. (Even while the CBC was pooh-poohing plans to shutter the Windsor outpost, I learned that some sixty-three employees would be terminated and regional broadcasts decimated. In spite of our efforts, we—Gray, Langdon, and I—could not change the outcome. Then again, the Mulroney Tories seemed so pro-American, they wouldn't care that a swath of southern Ontario would be "covered" and interpreted by Detroit interests, rather than our own: so, there'd be lots of news of gangbanger shootouts but much fewer about vultures picnicking on Pelee Island.)

Early in 1985, I buttressed the Action Group on Jobs, co-chaired by Knee-Dippers Lorne Nystrom and Langdon. We hit twenty burgs cross Canada. (This NDP manoeuvre was vital because Mulroney had greased his landslide by promising "jobs, jobs, jobs" but wasn't delivering.) Our resulting document, *Canada Unlimited*, stressed the need for municipal control of economic development as well as funding for worker-developed enterprise and co-operatives.

Thanks to the first budget submitted to the 33rd Parliament by the seemingly bloodless Tory finance minister Michael Wilson, I attained national prominence. Mulroney's guv'mint moved to de-index old age security—to let inflation ravage seniors' incomes. A fighting matter! That Charles MacDonald, a Windsorite, headed the National Pensioners and Senior Citizens Federation was a gift. I corralled him at once and helped to propel a national petition drive to oppose de-indexation. For weeks and weeks, Langdon, Gray, and I gathered thousands of signatures and submitted them to Parliament. We soon landed a political knockout. Vocal seniors' enmity for de-indexation was afforded an exclamation mark by a TV-worthy confrontation on the Hill between the prime minister and a feisty female senior who called the PM a liar, thus branding him as "Lyin' Brian," a moniker he'd never shake. The Tories had to kill de-indexation: Mulroney lost political capital with Bay Street and lost credibility with Main Street.

But the "other" demographic—youth and students—also hiked my status, for 1985 was declared the UN "International Youth Year." A boon for my profile.

Early that year, the CFS handed me a document, signed by Flora MacDonald, outlining a program called SELF. It revealed that the Mulroney Tories would spend 20 percent less on student summer jobs than had the Turner Grits the previous summer. As I peppered her with questions about the document, Flora at first denied knowledge of it but admitted subsequently that she had in fact approved the program cuts. To have embarrassed a minister, and an experienced parliamentarian to boot, and having caught her in a fib yielded me instant media glory. Already known for being quick-witted and a preacher-orator, I was soon topping polls as not only being one of the most effective MPs, but also as being the best-tailored, the best-suited (pun intended) male MP.

My next chance to humble a minister arrived when into my hands fell a letter signed by Andrée Champagne, the Secretary of State for Youth. Her missive, directed to Tory supporters, cited the potential of the student jobs program to recruit youth to the Progressive Conservative banner. Forced to apologize for this brazen essay to use taxpayer dollars propagandistically, the erstwhile "Youth Minister" lost her limo and was replaced by truly youthful Jean Charest.

At age twenty-eight, Jean—with those attention-grabbing "J.C." initials and a flopping mop of wild, Jesus tendrils—was the most junior Canuck ever to become a fed Crown Minister. Still, my gravitas was intimidating: Why not? I'd just brought down his predecessor! Even when he oversaw the demise of the youth-volunteer program Katimavik, we were more like sparring partners than battling pugilists, each striving for the knockout blow. (Upon learning that my daughter Linda would be vying in the high jump at the 1989 Jeux de la Francophonie in Morocco, J.C.—now Minister of Youth and Amateur Sport—bade me join his Canadian delegation to the event. A "sporting" gesture!)

That year, 1985, also witnessed the telegenic Ville de Québec "Shamrock Summit," so-called because summiteers Mulroney and Prez Ray-gun shared Irish roots and their "*Oireachtas*" occurred on St. Patrick's Day. There they agreed to negotiate a Canada–US Free Trade Agreement. In seeking the leadership of his party in 1983, Mulroney had opposed any such deal, pointing out that Canada-based US corporations would desert the country, costing Canada thousands of jobs.

What a difference Power makes! So, to "improve" Canada–US relations, Mulroney sold out our pharmaceutical companies and the patients who rely upon them by extending patent protection in Canada to US-minted drugs. Perhaps Mulroney had gambled that "Ray-gun" would reciprocate by taking action on acid rain. But the harmful rain kept pouring down while Canadians got soaked with stratospheric drug prices.

Mulroney's toadying to Reagan/Ray-gun (whose policies Canucks hated) opened the PM to scorn and derision. So, when Prez Reagan addressed a special joint session of Parliament, Les Benjamin heckled the B-movie, Tinsel-Town idol. Some thought his behaviour impolite, but he held that Reagan's proposal of a space-based, anti-nuke-missile system ("Star Wars") was implicit sabre-rattling, while the US funding of "Contras" to oppose leftist Latin American governments was explicit terrorism. I showed my disgust with *el presidente* by refusing to stand in respect for a man who had seized office by exploiting "Tricky Dicky" Nixon's "Southern Strategy" (to use "dog whistles" to curry favour with whitey-white supremacists) and who refused to act against apartheid.

Also in 1985, Flora MacDonald tabled her Employment Equity bill. (Employment equity is Canada-speak for "affirmative action," the US-speak for preferential hiring or placement.) I could not question her sincerity, but her legislation was much ado about little, merely asking Crown corporations and federally regulated employers to report periodically the numbers of women, Indigenous people, the physically challenged, and people of colour in their employ. Republican North types accused the Mulroneyites of pushing "quotas," but I excoriated the absence of strict targets to produce a public service that looks like Canada. The only penalty envisioned in the bill was a fine scaling up to $50,000 for any entity that failed to report. I mocked Flora's legislation as being only about "counting employees and counting them twice, to see which employers were naughty or nice."

Flora's good-intention'd bill passed—but with a poison-pill amendment. Report enforcement was left to the Canadian Human Rights Commission (CHRC). The problem? The CHRC was a white elephant of a bureaucracy (*Bureaucracy*? A pure, leisurely sinecure: / Ready-to-pour Scotch secreted in furniture…) and a paper tiger in terms of effectiveness. *Par exemple*: an African-Canadian woman from Colchester, ON, had been hired by Canada Customs and took up training courses for her duties. Because she was light-complected enough to pass for Caucasian, she directly audited racist advice ("training") to officers, directing them to prejudicially profile Black travellers. My office assisted the complainant in presenting her testimony to the CHRC. The response? Not a sigh! Not a shrug!

Finally, the CHRC Chief Commissioner, Max Yalden, materialized before the parliamentary Human Rights Committee. Here was the appropriate forum in which to question Yalden about what I saw (and see) as the CHRC's seeming inability to follow up and follow through on racism allegations. I raised the Customs case—plus others in which the investigative process (let alone prowess) was either retarded or MIA. Despite his background as a diplomat and his reputation as a mandarin responsive to minorities' concerns, Yalden became testy, scornful: "We have done quite a lot for YOU people!" His outburst reminded me of my Guardian Club, anti-racism campaigns, long ago, when, often, the most recalcitrant practitioners of "black codes" turned out to be the loudest "friends of (you) Coloured people." I felt ashamed for Yalden that he had tried to erase Black Canadian frustration with his bungling organization by attempting to racialize—that is, marginalize—me. Diplomacy vanished as (unconscious) prejudice got vented.

Then again, the federal civil service was (and is) the employer persistently most resistant to implementing fair employment. Although the government is immune to the market pressures to which the private sector must respond, the civil service is the consummate master of the arts of delay, denial, and diversion in response to discrimination concerns. (One irony of Flora's "flower power" approach to equity is that the federally regulated industries—banking, telecommunications, airlines—began to visibly diversify their rank-and-file employees, if not senior management, knowing that doing so would please urban markets. Notably, the federal civil service seemed to hew to a Social Credit vision of Canada as a Great White [Christian] North where "red Indians" are on reserves and anyone who ain't European and Caucasian "gotta go back to wherever from whence y'all came.")

In late 1985, I launched the New Democratic Party Task Force on Youth. From coast to coast, we held hearings at which some six hundred university students, high school students, street kids, Indigenous youth, and youth workers were able to convey their worries and wishes. After weeks on the road, listening and questioning, collecting narratives and testimony, confessions and memories, complaints and reflections, I sought to scribe an account that reflected what the assemblies had said. Yet, upon my return to The Big Zero in December, I was irked to find that Caucus Research had prepared a report that ignored my findings! Worse, their document was a miscellany of stats, stats, and déjà vu claptrap!

I rejected that crap outright, and Dan'l Loewen and I cogitated and typed steadily for four days—including forty-eight straight hours sans sleep—to file a report faithful to what we had heard many young Canadians say. Dawned Christmas Eve, 1985, as we finished our labours. (Time for eggnog and rum, to help along rumination.)

We observed that youths were fearful due to their lack of career prospects, the threat of nuclear war, and potential ecological catastrophe. They felt alienated and powerless regarding ruling-class policies and decisions that ignored their hopes. Many worried that university and college were priced beyond their means yet were prerequisites for success in the new economy.

Our report advised the creation of Youth Advisory Councils at every level of government. We also emphasized the urgent need for enhanced counselling, both academic and personal, in high schools. Our most important and most controversial rec? The provision of "Youth Prospects," that is, $2,500 grants for all high-school graduates to be used to cover the first two years of college, university, or apprenticeship study, or as seed money for young entrepreneurs. Mainly, we wanted to make post-secondary study affordable.

The report earned interest-group adulation, press notice, and politically flattering copycat policy rollouts from the Grits (who've never embraced an idea they didn't steal). But Mulroney toadied to folks for whom social policy means banning abortion, beefing up the military, and cutting taxes (or cutting abortions, beefing up the military, and banning taxes). So, his guv'mint cut back on education-oriented transfers to the provinces: Tuitions got hiked, student debt skyrocketed, and the working-class and marginalized couldn't afford the higher educations their tax-dollars sponsored.

Soon, controversy over the Tories' ham-fisted butchering of Katimavik cut my work from the headlines. A Katimavik booster, Hon. Jacques Hébert, launched a hunger strike in the foyer outside the Senate (thus imitating the IRA's Bobby Sands's fatal 1981 hunger strike in Belfast's Maze prison) to decry Tory "meanness." How appalling to see a senior statesman, pinstriped and gaunt, with his thinning hair, seeming to resemble Grandpa Munster, sprawled abjectly before the hallowed portal to the Red Chamber.

Anyway, as I boarded my Windsor flight, late Christmas Eve, 1985, I had to endure the kind of barb reserved for politicos. Eyeing me, a stranger ranted, "So, after weeks of doing nothing in Ottawa, you now get to go on vacation?" (Sometimes I wish I were a comic! I'd've said, "You know, seeing and hearing the likes of you, I don't need a vacation—I need exile!")

As the Knee-Dipper Youth Critic, I brown-bagged with students and the Canadian Association of University Teachers (CAUT); as the Science and Tech Critic, I held tête-à-têtes with the CAUT (again), plus other academics and scientists (such as the late great Fraser "Colonel" Mustard). Then, as the NDP Human Rights (International) Critic, I broke bread with Nelson Mandela in one suite (he named me a "civil rights hero") and sipped tea with the Dalai Lama in another (or so it seemed). *And* as a promoter of Black excellence and foe of anti-Black racism, I castigated everywhere wanton gun-and-badge murders of unarmed Black men. I was always on the go, always on call; never ever was I "off the road."

Too, during my first years in Parliament, I had residual obligations as a prof and scientist. I had to return to the University of Windsor to preside over oral exams for grad students. As well, I completed drafts of material for *Bergey's Manual of Determinative Bacteriology* plus two journal manuscripts. I was labouring—to cite The Beatles (or Tiny Yong)—eight days a week.

To conduct my critic posts, I staffed several committees: International Human Rights; National Health and Welfare; Research, Science, and Technology; Estimates; Private Members' Bills; Multiculturalism; *and* the Parliamentary Library Committee. My work life was a whirlwind. Did I still manage to jazz up the photo-ops and have a snappy quip to quiver the microphones? *Oui!*

My worst portfolio? Health! I was fuming nicotine at the peak of the anti-tobacco crusade! John Parry—a T'under Bay–Rainy River (ON) NDP MP—noted this anomaly but did so gently, dubbing me a "considerate smoker."

Even so, I sat on the Standing Committee on National Health and Welfare as it dealt with the patent drug bill. Canada had a system of compulsory licensing to produce generic versions of brand-name drugs. Before that smart move, Canucks paid the highest patented-drug prices

Howard with the Dalai Lama.

on earth. Under compulsory licensing, generic versions of drugs could be imported or manufactured, so long as a 4 percent royalty was paid the owner of the patent. So, not only were inexpensive generics available, the prices of patented drugs moderated. This policy raised the ire of the US-patented drug manufacturers. So Prez Ray-gun fired a phaser (particle-beam) blast at Mulroney.

Soon, Canadian economist Harry C. Eastman recommended that branded drugs enjoy four years of exclusive manufacture and merchandising—and then prosper from hiked royalties. He also proposed a Patented Medicine Prices Review Board. The Yanks saw Red(s)! They craved a longer period of marketplace exclusivity, and so Mulroney witch-doctored up Bill C-22. It okayed a decade of exclusivity so long as brand-name manufacturers pushed Canuck-based drug research expenditures to 10 percent of their Canadian revenues.

However, because levels of domestic investment in drug research were not stipulated in Bill C-22, the legislation was a mirage. Once the bill became law, research funding rose initially but never reached the 10 percent threshold. The drug prices review mechanism did lower the cost of patented drugs, but, ironically, generic drugs are now 150 percent more expensive!

In 1985, Canada spent only 1.25 percent of its GNP on research, compared to other industrialized nations that spent twice that. But our pharmaceutical research expenditures were low even when compared to research funds expended by other foreign-owned industries.

The Tories acted with typical sadism by slashing the budgets of both the National Research Council (NRC) and its Industrial Research Assistance Program, as well as the agencies that fund university research. These measures, ironically, were announced almost simultaneously with the award of the 1986 Nobel Prize in Chemistry—partially—to Canada's John Polyani. (Soon, he was appearing before parliamentary committees to vigorously critique the guv'mint science policy, which was, really, to borrow and buy and bag ideas *and* beg products from others.)

Every scientific and academic body in Canada opposed the federal cuts; so, doctorates in everything made beelines to my office. When Mulroney determined that Canada would help build the International Space Station, "the learneds" feared that government would abandon domestic scientific pursuits, to back Prez Ray-gun's "Star Wars" bid to weaponize space. Further controversy resulted from Ottawa's decision to locate Canada's space agency in Montreal rather than in the National Capital Region. Not rocket science? Aye, it was just blatant, classic vote-buying.

A lethal threat to domestic research and development (R & D) was the US-favouring bilateral Free Trade Agreement (FTA). Already, changes in foreign investment review laws had restricted the ability of Canada to impose conditions, including research levels, on foreign takeovers of home-grown companies. (France's Institut Pasteur's 1986 purchase of Canada's fabled Connaught Medical Research Laboratories was just one sorry example.)

Under the FTA, US-headquartered companies were to be treated as if they were Canadian; branch-plant operations could be transferred, along with their R & D facilities and personnel, to their US bases. Thus, the percentage of Canada's GDP devoted to R & D would become ever more minuscule compared to our competitors' outlays. The FTA also threatened to disassemble the Canada–US Auto Pact with its guarantees that *some* Detroit auto manufacturing and/or assembly would be done under the Maple Leaf, not the Stars and Stripes.

Another FTA issue? Exacerbation of Canada's Third-World-style reliance on resource extraction and export as a path to wealth. (Lookit! Thirty years on, in 2015, Canada's position as a supplier of raw materials for other industrial nations has not changed. Watch the Stephen Harper "Republicans North" go, hat in hand, begging the US to buy our poisonous tar-sands oil at discounted prices rather than see us refine it here or generate other secondary industries. Canuck *Kapital* has always been lazy and destructive: fleece the seas, axe the forests, gut the earth, pump the fluids. For instance, Alberta has always been ridiculously pompous about its oil-and-gas-generated "wealth." Yet, what real ingenuity or entrepreneurship is demonstrated by its profiting from having been one major site of the mass extinction of dinosaurs some 65 million years ago?)

In late 1986, the Standing Committee on Health and Welfare began a study of drug abuse (nicotine addiction excluded). Just as our hearings began, Prez Ray-gun declared his "War on Drugs," his repulsively Negrophobic rejoinder to Prez Johnson's "War on Poverty." By design, Ray-gun's domestic criminal assault would quadruple America's convicts, filling the jails with Blacks and Hispanics convicted of petty drug-dealing or addiction, while Caucasoid "recreational drug users" either just paid fines or got off scot-free. (White "blow" was okay; Black "crack" wasn't.)

Anyway, just two days after Ray-gun's proclamation, Mulroney echoed him with his declaration of a National Drug Strategy. Though I chastised the PM for misguidedly mimicking his mentor, Mulroney's policy stressed rehab, not "remand."

Over several months, our committee heard testimony from social workers, health experts, police, and vulnerable and demonized "users" in Halifax, Ottawa, Edmonton, and Vancouver. The most perilous—yet legal—drug? Alcohol. One BC doctor stated that alcohol abuse underlay the majority of preventable illnesses. (Too, alcohol was the "gateway drug" to needles and pills; marijuana was *not*.) Prescription drug addiction was a secondary offender. Tertiary in social damage were hard drugs such as cocaine and heroin. Intriguingly, the Canadians most likely to "get high" were coastal: Vancouverites and Haligonians. (Maybe salt-sea air spices up the smokes?)

While we audited many tragic tales of addiction and abuse, we also were informed of programs that could bring healing—if dollarized. Our hearings were also comic at times, as when one police chief explained painstakingly the import of such terms as "joints," "roaches," "roach clips," only to realize that we parliamentarians were already quite *personally* savvy about the slang!

Our chair was Dr. Bruce Halliday, a former family doc whose bedside manner (so to speak) was so collegial that even "Rat Packer" Sheila Copps accepted to be co-operative. She and I proposed opposing report titles; mine was adopted: *Booze, Pills, and Dope* (reflecting the order of importance of the abused drugs), subtitled, *Reducing Substance Abuse in Canada* (1987).

The report fielded recommendations on addiction prevention, treatment, and rehab. We sought heightened largesse for drug abuse programs for Indigenous persons, especially those off-reserve. Our work resulted in the creation in 1988 of the Canadian Centre on Substance Use and Addiction. We did suffer two setbacks: 1) the Tories refused to require warning labels regarding the perils of spirits; 2) they also balked at mandating banks to report suspicious financial transactions that could camouflage attempts to launder the profits of trafficking illegal drugs.

The next domestic stress to infuriate me was a long-dreaded bill to reinstate capital punishment—hanging—which got debated in the House in spring 1987. Since I had campaigned in the 1960s for the death penalty's abolition (effected in 1976), it was a debate that I approached well prepared. Although he argued to see his fellow citizens' necks stretched again, Deputy PM Don Mazankowski crossed the floor to express his admiration for the quality of my transcendent argument. The bill was killed, and many (very likely) poor people's lives were spared. (Death row wits aver, "Capital punishment means those without the capital get the punishment.")

Another domestic debate of import, in 1987, was a deal that Mulroney struck to get Quebec to sign on to the 1982 Constitution (patriated and amended by Pierre Trudeau with vast provincial support and public approval but with zilch buy-in from Quebec). That spring, at a meeting with provincial premiers at Meech Lake, QC, Mulroney had all but agreed to recognize Quebec as a "distinct society" (thus pleasing Premier Robert Bourassa), in exchange for everyone accepting enhanced provincial powers at the expense of federal authority. The agreement—dubbed the Meech Lake Accord—depicted unanimity that was fantastically phantasmal and fatally ephemeral.

When the Accord came before Parliament, all three parties approved the measure—partly because many prayed to prevent a new, divisive referendum on Quebec's future in Canada. I myself abstained on the ratification vote because I was concerned about minority (English and/or multicultural or diverse) language and culture protection in the "distinct society." I was not alone. Indeed, PET's essays and speeches against the Accord inspired all those who had grievances with Mulroney or who felt that Quebec was blackmailing the "rest of Canada" by threatening to hold constant referenda until it achieved outright independence or enough "concessions" from other governments that Canada would end up with its own "two-state solution." Other questions: What about Indigenous Peoples and their presence within Quebec's "distinct society"? What about gender equality? Could Quebec override the Canadian Charter of Rights and Freedoms by invoking the "distinct society" clause? And were not other provinces "distinct"? Newfoundland thought it was, and it was; it could not be confused for nearby New Brunswick, let alone distant British Columbia.

So, legislative redress proposed to enhance Canadian unity became, instead, polarizing. Many Québécois were feeling alienated because their "honour" was being "insulted" by Anglo-Canadian expressions of distrust over what Quebec might do if it had constitutional recognition as being "distinct." Yes, liberal and progressive Anglos had ammo for this view: the repressive Duplessis regime, the mania for Mussolini. Yet, contemporary Quebec was also the most progressive and secular of all the provinces—at least since the Quiet Revolution.

Ominously, a political price began to be paid by English premiers who okayed Meech Lake: a few got thumped at the polls, and new premiers rescinded their province's sanction. Some who hated the Accord simply hated Mulroney, some disliked Quebec achieving empowered saliency, but all of the enmity was toxic. The Accord's demise on July 1, 1990, helped sweep David Peterson from office and brought in Bob Rae as the first Knee-Dipper premier of "Loyal She Remains" Ontario; triggered the Charlottetown Accord referendum in 1992 (also lost by Mulroney); motivated a second sovereignty referendum for Quebec in 1995 (almost lost by the feds); and moved Quebec to adopt isolated self-development to establish its doubtless "distinction."

Uniquely among all MPs, I accepted an additional "shadow Cabinet" responsibility—to advocate for anti-racism and Black equality. Racial impediments were a minefield though. I was the MP for Windsor-Walkerville, not the de facto parliamentary flag-bearer for African-Canadians. But how could I abandon a lifetime of commitment to equality, justice, and human rights? I was the only Black MP. I had a duty to *represent* (to use Black slang)! I strove to air my critic complaints and to serve my constituents in a superior fashion; I strove to defend human rights at home and abroad. Yet, I am proud that never did I fail to speak out for African-Canadians. There is just no escaping who I am.

CHAPTER SIXTEEN:
FOREIGN "INVESTMENTS" & DOMESTIC "DUTIES"

SOUTH AFRICAN APARTHEID WAS THE URGENT HUMAN RIGHTS division internationally. From PM John Diefenbaker on, Canada had condemned white minority rule and had helped expel South Africa from the British Commonwealth. In an extraordinarily forceful speech before the United Nations in the fall of 1985, PM Mulroney echoed Dief the Chief. Condemning the racist regime, Mulroney pledged that Canada would sever all ties with South Africa unless apartheid were abolished.

Mulroney's stance had been previewed at the Commonwealth Heads of Government (CHOG) Meeting in Lyford Cay, Bahamas, in October 1985. There an Eminent Persons Group (EPG) was struck to press South Africa to change its evil ways or suffer the imposition of trade sanctions at a subsequent Commonwealth meeting. Canada's standard-bearer was Reverend Ted Scott, ex-primate of our "True North" Anglican Church.

While the EPG was investigating apartheid, Mulroney announced namby-pamby policies that negated his oath to sever relations with South Africa. Why? Prez Ray-gun and Brit PM Maggie ("Iron Lady") Thatcher wanted Canada to stay palsy-walsy with racists. Hell! I was having none of it! My public antipathy for apartheid included an appearance on CBC-TV with famed arms-and-foreign-affairs journalist Gwynne Dyer. I unleashed fiery anti-South African sermons before the general assemblies of the Inter-Parliamentary Union in both Buenos Aires (1986) and Pyongyang (1991). I also engaged with the Association of Western European Parliamentarians Against Apartheid (AWEPAA) in Amsterdam in 1985 and in Rome in 1986. At the latter, alongside MPs Charles Caccia and James A. McGrath, I relished a private audience with Pope John Paul II (only to endure yet another of his limp-wimp handshakes).

The Canuck anti-apartheid campaign was spearheaded by a host of religious and/or international-aid and/or peace bodies including the United Church, Amnesty International, Canadian University Services Overseas (CUSO), the Taskforce on the Churches and Corporate Responsibility, and the (British-based) Anti-Apartheid Movement, et cetera: leftism given righteous force.

Unlike the US, where no-guff, Af-Am civil rights orgs U-turned Prez Ray-gun's wobbly, pale butt, Black Canucks were invisible and silent on the anti-apartheid front. Artists United Against Apartheid (AUAA) alone gave a few "Africadians" a platform. The AUAA invited freedom tunes from jazz pianist Oscar Peterson and singer Salome Bey—the "Great White North" belting Black blues.

African-Canadians were absent from domestic anti-apartheid groups, but Black South African militants, notably African National Congress (ANC) reps, filled that vacuum. Also present were spokespersons from the South African Congress of Trade Unions (SACTU) and the South West Africa Peoples' Organization (SWAPO) of Namibia. The Southern African Institute for Policy and Research (based in Lusaka, Zambia) also circulated energizing info.

In 1986, I began treating with the ANC's Canuck rep: Yusuf "Jojo" Saloojee. We agreed that, because I wanted Canada to sunder ties with South Africa, I must oppose the invitation to Ambassador Glenn Babb to speak before Parliament's Human Rights Committee. My gambit got overruled; so, I seized the chance to confront Babb via several sharp exchanges. Impossible was his defence of an ignoble cause, that of the shabby theory of "separate development," which meant Caucasian tyranny and capitalist exploitation of the explicitly labelled "Black" majority. All South Africans would prosper, babbled Babb, if offshore meddlers would tend to their own sordid cases of domestic racism. Sanctions, he claimed, would harm Black citizens most. I characterized his specious thesis as a tacit rationalization for zwieback dictatorship. Though he and his ilk had a few collaborators—Uncle Toms and Aunt Jemimas—in their pockets, I said the ANC and like Black organizations were the only legitimate voices of South Africans.

But Babb knew that however tough be Mulroney and his ministers' rhetoric, Canuck mandarins would do nada. Mulroney barked—and his civil servants yawned.

South African and anti-apartheid NGOs pleaded for Canada to escalate sanctions, as had been oft urged. Sick of Canada's inaction and hypocritical rhetoric, I brought a motion, seconded by Steel-City-Gritty Sheila Copps, demanding that we shun South Africa. In committee, the measure was an easy sell; its passage gave anti-apartheid forces another goad to push Canada toward enacting truly harsh restrictions on South African-geared trade and travel. Did the government welcome that vote? Sure. It stiffened their spines versus redneck, Tory backbenchers and the drag-their-butts External Affairs bureaucrats.

Even so, South Africa's man in Bytown, Babb, was industrious in propaganda and skilled in smears. Evidence emerged of attempts to infiltrate some anti-apartheid groups and to launch fake letter-writing campaigns. Babb's embassy released reams of pro-apartheid op-eds; moreover, Babb could count on apartheid apologists within Mulroney's caucus. Zulu Chief Buthelezi—that lithe *comprador*—came to Canada and got toasted in business circles, which spurned Mandela, even after he became South Africa's first Black citizen to be elected prez. (One day, in the House, I referred to the relationship between Conrad Black and Buthelezi. Within a day, I received a note written in his Convicted-Pardoned Eminence's own hand threatening me with a lawsuit if I repeated my words outside the House of Commons! I scribbled on his letter, "You may be rich, but I am not stupid!" and sent it back. While "Lawd" Black was incarcerated in Florida from 2010 to 2012 as a convicted fraudster, I'd hoped he'd discover sympathy for the black, the brown, and the poor. Maybe one day?)

At many Canuck universities, including Queen's, campaigns to divest pension funds from South Africa were ratcheting up. In the House, I cited a letter circulated by Arthur J. E. Child, top dog of Burns Foods, among the Queen's U BOG. In his squib, Burns confuses South Africa with the utopian Dixie of *Gone with the Wind*, starring all those grinning darkies, capering to please their amused and devoted cracker masters. Said no-doubt "spoiled" Child, their homelands were well-designed;

Winnie Mandela did not reside in a shack; and crime was non-existent. Blacks thrived and wandered freely, going about their business (even if jobless, I guess). Thanks to bromides vomited by brown-nosing Black South Africans, Child also held that sanctions were inhumane. (Given his cheerleading—his shilling—for apartheid, Child deserved racist South Africa's Medal of Honour, becoming the only Canuck to sport that indecorous bauble. But he was pals with the Canadian South African Society, an anti-sanctions fifth column.)

Meanwhile, BC Premier Bill Vander Zalm hobnobbed with Babb to market prefab houses to South Africa (presumably for use in Black townships). Vander Zalm blessed the profit-making project and also schemed to increase trade in foodstuffs with the apartheid regime. No sanctions possible! Made sense: BC had neutered its own anti-discrimination statutes.

Babb had a trove of pawns to exploit in his upping of South Africa. He cruised a reserve and castigated Canada's racism toward Indigenous Peoples. He knew what most Canucks didn't (and still don't): apartheid was inspired by our home-grown "Bantustan" system.

Once, I attended a Canadian Jewish Congress banquet in The Big Zero where Babb was also a guest. I was unaware of the fact until the MC tactlessly referred to the presence of us both as indication that our "political" differences did not preclude our respectful camaraderie. How nasty a discourtesy! Herb Gray was so embarrassed that he walked out.

The EPG tabled its report at the 1986 CHOG gabfest in London. The conclusion was dismal. South Africa was increasing repression. High time to damage its economy, eh?

Brit PM Margaret Thatcher was pig-headed: her stentorian grunts nixed all anti-apartheid sanctions. But most Commonwealth nations, being melanin-positive, were eager for Azania's (South Africa's) liberation. The "paleface dominions" talked up "voluntary sanctions" (as toothless an affront as telling a neighbour that, the next time they're away, you won't set their garbage at the curb). Canada pledged money for anti-apartheid billboards (way to go) and to help finance schools in front-line states. Our mouths were rich with blarney, but we had no guts for a fight.

The next CHOG assembly in Vancouver was futile. Thatcher—the "Conqueror of the Falklands" (Malvinas)—continued to dig in her Yull Cheltenham high heels: let Afrikaners lord it over Africans, and let none protest. Her joint press conference with Mulroney was tense. Mulroney bleated for "racial equality"; Thatcher pleaded for Prez Ray-gun's love.

An observer in Vancouver, I got to converse with QE II at a reception for Commonwealth chiefs. I'd sidled alongside ultra-smiley-faced Afro reps who were plying Queen Liz with their practised pleasantries. Once the audience dwindled, I was the sole interlocutor with Her Majesty. She was petite in form, unflappable in manner. When I came out to her as a Canuck MP, she asked about my background as a fifth-generation "fugitive." We spoke for about five minutes during which I mentioned her visit to London II so long ago and the fate of our neighbourhood boys' "hideout." She was amused that her and her parents' visit had caused the City of London (ON) to demolish our tunnel'd quarters. Why not? Hadn't the British Empire been all about destroying other people's totems and temples, faiths and philosophies?

I was a backbench MP, yes, but my heritage positioned me at the centre of world affairs. So, I consulted with Southern Africa leaders including ANC head Oliver Tambo (whom I resemble somewhat), SWAPO Secretary-General Herman Andimba Toivo ya Toivo, and others.

In February 1987, à Montréal, the Canadian Council for International Cooperation convened a conference on Southern Africa. There, I conferred with Thabo Mbeki, a future South Africa prez. Our rapport was immediate. We talked for about an hour in his hotel room as he sat relaxed on his bed. He wanted my opinion of the Canadian anti-apartheid campaign and my view of Mulroney's policy. He was astute in commentary but diplomatic in assessment. (I'd admired Mbeki instantly, so I was grievously saddened when, as South African prez, he termed the AIDS epidemic an international conspiracy by the pharmaceutical industry to exploit Africans, thus denying its viral cause and condemning the value of anti-retroviral drugs. *Pity!*) The Montreal conference was a solidarity love-fest. Some six hundred international, anti-apartheid delegates communing. After debating day unto dusk, we boogied to African beats till dawn.

Alongside Walter MacLean, a Red Tory, and Don Johnson, a Grit, I condemned, at our panel review, Canada's failure to ratchet up sanctions. I urged that we send non-military aid to the front-line states to help them resist South African attempts to undermine their admins. Johnson drew the wrath of the audience due to his implicit allegation that Black governments were less trustworthy to treat with than were gun-toting, fascists-in-their-ranks, racist "honkies."

Ol' Joe Clark promised umpteen million smackeroos in aid to the South African Development Coordination Conference (SADCC) to try to decrease front-line states' trade dependency on South Africa. That move was salutary, but Mulroney and Clark still wouldn't deem South Africa a pariah. Their government never did. Instead, decisive action came from a surprising source.

US Prez Ray-gun's "constructive engagement" policy was balderdash. The Yanks were anti-Russia, not anti-racist. For them, the ANC spelled out USSR. They fretted: ain't Mandela a Marxist? Too, Castro's Cubans had crushed the pro-apartheid axis in "heavy-metal" tank battles. In his contest with the Iron Curtain, to be anti-Red—for Ray-gun—entailed being pro-white supremacy.

Even so, by 1986, the US domestic anti-apartheid push was paying off. The Congressional Black Caucus saw a law passed that, overriding Ray-gun's veto, imposed financial stress on South Africa. Due to tougher European censure too, South African capital began to choke, and "one person, one vote" began to seem a nicer option than Caucasian unemployment and/or a lily-white draft. Better to have Black majority rule than to see the pension plans go "poof" or see pale sons carted home in black body bags.

The next offshore crisis on my agenda? Haiti. This poorest nation in the Americas still bears the legacy of retaliation undertaken by its former colonizers (and Yanks) for being the only republic ever constructed outta slave revolution. (Versus Egypt, the Hebrews had divine assistance, so it's not equivalent to knocked-down, dragged-out, in-the-trenches struggle or against-all-odds success!)

Centuries ago, Haiti had been, due to impressed slave labour in sugar and rum production, the outsize contributor to French coffers. But after Haiti's ex-slave, revolutionary generals defeated French, English, and Spanish attempts at reconquest, the French threatened to reinvade Haiti in 1825 and thus extorted an indemnity of 170 million francs ($21 billion USD in today's currency). It took Haiti 122 years to pay off this "tax," a kind of reparations-in-reverse, and so its government has been persistently insolvent (and not due only to domestic corruption).

Impoverished and isolated by the Europeans and the Yanks, who feared the impact on their own enslaved of the news of a give-no-quarter Black revolution, Haiti became a country wracked with internal divisions between its Black poor and "Mulatto"/Creole middle class. Thus, corrupt and brutal despots ruled Haiti for most of the nineteenth century; they extracted blood, sweat, and tears from peasants to send gold—80 percent of their income—to France, Germany, the US.

Dissatisfied with his share of Haiti's GNP, Uncle Sam seized control of the treasury (the Haitian national bank). For refusing to be worked to death, Haitians were to be taxed to death. Then, in 1915, Prez Teddy Roosevelt invoked the Monroe Doctrine and dispatched US Marines to begin a two-decades-long occupation. Until 1934, Haiti's bosses were all US clients; even after the Marines said *au revoir*, the country's finances remained subject to *Yanqui* diktats.

In 1950, the first-ever direct popular elections in Haiti ushered Colonel Paul Magloire into power, and there ensued six years of democratic stability. But, in 1957, Dr. François "Papa Doc" Duvalier seized the palace. Initially *fêted* by Black proles, he morphed into a baleful dictator, utilizing his rebarbative private militia, the Tonton Macoute, to cow foes via torture and murder. Well, the anti-Red stance of the white-is-right West could wink at a Black lackey bumping off his own people.

Surprisingly though, Duvalier fancied himself a Haitian Martin Luther King! In the late 1960s, he posted me an autographed copy of the bio *A Tribute to the Martyred Leader of Non-Violence, Reverend Martin Luther King Jr.* Absurdly, Papa Doc addressed me as "a brother in the struggle"!

When Papa Doc—that Macbeth-n-Richard-III combo—gave up his poltergeist's soul in 1971, his cherubic butcher of a son, Jean-Claude, or Bébé Doc, carried on his pa's reign o' terror until a Black-fist uprising ensured his 1986 US Air Force flight to Paris and the Riviera, all champagne and white gloves. (Returning to Haiti in 2011, Baby Doc was jailed; he died in 2014.)

In 1987, a new constitution touted wide approval, but subsequent elections were aborted by the military who, aided by the Tonton Macoute, oppressed anyone left-liberal. (No liberal was left alone.) Thus was Machiavelli shortened to Macbeth; Richard III elongated to Richard Nixon. In 1988, an army-run election (boycotted by 90 percent of voters) delivered the Haitian White House to Christian Democrat Leslie Manigat. Canada, the US, and France cancelled all aid at once. In Montreal, the Haitian-Canucks called on Mulroney to help restore democracy.

In late January 1988, Knee-Dipper Bill Blaikie asked Joe Clark to dispatch a tri-party parliamentary delegation to Haiti. Clark agreed. I was tapped; to Haiti I jetted. Led by Jean-Guy Hudon, parliamentary secretary to Clark, our delegates were gravel-Gritty André Ouellette (Papineau), sandpaper-Gritty André Harvey (Chicoutimi), Tory Léo Duguay (Saint-Boniface), *et moi*—the one Anglo. Wouldn't my French get a workout! Before departure, I familiarized myself with Haiti's history and spent some time with Frank Chauvin, the Windsor ex-cop directing a Haitian charity. Even his sober account of the dire state of the downpressed could not prepare me for the unmitigated misery I surveyed.

February 17, 1988, commenced our four-day visit. Stark were the social-economic cleavages. Driven to a hotel on the hills of Pétion-Ville above Port-au-Prince, our quarter housed gated mansions, hotels, pools, restaurants, and high-end bars overlooking teeming, fetid, noisy slums. The "brown" ruling-class squatted *above* the massive majority of those whose complexions showed undiluted West African ancestry. And shit rolls downhill, eh?

In Port-au-Prince, I toured shoe-string-budget hospitals, orphanages, and missions plunked amid rickety shacks jumbled about stinking ditches brimming with human and animal feces and garbage. Nearby, toddlers gamboled and gangstas rumbled. Outside the cities, the soil was ochre dust, a virtual desert. (Because trees were kindling, no greenery could hold moisture in the earth.) I've seen squalor in South America, Africa, India, and other Caribbean isles, but Haiti was—is—incomparably destitute. Urban dilapidation; rural desiccation.

Intolerably, abysmally, the coffee-cream-complected elite rode the backs of their dark compatriots. They purred Parisian French, not the bubbly Creole of the masses. They were a domestic colonial class: brown Boers, caramel *pieds noirs*. So remote were they in their gated redoubts, they could not deign to mention voodoo, that jungle-vibrant Catholicism with its own saints and African gods equal to any in the Christian pantheon. Thus, only in sessions with labour reps and NGOs did we hear of the destabilization wrought by missionaries desecrating the voodoo culture, which is the one faith in which poor Black people pray to a god who loves and upholds them for who they are. Thus, plebeian rum may double as holy water.

The stark rift between the bourgeois lords and the lumpen serfs was *insupportable*. So, in my slow-spoken but frank French, I lectured Haitian poobahs on the significance that Haiti held in the hearts of Black people globally. I lauded the inspiration of the slave revolution that produced the first Black republic. I referenced how anti-colonialism and anti-apartheid movements in Africa itself were informed by study of Haiti's self-liberation versus the armed might of Europe's conquistadors. Even the Harlem Renaissance was influenced by Haiti's stellar feats in visual arts, music, dance, and literature. I held that the failure of the governors to build a nation that lived up to the promise of its revolution therefore concerned African peoples everywhere. A screaming silence met my sermon.

The NGOs told us of a culture of baksheesh and extortion, of aid supplies and money being siphoned off by officials for their own enrichment, and of the army's alliance with the drug lords. So, how can Haiti achieve democracy? Only when the army gets confined to barracks.

Prez Manigat was, I perceived, an impressively cultured gent conversant with Enlightenment liberalism. But his military was his master; he was a puppet. Worse, a zombie.

In our unanimous parliamentary report, we saluted Manigat's intentions but saw his position as untenably tenuous. To reach the Haitian people, Canuck aid had to be channelled through NGOs, we said, and should prioritize wells, seeds, medicines, and schools.

As predicted, as soon as Manigat tried to command the army, General Henri Namphy effected a *coup d'état*. Soon, the Tonton Macoute—backed by cops and troops—executed the horrific St. Jean Bosco massacre in the parish of Jean-Baptiste Aristide, a liberation theology priest and future prez. The liquidation of dozens was the outcome of a three-hour siege of the church (itself torched) where one thousand unarmed worshippers prayed. This incident precipitated a second coup; thus, General Prosper Avril turfed out General Namphy, giving the latter a taste of his own putschist poison.

In my opinion, Haiti will never know true liberation until the West ceases its interference (including backing despots), repays the Haitians the billions they are owed, and allows Black Haitians—the vast majority— to vote themselves social democratic governments to permit appropriate social spending and redistribution of wealth. Or Haitians *must* enact a new, Cuban-style revolution to allow them to finally have a government by the people, of the people, and *for* the people.

Although my caucus critic portfolios involved domestic and international causes, I also took on many parochial predicaments, most environmental. The first of these? The "blob" of chemical contaminants colonizing the floor of the St. Clair River. The Canada–US International Joint Commission (for the Great Lakes) and allies pressured firms whose spills and dumps whelped the toxic menace to dissolve the tumorous mass into flushable bilge. (Intriguingly, the "blob" had been "fathomed" in 1984 by the University of Windsor's Great Lakes Institute for Environmental Research [GLIER] when I was still the U Windsor chief biologist. Yet, then-GLIER chief "Doc Humbert Humbert" never bruited this biohazard. Perhaps his practised ignoring of me explains why an MP with no scientific background—Langdon, an economist—received Humbert's gifts of headline, newsworthy info.)

In 1986, Tecumseh and East Windsor were so alarmed by flooding from Lake St. Clair that sandbags were trucked to residents, including me. Fielding an emergency query from Tecumseh mayor Harold Downs, I called for troops to aid in flood control. My questions and letters directed to Environment Minister Tom McMillan encouraged no relief, but the Tories did approve $8.4 million for flood-plain mapping.

Also in 1986, Detroit fast-tracked a garbage incinerator, which, lacking state-of-the-art emission controls, still had approval-to-pollute from Yank regulators. Ontario's Grit government ignored the irritant until cross-border opposition to the towering "tailpipe" mounted. But 400,000 anti-incinerator signatures—and belated Canuck protests—were of no avail. My attempts to convince the recalcitrant Detroit mayor

Coleman Young to improve emission controls for the smokestack were dismissed, and contemptuously. Just as foreseen, the incinerator was soon the chief source of cross-border air pollutants. Young "blew his stack," yep, and soiled his reputation and poisoned his own citizens.

Deathless dispute arose over Detroit's Enrico Fermi Nuclear Generating Station, which is visible from Amherstburg across Lake Erie. So plagued by structural flaws is its antique design, it blows more hot air (steam) than it can stream electricity. The US Nuclear Regulatory Commission (NRC) lets Fermi operate at full bore despite the risks, thus stoking fears of a meltdown that would so X-ray Canadians that our hair would fall off our skulls and our skin fall off our bones.

Gray, Langdon, Caldwell, and I petitioned the International Atomic Energy Commission to intervene, but the Reaganauts rejected our entreaties. Citing its many malfunctions and safety violations, we asked the NRC to mothball the relic. But the NRC is captive to capital, and so the plant fumes on. (The only palliative for any China Syndrome–like disaster is an emergency measures plan that would permit just enough time for prayers.)

Plant closures and job loss were endless grief. Too, by 1987, Korean and Japanese car manufacturers had set up shop in Canada. Though not subject to the Auto Pact, they still skipped paying substantial duties on imported parts. Langdon, Gray, and I teamed with the Canadian Auto Workers (CAW) to demand that the Pact cover Asian carmakers. The Tories refused. Of course! Weren't they already floating "free trade" as a means to lessen Labour's clout?

Meanwhile, GM decided to "rationalize" its Canuck and Yankee car production. They'd move GM parts manufacture from a Windsor plant to a US facility despite the former's well-documented superior quality and efficiency. To me, the decision was payback for a CAW 1984 strike that idled GM's US operations. Indeed, during the strike, management asked CAW members at the GM Trim Plant to switch to being UAW members so that assembly could continue. GM's prez even suggested that Trim Plant workers observe US rather than Canadian holidays. But the union refused to bend, and the Windsor factory closed, killing 1,200 jobs.

Then, Ford closed its Windsor export supply office, casting off another 180 workers. Chrysler built an engine plant in Michigan rather than reopen its Windsor facility. The wheels were coming off Canadian carmaking.

Bought by US-based International Carriers, Yellow Freight System Inc. promptly jettisoned 70 percent of its workers. However, we three opposition Windsor MPs gained their reinstatement by demanding that the purchaser meet Foreign Investment Review Agency (FIRA) conditions. Yet, when LaSalle Machine Tools was shuttered by its US owner, thus cutting forty jobs, FIRA was MIA and workers were SOL.

The looming FTA could only aggravate matters at a time when Windsor's jobless rate was near 10 percent. Thus, I advised Mayor Dave Burr to initiate a task force of mayors of auto-industry municipalities. Nine mayors signed on. Burr appeared before the External Affairs and International Trade Committee where he defended the Auto Pact and advocated for a Windsor location for the new joint venture between GM and Toyota.

The committee report stated that Auto Pact standards must be applied to offshore carmakers, while pointing out areas where the Big Three faltered in their commitments. Despite the pleas of the mayoralty nonet and our MP trio, Regional Economic Development Minister Sinclair Stevens refused to advise a Windsor site for the GM and Toyota initiative.

Another peril to Windsor jobs was a proposed hostile takeover of Hiram Walker distillers by Gulf Canada, a subsidiary of the Reichmann brothers–owned Olympia & York (O&Y), an international property development firm. However, Allied Lyons of Great Britain, who were willing, unlike O&Y, to guarantee union jobs and for whom Hiram Walker was a "no-brainer" fit, had in play a formidable offer for the distillery. To stir the whisky further (*ahem*), Allied Lyons was itself facing a takeover by Elders IXL of Australia, and that would have scotched (yes) the British bid. Still, the union favoured Allied Lyons, and I stood with the union.

Somehow, though, the Reichmanns imagined that I could influence the liquor Labourites. Thus, I was in the House Opposition lobby when I was directed to a plangent telephone call. Ahoy! 'Twas the senior Reichmann, Paul, phoning from his jet to schedule a face-to-face. I soon met Paul and bro Albert in their O&Y digs in the Big Smoke. Oozing schmooze, they said they'd preserve jobs at Walker's if their bid won. But I'd not trust in signatures only. The bros were the acme of politesse, even humble, and—I wagered—sincere, but they'd guarantee nada.

I transmitted the content of our conversation and my impression of the Reichmanns to the union. But some thought I was being an ambassador for O&Y, that I was a shill for capital rather than a defender of jobs. (The latter 1980s—as consecrated in the 1987 movie *Wall Street*—was all about capitalists cannibalizing each other, to "create wealth" by buying up the assets of other corporations and companies, then liquidating them or selling them to yet other buyers. Often, in these cases of corporate concentration, workers lost jobs and retirees lost pensions.) In any event, Allied Lyons won.

Generally, I collaborated just fine with Labour. Indeed, I tapped funding for the Unemployment Help Centre. Too, often, I joined strikers—even provincial public sector workers—on the picket line. Still, some workers be reflex jerks. When Air Canada employees walked off the job, I caught hell for crossing a picket line: But how was I to get back to Bytown, to serve my constituents, otherwise? (I did pay an instant price for catching that flight! The plane was an eight-seater turboprop. I felt every bump, every wind gust; worse, my eardrums got pummelled by the loud, arrogant rants of Hockey Canada's screamingly loud, plaid-jacketed version of Rush Limbaugh.)

Soon, I negotiated with Hon. Benoît Bouchard to obtain $200,000 for the City of Windsor to draft a strategic economic plan; I turned up a Canada Works sum of $600,000 to help improve the Drouillard Road community.

I also arranged $350,000 in Ottawa moneys for an entrepreneur's development project. Because the gent benefiting was a Tory, my assistance incurred criticism. My response? The Tory enterprise would require union jobs. Who *dast* complain?

Still, federal politics were alienating. I felt divorced from my electors. Because only weekends could set me in the riding, I relied on my constituency aides to answer voters' needs. Then again, many of the problems reaching my office were municipal or provincial or concerned a different riding. Thus, we built co-operative relationships with other politicos' offices and with public agencies. Our reputation for serving our constituents, then, was unmatched.

Although I was a backbench, Black, socialist, rookie MP, I bonded well with a few Mulroney Tories. Chief among them was the Rt. Hon. Joe Clark, who, in 1988, appointed me to accompany Hon. Ethel M. Cochrane (Senator) on a special parliamentary delegation to Africa. We visited Côte d'Ivoire, Ghana, Nigeria, Zambia, Zimbabwe, and Botswana. It was just a courtesy and info junket. For me, though, it was my first foray to the continent of my ancient ancestors. In most, I was huzza'd as an expat bro—except in Zambia. Although she knew zilch about Africa, international protocol made Senator Cochrane the queen of our delegation. That did not explain the extent to which "K.K."—Zambia's head of state, Kenneth Kaunda—ignored me while gliding Cochrane about his sumptuous palace and his personal golf course. (If he'd just added a third "K" to his initials, I would've understood his preference!)

Although ruled by the firing-squad-trigger-happy dictatorship of former Ghanaian Air Force Flight Lieutenant Jerry "J.J." Rawlings and his Provisional National Defence Council, Ghana was, by African standards, booming (and not just via gunfire). Almost $2 billion (US) flooded into Ghana from 1987 to 1989, thanks to Rawlings's decision to let prices soar, devalue the currency, and adopt other International Monetary Fund (IMF) "stimuli." This windfall of foreign capital, if with strings attached, coincided with our visit. Warm to Canadians, Ghanaians greeted us with red-carpet-and-floral-bouquet enthusiasm. We dined with politicos and civic leaders, eyed the magnificent Volta River project (the Akosombo Dam), and peeped about the former home of the post-independence PM and Prez—and incendiary Pan-Africanist—Kwame Nkrumah.

My impression of Botswana? The most stable, democratic, and prosperous of sub-Saharan African countries. However, we spent little time in the capital, Gabarone, and saw little other than well-tailored, sweetly cologned "suits," all consummate, dapper, reticent Negro Europeans.

Nigeria's Lagos airport? Chaos eased by corruption. Clearing Customs and Immigration meant pacing a gauntlet of rude, raucous interrogatives and boorish behaviour only alleviated by the passing of baksheesh (bribes). Luckily, the Canuck embassy staff were able to use their own high-priority status to usher us past the grasping hands and onto the clenched fist that could, would, and did stamp our passports. The drive downtown: trucks snorted like bulls; drivers screeched toward ghastly collisions that somehow never happened. Scooters gunning and motorbikes revving. Air that was diesel-and-palm-wine-dizzying clotted; honking echoing the House of Commons question period!

We hung out at a nightclub that recalled those in Detroit: a smoke-tangy and perfume-sultry atmosphere and African-American music, somehow a bit more African on the east side of the Atlantic. Next day, I putted golf balls over unique mud greens (putting greens made of dirt).

We hopped to Harare, Zimbabwe, hoping to face ANC heads and Members of Parliament. But no invitations greeted us; no reservations got made; no revelations were divulged.

In Ivory Coast, we navigated the capital, Abidjan, and its exurbs, including cocoa plantations, schools, colleges, and Canuck-sponsored women's projects. We chatted with local parliamentarians and our expat NGO reps.

By the end of my first term, I had national profile, local swagger. Yes, being the only Black MP guaranteed that I'd stand out. Also, being a strong critic of the Mulroney Tories and an advocate for Windsor and for human rights, I attracted notice. Nor did it hurt that I was chosen by the CBC to flank Suzanne Fortin-Duplessis as co-host of a televised showcase of Canadian talent to honour the delegates to the Inter-Parliamentary Union conference in September 1985. More substantially, the *Toronto Star* named me one of "The 10 Best MPs" and *Maclean's* magazine listed me as one of "the most promising MPs." I even topped Parliament Hill's "10 Best-Dressed MPs" poll, a piece put together by staffers (or reporters) seeking a bit of levity. I was also complimented by the Hon. George Hees (the Veterans Affairs minister), who said, "I have been watching you, McCurdy! You are going to be here for a long time!" Well, his statement was true only if we accept that, as the old saw goes, "a week in politics can seem a lifetime."

Nevertheless, soon the voters of Windsor-Walkerville would decide whether I was truly one of the "10 Best" MPs in accomplishments (if also in wardrobe) or whether I should surrender my House of Commons megaphone and "get back" to my University of Windsor microscope. Yet, I wished to remain in The Big Zero—despite the winters and the "inescapable lousiness" (to borrow an Irving Layton phrase) of aspects of public life. As exciting as gliding bacteria are for this scientist, there was something heart-palpitatingly noble about *representing* sistren and brethren Windsorites as a scientist gone patently political.

CHAPTER SEVENTEEN:
TILTING AT "FREE TRADE"

I ENTERED CONFIDENTLY THE FEDERAL ELECTION CAMPAIGN OF October and November 1988—that seven-week or forty-nine-day ordeal. Indeed, I had a new team of staffers in place in The Big Zero, whose labours also assured that I should have wind in my sails.

A redhead firecracker of zest and efficiency, Nicole Charron seemed equipped to do everything at once—and twice more in the "other" official language. The office was all pep, thanks to her hustle and bustle, setting up distribution of my "householder" info pamphlets to constituents as well as ensuring deliveries of Scotch along with freshly pressed suits. She was an office manager *par excellence*: no message was missed; no instruction was ever misinterpreted. Moreover, never did she lose an ounce of her bounty of good cheer.

George Elliott Clarke was editing a tiny Black community newspaper in Halifax, Nova Scotia, when I called him up in September 1987 and interviewed him to become my Constituency Communications Liaison. He was the first Black to be hired to work for an NDP MP (and later I would also hire the second). I knew that he had a background in English and was writing poetry (sometimes—*ahem*—during office hours). But his writing style could echo my own, and I trusted many vital letters to his pen, while all signatures were reserved for me. That George hailed from "another" Windsor (in Nova Scotia) and had counted Rocky Jones as a mentor, was endearing—as was his gargantuan laughter—if not his appetite for my Scotch! (Clarkie thought his gulps were mere sips!) But I am also proud that he saw my example as a doctor-prof as one worth pursuing, and soon he was Dr. G. E. C., orating to classes at Duke and then Harvard.

Don Lenihan was pursuing a doctorate in philosophy but accepted to work as my critic-area researcher. He was affable yet earnest; professorial and detailed. All he was missing were the stereotypical elbow pads. He could digest scads of contradictory arguments and party position papers plus the exhaustless propaganda of militants and then help me fashion a substantive speech—all facts and figures and graphs but with exclamations "in." Soft-spoken but laser-focussed. That was the man: to the tweedy clerisy born.

However, before Don got my nod, Aileen Leo was my issues researcher. Dark-haired, serious-eyed, taciturn except for emitting snippets of dry, chuckling wit, she was already the sombre epitome of the science-savvy communications savant (especially in social justice advocacy) she would later become in her career choice. Like Clarkie, she spent the 1988 federal election campaign in Windsor.

The overriding, existential question of the 34th federal election campaign was the Canada–US Free Trade Agreement. My Ottawa and Windsor staffers knew—as keenly as I—that it would be the capital obsession, and our success would hinge on putting our concerns about the agreement before the electorate and asking them to say *NO* to Mulroney by saying *YES* to McCurdy; to vote *NO* to transnational corporate dominance by voting *YES* for Labour.

So, through 1987 and 1988, I tore apart the FTA; I ripped up the FTA. Union audiences raved about these speeches! The people had had no vote on Meech Lake, but here was a chance to nix the FTA and perhaps also rid us of Mulroney, whose charisma had faded to the blarney of a cartoon charlatan—though corporate Canada (branch-plant, US-bossed firms) rallied to his side. Yes, as with the Meech Lake Accord, the FTA was becoming a referendum on Mulroney. My analyses tapped into the widespread sense that Mulroney could not be trusted; that he had—as the "gritty" John Turner said during the pivotal leaders' debate—"sold us out." By toadying to Ronnie Ray-gun on everything, Mulroney had morphed into "Lyin' Brian."

So, my screeds heaped scorn on buddy-buddy Mulroney and Reagan and on the Tory willingness to kowtow to the US, which I viewed as declining while Canada was rising. I pooh-poohed the idea that we should surrender our never–properly exploited comparative advantage in energy and natural resources. I also stressed the danger to industrial advancement that was inherent in our lack of sufficient investment in scientific research and technological development. I also popularized these concerns in tabloid op-eds and in magazine articles. (A model speech was one given in the House of Commons; see Hansard, 33rd Parliament, July 5, 1988. Was it—as George Grant said of Diefenbaker's last parliamentary speech as PM, on February 5, 1963—"a great document of Canadian nationalism"? Mine expressed perhaps even fiercer anger?)

Ultimately, negotiations reached an impasse over the trade-dispute-settling mechanism, but this was overcome, and the FTA came to Parliament for ratification. In the fervent, pursuant debate, I studied the effectiveness of Turner's ploy to wave the Maple Leaf flag versus Mulroney's soiled white-flag-of-capitulation to US interests. In contrast, Leadbelly was waving the (A&W) orange-soda-and-root-beer-coloured flag of "Let's all chill at the barbecue!"

Despite Leadbelly's socialism-marinated brain-pan, he'd accepted two false polling results: 1) that Canucks would elect him—and the NDP—based solely on his likeability versus the hated (in English Canada) Mulroney; and 2) that Canucks distrust the NDP on economics. But the first poll reflected a summer 1987 love-in with "Uncle Ed," the kind of guy to snooze on your patio after burping his beer and burger. The second poll misconstrued the FTA as a pocketbook matter; it wasn't. For much of English Canada, the FTA was akin to treason.

Both Grits and Knee-Dippers demanded a people's vote on the FTA. Although it passed in the Tory-dominated House, it was stopped in the Liberal preserve: the Senate. Thus, an election was called on Saturday, October 1, 1988. Immediate battle lines got drawn. The Commons versus *Kapital*.

I plucked Clarkie from his digs and we sped to Windsor. Both of us railed against Broadbent's blunder at the NDP campaign launch. Playing his "Uncle Ed" shtick, Leadbelly had striven to appeal to working-class suburbanites, not realizing that Labour needed to see flames shooting from his mouth, not his patio grill! Upon arrival at our Windsor committee room, Clarkie dumped all that "Uncle Ed" crap in the trash. Our mission? *Stop Free Trade!*

No wonder hundreds of unionists to whom the FTA and the gutting of the Auto Pact were visceral treasons swelled our Windsor-Essex campaign rally. Langdon and I both pledged a vigorous fight, thus winning rowdy applause. Then, funereal Leadbelly croaked his effete nostrums, downplaying the FTA and upselling his "brand." Damn! He ceded patriotism to Turner, thus revitalizing the Grits and leaving Knee-Dippers to choke on Leadbelly's flash-in-the-pan cookout ash.

Shortly, viewing the Grits' incendiary TV ad in which the Canada–US border gets erased by the Yank FTA negotiators and then the Liberal Maple Leaf logo flutters over the screen to both the rattle of warrior kettledrums and the first notes of the national anthem, my Black poet-staffer practically blanched, and I leapt up, yelling, "There goes my seat!" Assuredly, to defeat the resurgent, insurgent Liberals, we did really have to ditch Leadbelly's Pollyanna jive.

My opponents for re-election were Shaughnessy Cohen (Lib) and Bruck Easton (PC): solid candidates with superior credentials. A pro-gressive lawyer, well-read in English lit and sociology, Shaughnessy and her husband, Jerry (a Windsor psych prof), were friends with me and my kids. Jerry had worked with my daughter Leslie on a science fair project. I'd visited severally their splendid riverbank home where my kids would fish off their back deck. And the couple had partied (non-politically) at my home. Born Irish (née Murray), Shaughnessy had taken Jerry's sur-name so she could also be Jewish. She was a congenial adversary, but I still had to prevail: no hard feelings!

The son of Mary Easton (with whom I'd served on the St. Clair College BOG), Bruck was, like Shaughnessy, a lawyer—and a true-blue Red Tory: heart on the left, wallet on the right. And he just loved political life in a non-partisan fashion; he admired folks who threw their hats in the ring, fought each round, and went the distance. Never could he be a sore loser.

Note: Bruck was crucial to my chances, for, though the Tories were championing free trade, the idea itself was a classic Grit policy. The com-mitted Tories in the riding were few, and the socialists who'd vote Tory were close to zilch. So, Bruck's campaign could only flourish by attracting the votes of pro-FTA Liberals (especially among professionals—lawyers, managers, etc.). The better he did, the worse for Shaughnessy. However, Shaughnessy could only grow her campaign by attracting Knee-Dippers prepared to put more trust in Big Biz lawyer Turner (who, upon becom-ing PM in 1984 had insisted, albeit briefly, on keeping his nine corporate directorships *while* he also had access to confidential government docu-ments) than in the avuncular but now irrelevant Leadbelly. Aye, Shaughnessy was a hazard to me on my left; but Bruck, who owned the riding's pro-FTA vote, was her dread menace on the right. To outpace my middle-of-the-road opponent, I'd have to run further, faster, and harder to the left than could Shaughnessy or her leader, Turner, to keep the NDP vote and also attract Grits who pined for the clarity and charisma of PET and who chafed at Turner's bum-patting chieftaincy.

Steelworker Ron Varley geared up to guide my campaign. His gruff talk matched his line-laced face, which recalled the Marvel superhero The Thing, if outfitted with wire-rim spectacles. But his shirt, tie, and suspenders revealed his build to mirror that of another Marvel character, The Hulk. Yes: he had the physique and visage of an ex-boxer—and a tough, no-BS attitude. And academic me appreciated the could-be-brawler sidekick. Here was street cred incarnate!

Our office team included canvass organizers John Whalen (with one foot in a kind of cast and sandal) and Clarkie (who was adept at convincing guys and dolls to buzz doorbells to identify "my" voters); plus Bev Wood back as office manager and sandy-haired Joe Comartin as treasurer; plus John's cheery, blonde wife, Lena, helping out with clerical duties and coffee; plus dozens of canvassers, from nerdy high schoolers to commie grannies, from crewcut engineers to "flying squads" of union picketers. (When Clarkie came face to face with the Caucasian picketer George Clark [no terminal 'e'], he was surprised, apparently never before realizing that the Scottish Clarks and the Irish Clarkes were slaveholders!) Nor can I omit Dave "Cookie" Cooke—as thin as the cigarette he was always holding as if it were chalk and he a prof—nor my Windsor staffer Jamal "Jim" Shaban (as equally loquacious and charismatically garrulous as his slightly older lookalike, the Big Smoke and Broadway impresario Garth Drabinsky).

The committee room atmosphere? Smog! It sashayed and swished, gave devils halos and saints halitosis; it scraped the eyes; it raped the lungs. That blue-grey blob of haze also separated our realm from the square world of mere voters, who did not sit with cigarette and Styrofoam cup of coffee (or black lava gruel) and convince each other passionately that only a new McCurdy mandate could send "Uncle Sam" Mulroney skedaddling to Wall Street. We were not a cult, we were not a cabal, but we had the zealotry of cults and the commitment of cabals.

My candidacy required plant-gating at 5:00 A.M. and at 5:00 P.M.; constant canvassing; chats with interest groups; media interviews; hurried huddles with Ron et al. to determine strategies and tactics; plus prep for candidates' debates. Democracy depends upon red eyes and sore feet.

Having trashed all the "Uncle Ed" posters and pamphlets, I had Clarkie design a leaflet that would highlight me and explain the FTA's flaws so that even a grade-6-schooled "Joe" or "Jill" could know why the treaty was evil. He drafted an electrifying, white-letter-on-black squib that featured me, looking fierce (a Malcolm X pose, my finger jabbing at you, my head backlit), and the inner text listing "10 Reasons to Vote No" (to the FTA). The back featured a nice pic of Leadbelly *et moi*, plus a Maple Leaf flag image twice the size of anything Shaughnessy was flaunting in her printed matter. Heck, we couldn't keep that leaflet in the office! All Windsor wanted it because it put the FTA dangers so patently. Teachers and entire classes came in and grabbed it, and it seemed that anyone who read it had to *Vote No* by casting a vote *for* yours truly!

I started the race with superb confidence, but it was not all easy as pie. The Grits were give-no-quarter contestants for the anti-FTA, NDP vote, but the real spoiler for me? *Abortion!* In January 1988, the Supreme Court had declared Canada's abortion law unconstitutional. Mulroney essayed to pass a bill restricting late-term abortions, but it died fast. Because abortion access was no longer regulated, the election campaign offered pro-life activists—supremely Vatican-agitated Catholics—a perfect time to either coerce me into an anti-abortion commitment or trigger my defeat. The unmitigated hazard to my re-election came from anti-choice Knee-Dippers and was spearheaded by Lucien "Kit" Lacasse, the *Tecumseh Tribune*'s publisher and editor.

Running left of the Liberals on the FTA, I was right, but being pro-choice or pro-woman, I was "wrong." In my own bailiwick of Tecumseh, Lacasse ginned up the New Democrats for Life, to woo any neighbours who were saps. Damn! I urge moderation in regard to abortions after twenty weeks, but I consider it a personal, medical matter to be decided between patient and doctor. Yes, I hold that the rights of a rational, able-to-conceive-a-child citizen do supersede that of tissue that is yet-to-be a visibly separate person. (Anti-choice folks want to police women's sexuality—and thus enslave their bodies. Their attitude is the same as that of racist Gestapo toward Black bodies: to inhibit, if not prohibit, our freedoms to be, to breathe, to move.)

Naturally, it was these same loutishly "compassionate" Christians who fomented ugly racism. A nameless *artiste* of Negrophobic ilk circulated a cartoon: a predatory, charcoal cat depicted *moi*. My unadulterated friends—long-time CAW militant George Johnson and his wife, Jo-Anne—knew the culprit but did not name him until I was re-elected. Their reticence kept me from suing the miscreant, a village idiot and auto-prole who published a local ad rag.

Critical were candidates' debates. Staged mainly before high school students, they played to my strengths. Even at Tecumseh's École secondaire catholique l'Essor, an anti-choice redoubt, I drew avid applause. An expert debater on the hustings, I dominated by making the FTA and Canada's future my focus. Bruck talked of profits; Shaughnessy spoke of her silver-haired, once-golden-boy *chef*, Turner (who'd danced with Princess Margaret); I damned Mulroney and demanded an independent, prosperous future for a proud nation of inventive and hard-working patriots.

I kept my seat; Langdon held his. I was re-elected with an increased plurality, a landslide victory of some 14,000 votes, while Cohen finished second, having taken Tecumseh as predicted. Easton finished third. (Bruck and I had a celebratory breakfast the very next morn: Tuesday, November 22, 1988. Had he not siphoned off much of Shaughnessy's vote?) Yet, although the New Democrats secured a record number of seats (forty-three), John Turner's impassioned, anti-FTA crusade returned the Grits with even more (eighty-three), thus consolidating their position as the Official Opposition. How did the Tories win? By holding Quebec (thanks also to its embrace of the Meech Lake Accord), taking a third of Ontario and a chunk of the West, and destroying Turner's credibility via TV attack ads (a Yank-cranked tactic that would backfire drastically upon the Tories in 1993).

Lookit! The Knee-Dippers had blown a chance to displace the Grits! Hadn't Leadbelly let the Liberals steal a socialist policy? His electoral leadership had been blunder upon fiasco. How could he stay? Time for him to vacate the Big Zero and kick back in Havana, puffing on cigars that, as Freud would say, need not be any kind of symbol.

CHAPTER EIGHTEEN:
THE MIS/ (OR MS.)/ LEADERSHIP CAMPAIGN

YEP, FEDERAL NDP BOTTOMS WARMED MORE PARLIAMENTARY seats than ever before: forty-three. *Oui*, that was twelve derrières better than the previous benchmark of thirty-one—accomplished by leader David Lewis in 1972. However, Lewis had secured 12 percent of a 264-seat chamber. Too, Lewis had been able to extract social-welfare legislation from P. E. Trudeau in trade for backstopping his minority rule. Now, sixteen years later, Broadbent had taken 15 percent of the 295-seat House. Yes, a 3 percent gain over the 1972 results, but now, with a Tory majority, we'd pass few progressive laws; plus, the Grits were back, and we were still third. So, when he greeted the new caucus, Leadbelly surveyed stormy, gloomy aspects. His failure to contest free trade had cost many Knee-Dippers their seats (by razor-thin margins). Windsor New Dems had only secured our seats because we'd junked the "Uncle Ed" paraphernalia and run independent campaigns, ignoring Broadbent's "Mr. Congeniality" emphasis.

Not just disingenuous but self-disparaging was Leadbelly's rationalization of (his) failure and rejection of the criticism of a strategy that let the Grits cultivate natural NDP turf. Cornered, Leadbelly played off as papal, lecturing *ex cathedra* against anyone who questioned his "bull." After bandying words with the patronizing *pater*, I muttered, "I'm tired of this shit." Anonymous auditors then tattled to the press that I'd accused Broadbent of racism. Muckrakers panted to corroborate the allegation but could not; thus, they stood up to their mouths in their own sloppy feces.

Unable to withstand the withering carping about his election peccadillos, Leadbelly bowed his slack backside out the door, cometh March 1989. Speculation put Stephen Lewis, Ed Schreyer, Bob Rae, Bob White, and Roy Romanow in the top tier of candidates to replace "Ed the Sock." In fact, I lounged with Romanow in a hotel where we talked about his leadership chances before embarking together (at his invite) to sample Big Smoke night life. He deemed his prospects as dubious, given his responsibilities in Saskatchewan (where he would soon become the premier). In the end, Romanow did not run, nor did any of the other prominent prospects.

Upon my re-election, I retained shadow critic responsibility for Human Rights (External) and Industry, Science, and Technology. In the former portfolio, I saw signs that South Africa would soon move to free Nelson Mandela and institute democracy, thus ending Dixie-style-minority rule. *Progress!* But China shocked the world with a repugnant massacre of (primarily) student protesters seeking democratic rights and civil liberties.

Peaceful demonstrations had been occurring in Tiananmen Square in Beijing for some weeks in spring 1989, seemingly with government acquiescence. (The atmosphere conjured the "Democracy Wall Movement" of 1978–79, when the Communist Party had permitted big-character posters to be pasted up publicly, exposing flaws in governance.) So, the West had cheered on the post-Mao leadership's display of tolerance. But Chinese officialdom began to sour on the protests after the summit meeting between the People's Republic bosses and the Soviet Union's celebrity reformer, Mikhail Gorbachev. Longing for a mascot for their dynamic interest in reform, students upheld Gorbachev and his programs of perestroika and glasnost as nostrums that China needed to pursue to realize a "Prague Spring" in Beijing. However, China's bosses rejected Gorbachev's liberalizations (fearing that they'd jeopardize authoritarianism) and were appalled by the appearance—amid the students' ranks—of the US Statue-of-Liberty-styled, ten-metre-tall, white foam-and-papier-mâché "Goddess of Democracy" figure. (Gotham City cachet? No, it was Hong Kong kitsch.)

The People's Liberation Army was tasked to clear the protesters. Sixteen hundred students were crushed under tank treads or riddled with bullets; thousands were wounded; others vanished. To stymie accurate identifying of the dead in their numbers, cadavers got carted off for mass disposal *somewhere*.

As Human Rights critic, I led a special emergency debate on the matter, resulting in the passage of an all-party resolution of condemnation. Consciences were salved and relations with China stalled, but serious rebuke was hobbled by the puissant economic stakes that relations with China involve.

Now, attention shifted back to the NDP leadership contest. Simon De Jong of The Queen City, Regina, Saskatchewan, launched his bid. He was so laid-back that he seemed as simpatico as Stan Laurel. Having been a toddler in a Japanese torture camp on Java, postwar, he'd sailed to Canada with his Dutch family. First a hippy artist, then a Vancouver social worker, he'd become a prized MP. A zero in The Big Zero, yes, but he ruled the "Sasquatch" Knee-Dippers.

Other prompt contenders? Roger Lagassé, a BC schoolteacher, and Edgar Ryan of Gatineau, QC. Ryan's ethics were his motivation, but the golden rule is obscured by politicos' smoke and mirrors. He announced, he got quoted, he disappeared. Although Lagassé was a fringe candidate, the BC press adored this eccentric. Was he the next "Wacky" Bennett or the next Amor De Cosmos? A *Vancouver Sun* headline on a *National Enquirer* story?

Vancouver-Kingsway's Ian Waddell—the BC Knee-Dippers' chair—now soft-shoed in. A lawyer, environmentalist, and Indigenous rights tribune, he was struggling with his sexual orientation, often pondering aloud whether he was queer. His half-closeted stance was a hindrance, but he had JFK's teeth, JFK's sandy-blond haircut, and a Glasgow brogue echoing JFK's Boston accent.

Next, Langdon offered. Though an ardent leftist, he left out his own constituents by proclaiming his candidacy in Ottawa: Did he prefer his former home, Ottawa, to Windsor?

Audrey McLaughlin entered the lists with lotsa caucus oomph. But her first backers? Greasy opportunists. She generated boffo press but zero zeal. Women and Prairie Knee-Dippers genuflected spasmodically to her mantra, "Time for a woman leader." (A mad proposition! By that measure, arch Tory Maggie Thatcher would have been an ideal NDP boss!) Having picked up a by-election seat in the Yukon in June of 1987, Audrey had been an

MP for only eighteen months when she declared her wish to lead us. (Though a neophyte, she got elected caucus chair in 1988.) Likeable in person, her House performance was lacklustre. But to hell with that! The zeitgeist desired a female *chef*. Buttressed by the National Action Committee on the Status of Women and the notion that having a distaff head would reap us votes, Audrey's momentum was unstoppable (I refer to Audrey by her first name because that was her "brand"). Hers was a "Ms." leadership campaign: hers to lose. But could it end in "misleadership"?

Though none of the declared contestants had my nod, I didn't plan to become a candidate until one day when Nelson Riis buttonholed me to tell me about a telephone call he'd taken from noted African-Canadian author Cecil Foster. Apparently, Foster had urged Riis to convince me to seek the leadership. Riis had no wish to do so. He blushed orchid-florid.

Once I realized that neither Stephen Lewis, whom I admired, nor Bill Blaikie, whom I vastly respected (and who conveyed genuine leadership stature), would run, I mused on my chances. My media assistant, George Elliott Clarke (who would achieve unexcelled recognition as a poet and author), took it upon himself to write a three-page argument in favour of my contesting the joust. My other two-term assistant, Nicole Charron, was equally enthusiastic.

As I pondered the marathon, I concluded that not only was I as well-qualified as the declared rivals, I had as much experience as any—and I boasted a superior national profile. Moreover, I'd inspired protest contra the Free Trade Agreement and credible skepticism regarding the Meech Lake Accord. Persuasively too, my oratorical skills had to be the envy of all the other contenders.

Given the impetus to elect Audrey, I knew my *odds* constituted a slant-rhyme with the *Ides* of March. Yet, if Knee-Dippers deemed it meet to pick a woman leader, I'd assert that it was high time too for the party to recognize that racialized Canucks could also lead.

I announced my candidacy at Willistead Manor in Windsor amid thirty vociferous proponents, including Dave Cooke and Gary Parent, prez of the Windsor and District Labour Council. Some folks present, like Councillor Dave Cassivi, had been claimed by Langdon for *his* column. So, I contacted Langdon to ask that he rectify his list; in reply, he implied that Cassivi and others were either confused or were shy to state their true loyalty. One of my militants, Tom Suffield, took strong exception, in a letter, to Langdon's outlandish inclusion of his name. But Doc Langdon, or his office, dismissed imperiously Suffield's objection. No matter—my Windsor base would prove broader and deeper than that of my caucus colleague.

The decision made, Clarkie and Nicole began to design my campaign in earnest. A political operative from Toronto, Ari Rozin, was hired as my national campaign manager, but it was Nicole and Clarkie and Ian McMahon and Jo-Anne Johnson in Windsor who would give impetus to an "impossible" campaign that would achieve a unique character and momentum. My slogan was "Passion" (Clarkie's notion); my colour was fuchsia (Nicole's idea).

In the period preceding the inaugural leadership debate, I summoned potential disciples and drafted my platform. Variously called a "New Vision for a New Canada" or a "Vision for a New Democracy," it stressed Canada's need to succeed in the value-added new economy. I urged that social spending seek to empower individuals rather than merely yield financial life-support. I also prized Canada's diversity as opportune; a base for global competition.

Preparing a platform, I consulted widely, even debating post-industrial economics with Doc Mel Watkins, the hard-lefty economist and an original "Waffler." But his analyses wafted still the dissipating vapours of the smokestack economy.

Winnipeg saw the first candidates' rhetorical matchup. Reporters wagered Langdon the victor, while Audrey scored second place for her dissection of Meech Lake. But one journalist averred that I had garnered an astonishing level of applause: the sound of things to come, eh?

Next up was Whitehorse, Audrey's home turf. She was a gregarious host and informative docent to us all, and I revelled in the stop. The debate yielded me a smidgen more "traction," for, like Audrey, I saw tacit racism in Meech Lake's requirement for provincial unanimity regarding the creation of new provinces, one or more of which could boast Indigenous majorities. How heinous it would be were paleface "settler" governments (even just one) to frustrate the rise to provincial status of an Indigenous-majority "territory"!

Edmonton, Vancouver, Victoria, and Saskatoon sponsored pursuant debates. Just as it had been during my NBCC days, BC was standoffish. Even so, my old friend Q (Quittenton), St. Clair College ex-prez, journeyed one whole day to sojourn with me for just two hours to tell me of his fervour for my campaign. Most BC delegates were either groupies of Audrey (a devotion half-*l'amour*, half-Louis L'Amour) or were lusting after the playing-extra-hard-to-get Dave Barrett, the one-term once premier of "Breeteesh Colombia."

While out on "the Left Coast," I heard Rosemary Brown, the pioneer BC MLA, address Vancouver women. She echoed Gloria Steinem, not Angela Davis—as if women of colour had the same resources as white women or that white women bear the same burdens as women of colour. *Being Brown*, how could she be my "Black sistah" in this "Ms.-begotten" race?

Memorably, in Edmonton, Saskatoon, and Calgary, I hit my stride. Wildly enthusiastic applause pummelled my eardrums in Calgary. So, a *Globe and Mail* journo floated a question that implied either marginalization or admiration: Was I imitating Martin Luther King or Jesse Jackson? Of course, it had to be one or the other: I was Black! Sidestepping the trap, I explained that Truth and/or good ideas always attract plaudits.

From then on, whenever my remarks drew extraordinarily luxurious clapping, critics would say I was "pandering." *Au contraire*: I was igniting audiences with the ardour of my delivery and the sincerity of my ideals. Thus, my campaign achieved liftoff—despite my "minority" status and persistent press reports that absented or belittled me. (In St. John's, one reporter noticed that I had aced the applause, while another stated that only the eight Blacks peppering the audience had given me the highest marks! Go figure!)

Now, the media scalpel descended to dissect my "character." On cue, my former Windsor Council rival Ron Wagenberg opined that I blame racism for all opposition to myself or my ideas. Bollocks! His plaint was itself suspect. Yes, I'm a civil rights apostle, as every thinking citizen should be. Problem was, I'd bested him as a prof—and as a politician. His swipe? His laughable reprisal.

More perversely, the press took persons whose commitment to me was of decades-long standing and twisted velvet observations into steel-wool-scathing rebukes. Case in point: Bob Doyle. My biologist bro got cast as regretting my tenure as Biology department head. He'd termed my style as aggressive—but *also* said that it had been a boon. His positive comment got inked as negative.

Moreover, both I and my staffers noticed that as Knee-Dippers reacted with increasing approval of my ideas, the media began to term me as "abrasive." This was an echo of long-gone *Windsor Star* headlines framing me as "angry" on the front page and "outraged" on page 2.

Manifest now was a wicked smear—the sequel to the malice engendered *ex nihilo* by my justified dismissal of Beth Rutledge a half-decade earlier. Purportedly undersigned by ten present and past assistants, the acid-oozing letter cursed me as being the boss from Hades. From what dumpster did it emanate? Everyone who worked for me, or who ever had, once told of the missive, disavowed its accusations. These foul lies even brought some ex-staffers to weep. (By the way, this scurrilous note only came to light when Lorne Nystrom got tried for shoplifting.

His exculpating defense was that he was so upset by the venomous squib that he had "absent-mindedly" removed contact-lens cleaner from a box, pocketed the item, then returned the empty box to a store shelf.)

The shadowy, septic campaign to undermine my candidacy intensified with every standing ovation I gained—especially after one pivotal Hogtown gathering. Beforehand, Audrey was seen as stepping blithely to a coronation; afterwards, she was death-warmed-over roadkill.

Why?

In mid-September, each contender had to make individual presentations to about fifty United Steelworker reps in Toronto. Audrey entered the room as *the* toast and exited *as* toast—all her pixie dust blown away as dust motes. In contrast, the Steelworkers extolled my "charisma" and my personable style of working through problems. Suddenly, I'd won over Ontario Labour.

That was my campaign's pinnacle—and my Waterloo: once the *Globe and Mail* reported that I was the Steelworkers' favourite, calls cranked up to get BC's Dave Barrett into the race. I wager that Barrett was pushed to run against Audrey *because* my ascendancy was revealing her abysmal weakness as a candidate. A Great White Hope had to be enlisted to forestall her upset and/or my coup. (Back in my Bytown office after my Steelworkers' success, Clarkie told me, "Howard, your ears must have been burning all weekend." Yes, there must have been a lot of scorched air about as the Anybody-But-McCurdy camp sought to pinpoint someone—anyone—to blunt my insurgency.)

Well, I did have the "Big Mo"—*Momentum!* In September, I opened a campaign office on King St. West in Toronto. By then my inclusiveness message had begun to take hold, inspiring my team to ill-advised flights of imagination. They had contacted both the entertainer Harry Belafonte and 1988 US Democratic Party prez nomination hopeful Jesse Jackson to see if they might assist our fundraising as well as burnish my international "box-office appeal." The idea was romantic but the reality not. Bluntly, African-Americans are always about America, and rarely Africa, and *never* about anywhere else. Neither socialist Belafonte nor "Rainbow Coalition" Jackson had any interest in aiding my campaign. After all, how would a Canadian spotlight benefit themselves or their causes? (Like many African-Canadians, I had rallied to Jackson's campaign to secure the Democratic Party prez nomination in 1988. He'd been the superior candidate to the eventual nominee, Michael Dukakis, but anti-Black racism sidelined him. Hell! Jackson's "non-win"—and the reason for it—foreshadowed my own campaign's end.)

Did I need either Black Yank? Nope!

My campaign catalyzed an unprecedented engagement of Black Canucks in politics. Inside a month of my entree into the race, the Friends of Howard McCurdy coalesced in Toronto. Headed by Denham Jolly, Al Mercury, Zanana and Isaac Akande, and other Black professionals, entrepreneurs, and politicos, they raised $7,500 at once. (All told, I estimate that Black community donations accounted for half of all campaign funds, with unions kicking in the second-highest level of contributions. Although it was reported that we had raised about $45,000, I was later told that the amount was closer to $80,000, which would have been the largest amount raised *and spent* by any candidate. I'd been "in the black"—literally!)

Wherever candidates' debates transpired in burgs with significant Black presence, *my people* delivered "McCurdymania"! Blacks in Halifax, Winnipeg, Ottawa, Saint John, and Montreal held fundraisers. In Halifax, Yvonne Atwell and the Jones militants—Rocky, Lynn, Joan—were hyper active. Few of these backers were Knee-Dippers, but all prayed to see me *represent* (I use Ebonics) on the national political stage.

Rocky Jones accompanied me on a picturesque drive along the Cabot Trail about Cape Breton for a campaign stop there. He was considering law school, and I think our conversation was a factor in his deciding to empower himself with an LL.B. When we returned to Halifax, Rocky and I met with Alexa McDonough, whom we both knew was anti-racist—and a feminist. She was frank about the pressure she felt to ally with Audrey, though she big-upped the merits of my campaign.

There were nine more official all-candidates' debates: in Sudbury, Regina, Montreal, Halifax, St. John's, Saint John, Charlottetown, Ottawa, and Toronto. I did rather better in Montreal than expected. While my French wafted a distinctive accent, my spontaneity in oratory was lauded—as was my statement that Quebec was the place where I had experienced, for the first time in my life, real acceptance as a Black man. Still, the Quebec delegation couldn't count for many votes.

My final campaigning entailed speaking to riding associations, provincial party and labour conventions, local union meetings, and at rallies touting my candidacy in Ontario, Manitoba, Saskatchewan, and Nova Scotia. In Ontario, I got to Elliot Lake, Hamilton, Brampton, Oshawa, and Thunder Bay. Ernie Epp, who organized a Thunder Bay fundraiser, was a 1988-election-defeated ex-caucus colleague. In Manitoba, I had dos in Winnipeg and Dauphin; in Saskatoon, I spoke at the local NDP council; next, I hobnobbed at the NSNDP convention in Halifax.

In Toronto, on the eve of the final debate, I faced a BIPOC audience. *That* was my fiefdom. My message to them had already resonated. Nor did

I relish only Black Canuck applause! Chinese and Korean Canadians flocked my way too. But few visible minorities would serve as NDP delegates; thus, I could have their fulsome adoration, but they could accord me few votes.

Still, at the Toronto City Hall debate on the morrow, I rocked the house to raucous ecstasy! I condemned the tsunami of greed that Mulroney had unleashed on the nation so corporations could export jobs to Mexico and tax collectors axe seniors' sustenance cheques to slivers.

Next, I stirred up a packed parliament of unionists in Chatham, ON. My speech? None equalled! I called for an inclusive country and party, for a Canada enriched economically by its diversity and a commitment to enhanced opportunity through training, education, and research. I plumped for an economy in which domestic innovation would create—out of our comparative advantage in energy and resources—new, value-added, tradable goods and services. The result? My standing ovation dwarfed the minuscule one-hand-claps others obtained. Even Langdon's wife, Shirley Seward, was thrilled: "I finally get what you are saying. It was wonderful!"

Most commentators now pegged me third, behind McLaughlin and Barrett, but surmised that I had the delegate strength to move up. Back in Windsor, developer Chuck Mady and Gary Parent held a $100-a-plate breakfast fundraiser at The Other Place restaurant. Never had bacon and eggs tasted so good! Mammon and Marx, figuratively speaking, agreed on my campaign: the silver spoon and the greasy spoon now spooning!

Soon, Garry Dugal, Nick Carlan, and Arlene Rousseau organized a Western Hoedown fundraiser at Local 444. Nashville in my cowboy hat, I was Motown in my groovy steps.

(Just six years later, Rousseau defeated me in my effort to secure the provincial nomination to carry the Knee-Dipper banner in the riding of Windsor-Sandwich. Her primacy was pyrrhic. On E-day, she had to dip her knees to Liberal candidate, Sandra Pupatello.)

In a bid to cement Labour's love, I went to Port Elgin; I shook hands with Bob White, the CAW chief. Unmoved by my "Big Mo," he was about as friendly as a corpse.

Back to Hogtown for the Ontario Federation of Labour (OFL) convention. OFL prez Gord Wilson endorsed my candidacy: a huge boost. Though Steelworkers District 6 chief Leo Gerard was noncommittal, I captured the United Steelworkers' rank-and-file affiliation. The Paperworkers and Ladies Garment Workers unions also hoisted me on their shoulders. The CAW Windsor delegates were so onside, they even furnished me with a bed in their suite.

My last major campaign hurrah was the Regina NDP convention. Saskatchewan fielded a delegate bumper crop, and so it was a must-win situation. Lookit! My reception was stupendous! After speaking to a crush of a crowd and raising a standing-room-only ovation, I got mobbed by well-wishers and autograph seekers. Many rated me as Tommy Douglas redux. One fan even called me the "Tawny Tommy Douglas"! By the time my campaign reached the decisive full-stop in Winnipeg, we had captured over two hundred Saskatchewan delegates.

After three more days of Toronto stops and speeches—and snagging *Pride* magazine's designation as "Black Man of the Year"—I jetted, exhausted, to Windsor. Here I was now honoured by a huge send-off party, arranged by my love, Brenda, and by businesswoman Gail Rogers at Cotton Club, a venue operated by barkeeps, blues aficionados, and brothers Ted and Ken Boomer. The joint? Packed to capacity with a who's who of entrepreneurs and *electicians* (to coin a word)—including photographer Spike Bell, public sector exec Jane Boyd, broadcaster and dude-about-town George Melbourne Macdonald, developer Bill Docherty, health advocate Dave Dubin, haberdasher Gerald Freed, auto dealer Ken Knapp, and politicos Mike Hurst, Al Santing, and Bruck Easton. I was Windsor's man—and I was elated!

But that celebratory night was my campaign's zenith (*pace* the Steelworker and Saskatchewan peaks). My health slid. After weeks on the road, getting zero sleep, and toiling unfazed through unrealized fatigue, the adrenaline was zero and my temperature a feverish 105. Every bone in my body cussed me out; every muscle was grumpy. But I flew straight from campaign to convention.

At Winnipeg, now, I arrived, high on meds, low on steam. Though feeling as sick as a kicked-down dog, I was uplifted by my campaign's vivid, visual show of delegate vigour: some fifty supporters shouting "Howard, Howard, the Passion!" serenaded Brenda, family, and me at the convention hotel. All wore the fuchsia T-shirts emblazoned with "McCurdy, Leadership, Passion." (This eye-catching garb became a highly prized convention souvenir.) It did warm us up—all that good cheer—fending off the frigid, Arctic-wind clime that is Winnipeg, capital of polar-bear-fielding Manitoba, every late-late cold-ember November.

But still "there was no rest for me"! Crucial delegates needed face time, immediately upon arrival; nor did that flesh-pressing throng recede until the wee hours. Energy was sustained only by my campaign workers' reports (and my own contacts with delegates) that reinforced our estimate that I'd attract about four hundred votes on the first ballot. Grassroots Saskatchewan and steel-and-auto Ontario infused us with confidence.

I'd heard floors tremble and roofs raised nationally due to the "Mc-Cur-dy, Mc-Cur-dy" shouts and ovations. (Eliot's "mermaids singing, each to each"?) I was upbeat.

From the stage during the bear-pit session, the sea of purple passion T-shirts before me seemed dominant, aye. But my performance? Sluggish. My brain was woozy, my headache a doozy. Not sounding incisive and decisive, did I seem fuzzy and hazy? I was groggy; I was foggy.

Well, I didn't have my A game, but my team brought theirs. Their skills had already helped me pole-vault over the heads of the NDP aristocracy and the frowns of pundits and the jesters of the press to land in Winnipeg with the status of being a Serious Contender. Catchy were our bilingual releases outlining my stands on the economy, women's rights, youth, the constitution, the family farm, international affairs, and defence. Our buttons and T-shirts vanished by the hundreds, to reappear (we prayed) on the lapels and chests of diehard McCurdy acolytes.

Truly, I had right-stuff people: Nicole Charron was the spark and livewire as my national coordinator; Ed Trapunski sweet-talked the media; and Ontario NDP exec sec Brian Harling was my floor coordinator. Ian McMahon, George Elliott Clarke, Jo-Anne Johnson, Monica Woodley, and Joe Comartin rounded out my team. They kept themselves and me busy, contacting delegates, recording all pro-McCurdy intentions, and issuing bulletins.

Gord Wilson and OFL apparatchik Ross McClellan collaborated to prepare my keynote speech for Friday night, December first. Their input? Desirable. But the result was piffle, to try to satisfy every faction as opposed to letting McCurdy be McCurdy. Sapped was the spontaneity inspiriting my oratorical power. I was a stentorian Samson flummoxed by two backroom Delilahs.

Entering the convention hall for my do-or-die speech, the floor demonstration by my partisans was pure purple pandemonium—all flourishes of fuchsia banners and parading TV-Technicolor-seductive T-shirts, all abundant in numbers consistent with our anticipated third-place finish on the first ballot. My red-carpet fanfare was fit for Prince himself (*that* pop-star Purpleness)!

As I seized the podium, I was flanked by nominators symbolic of all of the groups for whom I had fought to be part of a more inclusive NDP and Canada. Here was a telegenic staging of the differentiating message of my candidacy. Arrayed alongside of me were Doug Winsor, a man who had a physical disability; William Dennison, a senior; Lou Arab, a youth and labour activist and later spouse to Alberta NDP premier Rachel Notley; Monica Woodley, an African-Canadian and an education consultant; James R. H. Knudson, an Archerwill, SK, farmer; Robert Dupuis, a Québécois francophone; Cathy Goodhew, a single mom; and several others.

My nominators buoyed me, but my speech floundered. I was extemporaneous, yes, but not as emotively spontaneous as I had so boldly been on the hustings. Pain seared my brain; chills wracked my frame. I felt rushed, scattered in trying to cover all the points that my advisors wanted made. Despite the inclement conditions afflicting my delivery, pundits were awe-struck by my ability to speak minus notes. Nor were my militants downcast. Apparently, I was the one disappointed by my inability to take real advantage of what had been my strength on an occasion when it might have made a difference.

Still, I collapsed into bed that night, expecting that our projections for a third-place finish in the first round of voting the next day would prove accurate and, were I to fall short, I would still be dubbed the "kingmaker" or a "queen maker."

So, yes, the debut balloting was shattering. Projections, prophecies, plans, and plots: all dashed! I finished fifth with but 250 votes, some 50 fewer than De Jong and 100 behind Langdon. *Shock and awe!* Bobbing his TV bobble head, Bob White deplored the fact that so many who had expressed support for me had, in the end, marked their ballots for others. Damningly, the Saskatchewan "loyalists" had served me savage disappointment.

I was done; *I'd been done in.* I pinned on Audrey's button. But several of my staffers spoiled fourth and final ballots by writing across them, "McCurdy: No Sellout!" We were glum, and booze was the opioid of choice. We also feared that Audrey's victory would be fatal for re-election prospects, not due to sexism but due to her lacking even the charisma of sand. Her bland persona was negatively disproportionate to her "electability," eh?

But I was wounded, dead in the water, and the journos sniffed blood. The *Windsor Star* quoted me as blaming race-bias for my loss and stopping just short of calling the party racist. In a letter to the editor, I noted that my experience was not unprecedented. Flora MacDonald was a leadership candidate for the Progressive Conservatives in 1976. She too had received far fewer votes than had been prophesied by prior estimates of her committed delegates. That result has been immortalized in the Canuck political lexicon as the "MacDonald effect," for political scientists still speculated whether Progressive Conservatives had been sexist or had been merely indicating doubt about whether Canadians would accept a woman as prime minister. Still, I had touched the "third rail" in Canuck politics, which is to call out the blunt racism of voters and the cosmeticized racism of elites. Canadians are awfully smug about our racism, glorifying it as polite and subtle, when it is toxic and insidious. We think that so long as we don't tote flaming crosses or don the white hoods, our racism is harmless. That lie corrodes our humanity and corrupts our society.

A few weeks later in the Centre Block cafeteria, I would learn what had happened to my once-secure, two-hundred-plus Saskatchewan votes. Once more, it would be Nystrom who would downplay Polonious by playing Pilate. "Howard," he said, as we collected our food trays, "I imagine you're still wondering what happened to your Saskatchewan votes. Someone you know convinced the delegates at the last minute that they couldn't possibly vote for a Black candidate because it would be impossible for Canadians to accept a Black prime minister."

I've oft speculated about who oversaw that direct racist assault. One of my suspects was a colleague whom I'd identified as a bigot and who I knew was sore about having a woman as leader. However, considering who had the most to gain within the Saskatchewan delegation, it's likely that I was betrayed by someone I'd thought a friend, by someone who feared that his own sway over Saskatchewan politics could be jeopardized if I were to sit in the "Leader's Office," signing the nomination papers and distributing all the third-party parliamentary largesse available.

I'll never know definitively. What I do know? My candidacy was wrecked on the shoals of the typical, conspiratorial, speak-no-evil variety of Canuck prejudice. So ended a period of my life during which I had considered myself uncommonly lucky to be able to pursue a new path after having cast aside the sense of betrayal I had experienced at the University of Windsor. But I had merely traded crying crocodiles for giggling hyenas. (Or do I have the metaphors ass-backwards?)

No matter—the Knee-Dippers embraced an operatic, show-tune "feminism" that could only thrill electoral masochists. Once the curtain came down on the convention, and the headlines and commentators warbled their falsetto arias about the seven-day wonder of seeing a woman lead a major Canuck federal party, it was predictable that Audrey would fade away into desperate irrelevance, her star turn having no encore, her "fat-lady" advisors falling incoherent when not merely mute. Audrey bagged the throne and then slumped into a stupor. *Negligence* got confused with *Elegance*. Her team thought they had top billing in *The Unsinkable Molly Brown*; instead, they were drifting cadavers off the lost bow of the *Titanic*.

CHAPTER NINETEEN:
34TH PARLIAMENT FREEZE-OUT

TO SLAP AN EXCLAMATION MARK ON THE "MS. LEADERSHIP" debacle, fresh bad luck skidded my way: a crack-up! Back in The Big Zero post-convention, I yearned to zip to Windsor for Xmas, to relax, to recuperate. The December morn was clear, bright, cold as I entered the ramp to the King's Highway 417—a.k.a. The Queensway—clipping westerly at just sixty kilometres an hour. But I couldn't accelerate! My wheels were slipping on black ice: I spun out, Ping-Ponging into barriers on opposite sides of the road. Wreckage, in slo-mo, rose before my eyes. And wasn't that a convoy of semis hurtling—with the rancour of firing-squad bullets—toward me? *Oh, how did they miss me?*

As I stood in frigid confusion, teeth chattering, my frame shivering madly in a thin cashmere sweater, a motorist parked behind my crumpled car. That Good Samaritan, William Sims, offered aid. *Why, yes!* So, from the shambled back seat he disentangled my Arctic-geared, wool winter jacket; next, he went to hail cops and a tow truck. Upon his return, he mused aloud about how I'd now get to Windsor. *How?* His response? "Take my car."

That I was en route to Windsor and unlikely to return until January 1990 deterred Bill not a jot. Moreover, he whipped up a coffee, a nip of brandy, and calming small talk before seeing me off. One caveat: "The car's transmission is wonky." True: it clunked out just past Woodstock, still 230 klicks from Windsor. Again, I needed a tow. I hitchhiked to town to find a garage and a car rental. The garage mechanics shrugged: the town's sole rental agency was closed. Nicely, they tracked down the agency's owner who was already into his holiday cups. No probs. Setting down his eggnog and rum, he soon set me upon four wheels.

The rest of the trip was without incident—but only barely, for as I stepped from the rental, now home at last, I saw that I had a flat tire! Was the cosmos itself punishing me for having had the temerity to vie for the fed Knee-Dipper leadership?

The new year, 1990, was just as hurtful, for I suffered a colossal loss in April: my uncle George McCurdy. He'd seemed robust, whacking golf balls lustily in retaliation for his forced resignation in 1983 as director of the Nova Scotia Human Rights Commission. (His unforgiveable faux pas? Inviting Siaka Stevens, the dictator of Sierra Leone, to Nova Scotia to celebrate the bicentennial of the arrival of the Black Loyalists. Yes, the optics were poor: a human rights tribune beckoning a tyrant. Yet, we both knew that if he had invited an authoritarian, paleface *baas* to the province, Big Biz bigwigs would have clamoured to sign "Team Nova Scotia" contracts with the autocrat.) But Uncle George's hips were faltering. He agreed to surgery to replace those bones and recovered apace. But bacteria smelled blood and gobbled his cells as their buffet. Complications assailed his heart. Just seventy-one when he perished, his absence rendered my heart an aching abscess. My favourite uncle, George had also been my best friend, confidant, and ally in the anti-racism fight. Seldom a week had ever passed without our speaking to one another; so, for months after, each time the phone rang, I expected to savour his voice, that cross between gravel and smoke.

Though my avuncular éminence grise was no more, my political toils and travails did not abate. No chance to mourn. I was the NDP critic for Human Rights (External), and South Africa was heating up as apartheid was melting away. As it turned out, the pressure of economic sanctions—as well as the indefatigable, Black intifada versus the Boer regime—had persuaded corporations to jettison segregation and exalt colour-blind capitalism. Frederik Willem de Klerk had replaced P. W. Botha as South Africa's prez and had already freed most political prisoners and unbanned the ANC. He then shook the world by abolishing apartheid and commencing talks to transition the nation to a democracy. On February 11, 1990, after twenty-seven years behind bars, Nelson Mandela was released,

Walter MacLean, MP, Nelson Mandela, and Howard, in Namibia for Independence celebrations, 1990.

thus stoking global euphoria. In Mandela's first public speech, he warned that although apartheid was ending, international sanctions remained *de rigueur* to ensure the birth of a true republic.

Mandela undertook a pilgrimage of appreciation now, jetting to every nation that had offered the ANC succour, an itinerary including touch-downs in Havana and Ottawa. But his first trip abroad would be—de Klerk alongside—to next-door Namibia. Once a South African vassal, the new state was exulting in its independence as it swore in Sam Nujoma as prez. A Lutheran as radical as Martin Luther, Nujoma had swapped South West African People's Organization battle fatigues for the bourgeois suit and tie of the *electitian*. Now, Mandela would replicate the process, trading in the ANC's classic, Soviet-produced AK-47s for presidential command of South Africa's (rumoured) nuclear arsenal.

Joining the Canadian delegation to the fiesta, I made my second eventful trip to sub-Saharan Africa. First stop: the Semitic and Rastafarian Holy Land of Ethiopia. Famine wracked that nation, as did criss-crossing bullets that disrupted the trucking of food. The logistics of hunger relief were flummoxed by the Mengistu regime's bombing and strafing raids and/or ground assaults by dollarized bandits, all so as to hinder convoys from relieving the dissident, starving regions of Tigray and Eritrea. One solution? Ship food via the northern port of Massawa, ruled by Tigrayan rebels but suffering steady Ethiopian bombardment.

From left: Brenda McCurdy, Howard, Kathleen Davis, Ontario Premier Bill Davis, Prime Minister Brian Mulroney, Nelson Mandela.

To tell the despotic and genocidal Ethiopian president, Mengistu Haile Mariam, to cease the Stuka-style attacks on Massawa's shipping to let foodstuffs be offloaded came we Canucks to Addis Ababa.

Thus I viewed, finally, the legendary land my mother had identified with my African ancestors—with gilded kings and bejewelled queens. However, Addis Ababa was bereft of the opulence my boyhood mind had furnished. Too dusty to be Xanadu, too dreary to be Oz. Its bravest denizens were wild dogs; its only colour was that of "Red Terror" graffiti, posters, and billboards brandishing the red hammer (to crush heads) and red sickle (to slash throats).

The *Duce* who shook our hands was but the stunted shadow of that noble but flawed "god" of Rastafarianism, Haile Selassie, whom Mengistu had overthrown (and then had likely had strangled in his bed). Mengistu in his palace mirrored Hitler in his lair: a sadist of appalling brutality, of weaponized anarchy, of fiendish authority. Starvation was his law: to famish, not to feed.

Surreal was our eve of feasting and hotfooting in the hotel bar. Our chic dance-mates were as sepia as Iman, as cinnamon as Katrin Quinol (the face of Black Box's hit, "Everybody Everybody," which was everywhere), as mahogany as Foxy Brown, and as ebony as Grace Jones. Hard it was to square the Red, ruddy rule of the Derg (I prefer to pronounce the name of the state apparatus as *dirge*, which is most fitting) with the black discs circulating Af-Am-echoing Ethiopian pop. A "Jonestown" regime with a Motown vibe: Mengistu's version of a "Mephisto Waltz."

Being the singular Black Canuck, I aroused much curiosity. Ironically, the Ethiopians swore that I had to be one of them. They refused to credit that I could be from the Great White North. (Their adoption of me would've delighted my mama, Bernice!)

In Namibia, we holed up in a brand-new motel nigh Windhoek. Among the other dignitaries there domiciled were pistol-holstered Yasser Arafat and the blab-upholstered Jesse Jackson.

The Palestine Liberation Organization chairman, Arafat spearheaded a rapper-level entourage, laden with AK-47s, who, to accompany the leader's forays and sorties, jogged military fashion through the motel hallways. Deadpan, comic opera, it was reminiscent of the cancan-dancing Nazis in Mel Brooks's satirical flick, *The Producers*.

The Maximum Leader of all Black People on Planet Earth (or maybe just Planet Hollywood), Jesse deigned to breakfast with me on my first full day on site. The fare and talk were both digestible until an aide whispered that Mandela was nigh. Abruptly, yet tearing himself regretfully from his repast (pork and yolks), Jesse up and ran—to snag, bag, or beg a photo-op with Mandela.

All us motel dwellers had to assemble for bussing to the Windhoek *fête*. As I was about to board my bus, two bawling children drew nigh to ask if I'd seen "our pops," namely Jesse. I calmed them and said I'd locate him. I knew Jesse was playing de facto US ambassador in his sit-down with Mandela. I passed along his kids' tearful fears to the wannabe-prez, who displayed merely irked indifference. More urgent was it to fix his place in flashbulb history!

Windhoek? An insignificant, cracker-citizen'd burg. The next-door Afro township of Katutura swelled the capital's population to 200,000. Katutura, meaning "the place where no one wants to live," received that moniker because the South African mandate quislings forced Blacks to move there to make space for la-di-da Caucasian interlopers. In Katutura, folks inhabit cheek-by-jowl, seven-metre-by-seven-metre rental cottages. Despite this ticky-tacky "urban planning," the homes were remarkably neat and tidy, the dirt paths between kept swept-clean.

In one immaculate hut, the owner—the epitome of hospitality—entertained a phalanx. O! How she recalled to me the Afro belles of Essex County! Like them, our hostess was unfazed to cram a dozen more into her already body-glutted home. Plates turned mountains; glasses fountains; laughter and song jockeyed for mouth-space with spicy food and stupefying drink.

Celebration razzmatazz'd Windhoek. At bars, Namibians—white, brown, black—partied like it was already 1999. Euphoria fostered phantasmagoria! The independence protocols and fanfare for Prez Nujoma unfurled in a standing-room-only stadium. Dignitaries, global, witnessed the moment epochal. Mandela and de Klerk even sat side by side. Now, *that* was a Nobel Peace Prize–worthy photo-op.

At a state reception, trumpeter Dizzy Gillespie and stellar Canuck pianist Oliver Jones floated notes—jazzy, percussive, and ethereal—into our ears. Pumped was I to press their palms.

But alarming was it to find, as I packed to exit the next day, that my plane ticket and some $1,000 in travellers' cheques had "flown"—doubtless due to a thin-fingered stranger (who should have utilized his light touch to tickle ivories rather than pick through pockets). Luckily, local officials ensured that I'd know neither anxiety nor deficit. Though South African Airlines was blameless for the dings I'd incurred, its agent was pure cordiality, generosity, and charity: Not only was I handed new tickets for flights to Johannesburg, London, and Ottawa, I also picked up swag: ritzy toiletries and a suave nightshirt. The agent even limo'd me to the airport and saw me onto the plane. (Dizzy Gillespie was also a passenger, and since we had to await our connecters in Jo'burg, I absorbed the transcendent rapture of the trumpeter's repartee: down-to-the-earth salty, salt-of-the-earth earthy, all deliciously anecdotal but religiously sacerdotal in gravitas.)

Aloft, London-bound, I savoured the swishy upper deck of a 747, where my Scotch thirst was quite adequately acquitted and my salmon hunger quite quickly requited. Simultaneously, we first-class aeronauts were kept in gut-busting stitches by a cherubic gay steward whose comic patter defied all censorship while never transgressing the outer bounds of civility. (Some weeks later, American Express sent copies of my travellers' cheques, all bearing my passably forged signature. I confirmed that the florid *Howard McCurdy* on the cheques was an imposter of the flamboyant Howard McCurdy of Parliament. Thus, I pocketed a refund.)

Wheels down in "Otter-wah," I found Canada in turmoil (again) over Quebec's demands—really—for R-E-S-P-E-C-T versus the whining of *les maudits Anglais* for federal oversight of "*la belle province*." Yet, I'd just returned from Namibia where Canada had counselled the newly free state to guarantee, constitutionally, all citizens equality. No fuss, no muss. (Were we not poor teachers to our much better students?)

Once a "dove" symbolizing federal-provincial concord, by April 1990, the Meech Lake Accord (MLA) was a dead duck. The *dégringolade* had begun with New Brunswick premier Frank McKenna's refusal, in September 1987, to salute Mulroney's constitutional one-upmanship of PET.

Although a Jean Charest–led commission persuaded McKenna to drop his objections to the MLA, dead-ender nationalist Lucien Bouchard and other hard line Québécois—all discombobulated by efforts to downplay the MLA's designation of Quebec as constituting a "distinct society"— deserted Tory and Grit caucuses to form the breakaway Bloc Québécois (a block of single-minded blockheads).

Given delays, Senate hearings, and the requirement for the agreement of too many parliaments, plus the sudden precedence of the FTA (for the Mulroney Tories), the MLA got placed on life-support in two provinces. In Manitoba, where legislative unanimity was required to enable the MLA to be even introduced for debate, odd-man-out, Indigenous lawmaker Elijah Harper, while holding up an eagle feather of dissent, said softly, repeatedly, "No," thus nixing the move. (His dissent arose from the MLA's cavalier disregard for the Indigenous interest in self-government.) Once the MLA failed to even gain entree to the Manitoba legislature, Newfoundland deemed its consideration moot, and so no vote was held upon it there. Because unanimous passage in a baker's dozen of legislatures had not been won, the MLA died at noon, EST, on Canada Day, 1990—just as Jean Chrétien was being elected federal Liberal Party chief, bum-rushing John Turner out the emergency exit.

Yet, as much as Anglo bigotry catalyzed the MLA's defeat (for instance, news footage displayed redneck fogeys wiping their feet on Quebec's fleur-de-lys flag), Quebec—under Premier Robert Bourassa—was no innocent bystander. "Boo Boo" stoked suspicion about what a post-MLA Quebec might do regarding minority communities when, in exchange for Western bolstering of the Accord, he made cynical trips to Alberta and Saskatchewan in 1989 to okay their legislation to publish laws in English only (thereby nullifying legal—but unenforced—bilingualism that had been in place since the former territories had become provinces in 1905).

The demise of Meech Lake, the rise of the Bloc Québécois and of the Western-based Reform Party, and then the rejection of the Charlottetown Accord in a national referendum in the fall of 1992 not only prefaced the catastrophic Tory defeat in 1993, but also prepared the near-breakup of Canada in 1995. The Chinese curse "May you live in interesting times" was bitterly accurate prophecy.

In June 1990, Nelson Mandela and his wife, Winnie, canvassed Canada, and he addressed Parliament. Audrey McLaughlin and I were granted an hour-long session with Mandela. Frail, tired? Yep, but he was a seventy-two-year-old maintaining a twenty-seven-year-old's stamina— after twenty-seven years in prison. In his humble, decorous tones, he thanked us for our concord, while outlining the hazards ahead and the need to keep squeezing the Stars-n-Bars Boers so as to establish veritable democracy.

Soon I attended a Toronto $100-per-plate fundraising dinner for Mandela. After that lucrative gig, he spoke to fifty thousand ecstatic admirers at Detroit's Tiger Stadium. In parallel with that, an initiative in aid of the new South Africa—the Nelson Mandela Fund—was announced. All three major federal parties backed the bank. Led by Anglican Archbishop Ted Scott (of not only the International Defence and Aid Fund for Southern Africa, but also of the Commonwealth Eminent Persons tasked with urging South Africa to democratize), its "names" included Hon. R. Roy McMurtry, Gabrielle Lachance, *et moi*. Later, the governing board boasted such figures as Georges Erasmus, Carlton A. Masters, Bridglal Pachai, Rabbi W. Gunther Plaut, and Juanita Westmoreland-Traoré. The fund was to bankroll education, so as to tutor the once-voteless Black underclass to be discriminating electors. We Mandela Fund deputies had sought Mandela's signed endorsement during his Ottawa visit; however, red tape had hog-tied the legal dox. So, being the most visible (and audible) Black Canuck anti-apartheid activist, I got tapped to fly to Abuja, Nigeria, in May, to meet Mandela at a Commonwealth Foreign Ministers' confab. Thanks to the "Right On" Joe Clark, I conferred again with Nelson and Winnie. Belying the heinous accusations muttered against her in the gutter press, Winnie was—to me—a swimsuit-style beaut. Her complexion: copper sunlit by an ivory smile. (Back when her wardrobe was combat fatigues, Ms. Mandela may have instigated or abetted several Soweto homicides. Certes, she was convicted in the kidnapping of one youth, James "Stompie" Sepei, who was stabbed to death, post-torture. Was she more Lady Macbeth than she was "Lady Madonna"?)

Though pro-biz PM Mulroney big-upped Mandela, the eponymous fund could not raise donors. Canuck execs wanted Mandela to play Martin Luther King, but Castro had come to his aid, not *Kapital*. Although federal and provincial governments declared a Nelson Mandela Day to mark the anniversary of his release from prison, Bay Street proved unwilling to pony up a measly $2 to 3 million for the fund's kitty. Yet, every top-hatted executive fop sought a photo-op with Mandela. (He should have billed each a million bucks a "hit.")

Back in South Africa, Mandela and de Klerk blueprinted a non-racial democracy. Opposition? Vicious and tri-polar: Nazi zwiebacks on the right; Chief—"*Baas*"—Buthelezi in the dagger-gripping middle; and Black rads on the left, Molotov-cocktail-tossing fringe. Because Buthelezi directed his Inkatha Freedom Party to carry out terror in collusion with Caucasoid South African dirty warriors, a state of emergency soon hammered down Natal.

For making nice-nice as leaders, de Klerk and Mandela garnered the Nobel Peace Prize. Then, in 1994, Mandela became the debut Black prez of "Azania": the ANC kicked ass in the post-apartheid election. My joy in that outcome was tempered only by the Knee-Dipper choice of Svend Robinson rather than me (despite my front-row role in the anti-apartheid action in Parliament) to be our appointee to the South African Election Observer Group. (For me, "NDP" was becoming the acronym for the "Negro Disappointment Party.")

I did, though, return to South Africa, thanks to the recommendation of Andre Killian, the new South African ambassador to Canada. Babb's replacement, he was Babb's better. Finding that we were both avid baseball fans, we became comrades. While our plan to scope out a Bytown baseball game together was aborted because of my election loss in October 1993, it is probable that Andre facilitated the official, all-expenses-paid invitation to me to address a South African group in 1995.

Upon touchdown in South Africa, an India-descended civil servant slid me by limo to my tony lodgings in a high-end, Jo'burg suburb. Thoroughly racially integrated a hotel, my sortie to the lobby bar drew scant notice. Flying to East London the next day, I eyeballed the storied beauty of the South African *paysage*: green veldt, gold vineyards.... My East London talk on Canadian democracy prompted cordial applause. My audience yawned at chat about the constitution: they were most intrigued by the presence of a Black ex-politico from a country they had visualized as wholly Caucasian, due to "Great White North" propaganda.

Yet, East London itself seemed predominantly ofay! However, I toured a market in the Ciskei run by women whose gold-brown or ochre faces vaunted Negro-plus-Asian features. I pondered Africa's ancient commerce with China. Did these women reflect that historical admixture?

Back in Jo'burg, I scouted out Soweto. My guide took pains to point out the mansions of the prosperous; even so, the tightly crowded huts of the poor could not be obscured. Next, I spent three days at a game reserve where Mandela and de Klerk had carried out part of their negotiations regarding South Africa's transition to democracy. I savoured my private cottage and my treatment—by mainly Caucasian staffers—as an honoured guest. Enjoying both day and night safaris, I viewed the full array of South African fauna. The most arresting specimen? A female cheetah who ignored me, though I stood but two metres off. After a successful high-speed hunt, she was more interested in digesting game than in being game for being framed!

So, by 1994, once brazenly racist South Africa was commencing a journey toward racial equality.

Events in Canada reminded me, though, that intolerance was alive and well here. Notably, controversy raged over the infamous racial-superiority bugling of J. Philippe Rushton, a Western University psychologist whose "science" was salaried by the Pioneer Fund, which trumpets discredited eugenics. In one "study," Doc Rushton used shopping mall surveys of Asian, Black, and Caucasian teens to try to correlate IQ variations with penis size and sexual activity (or not). According to Rushton, because they practise "sexual restraint" (a notion that the population sizes of China and India contradict), "Orientals" best Caucasians; yet, both are superior to "Negroes," whose outsized manhoods and huge sexual appetites reflect stunted IQs. In sum, Asians have brains, ofays have money, and Africans have fun. This non-science—or nonsense—modified the racialist lucubration of Darwin's heirs, who justified Euro imperialism by asserting that Caucasians were the supreme beings of evolution, "Orientals" stuck in the servile middle, and Negroes on the enslaved bottom. Based on cranial and penis gauges, Rushton's IQ thesis belonged to the pages of Sade.

In February 1990, the esteemed geneticist and TV host David Suzuki debated Rushton in a CBC showdown, in which Suzuki debunked Rushton's work as fallacious. (Yes, fallacies about phalluses.) I chanced to run into Suzuki later at Pearson Airport. He seemed chuffed by his talking-head star turn. But I thought his arguments both hot-air shallow and scientifically hollow.

Criticized by many—even publicly by the Grit Ontario premier—and chastised by sundry scientists for grossly inappropriate methodology, Rushton was upheld by Western University via the rubric of academic freedom, which whitewashed his association with unapologetic white supremacists. Hailed to Western by Black students, I spoke in their support and excoriated the university for according academic credibility to Rushton's toilet-stall-peeping balderdash.

Although the Rushton controversy pushed Western to adopt an anti-racism policy, the institution seemed careless—or callous—about the well-being of Black students. I shot off a letter to Western's prez to say so, and it struck a nerve but missed his heart. I also rebuked Western's student council for attempting to withdraw moneys from a Black campus group protesting Rushton's research.

Then, in April of 1990, I rose in the House to demand the cancelling of Canuck Army recruitment ads depicting a Black man, an Asian man, and a white woman—all in subservient roles: the Negro was a chauffeur, the Asian fellow a cook, and the lady aproned. The military brayed that focus groups had okayed the commercials. But it was inconceivable that the portrayals could have been approved by any of the groups so stereotyped. Expressing meet mortification, Hon. Mary Collins—jointly the Minister for Women's Status and National Defence—had the offensive images yanked.

Later that same spring, answering a request from Bev Folkes of the Black Friends and Inmates Association, I decided to investigate Negrophobic racism in the Canuck penal system. With Clarkie alongside, I zoomed to Millhaven Penitentiary and the Prison For Women (known jocularly as "P4W"), both in Kingston. My most detailed consultations were at the Kingston Penitentiary (KP), which we twice eyeballed.

In the prison library, we convened some twenty-five inmates: Black, Indigenous, Caucasian. The old-timer prisoners imposed discipline, so what we heard—a litany of abuse claims—was attested to calmly. Apparently, racist epithets were lingua franca among the guards. One, they said, sported the initials KKK on his forehead. Another—ID'd as "Boudreau"—sported a lapel pin portraying an African man in a loin cloth, a South Asian man in a turban, and an Asian man in a coolie hat and flaunted the caption, "Who is the Minority in Canada?" One gang of white-is-might guards dubbed themselves "The Devious Few" and meted out insults, threats, drubbings, and clubbings. A blind inmate, I ascertained, had been duped into signing a document that affected him adversely. Horribly, we were informed of an Indigenous prisoner whom guards beat to death—a murder for which no one was held accountable.

I raised in the House of Commons the affront of Boudreau's racist lapel pin, and KP Warden Tom Epp responded by suspending him and ordering the suppression of other racist paraphernalia among the guards, whose union—tacit NDP allies, but implicit white supremacists—spoke rabidly about their "free speech." (Approximately five years later, with my good friend Herb Gray presiding as Solicitor General, the existence of a cell of racist guards at KP became public knowledge.) Nastily, Boudreau defended himself by declaring, "With Meech separatists, French this and French that—you see nothing about the white male—the white male is in the minority." (He should have studied Rushton; therein he would have understood that the problem was not in his head but in his loins.) Boudreau was not alone in voicing that refrain; it had become a mantra for Euro-Canucks fearful that egalitarianism would revoke their unearned privileges.

On our first KP tour, I'd not treated with Warden Epp. Take two: Clarkie and I saw a co-operative hombre, who even gladly pointed out the records kept by the first KP warden and also displayed some of the now-deplored whips and restraints, medieval enough to outfit a Grand Inquisitor. The inmates—interviewed a second time—said that Epp was trying to respect their complaints. Yet, clearly, the intolerance fomented by the guards was, for Epp, ultra vires.

Racism also catalyzed a major eruption in response to the intention of Mayor Jean Ouellette of Oka, Quebec, to expand a private golf club and construct condominiums upon lands sacred to and claimed by Mohawks, including a cemetery. Despite the pleas of Quebec Minister of Native Affairs John Ciaccia, Ouellette refused to retreat from his vision of pale, lard-assed, balding duffers trundling golf carts over Indigenous bones. To forbid that ugly scenario, the Mohawks constructed blockades to forestall any development.

Ouellette called in the Sûreté du Québec (SQ)—including a few trigger-finger hands—to dismantle the barricades. Their playbook? Hurl flash-bang grenades and stage a firefight with Mohawk "Warriors." Sadly, that skirmish saw an officer killed. Due to this deadly snafu, the SQ skedaddled, abandoning some heavy weapons to the Warriors, but also now choosing to besiege Kanesatake, the Mohawk territory adjacent to Oka on the North Shore of Montreal.

Upon this event, Indigenous "freedom fighters" (hailing from a miscellany of Canuck reserves and Yankee reservations) rallied to gird the Mohawk Warriors. To aid their Kanesatake brothers, members of the neighbouring Kahnawake Reserve barricaded the Mercier Bridge, cutting off the South Shore of the Saint Lawrence River from the Island of Montreal. Now, frustrated commuters *de souche* vented racist profanities at the Mohawks—and, in one incendiary incident, before TV cameras, palefaces stoned a convoy of Indigenous-driven vehicles. Oka was suddenly a replica of apartheid-era South Africa.

With the SQ at bay and tensions escalating (despite a fed gov decision to purchase the disputed land), the RCMP suited up, booted up. But the Mounties were fast overwhelmed and forced to retreat: ten of their contingent were injured.

Quebec's Premier Bourassa now asked PM Mulroney to activate the famous "Van Doos"—the 22nd Regiment—to repulse the Warriors. Once the soldiers trooped, the bridge barricade soon buckled. Not long after, at the site, I met a dispirited Mohawk remnant, tossing their firearms into a bonfire.

Though ofays never got their golf course, neither were Oka's Mohawks honoured. Soon, their protest would urge the rejection of the Meech Lake Accord (MLA): recall Manitoba politico Elijah Harper's breathtaking raising of an eagle-feather pseudo mace and his intoning of "No."

That summer, Ontario's Premier David Peterson cynically requested what abruptly proved to be a sudden-death election. Polls had shown the Grits at stratospheric poll heights. But the snap election call was venal, and Peterson's thumbs-up for Meech Lake was suicidal for an electorate angry about the FTA, hostile to the MLA, and fuming about a federal 7 percent Goods and Services Tax (GST) that would transfer directly to consumers a fee once only hefted by manufacturers. Disgruntled Ontarians could not (yet) punish Mulroney, but they were set to trounce Peterson for being too shoulder-to-shoulder with a politico now lampooned as a double-chinned, Gucci-loafered snake-oil peddler. Still, no one was more surprised than those of us backing Wayne Lessard in Windsor to hear that not only was he elected, but democratic socialists would command the Treasury. My pal Bob Rae was now the 21st Ontario premier—and the first New Democrat to acquire that title.

Good news! Bad news? Rae's caucus—novices, with paltry experience and lean credentials—were leftists in principle but all left feet in practice. Predictably too, the FTA wrought recession; next, a scurrilous billboard campaign and other Big Biz propaganda eroded public trust in the pro-worker government. Too, Rae pissed off many neophyte NDP voters who trusted that they'd soon be able to buy beer and wine in grocery stores and see pricey auto-insurance premiums reduced: Rae shed instantly those headline pledges. In the first case, alcohol unions said *nyet*; in the latter, auto insurers trotted tearful secretaries before news cameras to boohoo that they'd be out of work if Ontario regulated auto insurance. Fooled by this hooey, Rae chose to disappoint millions of drivers rather than promise the grieving but telegenic secretaries that they'd find new, better-paying, secure, unionized jobs with a taxpayer-funded, government-managed auto insurer.

Rae's two-left-feet team never did find its footing. Their defeat, in 1995, was vouchsafed from the moment of their unexpected government formation in 1990. But Rae's downward trajectory—shedding union support—also contributed to my electoral downfall in 1993.

Apart from my anti-apartheid and pro–human rights efforts as Human Rights Critic (External), my other principal duty was participation in the parliamentary committee on Industry, Science, and Technology (IST). Thus, I interviewed expert witnesses and inspected labs, factories, and universities so I could make reasoned recs regarding Tory science policy. Our committee also took to London and Paris to study science and research policies overseas. (What a difference to be undertaking such high-flying travel when, as a student scientist, I'd been so familiar merely with the roads between London and Paris, Ontario!) French officials were confreres, but England's minions scorned our accoutrements and scoffed at our accents.

Helping to oversee the Business and Labour Trust Program, I viewed the impressive Alcoa plant in Shawinigan, Quebec. Thus, I got schooled in aluminum smelting, recycling, manufacture, and research. The smelters were sweltering, but the hospitality was sunny honey. The IST Committee released its *Canada Must Compete* report in September 1990. Being the solo scientist "in da House," I proposed twenty of its thirty-five recs—including calls to invest 2.5 percent of GDP in R & D by 2005; to use government procurement to increase industrial research; and to launch a national scientific mission to develop a hydrogen fuel cell. I spearheaded a parliamentary debate on the matter, proposing that, based on its petroleum industry infrastructure, Canada could have a comparative advantage in developing a pollutant-free fuel, all green for go. What did Mulroney do instead? Abolish the Science Council of Canada! The successor Jean Chrétien and Paul Martin governments did utilize my recs, however. (Gross Domestic Expenditures on R & D actually reached 2.05 percent by the year 2005 but dropped off markedly under the Stephen Harper regime—so hostile to science, that is, to curiosity, perhaps even to dreaming.)

In 1991, the IST Committee became embroiled in a controversy at the National Research Council (NRC), whose imperious prez, Pierre "Juan" (I'll say) Perron, wished both to "innovate" and institute "fiscal austerity." That schizoid balancing act saw Perron alter the size and mission of the Industrial Research Assistance Program (IRAP), which was missioned to provide expert scientific assistance to small and medium-sized firms. Perron's oversight saw the sacking of IRAP head Shibly Abela and the protest resignations by members of its advisory committee. I must register that Abela was an Egyptian-born civil-servant scientist in a public service often unkind to "visible minorities" or BIPOC employees. This point is not editorial but factual.

Perhaps the most blatant case of implicit NRC racialism was the dismissal—in distressing circumstances—of Dr. Chander Grover, a first-class physicist and front-rank optics researcher. In spite of repeated findings of racial discrimination by Canadian Human Rights Commission tribunals, who said that NRC managers thwarted Doc Grover's advancement, humiliated him, unfairly fired him, and then tried to intimidate witnesses from testifying on his behalf, the NRC refused for years to comply with the mandated settlement provisions: to appoint Doc Grover to a senior post and to pay him his withheld wages. The NRC preferred to outlay a million dollars to flout the settlement, thus stalling and destroying the optics physicist's professional career. Much of this gross mistreatment occurred under "Juan" Perron—make of that fact what you will.

In the IRAP case, Perron moved to place it within the NRC so as to emphasize the targeted transfer of NRC R & D to meet industry's priorities. Perron also imposed managerial changes that robbed IRAP of its institutional memory while a new strategic plan was being foisted upon its advisory committee—sans consultation. When IRAP advisory committee members took this problem to the IST Committee, Perron (as if influenced by his partial namesake, the Argentine *baas* Juan Perón) disbanded the advisors because they'd dared speak out—an act that, in my minority report, I deemed contemptuous of Parliament. Committee Tories refused to condemn Perron's authoritarian-style management for what it was: oppressive of informed dissent.

The IST Committee did find extra bucks for the IRAP, but we also held that, even within the NRC, it be independently managed; that research from non-NRC sources be sought; and that the advisory committee be reconstituted and its role defined. Thus, "Perónism" was repudiated, though Perron survived into 1994. (Perron announced his intent to resign as NRC prez in an August 1993 letter. That was a prescient move, given Tory PM Kim Campbell's looming epochal defeat in October 1993. Incidentally, the NRC's website history for Perron is—to my eyes—so much doughy puffery.)

In October 1990, my father was hospitalized. His health had been deteriorating for a while. Evidently, his death was near. As I stood by his bed, he said what he had never *said* before, "I love you and I am very proud of you." These were his last words to me. And they made a difference—though so, so late arriving, this declaration of respect and devotion. I'd always felt his admiration, and even his adoration. But that man's need to "show strength," to be the paterfamilias, had meant that he could not avow the simple-simple fact of his love. And yet I can name no demerit to his character. Had he not always been there? Brutal was my grief.

(I confess that I have inherited the same stern and taciturn "tude" toward my own loved ones—out of the bogus fear that affection is weakness. I wonder if Black men, more than most, are subject to this "holding back" due to an adaptation to enslavement: that to love a spouse or child was impossible given the high probability that either or all could be sold away—or, worse, tortured, raped, or slain wantonly—at the pleasure of the master or the overseer. I don't make excuses for my failings, but I also *cannot* ignore the trauma of centuries of cold-blooded, Euro-"Christian," deliberate fracturing of Black families.)

Upon my black-suit return to The Big Zero in the wake of my father's funeral, a new brouhaha blizzarded: a storm of pale macaroni! Why? I'd been reappointed to the post of NDP Critic for Post-Secondary Education and Youth, just as the Mulroney acolytes had stoked the ire of college and university students by imposing a 3 percent surcharge on their loans. As I entered the House at noon on Wednesday, October 17, 1990, I hadn't planned to query the Tories on the matter. Yet, it was National Students' Day—and given Canadian Federation of Students (CFS) rancour, Nelson Riis slotted me to pose a question.

Then, as I rose to speak, the House was pelted—raucously—with uncooked Kraft Dinner pasta. Oodles of dry noodles blitzed brunettes and blondes, bald heads and bewigged, toupees and tonsures, straight-haired and curly, redheads and grey eminences…. The baby-shrimp-sized projectiles clattered on desks and speckled the chamber's fabled green carpet, crackling underfoot. Immediately, Tory MPs—with evident sympathy from the Speaker—accused me of having colluded with the demonstrators!

That charge soon animated a point of privilege finagled by Albert Glen Cooper, ex-Parliamentary Secretary to the Minister of Justice and the Attorney General of Canada, who moved that I be held in contempt of the House. His request of the Speaker stemmed from the truth that some students had received House gallery passes from my office. Thus, Cooper alleged, I and other Knee-Dippers had approved the pasta fusillade, that macaroni cascade.

I fought his incendiary with the oxygen-deprivation that is fact: I observed that, given the snappy Tory comeback to my question, the government itself must have had pre-knowledge of the student disruption, not a jot of which had been shared with Opposition MPs. I reminded all that I'd only arrived in "Cap City" late that morning, that my question was spontaneous, and that the issuing of passes—a routine courtesy—was hardly incriminating. Moreover, the CFS prez denied any collaboration on my part, and he apologized for the undeserved harm to my reputation due to the CFS stunt. His statement shut up Cooper and shut down his charge.

The point of privilege was denied. I then lodged that, in parliamentary tradition, a member who brings a false charge of contempt must face a contempt charge himself. Now, Cooper had to sweat through his used-car-dealer-quality suit. Regrettably, Speaker Fraser kiboshed my counter claim, perhaps because he had himself seemed initially to think me guilty of misconduct for which there was not a scintilla of credible evidence. How sad! That stand-up man brought *shame* upon his judgment!

No matter the Bytown shenanigans that I had to negotiate, my principal concern was Windsor. Two developments there soon had all my attention. In the early 1990s, Ontario hemorrhaged manufacturing jobs. The Canada–US Free Trade Agreement (FTA), high interest rates, and a high Canuck buck put our industries in a lose-lose situation. Inside a year, Windsor lost eleven automotive parts plants. Increased cross-border shopping by Windsorites but a sharp decrease in border-hopping Americans hollowed out the downtown. Jewellers became pawn shops; hotels barely ran their elevators. Unemployment hit 17.4 percent, and with the downloading of the burden of many social service costs (including welfare) to the municipalities, the city and county were tapped out.

Into this depressing environment the Economic Strategic Development Committee (ESDC) released its report, *Prosperity 2000*. Inspired by my proposal for "the Committee of 100," realty tycoon Chuck Mady and unionist Gary Parent co-chaired the ESDC, whose members represented capitalists, pedagogues, proles, artistes, local government, and civic boosters. I obtained $250,000 in federal funding for its strategic study, but Windsor City Council was slow to ratchet up the matching bucks required. In an almost unprecedented intervention by a sitting MP, I went before council to say that it was their duty to grow a quarter-million-dollar investment into a half-million-dollar one. Unanimous approval was thus secured.

The ESDC hired William Marshall as its chief executive and struck subcommittees to report on various economic sectors. But where was the focus on research and technology and academia as catalysts for economic development? (To document my misgivings, I presented a paper before a special forum on science and technology co-sponsored by the Science Council of Canada and the ESDC, which also got published in the *Windsor Star*.)

Eventually, the ESDC posited several proposals:

1) Wrangle high-end retail for the downtown, to model Windsor as a Great Lakes Riviera;

2) heighten Windsor's share of government and white-collar jobs;

3) stimulate tourism via an aquatic park;

4) refurbish dismantled factories and warehouses as student residences and artists' centres; and

5) transform the riverfront into a garden, park, and alfresco sculpture showcase.

The ESDC essayed to revivify manufacturing and agriculture. Finally, Mady et al. sought to merge the Convention and Tourist Bureau with the Development Commission (to create the "CBD")—for savings, yes, but also to centralize the dreaming up of lucrative downtown enhancements.

The report was widely hailed for what it was—the first systematic approach to an economic development strategy the city and county had ever had. Dismally, it would be the dire economic problems it attempted to address that would abort its full implementation. When the ESDC asked that a "Prosperity 2000 Consortium" be struck to implement the report, it was "no probs"—on paper! But the Convention, Tourism, and Development merger idea died at birth; thus, $400,000 in savings—that could've financed fresh blueprints—went poof! Next, the po-mouth county balked at paying its share, allotting but $25,000 of the $1 million required from tri-level government. By 1991, the grand plan was vapour.

Although the ESDC report was stillborn, it conjured benefits: the Windsor Casino; the provincial labour office; the art museum; Government Square; the new courthouse; the riverfront development; and initiatives for the aquatic centre and plans for university and college facilities—all based downtown and all consistent with *Prosperity 2000*.

Approved by Ontario's NDP government, the Windsor Casino initially opened in 1993 at the site of the Art Gallery of Windsor. (Later, it enjoyed a grand reopening as Caesars Windsor, operated by the Caesar's Palace brand.) While this socialist-sanctioned "casino capitalism" yielded hundreds of union jobs, it did not revive Windsor's moribund CBD. Plus, its initial attraction for US high-rollers—based on our low dollar and our being, literally, "the only *gaming* in town"—soon vanished as the Canuck buck neared parity with the Yank greenback, and Michigan legalized casinos.

In December of 1990, an announcement was made that provoked a unified cry of outrage from Windsorites. Enduring over $100 million in new budget cuts, the CBC now carried out its 1984 threat: to discontinue all Windsor TV broadcasting, cutting eighty-four jobs; Windsor news would now be selected, edited, and broadcast from Toronto. The Big Smoke would call the shots on what was our local "news."

What a stunning blow to one of the few stations in the CBC system that had been profitable—despite being situated amid the loudest din of radio and television broadcasts, virtually all American, in the world! What an exasperatingly short-sighted abandonment of a vehicle by which an American audience gained an understanding of Canadian culture and perspectives!

I received the CBC's announcement while in my Ottawa office. As it happened, Windsor Mayor John Millson was in town. I contacted him and arranged a press conference in the National Press Gallery, where he initiated Windsor's response, including the formation of the mayor's task force, of which I was instantly a part. This task force soon joined with the Friends of Canadian Broadcasting and the Windsor and District Labour Council to form the Coalition to Preserve Public Broadcasting (CPPB).

Acting jointly, Steve Langdon, Herb Gray, and I launched a petition drive that overnight netted some 47,000 signatures. We also peppered and salted the government with statements and questions, all insisting that the CBC budget cuts be rescinded.

The CPPB examined all possible recourse—even demanding that the Canadian Radio-television and Telecommunications Commission (CRTC) cancel the CBET TV licence. Also considered were a lawsuit, securing local funding and/or ownership of news broadcasting, and/or finding an ambitious start-up broadcaster.

In March 1991, five thousand Windsorites marched down Riverside Drive to an energetic rally at the CBET station. Labour activist Judy Darcy, Langdon, Gray, and I all told the protesters that we felt Windsor was being punished for being a city of working-class, Canuck nationalists, waving the Maple Leaf right under the beak of the American Eagle. How dare we affirm our Canadian identity in the face of a government that extolled Shamrock Summits and bilateral blarney!

Yes, the CRTC held hearings, and I was an intervener. But neither rage nor reason could change any Tory-appointee mind. Instead, the CBC was prohibited from soliciting local ads. This situation remained the status quo until 1993, when Baton Broadcasting obtained a licence for an independent TV outlet to serve Windsor (with what is now a CTV station). Then, in 1994, CBET resumed regional news broadcasts under the "Windsor Experiment," a procedure that multitasks journalists to do both reporting and camera work.

By then, I was an ex-MP, my political career seemingly as extinct as was the 34th Parliament itself. *Good riddance*, I could have thought. My Knee-Dipper leadership bid and its kneecapping, Negrophobic voters—and my complaints about it—all had cost me Caucasian backing in Windsor. Likewise, the Rae Government's decision to lower Ontario civil servants' wages fuelled union discontent with the NDP. Although I could bask in the success of my apartheid opposition, that foreign policy nicety was meaningless to most voters. And all my can-do, gung-ho boosterism could not recuperate factory shutdowns and jobs disappeared due to the cheap wages of the Mexican maquiladoras. But don't cry for me, Essex County.

CHAPTER TWENTY:
OUT!

BEING THE SOLITARY AFRICAN-CANADIAN MEMBER OF PARLIAMENT,
I was as good as adopted by many Caribbean nations. Several ushered
Brenda and me to their shores as practical Afro-Can ambassadors. Thus,
the Jamaican government beckoned us to kick back at the posh Montego
Bay Sandals resort. This rare luxury—a sun-sand-surf idyll—was damnably
cut short within forty-eight hours. I was called back to Ottawa to debate the
Canuck reply to the UN-mandated, US-led effort to oust Iraqi forces from
Kuwait, which strongman Saddam Hussein had annexed the previous
summer. (Clearly, the UN-sanctioned action would be a neat way to destroy
an army that constituted a present threat to every Western-propped-up
oligarchy in the Middle East. Lookit! H. W. Bush himself had smiled upon
"Saddam the Bad-Ass" when he was assaulting Iran. But that was yesterday.
"Sides" had shifted again like sand dunes in a windstorm.)

Having disappointed Brenda by accepting to return to The Big Zero,
I was irritated to no end when I was told that Simon De Jong,
Saskatchewan's Mr. Wishy-Washy, had not done so, perhaps presuming
that his role in Audrey's leadership win gave him carte blanche to put his
chaise longue before his Commons seat. Then again, no matter how loud
my ire, Mulroney would send five thousand Canuck troops to the
(Persian) Gulf War. So, why could I not have stayed in Montego Bay?

In February, Brenda accompanied me to Haiti because I was a Maple-
Leaf-flag delegate witnessing the inauguration of Jean-Bertrand Aristide
as the nation's first democratically elected prez in four decades. I was eager
to have Brenda along, due to the NDP's royal screw-up of our January
Jamaica stay.

We touched down after dark then limo'd to the prez-elect's country estate on the jumpy, bumpy road to Port-au-Prince. Unreal! Torch-bearing Haitians lined the route, casting out gloom with their blazing faggots. They feared an assassination attempt upon, and sought to pro-tect—via illumination—the man who was communicating hope: the peo-ple's prez.

Aristide's digs? A humble house a few strides from the road. Just as we sat to talk to Aristide, a blackout ensued. Instantly, the torch-lit-up crowd outside began to converge on us: they dreaded that the electricity fail was preface to a coup. Once the lights surged on again, the outdoors crowd stepped back. After our audience with Aristide, we Canucks, illu-mined all along by dark hands holding aloft blazing daubs of light, taxied to our Pétion-Ville hotel.

Pomp marked Aristide's installation in the albescent presidential palace. Uncountable Haitians—"ordinary" but exhilarated—were restrained by an imposing fence. Naturally, the faces of the gathered political, social, and military elite did not mirror the exultation of the thousands outside. Instead, their sneering contempt for the election result forecast a stealthy resistance that would undermine Aristide's pres-idency and lead to his ouster.

That same year, 1991, I attended the meetings of the International Parliamentary Union (IPU) in Pyongyang, North Korea, and helped draft a resolution branding misogynist violence a war crime. In searching for synonyms that would characterize wartime rape as heinous, I suggested the word *egregious*. Why did I proffer that word? Though *egregious* had been popularized in Canada due to the Meech Lake debates, two British IPU members—with typical harrumphing hubris—averred that English con-tained no such word. Thus, the committee suspended further deliberation until they could confirm its Anglo-Saxon heritage. Once they learned that *egregious* is an English word, the Brits reappeared—as red-faced as drunks.

Memorable was my experience of being in that isolated country: the Hermit Kingdom. We did have docents, who were unobtrusive but always at hand to pass on info and plan Pyongyang sorties. So obsequiously friendly, they were, but curious about Canada and anxious to convince us that North Korea was just as democratic. Long after our departure, I received amiable letters from my guide, still extolling the *res publica* talking points.

By occidental standards, our hotel was a three-star. But the star fea-ture of my roomy digs was a TV that revealed much about North Korea. Ads? Nil. But every movie and serial boasted a male hero who doubled for Kim Il Sung, thus was his deification even cinematic!

When not in talk-fests, I traipsed about a pseudo-business district where, at broad street intersections, women in trim uniforms directed non-existent traffic with sharply executed arm signals. I also observed platoons of uniformly clad schoolchildren marching hither and thither.

Near the hotel was a subway station; it typified the monumental scale of so many Pyongyang edifices and boasted within omnipresent murals depicting the Great Leader. Awaiting their trains, the platform crowd looked passive, disinterested, unsmiling—exactly like the denizens of Orwell's bleak dystopic novel, *1984*.

The most revered sites in the Democratic People's Republic of Korea were Kim Il Sung's modest birthplace (now a shrine) and the massive, one-hundred-foot-high bronze statue of him near the stunning Liberation War Memorial. The latter vaunted huge red granite flags as a backdrop for about a hundred granite soldiers gunning for the enemy's rout. These displays dominated a huge plaza facing a magnificent pillared marble building bearing a humongous mural of mountains.

The granite Juche Tower, slightly taller than the Washington Monument, commands the riverfront across from Kim Il Sung Square and the deceased founder's larger-than-life mausoleum. My guide informed me that *Juche* (almost rhymes with *Duce*, the Italian term for a [the] Fascist leader) refers to the official state philosophy as articulated by pop-star Andy Kim. (Just kidding!) In any event, I cannot claim to have deciphered *Juche*— beyond its connoting a combo of self-reliance and hero worship.

The hollowness of North Korea's *Juche* faith was, yes, architectural: many grandiose edifices in which there was nothing doing and no one working (except for the top-secret nuclear war planners and the rockets they were concocting in subterranean bunkers).

Culture was the cultivated difference. We reviewed a dance program offering beautifully costumed female dancers whose skills were Olympic-gymnast quality. Our intro to "Arirang," the ancient Korean folk song that is included twice on the UNESCO Intangible Cultural Heritage list? Cavorting acrobats involving the synchronized movements of some fifty thousand children and adults in a portrayal of North Korean history.

We also ogled Yeonyong Falls. En route, we dined at a restaurant whose elegance and gourmet menu seemed to mock the fare of most North Koreans. Poised on a hill, its views astonished us while we knifed astonishing Korean beef.

To reach the stupendous falls, we crossed—with much trepidation— steep gorges on rope bridges. Not for backsliders!

However, it was the return to Pyongyang that was indelible. When we had left, hundreds of workers were toiling in a field at the city limits, possibly preparing a construction site. On our midnight bus back, still they toiled, sweating by torch light.

Our next stop was Beijing—a breath of fresh, food-perfumed air after the sterile, starved vistas of the Hermit Kingdom. Where Pyongyang was desolate, Beijing streets throbbed with shoppers, were splashy with bicycles. We had no chaperones and were left to our own devices. A nearby super-provisioned supermarket carried everything to answer every craving.

"The Russian Square"—the fave mart of Russian expatriates in Beijing—was a must-see. No wonder! Items made for Western markets got sold at manufacturers' prices—no markups. Thus, knitted sweaters fetching $100 in Canada sold here for just $15.

We jaunted about Tiananmen Square, named after the main gate of the Forbidden City, which opens onto its expanse. Absent was any taint of the slaughter there just two years previous. This historical complex of red-painted architectural wonders of brick, wood, and rice cement had been the residence of generations of Chinese emperors and their royal courts. Also at Tiananmen Square is the Great Hall of the People where we met, in a courtesy call, a stern-faced panel of officials. A congress of ignoble toadies? (Well, dreamers make revolutions that clerks revise.)

Startling and stupefying was the Great Wall of China, which I strolled with Liberal MP Bob Speller. A world-class wonder, it stretches for 21,000 klicks—definitely outdistancing Toronto's Yonge Street of 56 klicks—and is wide enough on the top, in places, to accommodate vehicles.

Landing at Kai Tak Airport on Kowloon Island, at Hong Kong, was death-defying sport. Our pilot had to manoeuvre nimbly to veer past the mountains and encroaching skyscrapers. But to enter "HK" itself was to experience a city-state, never sleeping, never still. About our hotel, people resided in vertical stacks of crowded apartments on narrow streets overseeing insomniac merchants rowdily hawking foods and household merchandise, 24/7.

Among the gleaming towers, "suits" scurried to and fro. Barkers sold all. One yelled, "Genuine imitation Rolex watches! True to the hour and true to you!" Tailors could cut a suit within twenty-four hours. I bought one for $300 and several silk ties for $5 each.

On July 1, 1991, Canada Day back home, the Spicer Commission ended its mission. After the collapse of the Meech Lake Accord, its members had journeyed the country to pinpoint the malaise that had sucked down the Accord. Their only constructive proposal was the need to consult Canadians on any constitutional change. Yet, consultation would only spotlight hatred for Mulroney, antagonism toward bilingualism and Quebec, and hostility to multiculturalism. Indeed, the Spicer Commission surveyed a rural Canada that was US-Republican-Party yahoo in sympathy, if still nostalgically monarchical. Gung-ho for the noose and gaga for Walt Disney, for them, Moses bears arms and Jesus's arms bear tattoos. (Thus, Keith Spicer identified the electorate who would flock en masse to the angry-white-guy idol Mike Harris in Ontario in 1995 and who shunned me, federally, in 1993.)

Meanwhile a Senate–House body chaired by MP Jim Edwards (Tory) and Senator Gerald Beaudoin (Grit) held that any future constitutional amendments be put to the people in referenda to be held concurrently, province by province, territory by territory. A democrat's dream, a politico's nightmare. To put a constitution before the whole electorate would see some demand that English be the sole official language, while others would want to make Calgary the capital. Debates about choices would become alphabet soup and/or a dog's breakfast: a gigantic mess.

When we federal Knee-Dippers convened in Halifax, we proposed that a constitutional assembly, *not* a national referendum, be the legitimate forum for advancing constitutional change. I did not believe that the complexities of governance would be understood by the average elector; moreover, I believed each amendment, taken in isolation apart from the requisite historical and socio-political context, could generate fatal opposition. And my fears were correct.

New Democrats also proposed a Social Charter, which I lobbied to see enacted—and enforced. However, the flawed document did not demand equality for racial minorities. Instead, the vapid slogan, "promote the multicultural nature" of Canada, got tabled. Meaningless, the phrase could allow even the Ku Klux Klan and neo-Nazis to seek protection for their hateful views by declaring themselves to be representing a cultural perspective!

Not theoretical, eh? Spicer's commission had uncovered a cesspool of animosity for multiculturalism. Because state multiculturalism had evolved to mean—for Jean Q. Public—taxpayer funding of the exotic cultural practices of immigrants, *that* could mean, said rightists, the succouring of anti-feminist and anti-civil-rights ideas.

George Elliott Clarke (who would become one of Canada's greatest poets) was yet my parliamentary aide. We co-authored a paper for *Policy Options* entitled "The Demolition Clause in the Charter of Rights," in which we exposed and opposed the fact that the equality of racial and other minorities before the law—as posited in Section 15 of the Charter of Rights and Freedoms—can be overridden by Section 33, the "notwithstanding clause."

Years before, at a Knee-Dipper presser in Toronto, I had engaged in a testy hotel-room analysis of the clause with Saskatchewan premier Allan Blakeney. His Puritan position was actually adopted by supposed social democrats: "To ensure that the people and not the courts prevail, the Party supports the retention of the notwithstanding clause."

I answered Blakeney by juxtaposing his formulation with that of US Dixiecrats, who would have maintained white-supremacist-sponsored "black codes" had state governments been able to lisp, "notwithstanding" to the US Supreme Court. I was blunt: "The notwithstanding clause is a gun aimed at the Equality provision of the Charter. It makes possible a repetition, for example, of the incarceration of Japanese-Canadians—as happened during the Second World War."

Margaret Mitchell and I, being co-chairs of the Minority Caucus, submitted an amendment to the NDP constitution proposal, arguing that Section 33 must not apply to Section 15. Prez of the National Action Committee on the Status of Women, Judy Rebick, affirmed us—to our faces. Still, the party brass was duly negative until we threatened a public tongue-lashing. The Minority Caucus also pledged to quit the convention if our concerns went unheeded. Michael Lewis, brother to Stephen and sympathetic to minority, antiprejudice demands, was charged with finding a compromise. (Dammit! How was my equality subject to any compromise?)

Even so, the Minority Caucus lodged a bozo bromide: we asked the Constitution Committee to review the "possible effect" of the notwithstanding clause on Section 15. Given that the "possible effect" is nullification, we simply expanded opportunities for shilly-shallying.

Thanks to the alliance that Clarkie and I forged with thirty-three minority and ethnic organizations (under the title "New Vision"), we got the party to ask the government to amend the multiculturalism clause (Section 27) of the Charter to state: "Governments are committed…to the preservation and promotion of ethnic and racial equality in the country." (How I craved to add, "Notwithstanding the notwithstanding clause!")

Further progress? The NDP, in saying *oui* to the constitutional process, was permitted to voice our ideas in six constitutional conferences in major cities. Now, ex-PM Joe Clark headed up the constitutional folio. Natch: he was likeable, but Mulroney was loathed.

Lorne Nystrom steered NDP constitutional strategy. We stressed the need for a Social Charter (I had identified a prototype in the European Union) to prevent beggar-thy-neighbour diminution of social programs in the face of the pro-business (anti-worker) provisions of free-trade deals.

In assessing these constitutional positions, Ian McLeod, in *Under Siege: The Federal NDP in the Nineties* (1994), tars me as having reacted with "a predictable explosion of fury" (p. 76) for not having been consulted by Audrey McLaughlin regarding court enforcement (which I opposed) of the Social Charter. (Did McLeod choose to vaunt stereotype—*predictably*—over analysis?)

Truly, I demanded the protection of social programs, health care, the environment, collective bargaining, and education in a document now dubbed the "Social Covenant," which became a constitutive part of the "Social and Economic Union" in the committee's final report. (Look it up!)

Thwarted, though, were my committee efforts to forge an accord to limit the application of the notwithstanding clause—even though Clarkie and I (with assists from José Aggrey, Andrew Cardozo, and others) mobilized our New Vision coalition to voice our concerns to the committee at Ottawa, Halifax, and Toronto hearings. Unhelpful, though, was the decision of the New Vision "seers" to accommodate themselves to the mealy-mouthed NDP pledge to research the impact of Section 33 on Section 15. Piffle!

Black lawyer Donald Oliver from Nova Scotia was a just-bo'n Tory senator. He too served on the Joint Committee. For our hearings in Halifax, I'd scheduled presentations by Black activists Yvonne Atwell, Lynn Jones, and Joan Jones. Thus, I asked Oliver to stand with us to see equality rights protected within the Charter. Hell, he refused! He wouldn't jeopardize his (unelected!) "political position." Harrumph!

The committee heard seven hundred witnesses and received three thousand typed submissions. Deplorable it was, though, that no Black Torontonian *chef* (think Carlton A. Masters, Black Business and Professional Association prez) showed up to argue for the preservation of minority rights versus pasty-faced supremacist and/or "nationalist" governments, who'd demonize the "other" to capture or keep electoral office for themselves. (To rob Gandhi to pay Duplessis?)

That Black Toronto fielded Ralph Ellison–style "Invisible Men"—castrati—when we (they) should have appeared as an opal phalanx, hinted to the milquetoast, Wheaties-slurping committee members that we African-Canadians could care less about the Charter's equality guarantee. (*Grazie,* Carlton!)

Provincial premiers' resistance was exemplified in a reprise of the debate I'd had with Blakeney. Next, Rebick canned our reforms to Section 27 on the incomprehensible basis that minorities would thus gain "special rights." "Special" rights? A *guarantee* of our equality rights would be ultra vires?

Our committee's report? "A Renewed Canada." Along with the Social Covenant, it sought an elected senate that would reflect regional diversity and set aside seats for women and minorities. In recognizing Quebec as a "distinct society," it sought to protect francophone minorities in all provinces. It did not remedy the potential evil of the notwithstanding clause or include a revised Section 27. Well, *tant pis!* In any event, Canadians rejected the Charlottetown Accord in toto.

In Ontario, the Rae Government boosted noticeably the presence of racial minorities in the bureaucracy and the cabinet. (An "angry white men" backlash foreshadowed just what Prez Obama would face from "Tea Party" Republicans.) Zanana Akande, the first Black woman elected to Queen's Park, became a minister; banker Carlton Masters was appointed Ontario's Agent-General in New York; Fran Endicott got to head the Human Rights Commission; and Juanita Westmoreland-Traoré led the Office of Employment Equity. Other African-Canadians worked in the premier's office and in the caucus. Progress!

Even so, the Ontario NDP Black Advisory group, which had sought to strengthen the equality clause in the Charter, failed to convince Rae to advocate their position to other first ministers. At their request, I treated with Rae, who was initially resistant to amendments, being committed to the compromise that had been reached when the Charter was first negotiated (a deal to which he'd had a front-row seat). After a debate between us two, Rae accepted our concerns as legitimate and agreed to raise them during the Charlottetown Accord negotiations. Did he?

In the early 1990s, several incidents (in addition to others already cited) validated the need to strengthen the Charter's equality clause for racial minorities. For instance, in Halifax, the mayor and city—sans environmental hearings—okayed the building of a two-lane road that would bisect Seaview Memorial Park, which commemorated Africville, the Black village that had been demeaned and destroyed in the 1960s and whose citizens had been relocated. The Africville Genealogical Society caterwauled, but the mayor stonewalled. Nova Scotia's NDP leader Alexa McDonough, Mary Clancy (a Liberal MP), and I castigated Halifax's Africville-dismissive proposition. My scathing letter dinned into the ears of the Haligonian legislators.

Racial tensions—coupled with a soup-kitchen economy—trigger deathless division in Nova Scotia. So, in 1989, Black and Caucasian students at Cole Harbour High School brawled in a schoolyard. Eighteen months later, in 1991, after Blacks were denied entry to a Halifax bar, some twenty persons were injured in riotous melees. Halifax's Alexa and I identified joblessness as one cause of strife, but also called out the failure of the Nova Scotia government to implement effective employment equity and to fund adequately the Human Rights Commission and Office of Race Relations.

In Montreal, too, racial tensions were heightening. With his pregnant girlfriend beside him and his mother in the back seat, Marcellus François was shot dead—through his windshield—by fleur-de-lys cops, whose unmarked cars had boxed his in. His offence? Driving while Black. *Les flics* fired willy-nilly and slew an innocent man.

Other Montreal upsets? Baton-wielding officers thrashed Blacks exiting a night club; a Black woman's arm got broken as she was being handcuffed; et cetera.

Previous incidents had led to demos in Montreal, in which I participated. I'd also critiqued killer Stasi at Parliament Hill protests. My upraised voice at a Montreal march drew a letter to *Maclean's* magazine from Mordecai Richler, condemning me for my "interference in Quebec." His tone? So reminiscent of the complaints of southern segregationists upset by northern "busybodies"! Being a scribe excoriated regularly by "*Québécois de souche*," what was the point of Richler's carping? That only he had a moral right to quibble with Québécois affronts to minority rights? *Merde!*

Anyway, Toronto too had witnessed a spate of questionable police shootings of Black men. Was there an open season on *us*—all over North America?

On Monday, May 4, 1992, Dudley Laws led five hundred folks to the US Consulate in Toronto to decry the acquittal of cops who videotape had caught viciously beating Rodney King, an African-American, in Los Angeles. Marchers also attacked the shooting of Raymond Lawrence, a Black Torontonian, on May 2. Peaceful was the demonstration—until a rampaging, masked gang of mostly ofay hooligans turned it into "the Yonge Street Riot." These ruffians splintered windows, looted storefront displays. The prized products of most "smash-and-grabs" that day were boom boxes ("ghetto blasters") and other personal electronics. By its end, some thirty people were arrested. (So reminiscent this was of the March 28, 1968, Memphis, TN, anti-racism march, led by Dr. Martin Luther King Jr., that degenerated into a brouhaha—conducted by "Black militants" or *agents provocateurs*? I believe this question may be asked of the Yonge Street "uprising" window smashers and Molotov cocktail tossers. How many were venting real grievances? How many were on police payrolls?)

The media bayed and brayed over the Yonge Street riots; so, tri-level government began to assess, finally, the insidious fact of police persecution of Black and Indigenous Peoples. Although I'd stood in the House before for constitutional equality guarantees, I now stood to confront increasing racist incidents. In the House of Commons, on May 5, in response to my question period request, Prime Minister Mulroney agreed to meet with me and leaders of the Black community. Furthermore, Justice Minister Kim Campbell agreed to weigh changes in the constitutional proposals that I said compromised equality guarantees.

Dan Heap demanded a debate on the Toronto ruction and conceded his place so that I could lead the deliberation. My speech lured plaudits for its moderation and non-partisanship; still, I minced no words. I observed that many rioters were white youth—frustrated and alienated, like many Blacks, due to lack of access to training and jobs of good income and prestige. I stressed the dangers inherent in the pressures to adopt the socio-economic values of the US with its race-inflected wealth disparities (less $$$ = more KKK). Yet, I also said that dominant-class authorities and citizens alike had failed to understand the discrimination faced by racial and ethnic minorities. Specifically, I called for an inquiry into discrimination in Canada's constabulary and judiciary. Blaming we victims, Campbell chose only to study policies on police discharge of firearms! She turned an issue of racist police culture into a question of firearms training. Typical Tory.

In Ontario, Bob Rae commissioned Stephen Lewis to review and report on race relations. Lewis did so and recommended the formation of the Commission on Systematic Racism in the Ontario Criminal Justice System. He said the right thing—and did the right thing.

To address youth disaffection, Rae appointed Hon. Zanana Akande as his Parliamentary Assistant. The first Black Canuck woman to hold a cabinet position, Zanana was the butt of much pseudo-racist opprobrium from the press, who act as if Black politicos should don sackcloth and ashes rather than "rock" Gucci and Patrick Kelly. Due to an exaggerated rental property dispute from which she was exonerated, Minister Akande had to resign from her post. So what? She designed the Jobs Ontario Youth Program, an unqualified success.

If Zanana heard snarl the hounds of racism, so did I—even within the hallowed halls of the House. During question period, Tory MP Jack Shields yapped, "Shut up, Sambo!" I didn't hear him myself. Nicely, Langdon lambasted the hurled insult as despicable. Shields denied what he'd said, but he apologized for—um—*something*. His grinning disavowal further degraded his person. On a TV talk show with gritty Sheila Copps— slagged as a "slut" by grumpy Tory Bill Kempling—she and I harmonized that sexism must not persist and racism must be erased.

Episodes of intramural bigotry in Parliament were rare, but there had been a previous incident. When I objected to the statement by John Oostrom (a Multiculturalism Committee member—bizarrely) that Europeans are the best immigrants to Canada because they adjust easily to winter, the Speaker admonished me for reviling as racist Dutch-Canuck Oostrom's remark. But how else to classify Oostrom's public doubting that Black people could survive the Arctic? (Obviously, Oostrom was unaware that African-American Matthew Henson, in 1909, may have been the first non-Inuit to reach the North Pole.) Retreating, the Speaker accepted my urging that a Parliamentary committee opposing sexism also spurn racism.

In August 1992, first ministers and Indigenous leaders reached a consensus on constitutional reform: the Charlottetown Accord. Next, the Accord had to pass a national referendum. A "Canada Committee" staffed by Progressive Conservatives, Liberals, and New Democrats was formed to buttress the "Yes" side. Opposing were Quebec separatists, the Western-based Reform Party, and Pierre Elliott Trudeau, again isolated and so dangerously pissed.

In Windsor, all three MPs formed "Yes" committees. My interrogation of the Accord went to every household. I highlighted positive *and* contentious provisions. While I stressed my concerns about the lack of any obligation for governments to guarantee racial equality, I said it was time for the people to decide. The *Hill Times*, in giving me the award for the Best Written Householder, cited my eloquent—if partisan—exposition on the Accord.

A victim of the concerns I expressed early on, the Accord failed in the referendum. Supported in my constituency and elsewhere, it was picked apart by rightists from the West, leftists led by Rebick, Quebec separatists, and PET, enjoying insurgent and resurgent popularity now that he was no longer ensconced at 24 Sussex Drive. Rebick's Accord discord—spawned by her fear that gender equality was not enough guaranteed—was righteously galling to me, given her nixing of our efforts on racial equality, a heartfelt concern upon which I had compromised to put first the general (NDP, Negro Disappointment Party!) good. Too, mass loathing of Mulroney, with whom the Accord was so identified, had to assure its defeat.

Indeed, the arithmetic of Mulroney's subpar approval ratings was full of negatives for me. In truth, Mulroney's ascension in 1984—and the collapse of Windsor's Liberal vote—had made me an MP; now, the public's hatred for "The Chin," the fracturing of the Tory vote, and the irrelevance of us Knee-Dippers (dipping ever lower under Audrey's minus-sign leadership) had to diminish my third-term hopes.

Not only did the Charlottetown Accord debacle subtract from my re-election chances, the North American Free Trade Agreement (NAFTA) that added Mexico to the original, bilateral Canada–US Free Trade

Agreement (FTA), flagged another ominous omen—yes, for me, and for all Canuck workers. NAFTA's harm went further—and farther—than the FTA, for now, US companies didn't just relocate ("rationalize") production to their fifty states. Nope. Now, they outsourced manufacturing to dirt-poor-pay, ecologically toxic, Mexican maquiladoras. The FTA screwed Canadians, but NAFTA screwed everyone. Its deleterious impact catalyzed the US prez candidacy of the once-obscure Ross Perot. He emphasized its harm by saying (during the election campaign that put "polecat" Bill Clinton in the White House), "Y'all will hear a giant, sucking sound"—of US jobs getting hoovered up by Yank factories relocated to Mexico. Fat profits for the Fortune 500, tight belts for all else.

By spring 1993, then, Mulroney had plummeted precipitously in the polls. He resigned. Still, he'd been the first Tory PM (not counting "Unionist" Robert Borden) to engineer two back-to-back majorities since Sir John A. In the pursuant leadership race, the young, people's-choice candidate Jean Charest (Mulroney's protege) jousted with the flirtatious and enigmatic Kim Campbell. Campbell ascended on the toss-up third ballot to thus become Canada's first female prime minister. However, as with Audrey, her flash-bulb charisma soon blew out, that is, became smouldering ash. (My critique ain't sexism: a similar post-leadership-win vacuity afflicted both John Turner and Paul Martin. Like Audrey and Kim, they'd looked unbeatable as heirs-apparent, but once they assumed office and the ballroom balloons had deflated, flatulently, they were soon exposed—like the Wizard of Oz—as nude emperors.)

If the Tories, with Kim (not Jong-Il, not Kardashian) at the helm, seemed "ready-set-go" for the next election, we Knee-Dippers were not. Bob Rae's buckling economy was crippling us. Sadly, Rae came to power in Ontario after the Grits, now settling their rump's haunches onto Opposition seats, had racked up a $9 billion structural deficit. Rae got handed the keys to a ransacked house. Too, interest rates were menacingly guillotine-blade-high, the dollar overvalued, and three hundred thousand manufacturing jobs wiped out. Then, amid a sharp recession, Mulroney Scrooged on transfer payments. Next, in a tactic echoing CIA disinformation campaigns, "*Das Kapitalists*" ran a corrosive, insidious propaganda campaign, blaming democratic socialists for the industrial ruin that the branch-plant plug-pullers had wreaked upon Ontario.

Still, Rae accomplished much that should have pleased Labour. He'd passed anti-scab legislation and strengthened unions' hands in gaining certification. He saved Algoma Steel, saved Kapuskasing paper mill jobs, saved airplane manufacture at De Havilland. Confronted with mounting job losses, Rae cut taxes on low-income earners and introduced the

Ontario Jobs Program, creating fifty thousand posts. Poor Ontarians saw hiked expenditures on child care, plus—thanks to the Trillium Plan— lower taxes and lower prescription drug costs. Toronto got the new Sheppard-Yonge subway line; Windsor (which received unprecedented attention) got the new tax-and-income-generating casino and a new courthouse; the GTA got a turnpike—Highway 407—to help relieve congestion on the regular 400-series highways in the region. More Bill Davis than Vladimir Lenin in modernizing Ontario, Rae still got demonized as if he were Vlad the Impaler.

Yet, Labour could not approve all that Rae did. To open up Sunday shopping dismayed those who valued a "day of rest"; not to proceed with public auto insurance had to disappoint drivers. Too, numerous Labourites cursed Rae's actions to uplift minorities. Thus, an Employment Equity Bill raised hackles—with racist overtones—from unionists (see the Oshawa CAW) who railed against "quotas," which had not been proposed! So, ignoring my warnings, the Minority Caucus agitated for changes to the employment equity legislation that delayed its passage. The result was a bill too extreme to defend—and thus an easy target to maul in the 1995 provincial election campaign that turned shamefully upon the scapegoating of minorities and immigrants of colour.

The good relations achieved between the Rae NDP and Black Toronto were soured by the Carlton A. Masters (CAM) controversy. Ontario's trade rep in NYC, CAM had been accused of sexual harassment, then, denied a fair hearing, dismissed. Many Blacks felt he'd been railroaded; so, in protest, Hon. Zanana Akande resigned her seat and quit the Negro Disappointment Party. The matter was besmirching. Rae's outside investigator concluded that CAM had sexually harassed *seven* women. Rae then reassigned CAM to a new position, from which CAM resigned. Soon, CAM litigated his removal as Ontario's Agent-General in Manhattan, citing a lack of due process. No help. Because he served at the pleasure of the premier, CAM could be removed whenever Rae decided, and notions of "due process" did not apply. Case dismissed.

Never mind the typical ups and downs of polls and the ins and outs of policy implementation that test a government, it was Rae's breaking of contracts with government workers and reduction in their pay (via assigned, *unpaid* days of leave)—to try to reduce Ontario's $12 billion deficit—that ensured his government's defeat in 1995 and the federal NDP's loss of official party status in the House of Commons in 1993.

Rae strove to negotiate a "Social Contract," that is, to ask public service unions to co-operate in achieving savings of some $2 billion in labour costs. But the unions said *never*. They saw the Social Contract as nixing collective bargaining. Canadian Labour Congress (CLC) chief Bob White didn't even deem the deficit a problem. He mused that Ontario could just go bankrupt!

Sensing no compromise, Rae legislated the Social Contract. It imposed what would be called "Rae Days" that required public servants making over $30,000 per annum to take twelve unpaid leave days per year. It dinged higher-paid workers (teachers and other professionals), while sparing the last hired and the least paid, mainly women and minorities. It would stanch the province's red ink but stain the Ontario NDP (ONDP) as anti-Labour. Soon, in union halls everywhere, Rae was damned for his assault on collective bargaining and his abandonment of socialist principles. Yet, all he'd done was ask the well-compensated employees to sacrifice a little so that all Ontarians would not see government cuts to social services. To me, it was the unions who abandoned socialism, not Rae, who had to govern for the welfare of all Ontarians.

After an anti-Rae rally in Windsor (to which I was not invited), Langdon came to the federal NDP caucus meeting to table a letter condemning Rae. Many of us shared his concern but wouldn't attack a leftist premier trying to set right provincial coffers. Too, we interpreted Langdon's letter as a push to undermine Audrey (see Ian McLeod, *Under Siege*, p. 64). Instantly, she sacked him as the party's finance critic. (Did he not think twice before siding so grotesquely with the Bay Street boys' billboards and bullhorns?)

The Social Contract controversy exposed a dilemma too-long ignored: How can a social democratic party, including Labour as a signal ally, reconcile its role as a government, acting in all the public interest, and still satisfy Labour? The question is vexing in the absence of the discipline of the market—as Steelworkers, for example, knew; and the CLC should have pondered it before recklessly opining that *provincial* bankruptcy would be a painless matter for *public service* workers!

So, it was a mortally wounded federal NDP that contested the federal election of October 1993. Our leader was dull; the ONDP was despised. PM Campbell's campaign faux pas (including mocking the mug of Chrétien) assured the obliteration of the Tory vote. With few Knee-Dippers to gird me and no Tory candidate attractive to Windsor Grits, I was done. Like dinner. I was toast. Tossed.

I'd tried to stave off defeat by developing—alongside Langdon, Bob Mackenzie of the Steelworkers, and party researchers—a platform emphasizing job creation. Our Jobs Plan was rated as fiscally responsible and innovative. In party meetings across Canada, members were gung-ho for a document that asked little sacrifice to achieve long-term economic growth.

Alas! The doc was shelved; party boss Audrey shelved it—until it was copied in the Liberal "Red Book" campaign booklet. Jean Chrétien, the *always* savvy *"Tit gar de Shawinigan,"* was in sync with the zeitgeist when he declared (echoing Mulroney in 1984) at the debut presser of his campaign that his Grits would deliver, "Jobs! Jobs! Jobs!"

Windsor's Labour Day in 1993 was not the love-in with Labour that previous Labour Days had been, eh? No, it was just hostile territory. Handshakes but no backslaps, smiles but no bonhomie. The lugs scrutinizing me? Thuggish Alley Oop knock-offs.

Bob Rae came to town; I accompanied him on his stops at both the John Freeman Walls Historic Site and the Homecoming in North Buxton where we savoured hospitality. Black folks can always distinguish a helper from a hindrance, and they knew Rae was the former. For his part, he was self-effacing, kindly, and even apologized for the difficult electoral circumstances for me that his government's attempt to ameliorate economic hardship had fostered. Then, *Docteur* Professor Langdon *th'*economist— who'd writ that shamelessly opportunistic press release lambasting Rae— showed up. (He'd've been better off as a no-show.)

We were—ironically—in a big tent when a reporter requested an interview. Made sense: I was Black, at a Black historical site, a place close to my escaped-slave genealogy, dear to my Black-egalitarian heart. Hovering nearby, ever-over-eager for a photo-op, Langdon interrupted, diverting *cultural-historical* questions meant for *me* to *himself*. Furious, I told him that his gambit was an affront. Huffing, his hand shoved my shoulder. My dander? Up! I thrust that *mater-fouteur* up against a tent pole. I swore that if he ever lay a finger on me again, that digit would be busted, then his hand, then his arm.... And I could even have proceeded to his neck. No bluff!

Thanks to third-party sources, reporters knew about the bad blood twixt Langdon *et moi*—though we'd never yielded substantiation via public statements. *Au contraire*, even when we were leadership race opponents and he bested me, I gave him my delegate support, and he later nominated me to be the caucus chair. Still, I judged him persnickety. Were we rivals? I won't say so. But I did see him as an ivory tower carpetbagger, descending from Ottawa, a *pretender* (in my view) to the regard of the good folks of Essex County. Though some local yokels were anti-Black racists, I still felt I had more right to represent their interests in Ottawa than he; for I was of their corn fields, their harbours, their small towns, their pubs, their chapels, churches, and colleges. That's why I got along with Eugene Whelan and Herb Gray. We were of "the 'hood," and Langdon wasn't; and I begrudged his assumption—presumption—of belonging. Because he didn't.

The episode prefacing our near-fisticuffs was typical. As mentioned before, we tri-party MPs had agreed to co-operate closely to advance the Windsor/Essex County agenda. Frequently then, Gray, Langdon, and I would hold joint scrums. Well, Langdon would so monopolize the microphones—I felt—that I or Gray could hardly speak. When I objected to this vanity, his rebuff was that I was jealous of his superior ability to get press. Did he ever wonder that his *whiteness* might also play a role? Worse? Dude was "ig'orant" about the high profile that I had gained due to my Canuck civil rights struggle—*and* of that gained as a far-sighted Windsor councillor, *and* in other roles, including having been responsible for dubbing the CCF-ers "New Democrats." To me, scrambling for personal press flouted the idea of co-operation. (What are we, media sluts?) I warned: if getting press is the measure of super acumen, well then, watch me! Thus, I ensured that I was in the *Windsor Star* almost daily for the next two weeks—often concerning matters that I thought too trivial for the coverage they garnered.

During our second term, I began to suspect that Langdon or his office was the anonymous source for a scurrilous *Star* columnist, who loved to knock down "Cookie"—Dave Cooke, Rae's "Minister of Everything." The matter became so egregious that Robin Sears, Rae's Principal Secretary, summoned Langdon, Cookie, and me to a Queen's Park rendezvous to read the riot act to Langdon in our presence. "Bwoy" was ordered to cease and desist praxis akin to sabotage.

With the dropping of the writ for the federal election, our prospects were so poor that I considered resigning my seat. That the poll was held on October 25 was a mistake. Should've been on Halloween (although a Sunday). What went right? Only the Liberals. (I gotta pun!)

Ontario Fed of Labour prez Wayne Samuelson replaced Ron Varley as my campaign manager. Put simply: he was no Ron "Rainmaker" Varley. I felt I was running on a treadmill rather than for re-election. And the incline was steeply uphill.

All of my work on behalf of unions who'd convinced me to run in 1984 was now all for naught. My CAW campaign workers lacked heart; my campaign dollars could only buy sourdough (emphasis on *sour*) doughnuts. Subliminal racism among some CAW leaders became explicit: one even had the unmitigated gall to tell me that I no longer had his permit "for chasing white 'tail' in Ottawa"!

The electorate vented much unfair enmity toward me and the federal NDP. Blatant also was anti-minority and anti-immigrant hostility (that would soon blight the 1995 Ontario election). One voter told me proudly that she was going to vote for McCurdy. Yet, when I showed her a pamphlet with my photo, she asked, "Is that him?" *Yes.* She eyed me coldly: "Oh! I could never vote for a Coloured man!" On another stoop, a teacher denounced the Social Contract. When I stated that if the Ontario deficit were not addressed, schools might close and students be harmed, she barked, "I don't give a shit about students!"

In many instances, voters expressed no antipathy for me but were eager to punish Rae. One gent said, "Howard, you have been a great MP, but right now I can't stomach your party." Multiply that response several thousand times: my campaign had nowhere to go but belly up.

I lost—badly—as did Langdon (despite his union troupe). He fell to Susan Whelan; I to Shaughnessy Cohen: the ladies ascendant as heirs apparent. Federally, the party went from forty-four seats to nine. We went from a national vote percentage of 20 percent (in 1988) to 7 percent. Only the Tories fared worse: they were virtually annihilated in a campaign where its defeated leader squandered her initial stardom via a series of heartless remarks that told jobless Canadians they were hopeless.

As soon as my defeat was absolute, I went solo to the Liberal campaign party at the Caboto Club and gave a speech of concession and congratulations to the party and its candidate. It was an act of bravado, for I promised to return with a vengeance if their new member faltered. She did not.

Instead, Shaughnessy would die suddenly in her second term and be replaced by Joe Comartin. Joe had been the losing candidate in the previous election. His selection as the bearer of the NDP flag in the constituency I had carried for the NDP for the first time was conducted without any attempt even to ask me along to the nomination meeting! In posts of his bio, Comartin claimed credit—as merely my finance committee chair—for my parliamentary wins! Well, post–Bay of Pigs, JFK said it best: "Victory has a thousand fathers, but defeat is an orphan."

The day after my loss, I played golf—alone. This time, Frank, the course owner, did not refuse my green fee. No longer a parliamentarian, I was simply plebeian. Full stop.

CHAPTER TWENTY-ONE:
ELDER STATESMAN? OR JUST ELDER?

WAS MY DEFEAT A PERSONAL REBUKE? I HAD NOT DONE LESS than my best, and few would question my effectiveness as an MP. That fact was reinforced when a *LaSalle Post*-contracted panel of regional politicos and news columnists rated local MPs of the previous fifty years. I placed fourth—behind Herb Gray, Gene Whalen, and David Croll, all of whom had been Grit cabinet ministers. Though I had always been in Opposition, I still scored high marks for my service. Now that I was "a free man in Paris"—and London and Windsor, Ontario (to amend Joni Mitchell's lyric)—I was finding favour, even with former foes.

Led by Ian McMahon, Kim Hennin, and Joe Quinlan, the NDP Riding Association sponsored a testimonial dinner a few months after my defeat. There was a heartwarming video-profile of me, with witty teasing from my family and friends. Bob Rae, Ken Lewenza, and Bill

Tepperman were the star speakers. In the circumstances, there was much irony in having Rae (wounded by the unions) and Lewenza (union boss) sharing the dais.

Similarly, Clarkie, now "Doc GEC," arranged a House of Commons celebration for me in summer 1994, attended by chief parliamentary reporter Mike Duffy, as well as several senators and sitting members of the House and folks from the Ottawa Black community: all were eager to let me know how well I was appreciated. Another lighthearted event, it was also very heartfelt. While I took solace in positive post-mortems of my parliamentary career, I raged inwardly at the unfairness of having been punished for the actions of a provincial government in which I'd had no part and those of a fed NDP leader who flip-flopped between being inept and being incompetent.

One silver lining: more time for myself and my family. I was confident of an eventual return to politics. Perhaps I could imitate Tricky Dick's "rehab" and author a book? (That approach had worked well for Robert Bourassa, P. E. Trudeau, Jean Chrétien: all had recovered reps and new fans by penning policy ideas or tell-all memoirs.) I relished the instant karma (sorry, John Lennon) of being able to lounge on the sofa or even laze in bed. No more 5:00 A.M. coffees and the adrenalin-producing rush of sussing out scandal!

But who was I kidding? My defeat nagged at my ego. Was my loss due to some fault in me? Or was I the kind of hero that George Grant, quoting Milton's adjectives, "Unshaken, unseduced, unterrified," saw in vilified Dief? Or was I Ralph Ellison's *Invisible Man* redux, a Black man suddenly defamed and hunted and hiding? Flummoxed, I began to feel I'd been betrayed by many a leftist Brutus and many a racist Judas; nor did the University of Windsor offer me a post or sinecure. Depression began to gnaw or chomp at every organ.

Truth is, I'd loved being a Member of Parliament! It was employ wherein my upstart ego was checked by being kept under constant pressure—to do the right thing, for the public good, but also for my own sense of well-being. Yes, it was hurtful, painful, awful to descend from alternate adulation and, yes, severe criticism to being unimportant and irrelevant. I no longer had a race to run, a high bar to clear; the halo was off my head, even if the bull's eye was now off my chest.

Still, I was fortunate to have income from my parliamentary pension, Canada Pension Plan, and moneys from my university pension, for nevermore would I be gainfully employed. That fact arrived as a shock. I turned sixty-one within seven weeks of my loss and identified myself suddenly as a tossed-out senior, "ex" this and "former" that:

an unremembered (dismembered) parliamentarian and a forgotten (misbegotten) microbiologist. Lookit! Despite plural promises of ONDP appointments, nothing significant ever materialized for me; however, many others, whom I believed had contributed less, got favoured with oodles of boodle, with unlimited laurels and largesse.

The single appointment I did receive would prove as contentious as it was brief. The Canadian Blood Agency (CBA) asked for tenders for a blood fractionation plant. Among the responses, only the Canadian Red Cross (CRC) vaunted partnership with a US company, Miles Laboratories (makers of Alka-Seltzer), that warranted further exploration.

Now Canada's health ministers formed an experts' panel to assess the risks and benefits of the CRC plant—plus the aptness of its planned Halifax, NS, locale. In spring 1994, Bob Rae bade me join an advisory panel whose members counted Dr. Christopher G. Knowles representing business; Dr. John Langstaff, a fractionation expert; and Iain Stewart, a technocrat. I was elected chair. Our two medical advisors? Dr. Georges-Étienne Rivard and Dr. Ken Shumak.

Our deliberations occurred alongside those of the Krever Inquiry (on the Blood System in Canada), which was pondering the culpability of the CRC in disseminating diseased blood to Canuck patients. Hell! Blood contaminated with Hepatitis C and/or HIV got transfused into—poisoned—thousands. Hemophiliacs knew the most drastic harm: 94 percent of those who received tainted blood became infected with hepatitis.

Our panel heard submissions from the CRC, the CBA, the Canadian Hemophilia Society (CHS), Miles Labs, and our medical advisors. Tensions were hypertension (ahem). The CRC reps, pompous, stonewalled, and the CBA and CHS put defiance ahead of science. Yet, we okayed the plant's being erected subject to conditions—including reconsidering its location, its financing, board membership, and operational control. We judged the CRC persona non grata.

Our panel report had narrow parameters. The fractionation plant: Yes or no? Plant it in Halifax or not? The desecrated blood horror was not our focus. Even so, my University of Windsor ex-colleague, Durhane Wong-Reiger, now CHS prez, lambasted us for "ignoring" the tainted blood scandal! Her plaints were, to my ears, just grandstanding, for she must have known that the Krever Inquiry's report would address CHS concerns. (Were her motives partisan? She was a losing Tory candidate in the Ontario election of 1999....)

Inevitably, the Krever Report damned the CRC for letting virus-plagued blood seep into transfusions. So, the Canadian Blood Service replaced the CRC, which was also penalized by fines and the criminal indictment of some of its officers. That was positive, but the value of Canada having its own fractionation plant evaporated in the searing negativity over the CRC.

I pivot now from blood to "race." Just as my science background was voided in the emotive fractionation plant debate, so now did I find that my decades of civil rights and human rights agitation were meaningless to the Negro Disappointment Party. Let me explain.

The NDP's Participation of Visible Minorities Committee (chaired by Margaret Mitchell *et moi*) had demanded a program of affirmative action to ensure BIPOC representation, top to bottom. So, one fed NDP veep had to be a BIPOC soul. I'd been elected a veep in 1992. But I was a member of the national exec during an excruciating period. Not only had our Commons caucus been axed to a rump of nine in 1993 (so we'd lost official party status), we were broke. We owed $6 million to our financiers. Focus had to be on moving from red ink to black; and so, the already postponed biennial convention scheduled for 1994 was delayed again, our federal office building sold off at a huge loss, and many staff pink-slipped. Our budget woes reflected the stunning downfall of a party that short years before had looked sure to become the Official Opposition.

What happened—and *why*? Well, the subtle role of "race" was again overlooked.

Yes, the electorate's determination to terminate the Tories triggered our *dégringolade*. Nor had we forwarded a credible alternative. Our campaign? A fount of airy nothings emanating from a flat-lining leader. Yes, Rae's downward spiral depressed us too; yes, the CAW and public sector unions declared war on every fed NDP Ontario seat. Outrage over the Meech Lake and Charlottetown deals, plus Mulroney–Thatcher–Reagan neo-liberalism, plus the Goods and Services Tax and the persistence of high unemployment and low growth could not benefit us politically, for we would not profit from disaffection by blaming the marginalized for the economic malaise.

Now, "race" becomes a factor: Preston Manning's Reform Party accrued much of the populist support once garnered by Knee-Dippers, for he catered to those inclined to blame their plights on immigrants, Indigenous Peoples, and the indigent. Seriously, Reform was Social Credit (the folks who invented forced sterilization) reborn. This unholy demonization of the poor and the powerless inspired the Mike Harris Ontario Tories to follow suit—in their electorally profitable "Common Sense Revolution"—in 1995. Coded appeals to white supremacy had to be countered by the NDP if we were to attract BIPOC Canadians. That was job one. Could we do it?

Too, our bond with Labour, on life-support, needed critical care. We socialists had failed to mount a scorched-earth campaign against the beggar-thy-neighbour trade deals, ceding our turf to the Big Biz Grits, who, come elections, love to top their pinstripes with hardhats. The Dick-Tracy-faced Bob White was so disaffected with us that, under his leadership, the CLC began to stress alliances with social action (civil society) groups rather than with Knee-Dippers.

Indeed, in spring 1993, White hosted a mass rally on Parliament Hill at which lobby groups such as the National Action Committee on the Status of Women (NAC), the Action Canada Network, the Native Council, and various unions and their leaders spoke. Fifty thousand souls attended, along with Audrey and our caucus. But because the event was declared "non-partisan," we stood muted, while our "allies" kneecapped us Knee-Dippers but played footsie with the Grits. *Incroyable!* A leftist gabfest at which no elected leftist was permitted a say. And yet all our seats were on the line!

Our renewal process had to scrutinize the party's relationship with Labour. *Certainement!* Labour determined our governance and contributed mucho moolah and many campaign workers; yet, less than 20 percent of eligible locals were affiliates. So, we were an empty threat to *Kapital*—like a troopless Trojan horse. We were a "Labour" party, eh? Yes, but we had zero clout with most unionized plebes. Damn! No wonder so many of them could vote—in a nanosecond—backward Tory or reactionary Reform! They saw us as just another class of politicos, not as militant advocates for their interests. Conversely, a handful of union bosses could virtually guarantee our defeat if the public good was seen to contravene the private interests of their fiefdoms. We needed to decide: Are we "radical" socialists, "electable" social democrats, or just bleeding-heart liberals? Maybe radicals belong on barricades and democrats in legislatures?

Our relationships with other "allies" were just as frustrating. We saw ourselves as assembling a "big tent" array of socio-political and special interest groups, each of whom expected strict adherence to their separate agendas. We'd gone broke by trying to be a brokerage party!

NAC was Exhibit A. Annually, our caucus dipped knees in homage to the NAC's politically puritanical, roundhead reps. O! How they loved to give us marching orders! Vassals we were to them but "nonpartisan" were they.

Bully for the NAC that it scolded we Knee-Dippers into electing odd-duck Audrey as a swan-song chief! But shame on the NAC for blaming Audrey's defeat in 1993 on her alleged failure to make women's priorities our campaign focus. The feminist "fatales" didn't "get" that Canucks yearned to kayo Mulroney but had to settle for kicking pant-suited Kimberly Campbell instead, for "The Chin" was already long gone supposedly with the metaphorical silverware.

The NAC was also offside in the constitution debate; they opposed the NDP's "YES" on the Charlottetown Accord referendum because the deal did not institute equal representation of women (and proportional representation of minorities) in the Senate. But, geez, Judy Rebick, NAC's prez, a Knee-Dipper herself, sat in on our discussions. So, she'd side with us one day and deride us the next. (To me, Caesar's last gasp— "Et tu, Brutus?"—is apt.)

Hard it was to find "J. R."—"Junior"—honourable. She claimed to back BIPOC. Yet, after first backing our opposition to the notwithstanding clause, she then backtracked on the basis (as she told me) that a new equality clause would accord us "special status." Huh? Constitutionally guaranteed gender equality was right and proper but not racial equality? Huh?

The *beau risque* presented by NDP alliances with NAC and Labour was multiplied many times over, in other "theatres," due to the many other special interest groups (some in conflict with one another) with which we identified. We fawned over students but also teachers. We loved loggers but also tree-huggers—or did we? We said we were anti-poverty, but would we build public housing over realtors' objections? We were for international aid, but what about the Third World conditions on Indigenous reserves? Our interest was pleasing every interest group possible, so our policies were Newspeak to some and "Greek" to others.

Too, the party now eschewed policies of public ownership; we prayed, instead, that steadily increasing wages—and the generous provision of social programs made possible by a prosperous economy—would serve to ameliorate boom-and-bust cycles as well as occasional inflationary shocks to people's purchase power. We'd failed to reckon that globalization of the economy (that is, the empowerment of corporations versus the commons), allowing capital to flow anywhere while Labour could only "pool," demanded imaginative policies to foster wealth, promote social justice, and *not* befoul the environment. (Keynesians! Where art thou when we needs ya? To *regulate* how and where *Kapital* flows and how and where *Labour* pools?)

In our renewal exercise, many argued that Knee-Dippers needed to be more democratic. If we could get back to our roots, just be down-to-earth, we'd avoid becoming business-class clones. Inspired was the rhetoric; intransigent was the status quo.

Only a few ideas were truly progressive. Hugh Mackenzie of the Steelworkers defined the role of a social democratic government in ways distinctly in concert with mine. Opting not to contradict the socialist thrust of the CAW in seeking new socio-economic alternatives, Jim Stanford was vague in asserting what they might be. Yet, both Mackenzie and Stanford rejected Bob White's notion that deficits don't count. (Hey, stupido! Deficits enrich the rich!)

In my view, social democrats must seek economic growth through empowering citizens in areas where private enterprise will not. Our governments must ensure equal opportunity and access of all citizens to income security, health insurance, housing, and training and education to post-secondary levels. We must also uphold basic research and construct the infrastructure necessary to sustain commerce, public health, and public safety. We must affirm wealth derived from furnishing finished goods and services that the world admires and desires, not just that got from chopping trees, pumping oil and gas, and strip-mining (and poisoning) the earth.

Internationally, Canuck democratic socialists should join with like parties in achieving a social charter among trading nations that protects social programs, workers, human rights, and the environment. Moreover, we require an international tax and regulatory regime to ensure that corporations do not escape their obligations to citizens (not only shareholders)—to protect the environment, ensure health and safety *for* their workers and *of* their products, and support the treasury (*not* undermine representative governments).

The fed NDP review, while constructive, exposed our paucity of intellectual depth. Rather than tussle for policy renewal, Audrey resigned, and we pursued the panacea of selecting a new *chef*. Thanks to a revised voting process (which employed regional primary polling to qualify candidates), Alexa McDonough upset—in fall 1995—both Lorne Nystrom and Svend Robinson.

In spring 1995, Ontario's provincial election was nigh, but the Windsor-Sandwich riding association lacked a credible candidate. Both NDP provincial secretary Jill Marzetti and Premier Rae asked me to run, which I was loath to do, for I yearned to return to The Big Zero. They promised to make the riding a priority in terms of ONDP resources. In spite of my qualms, I acceded to the pressure and met severally with Elmer Brian Kersey and Sungee John—prez and veep respectively of the Windsor-Sandwich association—who pledged a vigorous campaign. Yet, their association had a history of disorganization and ineptitude that had seen candidates lose despite strong NDP comrades in the constituency.

Nevertheless, Ian McMahon, Kim Hennin, and I commissioned a poll by the University of Windsor political science department. The results indicated that I could top any Liberal candidate by a lopsided margin. I thus allowed my name to stand for nomination. By that time, Arlene Rousseau had become a dark-horse entry into the race, and the deadline for signing new members had passed. An ex-Yank party militant, Rousseau was a friend whose activism I'd assisted and whom I'd helped out personally. Her children even called me "Uncle Howard." If she was a last-ditch candidate, she'd be a first-rate "also ran."

Once my candidacy became public, a delegation from the Windsor and District Labour Council pilgrimaged to my home. Obvious was their hostility as they queried me about my view of Rae's Social Contract (deficit-cutting) law. My reply? I'd seek the law's revocation and a return to collective bargaining (a position that I had led the fed NDP to adopt). However, I did scruple to advise my guests that the Social Contract was not only about "Rae Days," but an effort to protect from job loss the newest hires, chiefly visible minorities. It also freed up money to assist the greatening numbers of unemployed. I figured that for some well-compensated *public servants* to sacrifice a scintilla of income, so as to ensure the continued employment of the majority, was a sensible *temporary* measure, consonant with *socialist* democracy (Cuban in spirit, if antithetical to Milton Friedman's slash-and-burn economics). In effect, it was a form of socialized "strike pay"—an expression of solidarity vis-à-vis the crisis wreaked by globalizing capitalism.

Moreover, I averred that the Social Contract imbroglio was a result of Knee-Dippers and union militants having refused to contemplate the inevitable conflict between our alliance and the responsibilities of an NDP government to *all* citizens. This problem was poignant and cogent for civil-servant unions, for whom, unlike private-sector workers, the do-or-die discipline of "market forces" was never a sobering possibility. Insulated from balance-sheet realities, public-sector unions could afford to be blithe about their salaries and benefits.

Though I undertook to uphold Labour's position on the Social Contract and a return to collective bargaining, I could not spurn Rae. Despite a NAFTA-induced recession, Rae had kept workers working, had delivered Windsor a new courthouse and casino, had extended tenants' rights, and had promoted women and BIPOC citizens. I deplored criticism of that viable and most honourable cabinet minister, Dave Cooke, and I lauded our local NDP MPPs, namely George Dadamo and Wayne Lessard. My interlocutors thought my stance responsible and reasonable but refused to commit their votes to me. That spelled majuscule, major-league T-R-O-U-B-L-E!

Preparing for the nomination meeting, McMahon, Hennin, *et moi* contacted the entire Windsor-Sandwich riding membership to seek their votes—and to offer rides and any other assistance anyone might need to attend. Eighty members said I was their man, so we were confident of a win, even though we knew the CAW opposed my candidacy. Sensing an upset, practically as many reporters showed up for the nominating meeting as did Windsor-Sandwich voting members.

Now, I knew I wasn't going to be a Bill Clinton–style "Comeback Kid" but more like Billy the Kid facing Pat Garrett's smoking pistol! Even so, once the votes were tallied, Rousseau was markedly stunned by her unanticipated coronation. Just as stunning was the instant vanishing of the ONDP reps in attendance—without a word to *moi* whose candidacy they'd urged. The CAW denied involvement, but, according to Gary Parent's comments in the *Windsor Star*, the autoworkers had engineered my loss.

What goes around comes around, eh? "Gritty" Sandra Pupatello triumphed in Windsor-Sandwich, tapping 47 percent of the vote to Rousseau's 25 percent. But the veritable victors were the Tories, headed by the unapologetically regressive Conservative, Mike Harris. The true-blue "lefties" of the CAW and its civil-servant confreres could now gloat over having helped to elect the most extreme right-wing, anti-worker government in post–Second World War Ontario. How frothy but vapid their vengeance was: Harris quick took a buzz-saw to unions. Worse, he sicced the OPP on Indigenous protestors, resulting in activist Dudley George's death. BIPOC citizens were told again to sit at the back of the segregated bus.

Apart from my loss to Rousseau, my debut excursion into provincial politics exacted extra personal cost. A short-list applicant for the just-born James Robinson Johnston Chair in (Canadian) Black Studies at Dalhousie University, I flew to the campus for interviews and made a passionate presentation to people my ex-aide Clarkie (then a Duke University prof) dubs "Africadians." I underlined the similar experiences and histories of the Black communities of Southern Ontario and Nova Scotia. Plural ovations ensued. Since I'd been previously much engaged with the "Africadians" and my Uncle George had directed the Nova Scotia Human Rights Commission, I was *the* front-runner for the position in spite of my scientific background. (Most appointees have been lawyers or social scientists.) Then again, one of my former grad students, Tom McRae, was head of Dal Biology. One delightful aspect of my Halifax visit was to see Dorothy Wills for the first time in years, for she sat on the Johnston Chair selection committee. Regrettably, I had to withdraw my name—to stand for the Windsor-Sandwich Knee-Dipper nomination.

In 1996, Bob Rae, in the wake of his government's defeat, resigned both as Leader of the Opposition and as an MPP. In the subsequent campaign to replace him, the front-runners were Frances Lankin and Howard Hampton, both of whom wooed Windsorite Knee-Dippers. Advising both, I pressed the need for the party to emphasize economic policy, research and development, and education—early childhood education in particular. Hampton became leader, and soon Dave Cooke resigned. A by-election for the Windsor-Riverside riding was in order. Again, I was pushed to seek a provincial nomination—with the assurance of a cabinet position were I elected and the party to form government. Again, polling indicated that I was the front-runner for the Windsor-Riverside electorate. Defeated in his own riding in 1995, Wayne Lessard could run again. I tried to convince him to hail my candidacy. Nothin doin': Lessard also contested the nomination.

On Cookie's advice—and in spite of my aversion to seeming a union puppet—I agreed to mend fences with the CAW. So, Ian McMahon and I met with Ken Lewenza, who seemed too haughty to be anything other than hostile. True: some CAW honchos were heard making racially coded remarks. George Johnson, CAW retirees prez—and until then right amiable (being a frequent golf partner)—informed the *Windsor Star* that I was a candidate for provincial office only because I yearned to cram my wardrobe with more fancy suits!

The Windsor-Riverside nomination meeting, held at the Serbian Cultural Centre on a bright spring day, was a crusher. At first, I thought the mood festive; then I saw that the CAW had mobilized *again* a lynch-mob. My daughters heard, among the delegates, so many caustic comments about me, some racist and many just cavalierly evil, that they pressed me, in the wake of my loss, to quit the Knee-Dippers *now*. Once more, no leading NDP member offered a word of solace. I now understood that *I* was Windsor's NDP scapegoat for the CAW's ire over "Rae Days"; my being Black made my choice for inglorious victimization just that much more satisfying for my detractors. (I thought of Uncle George being driven from his Human Rights office for having tried to honour the historical bonds between Nova Scotia and Sierra Leone. I thought of Muhammad Ali vilified for refusing to help Uncle Sam kill Vietnamese, Du Bois self-exiled to Ghana, Paul Robeson blacklisted, Black Panthers railroaded to prison or shot dead in their beds.... Okay: I wasn't persecuted as they were, but almost no prominent Black man ever escapes—at the very least—character assassination.)

After that final electoral lynching-bee, I sped home to watch Tiger Woods win the Masters in a record performance. That is how I celebrated the last day that I would ever consider myself a member of the party I helped to name.

Weirdly, it was after I had become a Liberal that I was named the 2001 recipient of the ironically named J. S. Woodsworth Award, for contributions to the elimination of racial discrimination. Given Woodsworth's racist attitudes, it was an award for which he himself would have been ineligible! (Although I quit the Knee-Dippers, I lent Bill Blaikie the last iota of my socialist optimism in striving to see him elected fed NDP leader in 2003. Had this admirable, ex-caucus colleague succeeded, I may have renewed my party membership.)

Beginning in 1995, I became a political pundit on radio and television. For that year's Ontario election, CBC-TV had me on board alongside ex-premier David Peterson, and the very likeable ex–Mulroney cabinet minister Barbara McDougall. (Babs and I even counted a common friend in Bajan-Canuck author Austin Chesterfield Clarke.) Peterson proved irritatingly glib, as if *suave* could denote *savvy*. Casually uncouth, he made an edgy remark—borderline racial—about the shirt I wore. In that broadcast (as in a letter featured in the *Toronto Star*), I chastised both Ontario's Tories and Grits for scapegoating immigrants and minorities. My co-panelists resented my public rebuke of the subtle racism being espoused by their provincial parties. But *tant pis*, eh?

For two years, I was a panelist on *The Editors*, a PBS show, for which I jetted to Montreal for the tapings. Therein, I interacted with several household-name politicos and commentators, including Babs McDougall; future Canuck PM Stephen Harper; P. E. Trudeau-era cabinet minister Francis Fox; ex-Democratic would-be prez nominee Howard Dean; Af-Am journalist Tavis Smiley; Canadian journalist Chantal Hébert; Betty Franklin, another Af-Am and a senior editor of *Forbes* magazine; and Mairuth Hodge Sarsfield, Montreal-born author of *No Crystal Stairs*.

Nice as *The Editors* gig was, it had a nasty end. Among the PBS staff was a striking, amiable young woman who loved parrying puns. Our interaction was purely cordial, but a producer was bothered by it for reasons that I can only infer. Soon, my Air Canada tickets to Montreal were deemed more expensive than tickets from Washington and New York! My show appearances? Disappeared!

May I forget *ever* that a Black man of any age or accomplishment is a suspect? God help me if ever I do! Though I was retired from politics and microbiological research and was busy with golfing, boating, and the pleasures of family (most of whom, including my sister, now lived nearby in LaSalle), I could not retire from being Black! Indeed, an incident that occurred while I was shopping for a new boat prompted me to resume anti-racist activism.

I was on County Road 42, wheeling toward Puce when I eyed an Ontario Provincial Police (OPP) car trailing—or tailing. The speed limit was 80 km/hr, and I toed that line. Still, I slowed so that the cruiser could pass. It did not. Turning mistakenly down a dead-end road, I had to turn back. Reaching Highway 42 again, I saw that the OPP auto was parked opposite to me at the intersection. In wait! On finding the road, I made the right turn, and the OPP vehicle pursued, roof lights now ablaze. I pulled over. An officer demanded to inspect my licence, insurance, and registration. I asked him if I had violated any driving laws, but he couldn't name one. I refused, then, to comply until he named my infraction. Now, I was threatened with arrest. Still, I refused to yield any of my dox until he explained what law (or laws) I'd transgressed against. His silence said all: I was "driving while Black"! Thankfully, a car pulled up beside us, and the driver cheerfully asked why in the world the copper had stopped "Howard McCurdy? He's a pretty important guy." This spontaneous citizen interjection gave the officer pause. He sensed a potential imbroglio. With a substantially altered demeanour, he virtually pleaded with me now to give him some sort of ID. I was still not about to concede to being racially profiled. Instead of my licence, then, I showed him my credit card in the name of "Dr. Howard D. McCurdy." Sufficient? Aye, and away I sped—as fast as limit permitted. But I knew I was not the only prey of this "police procedure"!

Thus, when racial profiling spurred an urgent call from my cousin Raymond McCurdy in February 2001, once he was free of cop custody, I had to ask, "¿Qué pasó?"

The previous eve, he and two Caucasian pals, Kevin and Chris, were cutting through a downtown Windsor parking lot when two paleface flat-feet accosted the trio. Suddenly, one pushed Kevin up against a shop window, after which they released him and told him and Chris to keep walking. Next, they threw Raymond face down to the ground to cuff and pummel him, while screeching, "Stop resisting!" Kevin and Chris swore that Raymond was passive. Clearly, the "stop resisting" line is a Stasi ruse to con any witnesses into thinking that the percussive abuse was justified.

After allegedly being pepper-sprayed, Raymond, gasping, got shoved into a paddy wagon. He was jailed until ten thirty the next morn and was never permitted a phone call. Though he was accorded no test for intoxication, Raymond was charged with being drunk in a public place. (This is all a play-by-play forecast of my abuse by Canuck border cops recounted later in this chapter.)

With my aid, Raymond brought charges against the officers involved and sought to launch a civil suit. Before any of these actions were resolved, Raymond was once again tormented by Windsor's "finest" in May 2001. This time, Raymond had gone downtown at 3:00 A.M. to pick up his gal pal from her job. Again, his buddy Chris was in tow. This time, after buying a takeout soda pop and a donair, Raymond was confronted, he said, by a goon who cuffed him while announcing he was under arrest for being drunk in a public place. Down to the ground went his soda and sandwich; onto the hood of a prowl car went he. Other gendarmes piled on. One pulled Raymond's pants down to his ankles, Raymond reported, and forced him to stand, thus exposed, on the street for several minutes. Again, Chris witnessed all. Once more, Raymond was held overnight— and, again, no attempt was made to test for intoxication.

I believe Raymond's extra-legal persecution was attributable to his having earlier testified in a trial against cops facing assault charges. His own complaint had triggered a police misconduct hearing that, presided over by the constabulary, led to a predictable outcome: the judge ruled that, though the evidence demonstrated that officers had manhandled Raymond, it was not possible to identify who was criminally responsible; thus, no one was.

These incidents led me to wonder whether the Windsor and District Black Coalition (WDBC) had interrogated righteously the crisis of racial profiling. My son, Brian, had been stopped too often for no true cause— as had my daughter Linda. Both attested to this hounding and harrying, this dishonouring and harassing, as being a common experience among their Black friends.

Prez of the WDBC as well as the Windsor Urban Alliance (WUA), Clayton Talbert had done a fine job of keeping both organizations alive— pretty much on his own. I treated with Clayton at his WUA office. He acknowledged that racial profiling was a plague. He'd contacted the Windsor police admin about the problem, but their response was cordial bumf. We decided to hold a community forum on all justice system injustices.

Clayton convened the meeting in April 2001; about fifty Black Windsorites showed up. The session opened with the showing of a CHWI (Windsor) TV news clip that erroneously portrayed a downtown distur-bance as having been caused by Black hooligans when, in fact, even Windsor Police Chief Glenn Stannard agreed that Entertainment District drunk and disorderly behaviour was primarily the fault of fair-skinned US van-dals. Stannard even signed on to the letter of protest that the WUA sent to the local CTV (more-or-less) affiliate. We asserted that racial profiling is just age-old stereotypes recycled as fearsome thrills for Caucasian auditors. To be intimidated, threatened, humiliated, beaten, arrested, charged, jailed—and/or assaulted or murdered—by police was the consequence of their acceptance and actualizing of Negrophobic propaganda.

Our attendees also complained that the *Windsor Star* had begun to feature two neo-con, "Negroid" columnists, one of whom had upheld slavery (I guess, as either a means to convert "heathens" or as a solution for Black joblessness). I was delegated by the group to question *Star* editors regarding the broadsheet's intemperate insensitivity to Afro-Can citizens. Lunching with *Star* editorial-page editor John Coleman and an associate, I ascertained that the *Star*, now owned by the illiberal Canwest Global Communications Corporation, had had imposed upon it the—I'll say, "blackface"—columnists spewing sickeningly reactionary positions. Thus, Coleman said he'd welcome op-eds from me and other Black Windsorites. But I was skeptical about his invite, for he'd already spiked my piece criticizing the white folks' brown-nosing columnists.

Yet, newsprint reiterations of Negrophobic natter are trivial compared to the life-and-death crimes perpetrated by cops and courts. Where to start? Police targeting of Blacks in multiracial disturbances; racial profiling; excessive use of force; harassment; trumped-up charges; a litany of unconstitutional abuses. When Black citizens become victimized suspects and defendants, they are frequently further victimized in a court system dismissive of well-documented racist attitudes in law enforcement and judicial decisions. Black youth are routinely failed by their attorneys, resulting in convictions that, in turn, serve to increase mean-minded, Gestapo-level persecution.

To take action against this thin-blue-line threat to Black lives, limbs, livelihoods, and property, the WUA membership agreed unanimously to revitalize the Windsor and District Black Coalition. United, we'd have strength?

I volunteered to investigate each allegation of police abuse, including taking affidavits from plaintiffs and witnesses. Further, as a WDBC member, I'd assist in registering complaints with the Windsor Police Department's Professional Standards Branch and/or in facilitating charges being laid against suspect officers where circumstances warranted. I also proposed instituting a 24/7 "hotline" telephone number—to be printed on cards distributed through schools, churches, and community organizations. Another idea was to coordinate a system of volunteer "court watchers" to document the treatment of Black defendants. Showing unprecedented solidarity, the Windsor Black Ministerial Alliance donated significant funds, as did Bishop Clarence L. Morton of the Mt. Zion Full Gospel Church. *Progress!*

Thus, the reactivated WDBC developed further responses to injustice and inequality—but not without the usual conflicts that plague grassroots organizations. Meetings were often derailed because of the refusal of some to respect rules of order; or malcontents would raise extraneous matters or launch ad hominem attacks. Frustration! Paralysis! Inaction! (But I knew that so many of us felt so silenced and/or unheard that activist gatherings became venues for "venting" or avenues for encounter-group sessions to redress many experiences of racist hostility, rather than strictly opportunities for weighing measures of concerted action.)

By early 2002, Clayton resigned as chair of the WDBC; a new executive was elected. I became prez; (Ethel) Andrea Moore my veep; Irene Moore, the secretary; and Eleanor Green, treasurer. Rodney Davis chaired the Employment Committee.

Now, I insisted on respecting rules of order, which aroused gripes, emanating most stridently—in my opinion—from Yvette Blackburn and Kim Elliott. Both Kim and Yvette seemed chummy with an outfit dubbed the Canadian Centre on Minority Affairs (CCMA), founded in 1998 and headed by Ian Francis, whom I knew (unhappily) from NBCC days. Kenny Gbadebo of Youth Connection (YC), plus Sungee John and (Elmer) Brian Kersey were also affiliates. Beyond its stated interest in building (visible) minority group leadership skills, it seemed inaudible and so low-profile as to be invisible.

In spite of the WDBC's refusal to bond with the CCMA (a reluctance for which I was blamed), we did extend them "associate membership." However, their dues went unpaid and no delegate ever again monitored a meeting. Nor did the CCMA engage in any action to address the issues that seized the WDBC. Nor were they ever any help to us. Indeed, the "court watch" program never attracted sufficient volunteer observers. The hotline became too expensive for us to operate and was transferred to Kenny Gbadebo's YC. The CCMA was MIA—or SOL. (It appears that the CCMA received a total of $455,055 in federal funds between 1998 and 2001 but went "inactive" sometime after it was officially registered as a lobby group in 1999. See lobbycanada.gc.ca/app/secure/ocl/lrs/do/vwRg?regId=493369&cno=12436.)

We, the WDBC, soldiered on, for most critiques of paleface boys in blue reached us by word of mouth. I handled most of these, and I sat in on trials that were torture because most defendants were poor and many were BIPOC. That their lawyers pled by rote and seldom questioned copper testimony made convictions as routine as hellfire sermons chased by collection plates. (One signal injustice? A Black defendant with an intellectual disability testified that a jackboot brute held him to the ground and, while punching him, pressed down on his chest with an instrument that had a definite pattern at its end. In spite of a well-defined chest bruise reflecting said pattern, the judge scoffed at the victim's word and his scar. Attorney objections? Nil!)

In addition to pursuing charges of justice-system injustice, the WDBC decided to survey Black youth for data on their law-enforcement contacts. The results? Jaw-dropping and eye-opening. A whopping 90 percent of Black males had been stopped at least once (and most more than once) by cops. Most stops fixated on Black motorists, but Black pedestrians could also attract unwarranted suspicion. About half said officers were "impolite," and another half said they were verbally or physically abusive (although racist epithets were seldom used—unless "you people" is considered such). Black females were less likely to be stopped, but when they were, their experiences were similar. Over a two-year period, we logged twenty-four 'plaints involving racial profiling, many of which were processed through the Windsor PD's Professional Standards Branch. Disciplinary actions? Zero.

One egregious incident entangled an immigrant East African family. Three teen girls scuffled with some Caucasian girls; then the father of two white girls assaulted two Black sisters. A weapons-wielding, "N-word"-shouting mob then converged on the African girls' home to threaten their mother. Once cops arrived, the two African sisters—one just thirteen—were handcuffed, solely due to the claims of pink-toned witnesses! In court, the Black girls' testimony was belittled, perhaps because they also alleged that the arresting cops wielded racist terms. Yet, the Black girls had never known trouble with the law or at school, whereas the cracker assailants were "known to the police." (In fact, the paterfamilias was in breach of his parole conditions.) Charges against the girls got dropped, but the court still announced, risibly, "No police wrongdoing."

This incident engendered a single positive: it coaxed Black leaders to act. Thus, the WDBC was able to convene an ad hoc community leadership forum—consisting of thirty-plus clergy and leaders of sundry community groups—to address the pernicious fact of racial profiling.

The forum members shuttled between Chief Glenn Stannard and his deputy, Roger Mortimer. Cordial were consultations; the top cops agreed that racial profiling equalled bad policing. So, the Windsor PD made some administrative changes, mainly to streamline the complaints procedure. Moreover, the WPD—in cooperation with the WDBC, CAW Local 444, and the city school boards—circulated a brochure to educate pupils on the correct comportment to demonstrate in the event of interactions with the police. (Reader, appreciate the horror of this paragraph! We were telling *schoolkids* how to *survive* cop stops!)

Not surprisingly, rank-and-file "bobbies" balked at donning name badges. Nor did they welcome the idea that all unsolicited engagements with free citizens be recorded—along with the age, gender, race, and ethnicity of those thus "stopped." The Caucasian force wanted to continue to exercise carte blanche (in other words, white privilege) in their dealings with "subalterns."

Simultaneous with the WDBC's efforts regarding this grievous insult to Black citizens, the Ontario Human Rights Commission (OHRC) launched an inquiry—chaired by OHRC chief, Keith Norton—into racial profiling. Asked to testify, I outlined WDBC initiatives to document profiling and listed our recs for combatting this nuisance *that is equally a menace*.

The late 2003 release of the OHRC's report attracted much media fanfare. In public speeches and panel discussions with flatfoot reps, plus broadcast interviews and letters to the editor, the WDBC won ground for our proposal that police sport name badges. However, beat-cop resistance to any constraint on their power was voiced obnoxiously via spurious arguments.

Finally, I prepared a brief on racial profiling that, subsequent to my resignation as WDBC prez, was put before the Windsor Police Services Board—but, curiously, only after the WDBC itself had asked coppers to give it a look-see. An act of courtesy—or cowardice? My brief called for:

1) the creation of a civilian complaints bureau;

2) provision of name identification badges for peace officers;

3) a new disciplinary regime for officers demonstrating patterns of abuse; and

4) provincial anti-race-profiling legislation.

I maintained that racial profiling is both a nuisance—in terms of exposing law-abiding citizens to undue harassment—and a menace, because unwarranted suspicion of innocent civilians can spur humiliating and/or violent and/or lethal use of force. Lookit! Racial profiling amounts to lazy policing: the "usual suspects" are oft *not* the right ones. Too, racialized and marginalized communities repay police harassment with distrust and repay police brutality with a "no-snitch" solidarity that only succours thugs.

Despite the facts and figures assembled, the sober and succinct prose utilized, the thoughtful recommendations presented, no specific response to that WDBC brief (presuming it was not gutted or redacted by the predator-protective vetting) was ever received from the Windsor constabulary insofar as I am aware. Nor did the Government of Ontario act to protect Black citizens from uniformed brutes. True: civilian complaints about cops may now be subject to independent investigation by the Office of the Independent Police Review Director (OIPRD). Time will reveal the effectiveness or not of this oversight agency. But justice itself is on the line: Are police *peace officers* or are they de facto paramilitary oppressors vis-à-vis African-Canadians?

The nuisance and menace of racial profiling is not limited to policing. The WDBC also identified its occurrence among Canada Border Services personnel and in the school system. Regarding the former, the WDBC considered a program to document racial profiling at the Windsor–Detroit, Canada–US border crossings but failed to implement it, in spite of an abundance of incidents. (I would myself become a victim of said racial profiling in short order.)

In our schools, Ontario's zero-tolerance policy (terminated in 2007) for misbehaving pupils seemed to urge the wanton suspensions and/or expulsions of Black kids. Hard numbers were (and are) hard to come by, but I wager that Windsor's stats were not far off from Halifax, NS, data collected by the Black Learners Advisory Committee (1987–1992), which asserted that while Blacks were only 8 percent of the Haligonian student body, they accounted for 16 to 20 percent of suspensions (see ohrc.on.ca/en/ontario-safe-schools-act-school-discipline-and-discrimination/vi-disproportionate-impact-other-jurisdictions). Parents decried such racism, especially in Catholic schools, where not one authority would address Negrophobia. Secular schools did boast a single Diversity Officer, Rachel Oliver, who was sympathetic to Black community concerns, not only in regard to profiling, but also in regard to the hiring of teachers of colour.

Our WDBC worry about the latter centred on the school board's tendency to hire recent university grads with no community experience at the expense of more mature and better trained applicants who were "indigenous Black" (a Rocky Jones neologism for the historical "Africadian" population of Nova Scotia that I think applies equally to the Underground Railroad-descended Blacks of Essex County, ON). The board rejected all proposals to consult with a community advisory committee to address these concerns. Why? A power play?

The WDBC did succeed in pressing the school board to accept Shelley Harding-Smith's motion to integrate African-Canadian history into the curriculum. (My Uncle Alvin would've lauded this measure. He recognized the urgent vitality of our history.)

In February 2004, I resigned as WDBC prez, having done as much as I was able to do and no longer being able to tolerate the malice of those keen to sabotage my direction. The über-capable Andrea Moore thus became prez, but ephemerally: sadly, Andrea passed away in 2005. Her death was a loss—for the WDBC and for our entire community. Indeed, she'd forged the Essex County Black Historical Research Society, and she'd spearheaded the construction of the Tower of Freedom (unveiled in 2001) near the Windsor riverfront. Featuring the work of master bronze sculptor Edward Dwight Jr. (whom JFK had tapped in 1962 to become the first Black astronaut, a plan likely scuttled by NASA hot-shot Chuck Yeager), the Tower of Freedom commemorates the arrival in Canada of fugitives on the Underground Railroad. It faces a corresponding sculpture on the Detroit riverfront that celebrates their flight from enslavement (or the threat thereof) in the States. The Windsor monument lists Underground Railroad militants, including my ancestor, Nasa McCurdy.

In 2002, I joined several Amherstburg families who proposed a reunion to be called the Amherstburg Heritage Homecoming (AHH). I became a member of its executive, chaired by Blair Harris. The AHH was scheduled for late September. I asked the group to feature the heritage aspect by highlighting the centrality of the town as the most vital terminal on the Underground Railroad. I prepared a brief history of Amherstburg for the AHH website, and I was the MC for the inaugural event (and subsequently).

At its outset, the AHH sustained overflow crowds, thanks to the efforts of Blair, Milton, and Janice Harris, and Wava and Eddy Hurst. But how long could the event endure with so much of the burden falling upon so few? Worse, the Town of Amherstburg introduced the Amherstburg Wine Festival to occupy the same calendar dates as the AHH. Efforts to coordinate the two events failed. Then, a growing dominance of fundamentalist worship led to diminished interest—and the demise of the AHH. (Damn! Ain't it devilishly hard for gospel shouting to sideline wine tasting?)

In 2006, I re-entered politics—one last time—to back Bruck Easton, once my Tory opponent, now running as a Grit in that year's federal election. No longer rivals for votes, he and I, now pals, were teetotally disillusioned with our former parties. Bruck lost to Knee-Dipper Joe Comartin, but for three years we bolstered the Windsor-Tecumseh Federal Liberal Riding Association.

As a result of my rebranding as a Grit, Ontario Liberal MPP Dwight Duncan suggested that I would be a valuable addition to the OHRC.

Beckoned to apply, I sent in my CV. Then, I waited for word about my prospects, the disposition of the Grits to my appointment. And I waited.

In the meantime, I became a victim of the most atrocious incident of racial profiling I'd ever experienced. I was en route home from Detroit at about one thirty in the morning via the Ambassador Bridge when I was stopped by a young, male Canuck border officer. Asked about my business in Detroit, I replied, "Visiting." The same individual had processed me previously while remarking on my garb and implying that I was in Detroit to pursue the "ladies." I was not about to be engaged in any similarly inappropriate chit-chat. I said nothing more. He asked nothing else.

I proceeded to the car-lane entry booth. Now, a female officer asked me how long I had been in the US. "A few hours." She wondered if I had done any shopping while there and whether I had anything to declare. "Nothing." Did I have any cigarettes? Liquor? Guns? "No." Dissatisfied with my primary responses, the officer had at me with the identical interrogatives for a second round. I again answered truthfully negatively. In frustration, I shrugged, "If you want to send me over (to secondary inspection), please do so." Now, the officer who had stopped me earlier came to the booth, spoke to his colleague, and looked like he was about to direct me to secondary inspection. I said dourly, "I know how to get there."

I wheeled to the parking area and started to exit my car when a sextet of cops swarmed, running from six cardinal points. One yelled, "Get back in the car!" I complied. But I was no sooner seated than another barked, "Get out of the car!" Yet, as I effected my egress, the tallest ruffian seized me and snarled, "I told you to get out of the car!" (How did I elicit such methodical wrath?) Now, he threw me to the pavement, screeching, "Stop resisting! Stop resisting!" As I lay passively on the asphalt while being tugged and shoved by several two-legged K-9s—their mountainous bulks avalanching heavy gloves—one barked, "He's not resistin'!" Of course not! I was following advice I had given to others. The only words I uttered during this KKKanuck affair? "They are going to give you idiots guns?" I was then dragged roughly into the Customs office where I was assigned a breathalyser test (negative). I promised the most oppressive aggressor that he would regret his actions.

I was imprisoned in a cell—in durable gloom and indecent quarantine—until 4:00 A.M. I was a municipal Mandela in a parochial police state. When released, I was informed that I would be charged with resisting arrest and obstructing a peace officer. Apparently, the Windsor Police had been in attendance (to jeer and sneer at my prone, manhandled form) and were to be consulted about my "offences." The stench all about? Sewer rats. Gutter rats.

My daughter Linda was my lawyer. Eventually, several border guards volunteered to aid in my defence; they savoured the help I had given them and their union in the past. Shortly, the charges were dropped, for there was no likelihood of a conviction. Subsequent news reports indicated that I'd been subjected to—guess what?—racial profiling.

When returning from Detroit since, I have not espied any of the KKKanuck Stasi. May I surmise that all have been demoted, transferred, or sacked? Or were they promoted and dispatched to other border crossings—to tyrannize and persecute other BIPOC citizens?

Almost two years later, Barbara Hall, the OHRC chair, came to Windsor to interview me. Our earlier set-to did not bode well for my long-dangled appointment. On that first meeting, perhaps in the midst of a leadership campaign, we disagreed about something I could not recall. But whatever it was, it seemed to have stuck in her craw. Then again, during the interview, her focus was on addressing sexism and homophobia, not racism, and she ignored totally all my recent and, one might think, relevant work against racial profiling—by cops, by judges, by teachers.

I did not get the appointment. Perhaps I was too old? In 2009, I turned seventy-seven. So ended my public life.

EPILOGUE:
LIFE LESSONS

MY LIFE HAS SPANNED THE GREATER PART OF A CENTURY IN A world that has much changed over that time period. No longer is it rare to see BIPOC evident and even flourishing beyond our once sharply delimited spaces of home, house of worship, and rez or plain old "ghetto." Lookit! African peoples are now everywhere—on the streets, on movie and television screens, in print media, and in legislatures, colleges and universities, and corporate offices. Stepin Fetchit, pickaninnies, and big-lipped, bulging-eyed depictions of Blacks are mainly historical curiosities. Racists and xenophobes now confront irrefutable evidence of our unstinting excellence. Blacks appear as heroes, villains, comedians, and ordinary folks in movies and plays that we may have directed, produced, or written. Blacks dominate the most popular sports—even hockey. Black music is accepted, emulated, and recognized as a fount of creative inno-vation. But we are also graphic artists and poets, economists, entrepre-neurs, executives, engineers, and scientists. Nobel laureates and Olympic medalists: that's us. The best of the best; the top of the top; *la crème de la crème*. The best science program on television is hosted by America's best known astrophysicist—a Black man (although, as late as 1985, there was not a single African-American in that field). We are conspicuous in pol-itics and in world leadership: as I write, the United States has a Black president; Canada has had a Black Governor General; and Nova Scotia and Ontario have had Black lieutenant-governors. The most respected icons of democracy and social justice on earth are Nelson Mandela, Martin Luther King, and Mahatma Gandhi.

Discrimination in employment, housing, or public accommodation has not disappeared but has become much rarer—because of legislation *and* changed attitudes. Now, in Canada, we may work and play and live where we choose, with whom we choose. White mothers and grandmothers with children and grandchildren of colour turn few heads now.

My children experienced less racism than I, even as I experienced less than my progenitors. My grandchildren with their multicultural friends are hardly conscious of it at all. Yet, I do fear they lack the armament they may need versus the vestiges of racism they may yet face. They need to know the history of our struggle. Not knowing, they may be tempted to believe that there has been no change—or be frustrated by what has not changed. It is from an awareness of the past that they can best meet the need to change what yet needs to be changed. That is as much the rationale for this book as the urgings of my friends to write it.

Herein I have described the influences of my family and its generations: how my mother provided pride in my African roots and the urge to dream, and how from my father I imbibed the virtues of discipline and hard work, and, most estimably, to concede superiority to no one, whatever their status—not in classroom or lab, not in office or on the track, not in leadership or in protest. In the deep roots of my family's involvement in the Underground Railroad and their fight for freedom and equality, I derived inspiration to continue the right and just offensive. But I learned too, in those same roots and in boyhood, that to confront white racism did not mean contesting all Caucasians, for in their number were not only antagonists, but indispensable allies. Assuredly, for most of my life, my closest friendships and even loved ones have spanned the races—as have my ancestors.

Moreover, I knew early that we were not the only people who suffered injustice because of prejudice, nor are we free of it. We were not the first to be enslaved. The very word *slave* derives from the ancient exploitation of Slavic peoples. Ordained even in the Bible, slavery is as old as humankind. Indeed, the enslavement of Jews in Egypt conceived the code words for our own underground, subversive, revolutionary, abolitionist struggle. Yet, even the Jews enslaved others. Nor were Africans guiltless in that trafficking, that trade, in precious human lives.

I also realize that antipathy to those who are different exists even among those who have been its victims. Blacks are not free of racism even against our own kind; Israel is not the epitome of racial tolerance, in spite of the Shoah. Religion remains the main motive for genocide *and* the exploitation and oppression of women. (Religion is the root of all *Evil*?) Persecution of others of different religion, ethnicity, gender, and/or sexual orientation leads to oppression unto death.

My political engagement was in opposition to all of the above ills and wrongs, and was undertaken for the achievement of social and economic justice and equality for all—regardless of race, ethnicity, gender, sexual preference, or religious belief. I credit that politics in all its forms—legislative and civil-society-agitation-provoked—is a transcendent, civilizing, and justice-realizing pursuit.

My family also taught me that if I was to excel in any activity in which I engaged, I must try to be better than good: excellence ain't second-best. Yes, there were lapses in effort sometimes, but I mostly strove to triumph and never allowed myself to be discouraged by anyone, Caucasian or Black, in that endeavour. In fact, besides my family and bursary-disbursing organizations, my most positive influences were educators. Thanks to their advice, aid, encouragement, and examples, mine has been a reasonably accomplished life—as a teacher, athlete, scientist, politician, and social activist.

One day, recently, a young man dubbed me "Canada's Martin Luther King." His praise was obvious hyperbole, but it is satisfying to be recognized as part of the Canadian struggle against racism and as a standard-bearer for African-Canadian political engagement.

To receive both the Order of Ontario and the Order of Canada was signal recognition that I have lived up to the distinguished legacy of those in my family whose accomplishments were more deserving of those honours. It is of that I am most proud.

I am also blessed to be a Canadian: it has been Canada's greater commitment (so un-American) to socio-economic justice that has yielded fertile ground for anti-discrimination legislation and greater acceptance of minorities, whether religious, ethnic, racial, or sexual. (Will my beloved country *ever* exempt visible minorities' rights from abrogation via the notwithstanding clause?)

That racism is not dead and that conditions could again promote its resurrection can be identified in the US where aspirations to social and economic justice seem to diminish day by day and where the negative legacies of slavery and segregation are congenital. However much I celebrated it, the ascendancy of Barack Obama in becoming the 44th president of the great republic to our south in 2009 did not signal the attainment of a non-racial society. All too clear is the truth that a solid 33 percent of the US population, led by Republicans, reject and fear the very idea of a Black president and especially the changing demography and BIPOC coalition that his election brought to the fore. (Many of that 33 percent also reject Latinos, women's equality and abortion rights, and disregard environmental protection; they

(ABOVE) *Howard receives the Order of Ontario on January 26, 2012. At right, Lieutenant Governor of Ontario, David C. Onley.*

(LEFT) *Howard receives the Order of Canada on November 19, 2012, from Governor General David Johnston.*

worship, instead, war on peoples of colour abroad and massacre by gun of their fellow citizens—also, often, people of colour.)

The positive forces that married racial progress and social justice in the US have been muted by a culture that is gloatingly one of unimpeded greed, propagandized and controlled by plutocrats and policed by municipally deputized militias outfitted with arsenals. Measures intended to improve the lives of ordinary citizens are execrated as "entitlements" by those who should represent them, largely because financial assistance programs might enhance the lives of racialized minorities. (Nor can we forget that much inherited white wealth is a product of centuries of unpaid labour extracted from

African-Americans.) Meanwhile, the privileges of the richest are enhanced by a Supreme Court that has given far more weight to their wealth than the votes of ordinary citizens, even as many are deprived of even that right. Wages are suppressed and unions disarmed—in the interest of global capitalist jousting—even while US public education trails that of most of the overdeveloped world. Slavery and apartheid have been replaced by a justice system that enslaves and deprives minorities of the rights of citizenship or subjects them to execution by cop or execution by judge. In the United States, *race* still matters, while allegiance to democracy is feigned.

Canada's "Red Tory," social democratic character created a more sympathetic context for racial progress. From the outset, I saw my political and anti-intolerance praxis as proceeding hand in hand, for the greater the extent of social and economic justice, the greater is the acceptance of differences. Indeed, in police-state plutocracies, resentments and scape-goating prevail. History is loud: not only did the fight against discrimi-nation advance furthest under good economic conditions, so did the so-called welfare state. Not only was there anti-discrimination legislation in that period, changes in immigration policy served to inspire the non-discriminatory acceptance of people of colour as citizens. Now, Canada considers diversity a strength. Even our constitution defines Canada as a multicultural nation.

But the old "Dominion" is not Utopia—yet. If multiculturalism comes to mean the perpetuation of cultural divisions, then it will strain the social fabric. Cultural prejudices are as bad as racial. Thus, Somalis can face discrimination not because they are Black, but because many are Muslim. Jamaicans may encounter more prejudice than Nigerians—or vice versa, due to different stereotypes attached to their different cultures. We need always to keep front and centre John Porter's analysis that Canada is a "vertical mosaic" of races and ethnicities, with WASPs and (now) fran-cophone Catholics at the summit and all others taking secondary and tertiary positions, region by region, but always with Blacks and Indigenous Peoples at the bottom of this hierarchy.

Other peril lies in an immigration policy that privileges the best trained, best educated, conservative elites of developing nations that are kleptocratic tyrannies. So, ironically, we beckon immigrants who reject the very social democracy that makes their acceptance possible in Canada.

Finally, in this "brave new world," workers—even professionals—are being displaced by machines that profit the few, while others struggle for their livelihoods. Indeed, the "filthy rich" and newfangled "robber bar-ons" exert too much economic *and* anti-democratic power to give a damn for the public good. That their excesses jeopardize the very survival of humanity and perhaps Earth itself seems beyond their understanding. To save the planet—and the species—we need socialism, or social democracy, or enforced sharing of resources. Or else!

My grandchildren may be freed from racism. Their future faces far graver challenges.

— *Dr. Howard D. McCurdy Jr., CM, O.Ont, PhD*

DEDUCTION:
LIFE LESSONS REDUX

No Beauty without struggle.

– REV. DR. ANTHONY BAILEY, "HONOURING HOWARD D. McCURDY (1932–2018),"
ST. ANDREW'S PRESBYTERIAN CHURCH, OTTAWA, ON, MAY 19, 2018

ONE OF THE PHOTOGRAPHS OF HOWARD DOUGLAS MCCURDY JR. that always seemed, to me, to reveal his extraordinary poise was a snap taken in the early 1950s when he is perhaps eighteen or nineteen. It depicts, in its black-and-white shadings, a lanky young man, lean and natty in a crisp, dark, pressed suit, in mid-stride, approaching the wide-eyed camera, polish sunshining each black shoe but a look—brazen, serious, charismatic—sculpting a face somehow as smoothly angular as a Benin bronze mask. Even at such a young age, McCurdy seems geared to ascend to a podium or lectern, to deliver an address, and the style is likely activist-professorial, a combo that he would soon refine outstandingly. Sharp logic wed to sinuous syntax, polysyllables unleashed against folderol, backward persons, and wrong-headed deeds: such was the McCurdy comportment, the action-and-glamour shot, all already communicated incandescently in that flashbulb instant, with the enlightenment of lightning.

That's likely why he appeared immediately unforgettable when I first met him, nonchalantly, insouciantly, being all of nineteen and a slapdash, Black "rad" outta the Haligonian 'hood. I just barged uninvited into a meeting of the floundering National Black Coalition of Canada (NBCC), which Howard had sparked to life a decade before. It was May 1979, and at that weekend Toronto conference gathered the who's who of African-Canadian politicos and activists, some elected to provincial or national office, and others who were movers of motions and/or shakers-up of their urban Bantustans. The assembly was an eye-opening mishmash of various tones of melanin, a mellifluous medley of accents, and a give-no-quarter cacophony of clashing ideologies. At the centre of the dynamic debates—almost indifferently Tory, Grit, socialist, Quebec nationalist—was Dr. McCurdy, whom I remember as being eminently dapper in suit and tie, estimably bourgeois, and producing loquacious eloquence intended to persuade even the most recalcitrant or insolent delegate into accepting constitutional governance. By that weekend's close, Howard was vice-president (veep) of the revivified NBCC but not until he'd had a fist fight with an "Island" gent who had posited that we native Black Canucks were a bunch of no-count, sad-sack Uncle Toms. Given his unparalleled lineage of abolitionism and civic activism—plus his wiry, athletic frame—it was likely to his advantage, Howard may have decided to set aside scientific objectivity and *Robert's Rules of Order* and just hit the sucker (brap!) upside his dumb-ass head: maybe a tap or two would tutor the miscreant in the history of African-Canadian struggle since he was evidently ill-read in the subject.

I'm not sure how I wound up talking with Howard during the confab, and our exchange was brief. I just see him smiling, doubling up with laughter, a cigarette in his hand. Being pretty secure in my own (political) smarts, I know I didn't hesitate to ask questions or to hobnob with this Afro-Can bigwig dignitary as I sought to establish my credentials as the self-appointed rep of the Central Planning Committee for the Black Youth Organization of Nova Scotia. (I was, *naturally*, the "Minister of Information.") Sure, I gravitated to Howard's orbit. To preen in his reflected sheen.

That slice of life is lodged deeply in my cranium. Eight years later, in late September 1987, when he called *The Rap* (my Halifax Black community newspaper) office to interview me to be his parliamentary-constituency liaison, I was able to recall meeting him and to update him about persons we both knew, such as Rocky Jones. Although my newspaper was a small monthly tabloid (7,000 circulation), only eight pages per printing (with one page reserved for poetry—always), I did earn national attention for a few news stories, and thus Howard had looked me up. I recall the probing interview well, especially the part where he said, "I can only pay you

$24,000 per year." I tried to sound miffed about that figure, but I was living on $12,000 per year, and I was twenty-seven years old and about to marry (for the first time). Yes, I said YES to his job offer PDQ!

So I removed myself to Ottawa, arriving on Thanksgiving weekend, and started working for Howard the day after the holiday. He was gruff and brusque with us staffers; often hounded or teased us; often barked at us to do better, work harder, be smarter; was belittling about anything that didn't measure up to his standards; and he treated us like serfs, slamming down his soiled shirts or suits on our desks so that we'd order up a parliamentary runner to speed all to a drycleaner's; or he'd have us dispatch a runner to ferry back Scotch from the House of Commons liquor store. (After we disagreed about who had gulped or sipped the best part of a bottle, we alternated our purchases!) Yes, he could be a difficult, prickly taskmaster.

However, I soon came to learn that beneath the very superficial flashes of anger or upset, the man nursed an unlimited fondness for each of us—but hid it because he was not one to show feelings that could render him vulnerable. After all, he'd been reared in the macho school of masculinity (*maybe not* sexist but definitely gendered "traditional" male). He treated us to meals in the parliamentary restaurant, gifted us with books (for Xmas 1988, HDM passed along to me *The Lynch Mob: Stringing Up Our Prime Ministers*, a series of commentaries on Canadian PMs, Macdonald to Mulroney, scribed by Parliamentary Press Gallery mainstay, Charles Lynch; Howard figured that I'd relish the black-comic significance of the author's surname), awarded us birthday parties (my thirtieth birthday bash on February 12, 1990, unfurled in Howard's inner office: a small gathering of NDP staffers, including my daughter's mom-to-be, about a birthday cake and a bottle of Scotch!), and splurged on praise for anything that he really thought had been done or written well. Whenever one of us quit his office, however, he'd fall morose, quiet, be unable to put together a sentence, and would appear dazed—until the new hire materialized. He seemed to take each departure from his office as a personal affront, a vote of non-confidence in his management or personhood, and so he'd sink into a dude's version of post-partum depression. Some staffers who left in a snit or a huff likely never knew how much their exit wounded Howard.

When I went to him in the fall of 1990 and said that I would leave to commence doctoral studies at Queen's University in Kingston, ON, Howard would not let me depart! Instead, he permitted me an absence, one day a week—Tuesdays—to which I agreed, and that extra year of nearly full employment got me through that first year at Queen's, where there was no money for the "extra" nine of us that the university had accepted.

When I did sidle out of Howard's office in fall 1991, I did so with teary eyes. Why? He'd been like a father to me, and I'd lost mine, in a sense, when my parents split up when I was twelve. Not only that, but Howard modelled for me the style of the activist and compassionate intellectual: to put progressive thought behind protest actions. (Nor was I the sole beneficiary of his incidental—and yet deliberate—mentorship. The Windsor-born documentary filmmaker Preston Chase; Howard's ex-staffer Jacqueline Lawrence, now the Diversity and Equity Coordinator of the Ottawa-Carleton District School Board; once-Ottawa-based Gwyn Chapman, journalist, TV personality, media relations consultant, and now the Senior Advisor to the City of Brampton's Black Empowerment and Anti-Black Racism Unit; and now-retired economist José Aggrey—all were energized by Howard's example of magnetic and propulsive *daring*.)

In addition to all that, in giving me a chance to launch out into a rewarding, adult life as a scholar and writer, Howard also touted my poetry, *before* I toted home any major prizes. When my second book was born, Howard threw a launch party on Parliament Hill, and the Right Honourable Joe Clark showed up and bought a copy! I doubt that there are many Canadian poets who can say that they had a Parliament Hill event wherein a former prime minister purchased a book! (In March 2016, I was asked to Windsor to give a poetry reading as Parliamentary Poet Laureate. Howard showed up spectacular: his fedora sailed through the room, dividing the light finely.)

Besides, those Centre Block House of Commons years were rife with adventure—viscerally in 1987–88 when we were booting up for the federal election campaign, and I was desperate to see Howard re-elected so I could keep my job! (I did not want to return to the mean streets of Halifax, where my future would be, could be, menial employ and police harassment.) I remain chuffed about our insight—as early as spring 1988—that the Canada–US Free Trade Agreement (FTA) would be the dominant concern of the nigh campaign, that it was an economic matter, yes, pitting blue jeans versus pinstripes, but it was also an existentialist provocation, worrying the worth and quality of "culture," "independence," and "nationhood." I think Howard's speech in the House of Commons on July 5, 1988, is one of the classic statements of Canadian nationalism.

As soon as the election was called, he drove me to Windsor and moved me into his home in Tecumseh. Then I spent forty-nine days in the trenches, as it were, convincing volunteers to knock on strangers' doors, block after block, to ID our voters so we could wheel them to the polls come E-day. And Howard was out, in running shoes, pressed slacks, sweater, and light jacket, daily—nothing ostentatious, but the perfect duds for a man "wukkin hard for yer votes."

When he was in the committee room, his cigarettes added to the cumulous cloud of blue-grey, lung-cancer-promising smoke that hunkered dead centre in the room. I'm a non-smoker (my only virtue?), so it took me a while to realize why I was coughing non-stop, my eyes red and sore and my nose running. I was inhaling the equivalent of umpteen packs of smokes per day, from 8:00 A.M. to 9:00 P.M., seven days a week. But I mustn't complain, for we won—Howard won!—despite the almost miraculous second coming of John Turner, a Bay Street boy wonder rebranded as Canadian nationalist patriot. The national Liberal campaign outflanked the fed NDP on the left, but our local NDP campaign outflanked the Liberals on the left. (The night before the vote, I spent the evening in the ultra-companionable company of author Alistair MacLeod and family; the Cape Breton author taught at the University of Windsor but summered—and wrote—in our joint pseudo-Xanadu of Nova Scotia. I somehow knew that a dinner party of Scotch and red wine and turkey with all the trimmings was a sign from on high that we'd triumph in the morrow!)

While his re-election in 1988 was a high point of Howard's political career, his 1989 defeat in seeking the NDP leadership against the front-runner Audrey McLaughlin was a blow that set him off-kilter. He felt betrayed—by stealth racists, by folks who smiled smugly in his face while lustily "burying the hatchet," yes, in his back. Throughout the leadership campaign, which I had urged him to undertake, he noted the steady rise of a membership momentum in his favour—despite all the naysayers and their anonymous noising off in the press. Yet, he had a stiff wind in his tacking sails, and everyone knew it—especially after he and his rivals appeared before the Steelworkers in Toronto in September 1989 and these take-no-guff unionists acclaimed Howard as the only capable candidate. Perhaps the ephemeral peak of his political life was his final leadership campaign debate in Toronto and then the Windsor send-off celebration, wherein he and his Windsor base anticipated either a first-ballot upset or a down-ballot third-place or second-place finish.

He'd loved winning a city council seat in Windsor in 1979 and then his House of Commons seat in 1984 and 1988. But he adored campaigning for the NDP leadership, first because he had led the drive to rename the former CCF as the NDP (so he viewed the party as his baby) and second because he got to parlay the McCurdy brand—barbed wit and captivating oratory—*nationally*. Oxygen to him were the lush ovations of the crowds in the provincial capitals and in major NDP ridings, surely. So his defeat on the first ballot, finishing absurdly *fifth*, was crushing: an ambush. He'd anticipated a multitude of autoworker votes and the solid support of the two-hundred-strong Saskatchewan delegation. Canadian Auto Workers chief Bob White—miked by the CBC—reacted to Howard's sorry tally by commenting, on live TV, that it was reprehensible of delegates to don McCurdy T-shirts and buttons and pledge Howard their votes and then desert him in droves. White's remarks hinted that delegates may always have been fickle, and one may infer that some, in the end, could not bear to black their ballots for a melanin-positive candidate.

If Howard's memory of Lorne Nystrom's purported statement—"Someone you know convinced the [Saskatchewan] delegates at the last minute that they couldn't possibly vote for a Black candidate because it would be impossible for Canadians to accept a Black prime minister"—is accurate, then he, with all his gifts of smarts, charisma, courage, matinee-idol looks, and excellence at almost everything, was felled by the foe against whom he had raged his entire life. If Nystrom's statement is as true as Howard reports, it is no wonder that my mentor felt so devastated: after demonstrating, nationally, that *he*—a Black man—was *the* candidate-of-quality, his potential high place in the balloting was denied by bigotry, a whisper campaign *within* the federal NDP, where "progressives" unknown had decided that the man who named the party could be discarded with aplomb and on the facetious basis that he could never be prime minister. (Um, what NDP leader was ever going to be PM? The point of being the leader of Canadian Anglophone social democrats is to be able to argue nationally for better social supports, better usage of taxpayers' moneys to benefit taxpayers, not to plan on redecorating 24 Sussex Drive!)

There's a major clue in Howard's memoir about who he believes shattered his Saskatchewan bastion: a person who feared losing clout with "his" Saskatchewan base. (If it was Simon de Jong, we will never know; he passed away in 2011.) The vital point is, Howard had believed his whole life that merit was its own reward. Once his apparent electoral viability—electability—was rejected on the basis of race (as he believed), he felt dejected, disjointed, *destroyed*: like Othello, destabilized by the thought that Desdemona had thrown him over for his Caucasian lieutenant, Cassio.

We can understand Howard's funk. As a microbiologist, he'd proven himself either equal or superior to the test of meeting standards of objective proof—ditto for being a professor. And then, as a human rights activist, he could measure success by inches of newspaper columns, numbers of headlines, reels of footage broadcast, and minutes sustained of applause. Not to mention legislation passed or practices of racism foregone, abandoned, finally *quit*. Thus, to be dissed and dismissed by so-called socialists to whom he had always given his all? 'Twas *dégueulasse*. *"Après moi, le deluge,"* Howard could rightly have thought. For, his betrayal in Winnipeg was followed by treachery in his third fed election race in 1993—and then in those two *provincial* (a term I wield pejoratively) NDP nomination campaigns in 1995 and 1997, wherein Windsor union activists determined that he alone had to pay an everlasting price for having backed Premier Rae's attempts to govern for all in the face of atrocious economic conditions.

Thus, Howard ceased to be a flagrantly fuchsia "socialist" and became a pastel, Parma-tint Liberal. Why not? Following a quartet of electoral letdowns, plus being attacked by Canuck border goons when he was seventy-five, Howard was fed up with fake liberals, specious humanitarians, and faux progressives and felt it meet to say, *Sayonara, connards*, to his two-faced nemeses.

Howard's defeats—*quadruple*—were comprehensively dispiriting. He lost his mojo, his bearings. His last years were almost aimless: some golfing, some boating, the enlivening circuits of family, grandchildren, and friends. But then came the rounds of doctors and hospitals to deal with the cancer that was chewing up his bones. Except for the medical appointments and the familial, homely pleasures, seldom could he feel grounded; rather, he felt grievously wounded.

This fact has me thinking, recognizing, that too many Black folk, despite lives of significant accomplishment, end up broken, reviled, impoverished, well-nigh forgotten, or prematurely dead due to incarceration—or assassination. (But character assassination is just as bad, save that one merely loses—maybe—one's livelihood.) Examples are legion: Paul Robeson, Huey Newton, Toussaint Louverture, Malcolm X, Martin Luther King, Marcus Garvey.... Too few are those whose trajectory moves from summit to summit and then to a final, relaxing plateau. For too many, trouble and turmoil, or bad health and bad debts, or almost total obliteration of their achievements and their legacies await after all the accolades and applause.

That this was Howard's fate speaks volumes about the devaluation of Black excellence and, for that matter, Black lives. Yet, that personage who was thwarted in his NDP leadership bid—and who was then tossed from the House of Commons and refused twice a chance to sit in Ontario's legislature—was no average or petty candidate. Among his legion accomplishments and honours (outlined in the preface and in Howard's own account) is the fact that when the Dalai Lama came to Parliament Hill to appeal for the liberation of Tibet, he made a beeline to Howard's office, perched eminently upon our sofa, draped Howard's neck with the gift of a scarf, and gave us his blessing.

Now and then, grad students whose dissertations Dr. McCurdy was directing made a Holy-Grail pilgrimage to Ottawa to take notes in Howard's inner office as he discussed their research into gliding bacteria. Then, phenomenally, after the student had left, Howard could rush down to the House itself and fire off a pertinent question to an embarrassed "Honourable" or speed demonically to the Macdonald-Cartier Airport and jet off to wherever, with a black leather man-bag/wallet-purse borne in his right hand. Perhaps to attend a protest against police killings (murders?) of unarmed Black Canadian kids. Or perhaps to go to the Soviet Union and research the treatment of Jews seeking to flee that tyranny.

So, after that lifetime of public brilliance and righteously articulated truth-speaking to well-heeled Klansmen and blue-collar rednecks or badge-and-revolver thugs, to be so cast aside and shrugged off because, suddenly, he was no longer a top-level microbiologist or a poet of civil liberties but just a "Black man," well, yessirree, this was most evil. Dr. McCurdy had a right to say, "A pox on all yas," to adopt abulia and set aside being gung-ho, and then pick up his golf clubs or go boating toward the blue meridian—or, very beautifully, to become, as he was in his last days, a painter of "Expressionist," primary-pigment bacteria, the focus of his scientific career. (Recall that Howard the boy was always drawing Second World War fighters and doodling classmates; he'd always had a hand for art and an eye for colour.)

I think that such callous disregard for the self-sacrificing activist that he was, for the principled tribune that he was, and for him to be buffeted about—roughed up, cursed out, flung face-down on spiteful asphalt by Canuck Border Services storm troopers, treating a distinguished man of seventy-five as a Detroit gangbanger—was despicable, disgraceful, and a dishonour to this monarchical people's republic itself. That Dr. McCurdy later merited the laurels of appointments to the Order of Canada and the Order of Ontario was befitting, belated acknowledgement of his struggle to make Canada *truly Canadian* in respect to enhancing egalitarian principles and uninhibited social-democratic public spending on health, education, R & D, and infrastructure. That such a noble figure, such a charismatic servant of the Canadian people, could be fettered and arrested, scorned and rebuked, and literally put down, low to the ground, as "a trifling Coloured man" tells us how thin lay the rhetorical cosmetics intended to prettify the brute features of Canuck racism.

I regret how isolated Howard must have felt himself to be at the end of his "public life," in which he had had to represent—solo, nationally— the fact of a Black citizenry. Why did he not have cadres of multicultural intellectuals to bear him up, buck him up, to assure that all of the marginalized—the poor, the visible minorities, the BIPOC, the sexual minorities, immigrants, and unorganized workers—could continue to be exalted and principles of equality elaborated?

Maybe one reason for his unfortunate animosity for the accomplished, heart-in-the-right-place, and very likeable Dr. Steve Langdon was Howard's back-o-mind bias that Dr. Langdon had come by his prestige and election too facilely, that he never had the struggles that Howard had—being a *citoyen noir* (and, no, it didn't count, for Howard, that Langdon knew and loved Africa): to enter the Academy, to become a scientist, to dispute simultaneously for human rights and civil liberty (and think how strange that must have been, to go from microphone to microscope, and back again, two or three times a week—or day), to then be entrusted with seats on Windsor City Council and then in the House of Commons, to be a de facto leader of all African-Canadians and one of the principal visages of the African diaspora, and to do all with vivid, breathtaking class—but so often alone. Thus, to believe himself to be disparaged (even if illusorily) caused Howard to take umbrage, to rankle.

Perhaps he saw Dr. Langdon as being condescending toward him rather than being punctiliously deferential. Perhaps he was also envious of his fellow academic's name branding a host of books. Sure, Howard's irrepressible egotism was a flaw, yet it also made him aspire to the saving grace of graciousness. (Despite his evident animosity for Langdon, never did Howard try to influence my own opinion.)

Apart from that forty-nine-day election campaign in autumn 1988, the next-nice spate of time that I spent with Howard was a weekend tour of the Maritimes during the 1989 NDP leadership contest. I had a chance to see him up close and personal as we flew to Halifax, ferried to Charlottetown, and then puddle-hopped to Saint John. In Halifax, we met the provincial NDP leader Alexa McDonough (once my kindergarten teacher), whose cordiality staged first-class theatre of courtesy; I mean, the amiable welcome came tinged with the frostiness of her evident first-ballot commitment to front-runner Audrey McLaughlin. Despite that blunt impediment to heart-to-heart camaraderie, Howard behaved with noblesse-oblige *politesse*, angling perhaps to secure Alexa's second-ballot support, if he did as well as he expected in the initial balloting.

Also attending that impromptu meeting—a tea setting—in Alexa's office was her ex-assistant, Rocky Jones, once Howard's colleague in the NBCC and also my mentor. Their mutual respect and admiration could have spurred someone to think, *If a Black man is backing a Black man, why shouldn't a Caucasian woman back a Caucasian woman?* However, this skin-deep analysis avoids the most pertinent question: Setting aside physical data best left to beauticians and morticians to ponder, should not a socialist promote the most adept, canny, and charismatic socialist?

Later that night, Rocky wrangled a swath of the Haligonian Black community to lift placards and voices for Howard, whose stentorian oration and deft responses to questions brought folks leaping ceiling-ward. The night was a success but, myself excepted, not one of the Africadians present would be voters at the Winnipeg convention. Even so, Howard was buoyed by their applause and by the hospitality and joviality extended him by the extended Jones's genealogy. He even managed to forget about my failure to retrieve his luggage from the Halifax Airport carousel when we'd landed that day! (I imagined that he'd pick up his own suitcases; he'd wagered that I'd automatically morph into his valet! No problem—one of Rocky's sisters gave Howard's shirt a fresh ironing, his pants a fresh pressing, and he was good to go.)

On the morrow, we boated to Charlottetown but travelled as foot passengers. Unremarkable? Sure, save that the ferry disgorged its cars and their drivers at a dock a kilometre from the terminal. So, there we were, MP and aide, striding through autumnal sunlight but full frontal into a bone-chilling, Atlantic-sourced, blustery tempest. Weren't we Lear and his Fool, out on the stormy moors? (Save that Howard was the wise "Fool" and I the foolish "Lear.") We were the only pedestrians forging our way through the wind that flapped our coats and slapped our ties against our faces, yet no one paused to offer us a lift to the terminal. (So much for the fabled East Coast hospitality!)

Worse, the Charlottetown sortie was frivolous, if not trivial; yet, Howard proved that his campaign was cash-flush enough that he could be there to debate Audrey, that he was no fringe candidate. Next, we were off to Saint John, where Howard was again leagued with his luggage. This stop netted Howard an Acadian delegate, and his visit also brought flocking Black Saint John—peeps who huzza'd his debate event and then packed into a waterfront soul-food restaurant for breakfast the next day. Howard had to orate extemporaneously but gained goodly donations. The crowd clamoured and stamped feet on floors in praise. The grits molten with syrup and butter and the potent coffee yielded not just a meal, but a festival. Our bellies were filled, our hearts were full. And Howard was in his element, royal molasses sweetening the salt-o-the-earth.

I gotta reflect on this luminous being, the solitary boy-engineer of blasts and tunnels, raiding the Amherstburg Library for everything it could tell him about the cosmos and about microbes; the teen finding solo honour by hurtling down a track and/or springing high into the air (and thus learning that, to be respected, he must place first, seize the medals, the ribbons, the trophies, the titles); the young man crushed by his passion for a white gal, whose leftist family was not leftist enough (along with Howard's own family) to allow the romance to continue. That disillusionment reinforced in Howard a determination to be self-reliant and self-protective, to secret his feelings, to never be so vulnerable again. Perhaps also it urged him into a monastic, workaholic lifestyle, because the lab (or the office) promised possibly racism-transcendent rewards of discovery and/or recognition.

Surely, there was less chance of mixed-up folks—venting hang-ups and humbug—intruding upon or hampering resolute study and articulation. Certainly, Howard seems to have entered his first marriage with some reluctance and then expresses immediate misgivings about his choice; and so, he preferred the rigours of the lab and the thundering strains of Beethoven to the pressing needs of "husbandry." Yet, he and Pat Neely had five children, and the birth of daughter Leslie generated the metaphor useful for his notable speech naming the New Democratic Party in 1961. In contrast, though, the loss of the first-born son, Frederick Douglas, in infancy must have again taught Howard that one mustn't invest too much emotion in too-vulnerable relationships, whether parent-child or husband-wife or boss-staffer.

Howard also realized, early on, that success was most easily secured via solitary study and the discipline essential to allow one to take one's lonesome stance on the loftiest pinnacle. But the cost of that alienated push to premiership—in sports, the academy, and social activism—was the excitement, yeah, but also the risk of being alone, even "in the presence of mine enemies" (says Psalm 23). If the foes—or inclement environment—persist, *excruciatingly*, who can be there to offer solace and support, the strength to persevere and overcome? Dr. McCurdy was a man who made allies and had friends, or had allies and made friends, but these bonds were seldom strong enough for either allies or friends to throng when tacitly summoned.

The image of him going alone to the partying committee room of the Liberal who defeated him in his re-election bid in 1993 and personally congratulating Ms. Shaughnessy Cohen; or the image of him retiring from his second failed ONDP nomination bid in 1997 and going home alone to watch Tiger Woods score a Masters' coup via master (golf) strokes—both of these portraits reveal *un homme politique* of awesome aloneness, divulge solitude as a beatitude. I think of his depression in learning of the death of his fiercely beloved Uncle George, but I also recall Howard's poignant desolation at hearing his father admit his love for his son, his boy, only as he, the paterfamilias, lay dying.

Howard had believed, his whole life, that he'd had to go solo into jousting for track trophies, scientific publication, headlining protests, and then to barge into the dens of the politicos, part funhouse mirrors and part Babylonian bordello. Intriguingly, he never cast himself in the mould of any heroic exemplar. He admired M. L. King, yes, but King presided over a movement of millions. Howard was alone—counting but a few disciples—in whatever organization to which he belonged. If he did identify with one suave, hieratic, singular tribune, it was his partial name-sake, Frederick Douglass (1819–1895), whose impress upon African-American history and polity arose from his mighty oratory, *not* because he led anything. (Douglass also set a daunting example for Howard by penning a socio-politically influential and deathless autobiography.)

Howard also had terrific respect for Pierre Elliott Trudeau—another shy and private intellectual who had accepted the public role of political primacy, partly so that he could reduce the glaring inequities in Canadian life arising from the antediluvian, *trop* Victorian British North America Act. Observe: Trudeau was another figure who built no mass movement and famously abandoned politics after taking a lonesome stroll in a Bytown blizzard. Perhaps Howard was also following Trudeau's lead by trying to have ethnic and racial minority rights exempted from the potentially disempowering enforcement of Section 33 of the Charter of Rights and Freedoms: the notwithstanding clause. If he had achieved that end, he would have placed his own egalitarian brand on the constitution.

Unsurprisingly, Howard was buoyed by the election of His Excellency Barack Obama, but also studied the ways in which Obama—for all his oratorical prowess and constitutional lawyer-prof acumen—could not push a Tea-Party Congress to enact legislation good for all (excepting health care) because too many Republican congresspersons vowed to obstruct the republic's first Black president. (The tragedy of Obama's failure to pass on a progressive mantle to his would-be successor, Hilary Clinton, spawned the iniquitous regime of Don John Trump.) Now an exalted ex-prez, and one whose bona fides and laurels have increased since he choppered away from the West Wing, Obama-the-Nobel-Peace-Prize-Laureate still gives dynamite speeches, particularly at funerals, but still heads no movement—not for peace, not for equality, not for social justice.

Despite my casual analysis that too many Negro politicos or pop stars (of bedazzling optics) fade from the spotlight—or fall from grace—and perish in obscurity, I remain startled by Howard's socialist individualism that eventually became a recluse's liberalism. Startling also is the relative absence of any McCurdy nostalgia or the museum fanfare of memorabilia that one might expect in Windsor, the city that he loved and served to help lead—as well as confronted for its racism—over five decades of personal struggle and personal sacrifice.

Perhaps because Howard became a university graduate and then a scientist and professor, that is, assumed a middle-class, gradualist position vis-à-vis Caucasian racialism, his means of organizing was to form interracial clubs and even help to establish non-racial organizations to push for integration and employment equity. Indeed, both the Canadian Civil Liberties Association and the Ontario Human Rights Commission emerged out of integrated Amherstburg or Windsor cocktail parties. (In Pat Softly's CBC-TV documentary *The McCurdy Birthright* [2007], Howard declares that the McCurdy clan has always rejected any compromise "on issues of race"; however, he later adds that his personal style was to "raise hell—and then negotiate." Negotiation implies compromise....)

Howard's organizations, like the Guardian Club, were often ephemeral; indeed, his contributions were often national, liberal, and professional—such as catalyzing or midwifing the Canadian Civil Liberties Association, the Canadian Association of University Teachers, the Canadian Society of Microbiologists, and so on. True: Howard did spearhead the creation of the National Black Coalition of Canada, prompted the mounting of a Black history exhibit that led to the establishment of the North American Black Historical Museum (now the Amherstburg Freedom Museum), and headed the Guardian Club and then the Windsor and District Black Coalition in anti-segregation and anti-racism initiatives. But seldom did he initiate or sanction popular mobilization. Few, then, were his apostles, his proteges. But Howard gained entree into both the Order of Ontario and the Order of Canada. Too, he is honoured in the bestowal of the annual Howard D. McCurdy Memorial Scholarship to a Black third- or fourth-year University of Windsor student who is excelling in STEM (science, technology, engineering, mathematics) study. This award represents a meet conjunction of Howard's interests in science and Black excellence.

Toward the end of his life, in July 2017, Howard reached out to me to edit his autobiography, and my companion, the poet Giovanna Riccio, and I visited him in LaSalle, near Windsor. We met a man who was dying but vaping away, talking up his new car purchase (of a Lincoln), and exulting both every time a CNN guest or reporter or anchor criticized the asinine policies of Prez Trump *and* every time Howard's dog jumped and barked at the window as a spray of water from a revolving fount slapped gushingly against the sunroom glass. I was so glad to see him again; Giovanna was so glad to meet him; and he was suitably appreciative of her style and

George and Howard, Christmas 1988, in Howard's Centre Block office, Parliament.

comportment. Then, he ushered us to view his paintings (one of which I now own) of primary-pigmented bacteria. He loved painting now, and one of his last public appearances was at a Windsor show of his art.

I say there's only one good thing about death: it clarifies what we know or think we know about someone. I hate the fact that Howard is gone. But our loss of him reveals clearly his irreplaceable worth. He looked a bit like Miles Davis and was just as mischievous (he'd sometimes shoot peas through a drinking straw at us staffers). Still, he was that elder Black male who had accomplished much, who was making a difference, who was giving back to the community, setting that example, being that role model, always *representing*.

No wonder that the speakers at his too-soon-arrived funeral included The Honourable Bob Rae and Percy Hatfield (MPP), plus jazz and gospel singers, while a trio of prime ministers sang his praises for his obit. In life, Howard "brought the noise," feisty eloquence and funky riffs; in death, he could be serenaded by politicos and sung by a multiculti *vox populi*. Now that he's reached Heaven, I's sure God be findin' it hard to argue with him!

Life is too short, as we all know, and it flees from us even as we are in its midst. So, I know that I must cease my perambulation about the life and meaning of Dr. Howard Douglas McCurdy Jr. with that train of estimable letters trailing after the denominated, biological, biographical fact of his existence. And so I do. But I say again that Canadians—African-Canadians—do not recognize the valiant, chivalric figure who dominated the social-justice, racial-justice landscape of the Dominion from 1960 to 2000 and registered the fight for Equality in elected councils, on the hustings, in boardrooms (remember that he arranged the first affirmative action program in Canada), and on the streets themselves, leading protest marches that would not be turned around.

If we do not know of HDM's deeds or his struggles, how can we understand correctly what we confront as we attempt to challenge settler-squatter illegitimacy and opposition to the erasure of Euro-supremacist and aristocratic privilege and power? No: the life of this man, this Black man, this African-Canadian of unmatched civic virtue and commitment to social justice is our beacon, our catalyst and prod to push forward and accomplish the most magnificent rebuttal of everything that forbids our collective betterment and our empowerment.

—*Dr. George Elliott Clarke, OC, ONS, FRCGS, PhD, LL.D.,* etc.
Parliamentary Aide to Dr. Howard D. McCurdy, MP, 1987–1991

ROLE MODEL:
A EULOGY REGARDING HOWARD D. MCCURDY

LABRADOR POET BOYD WARREN CHUBBS SENT THIS EMAIL MESSAGE on Saturday, February 5, 2022:

My dear George Elliott,

Upon learning of the passing of Mr. Howard McCurdy, immediately you were by his side, in my head. I recall, every now and then, when you were working with him, how you expressed to me your regard for his character, his mien, his vision, his commitment to ideals.

All of the aforementioned strengths I see and know in yourself.

The best of days; the best of nights.

Your friend,

Boyd Warren

Here is my spontaneous response to Boyd Warren Chubb's spontaneous email:

I check the mirror to see
The person picturing you
Is impersonator me—
Where your likeness falls true?

In reading your bio, I
Leaf—divine—deathless *Achievement*—
Nothing wrong to rectify,
Except *Belief*'s *Bereavement*?

Still, your model has bearing—
Imprint of *Experience*—
(By *Reverse Engineering*
Rehearsing mint *Innocence*)—

As pages turn and chapters
Unfold a man half-Einstein,
Half-Fred Douglass, what captures
Me is semblance by design—

A man whose character was
Singular, unparalleled,
Whose deeds—done—a hero does—
As witnessed here and beheld.

I trace your life and I face
The mirror that is my own:
A tracing that would keep pace
With yours—plus merge in *Renown*.

ACKNOWLEDGEMENTS:
THE PRINCIPAL PRINCIPALS

I KNOW THAT HOWARD (HDM) WOULD WANT TO BEGIN BY THANKING Brenda, his wife of forty years, and so I commence by thanking her too. Dr. Brenda McCurdy, PhD, has thoroughly midwifed both the authorship (in caring for HDM in his declining years) and the editing of this book (by prodding me to get it done and spell-checking names and fact-checking events and putting me in touch with persons in the know about aspects of HDM's life). Likewise, HDM's sister, Marilyn, and his children—Leslie, Linda, Cheryl, Brian—answered queries that Brenda relayed. All overflowed with enthusiasm for this project. In addition, Patricia Neely-McCurdy, BS, MS (Howard's first wife) for her help in identifying persons, places, and/or time-periods in some of the photographs herein.

Another McCurdy organized the manuscript before upon it I set my eyes: Norm McCurdy, Howard's cousin, contributed time and passion, thought and second thought. Howard was, recalls Brenda, enormously grateful for Norm's early involvement and guidance.

Because my editing was not, at first, assisted by a publisher's advance, Dr. Sonia Labatt, PhD (1937–2022) and Victoria University, via the E. J. Pratt Professorship at the University of Toronto, furnished me with travel funds, permitting me to visit HDM in July 2017, co-host a memorial service for him in Ottawa in May 2018, deliver the second draft to Dr. Brenda McCurdy in Amherstburg in May 2022, and undertake additional editing in Parrsboro and Ketch Harbour, NS, 2021–2022, and in June 2023 in Tropea, Italy. (I also thank Judith Bauer and Harvey Lev for arranging my residency at Main & Station Nonesuch, Parrsboro, in August 2022.) Apart from these few incidents of travel, the bulk of the editing was undertaken in Toronto.

For information on the McCurdy hometown and the 1930s to 1950s era of Amherstburg, I was assisted immeasurably by Meg Reiner and Kara Radmore Folkeringa of the Marsh Historical Collection, located in Amherstburg (although I did not actually make it to the premises of either the Marsh Historical Collection or the Amherstburg Freedom Museum, formerly the North American Black Historical Museum). I regret my absence as an on-site researcher, but I am abundantly grateful for the resources made available to me online and/or through email exchange.

Prof. Karolyn Smardz Frost of Acadia University is a top historian of the Canadian terminals of the Underground Railroad. She identified several Amherstburg slavery abolitionists.

Kate Akagi of Indian Point and St. Andrews by-the-Sea, NB, where she is currently deputy mayor, verified the family history of her older sister, Alice, who helped HDM nurse his broken heart in the summer of 1953.

Corpus Christi Parish Windsor forwarded photographs of priests serving at St. Gabriel's Catholic Church in 1962 when HDM and wife Pat had just moved into Windsor's Mt. Carmel 'hood. Of the two choices possible for the "enthusiastic" priest who welcomed the couple, I decided on Rev. Martin Johnston (over Rev. Aloysius Nolan) because he had also just arrived in 1962 and was seemingly young and perhaps extra gung-ho to expand the congregation.

Pastor Brian Harrison of Windsor's Parkwood Gospel Church identified for me a pastor instrumental to HDM's 1979 Windsor City Council campaign, namely Bishop Arthur T. Harrison. Likewise, Christine Chauvin of the Office of the Mayor (Windsor, ON) provided details regarding Peter MacKenzie, who served on Windsor City Council alongside HDM.

My former Windsor-based colleague in HDM's parliamentary employ, Ian McMahon, was always ready with information and recollections that bettered my understanding of HDM's Windsorite associates, backers, pals, cronies, rivals, foes, and chums. He was an invaluable interlocutor. Similarly, Lena Whalen, who I came to know as a committee room worker (alongside her husband, John) during the 1988 "Free Trade" federal election, was able to interpret personalities and explain conflicts related to not only that election campaign, but Windsor politics and the NDP at large. Her insights always exuded psychological acuity. Hon. Walter McLean kindly offered assistance with the photo of Mandela and Howard in Namibia.

A member of HDM's NDP leadership team in 1989, Edward Trapunski filled in some blanks for me regarding HDM's organizers, supporters, and bankrollers. He was a fount of information.

Ron Fanfair's article reviewing HDM's life and achievements is a must-read: search "Howard McCurdy" at RonFanfair.com.

See also Herb Colling's history, *Turning Points: The Detroit Riot of 1967, A Canadian Perspective* (2003), which includes many references to HDM's anti-racism activism and socio-political insights. Craig Baird's narrated digest of HDM's life on Canadian History Ehx is a superb summation of highlights.

Pat Softly's documentary *The McCurdy Birthright* (2007) anchors HDM securely in a genealogy of anti-racism activists, beginning with Underground Railroad agent Nasa McCurdy, continuing on with George McCurdy (grandfather) and George McCurdy (uncle), and then being extended through HDM's own activism. HDM is squarely present himself—and never in a circuitous fashion.

Stacey Janzer of CBC Radio (Windsor) interviewed me in February 2022, thus encouraging listener interest in HDM. Her outreach verified the significance of HDM's life story.

At Nimbus, Whitney Moran accepted the manuscript instantly, savouring the narrative as much as she lauded the style. I am thankful to both her and to Angela Mombourquette at Nimbus for appreciating HDM's life and story and being so caring about making it available for readers. Angela was also an avid proponent of conscientious diction and moral clarity. Similarly, Chris Benjamin edited the book's structure to the quintessence of readability. Nicely, Marianne Ward, the copy editor, chimed in with equal gusto, plus an eagle eye for error and a Renaissance rigour for prose improvement. Her unswerving sense of correct terminology and structure were unstintingly conducive to transforming improvement to achievement. Importantly, in reading the manuscript, they came to value HDM as much as I do.

Although HDM commissioned me in July 2017 to edit his autobiography, I didn't commence the process until a first exchange with Brenda in April 2019. Still, headway on it began only two years later in winter 2021, with the second edited draft being completed in May 2022. I pray that HDM is happy with it (!) and will not mind my "adjustments" and additions, elaborations and extrapolations. It was a privilege to work with all of the above to bring this manuscript to print, but my terminal expression of gratitude is for my companion, Ms. Giovanna Riccio, the excellent poet and heartfelt socialist, who met and liked HDM immediately in July 2017 and who was alongside me in Havana, Cuba, when we learned so sorrowfully of his decease. She has "Sister"-travelled with me through this journey of reliving and rethinking HDM's life through his words and has helped me to stay true to his spirit and committed to the task.

   – GEC

The text of *Black Activist, Black Scientist, Black Icon: The Autobiography of Dr. Howard D. McCurdy* is set in 12.5 pt. Mrs Eaves, a transitional serif typeface designed by Zuzana Licko, a Slovak-born American type designer. Mrs Eaves is a variant of Baskerville, which was designed in Birmingham, England, in the 1750s. Mrs Eaves is named after Sarah Eaves, the woman who became Baskerville's paramour and eventual helpmate with typesetting and printing. Like Howard McCurdy, Mrs Eaves is plain but elegant, self-evidently full of gravitas, and yet graceful.